Archaeologies of Slavery and Freedom in the Caribbean

Florida Museum of Natural History: Ripley P. Bullen Series

Archaeologies of Slavery and Freedom in the Caribbean

Exploring the Spaces in Between

EDITED BY

LYNSEY A. BATES, JOHN M. CHENOWETH,

AND JAMES A. DELLE

University of Florida Press

Gainesville

This book may be available in an electronic edition.

First cloth printing, 2016
First paperback printing, 2018

23 22 21 20 19 18   6 5 4 3 2 1

Library of Congress Cataloging-in-Publication Data
Names: Bates, Lynsey A., editor. | Chenoweth, John M., editor. | Delle, James
    A., editor.
Title: Archaeologies of slavery and freedom in the Caribbean : exploring the
    spaces in between / edited by Lynsey A. Bates, John M. Chenoweth, and
    James A. Delle.
Other titles: Ripley P. Bullen series.
Description: Gainesville : University of Florida Press, [2016] | Series:
    Florida Museum of Natural History: Ripley P. Bullen series | Includes
    bibliographical references and index.
Identifiers: LCCN 2016020153 | ISBN 9781683400035 (cloth)
ISBN 9781683400554 (pbk.)
Subjects: LCSH: Slavery—Caribbean Area—History. |
    Slaves—Emancipation—Caribbean Area. | Caribbean Area—History.
Classification: LCC HT1071 .A73 2016 | DDC 306.3/6209729—dc23
LC record available at https://lccn.loc.gov/2016020153

UF PRESS

UNIVERSITY
OF FLORIDA

University of Florida Press
15 Northwest 15th Street
Gainesville, FL 32611-2079
http://upress.ufl.edu

Contents

Illustrations

Tables

1

Introduction

The Caribbean Spaces in Between

JOHN M. CHENOWETH, JAMES A. DELLE, AND LYNSEY A. BATES

On a small island called Little Jost van Dyke, five kilometers from the regional population center of Tortola, sit the long-abandoned ruins of a house. Tamarind trees shade these ruins, their roots finding tiny spaces in between the stones and pulling them slowly apart (Figure 1.1). This island is known to the historical record primarily because of one of the people born there: John Coakley Lettsom, a white man of English descent who in the eighteenth century moved away from this poor island, gained an education, and established a successful medical practice in Britain, including treating members of the royal family. Such connections to power, money, and European elites are frequently found in the written record of the Caribbean. Moreover, these islands, large and small, supported European empires and formed the foundation for the economic engine that ran them, fueled by sugar, rum, and profits squeezed from the blood and sweat of enslaved people.

While much has been written of late about the archaeology of the colonial Caribbean (e.g., Delle 2014; Hauser 2011; Kelly et al. 2011) this volume explores sites, themes, and times often overlooked by historical archaeologists. The small, marginal site of Little Jost van Dyke exemplifies the central role often played by these neglected "spaces in between," revealing how the mainstream narratives of European empires and elites like John Coakley Lettsom are framed by often-untold backstories and simplifications. During his life, Lettsom had little to say about his modest "creole" origins or those whose labor paid for his education; they did not fit with the high society in which he circulated. Nevertheless, his racial identity allowed him to gain access to the elite circles of the imperial core, a privilege that led to a well-recorded life history present in the documentary record of empire.

Figure 1.1. Mid-eighteenth-century house foundations on the Lettsom Site, Little Jost van Dyke Island, British Virgin Islands. (Photograph by John M. Chenoweth)

Although the social and racial structures of his day allowed Lettsom to remove himself from Little Jost van Dyke, there were, of course, those whose racial identity prohibited such free movement. It was primarily the hands of the enslaved Africans of Little Jost van Dyke that built the walls that are now slowly being ruined by the encroaching forest, but little remains in the written record to document their lives. In recent decades, archaeology of the historic era has turned toward the stories of those "of little note" (Scott 1994): those literally rarely noted by documentary records but also seen as unimportant by the elites of their day, a view that archaeology aims to counter. Understanding the lives of the "invisible" men and women of the empire has long been a focus of Caribbean historians and archaeologists (e.g., Craton 1978; Handler and Lange 1978), but here archaeological work has the added responsibility of understanding the long, sinuous roots of empire: trading networks, military structures, and religious groups in addition to the plantation system itself. These were organizations that stretched worldwide but whose presence was often felt (and fought) in the microscale of daily life. Both of these avenues of research—understanding the sinuous connections between Caribbean plantations and empires and returning those edited out of history to their deserved place—are vibrant avenues of research that are far from exhausted. Yet the chapters in this volume seek to focus our attention on a different set of stories that have so far mainly fallen through the gaps in Caribbean historical archaeology.

The Spaces in Between

Michel de Certeau famously defined a difference between "place" as "the order (of whatever kind) in accord with which elements are distributed in relationships of coexistence" and "space" as living or "practicing" in this place, taking into consideration the "vectors of direction, velocities, and time variables. . . . In relation to place, space is like the word when it is spoken" (1984:117). We find this distinction a useful one in imagining the eighteenth- and nineteenth-century Caribbean. At first glance, few institutions were more emplaced—more stable, ordered, and structural—than the Caribbean plantation. The physical order of fields, village, and "great" house implies and creates social order of free and enslaved, wealthy and poor. But any student of the Caribbean knows that this stability is to some degree illusory. As "the street geometrically defined by urban planning is transformed into a space by walkers" (de Certeau 1984:117), so was the plantation landscape transformed by the active living of those who inhabited it.

In de Certeau's terms, space and place coexist since "space is practiced place" (1984:117). In life, even the most ordered of "places" were lived and negotiated as active "spaces," and the two are not separable—some areas being declared "places" and others "spaces." In this way, the "space" of our title is not literally de Certeau's, and his distinction of "space" and "place" is not necessarily played out in every chapter. Nonetheless, we find this perspective useful in directing us away from a view of ordered stability and the plantation core: a story of oppression and control that, although not wrong, is incomplete.

The site on Little Jost van Dyke described above was the subject of archaeological research that focused on the traditional plantation core of the site: the owners' house and the homes of the enslaved people held there (Chenoweth 2011, 2012, 2014). Even in this isolated setting we find evidence of the long economic and social arms of empire: manufactured goods, signs of broader religious movements (Quakerism), production geared toward the export of cash crops for the empire, and so on. A traditional focus on an "emplaced" plantation was not the goal here, and the site was considered as lived (as a space), but the focus remained on this core.

While valuable, an alternate view of this site and the empire to which it was tied is also possible. The slow growth of European empires within the island communities of the Caribbean was "enacted in regimes of everyday practices that [were] more mobile and flexible" than one might imagine but that nevertheless resulted in the development of cemented social and economic hierarchies (Hardt and Negri 2000:194). Even on the well-studied plantation, there are creative negotiations, "spaces" being made. While necessarily subordinate to many aspects of imperial goals, local people created their own spaces both within and outside of the imposed divisions established in the colonial world.

*　*　*

The oppressions of the European empires have been well studied by historians and archaeologists alike. While the stories in this volume frequently entail oppressions, our collective goal is to understand the strategies of people who sought to maintain their own spaces inside or outside the fixed borders of the plantation. All parts of the Caribbean were shaped by similar forces, including race-based chattel slavery, sugar production, capitalism, and the tropical and sometimes deadly natural environment. Embedded in these commonalities, however, is a great deal of diversity. Large sugar plantations populated by hundreds of enslaved Africans have rightfully received a great deal of attention from archaeologists, historians, and the public. They were, however, not as totalizing as a passing glance might reveal, and they cannot be understood simplistically as expressions of the wills of their white owners (Battle-Baptiste 2011; Fellows and Delle 2015; Hauser 2008; Singleton 2001; Wilkie and Farnsworth 2005).

At the same time, these sites do not account for the experiences of everyone in the Caribbean. Other large groups of people lived very different lives, including the great majority of free people who owned only a handful of enslaved people or none at all (Higman 2014:531), the free black population, and a sizable minority of the enslaved who were held on smaller operations. The authors in this volume use innovative techniques and perspectives to reveal stories of spaces and times where the rules of the sugar lords did not always apply. Some of these "spaces in between" hide within plantation landscapes and some are revealed by alternate views of landscapes dominated by the plantation economy. These time periods and sites have received less attention than the experience of being an enslaved person on a large sugar estate in part because the latter was a very common life of an inhabitant of the Caribbean and because of the rich documentary resources associated with large plantations (Higman 2014:531).

Other "spaces in between" are opened up by looking at a time when the plantation system as it had existed was being restructured during the transitions surrounding and following emancipation in 1838. As Kenneth G. Kelly, Mark W. Hauser, and Douglas V. Armstrong note, while slavery-era archaeology has spoken for those denied a voice in written history, "archaeology has not been similarly applied to the post-slavery period, and yet emancipation did not suddenly render workers 'with history'" (Kelly et al. 2011:244). And yet archaeologists have not been quick to investigate this period (although there are important exceptions, such as contributions to Barnes 2011). Particularly in the Caribbean, archaeologists have yet to fully realize the potential to consider this important time (Hicks 2007; Wilkie and Farnsworth 2011).

The authors in this volume aim to take up the challenges posed by these observations through the analysis of lesser known contexts, such as Dominica, St. Lucia, the British Virgin Islands, and the Dominican Republic, as well as the reexamination of unfamiliar settings in more well-studied islands, including Jamaica and Barbados. Despite grueling work regimes and the social and economic restrictions of slavery, people held in bondage carved out spaces in plantation societies ordered and "placed" by others. In similar fashion, studies of the lives, of non-elite Europeans, continental soldiers, and free people of color demonstrate that binary models of black slaves and white planters do not fully encompass the diverse landscape of Caribbean identities as they were negotiated both before and after emancipation. The studies in this volume employ innovative research tools and integrate data from a variety of historical and archaeological sources to better understand these alternate stories within and beyond the sprawling sugar estates and their modes of order.

Historical Archaeology in the Caribbean

While a full review of historical archaeological work in the Caribbean is beyond the scope of this introduction, our suggestion that the works in this volume expand in a new way on this body of work necessitates some discussion of its shape. There are a number of bibliographies and guides to the literature that expand on the discussions considered here. These are usually grouped by the colonial power whose colonies they concern, as in predominantly Spanish (e.g., Curet 2011; Deagan 1988; Ewen 1990a, 2001), English (e.g., Delle 2014; Delle et al. 2011; Hamilton 1996; Watters 2001), French (e.g., Delpuech 2001; Kelly 2008, 2009, 2014), and Dutch (e.g., Haviser 2001) settlements, but other subject-oriented bibliographies, such as Bell's (1994) on cemeteries or Orser's (1992) on plantation slavery also include much Caribbean material.

Historical archaeological work in the Caribbean can be loosely classed into five groups. The earliest Caribbean archaeology was concerned with the earliest European occupations. In the 1960s, archaeologists turned to documenting how the enslaved people who made up the bulk of the Caribbean population lived and saw the world. While the role the environment played in shaping human society was a key focus of processual work in 1970s and 1980s, in the late 1990s researchers began to study archaeological "landscapes," focusing on the way the physical environment was seen and shaped socially. Beginning in the late 1970s Caribbean historical archaeologists began to search for "Africanisms"—cultural survivals carried by African-descended peoples across the middle passage and into the New World. Finally, critiques of the search for such Africanisms led to a new focus away from "acculturation" toward "creolization," the creation of a new uniquely Caribbean culture, and its expression and negotiation. These categories are, like any such grouping, heuristic rather than absolute, and many works cross or blur the lines. For instance, the important theme of how African-descended peoples resisted their own enslavement and thwarted the ends of their enslavers rather than being passive victims cuts across several of these categories. Also, despite the roughly chronological sequence in which these trends appeared, it is not suggested that any one has or should replace any other, and high-quality work toward all of these goals continues.

European "Firsts" and Early Colonialism

The Caribbean islands have been seen as a microcosm of the larger economic and social processes of colonialism, and the importance of the earliest colonial encounters there is frequently mentioned. Yet records of these settlements are few and far between, and so these were the topic of some of the earliest historical archaeology.

The first "first" in Caribbean colonialism, is, of course, the landfall and legacy of Columbus, and there has been much effort expended to locate his ships' earliest stopping points in the New World (Brill et al. 1987; Hoffman 1987; Keegan 1996:267–268). A counterpoint to this work has come in a renewed focus on the people who "discovered Columbus" (Keegan 1992) and how they fared after their ill-fated discovery. Kathleen Deagan has authored some of the earliest and most extensive works on postcontact native life, and has examined the devastating results for some of the indigenous peoples of the Caribbean during the earliest years of contact, 1492–1520 (Deagan 1988; Deagan and Cruxent 2002). William Keegan (1996:268–270) describes the decline of native populations and the introduction of new domestic animals, which provide the best evidence of early European-contacted sites as opposed to European-sourced artifacts.

Obviously, the earliest European settlement in the Caribbean was Spanish in name and primarily Spanish in culture, and reconstructing lifeways in these settlements has also been a main goal of archaeology. Again, Kathleen Deagan provides an overview of this work on Spanish-American settlements that focuses on settlement patterns, reconstructing architecture, trade and the origins of European artifacts, changes to the environment as a result of colonization, and "syncretic" items representing crossover of native forms or materials with European ones (and vice versa) (1988; see also Thomas 1992 especially pp. 225–315). The alteration of European lifeways upon arrival in the Caribbean was studied by Bonnie McEwan (1986), who compares the sites of Puerto Real and Santo Domingo. In the end, her conclusion is that few changes were made to Spanish lifeways in Puerto Real because of greater access to wealth, and this is contrasted with Santo Domingo's less wealthy status, reliance on military supply lines, and long-term settlement, which forced them to adopt local foods and materials.

The Caribbean environment's role in the early development of European settlements is the subject of a comparative zooarchaeological analysis conducted by Elizabeth Reitz (1992), who compared faunal remains at four early Spanish sites. The role of the environment is suggested to have been primary, with Hispañiola providing a good breeding ground for European cattle due to the lack of indigenous diseases, other ruminants, or predators, while preexisting ruminant populations bearing diseases are suggested for the failure of domesticates to flourish at Cubagua and Spanish Florida, and the extreme heat of Nueva Cádiz and other sites made life difficult for all but pigs. In a work on the 1503 settlement of the Spanish at Puerto Real, present-day Haiti, Charles Ewen (1990b) attempts to understand explicitly how life for Europeans changed and "creolized" through the colonial process. He concludes that there is a broad pattern of Spanish colonial adaptation in which technomic (utilitarian) items were adapted from local materials and the common practices of enslaved Native and African groups, whereas sociotechnic (more socially significant) items were not and remained exclusively European in origin.

"Those of Little Note"

In 1994 Elizabeth Scott framed her book *Those of Little Note* as one that tells the stories of those rarely noted in the historical record. Archaeological inquiry is one approach to recapture some of those stories, and this has been a particular focus in the Caribbean. Jay Haviser (1999) explicitly cites a need to fill in the gaps left in written history as the reason behind his 1999 edited volume *African Sites Archaeology in the Caribbean* and laments the archaeological attention focused on the "firsts" noted earlier.

Armstrong's early work at Drax Hall in Jamaica traces how the Afro-Jamaican population "developed a new and distinct cultural context that drew upon a variety of African as well as European and possibly Amer-Indian patterns" (1985:262, 265). Lydia Pulsipher and Conrad Goodwin (1999) attempt to reconstruct the unrecorded "haptic perceptions" of the enslaved who lived on Galways Plantation, Montserrat, arguing that we must consider the "cultural meaning" of the landscape as experienced by past people if we are to reconstruct the lives of those who inhabited it. Historical accounts of chains and beatings cannot fully capture the oppression of slavery, and the long-term damage done to persons' bodies through repetitive work and poor conditions is revealed through direct analysis of burials by several authors (Courtaud et al. 1999; Jacobi et al. 1992; Khudabux 1999; Mann et al. 1987; Watters 1987, 1996). James Delle and Kristen Fellows (2014) use different lines of evidence, including documents and aboveground analyses of cemeteries, to consider the role of burial placement and commemoration in the negotiation of power between Jamaican plantation owners and workers both before and after emancipation. This account provides us with both an unwritten story of resistance and an account of identity creation and community building.

The institution of slavery makes race a paramount feature of Caribbean life, and of the study of the Caribbean past. However, people were also "little noted" on the basis of factors other than race. An attempt to consider social relations of gender is made by Erica Hill (1995), who associates women with thimbles through their work in domestic contexts using finds from several Caribbean sites and reports potential for gleaning information on women's household production, gender relations, and age from thimble analysis (see also Reilly, this volume, on a group of disadvantaged poor whites).

The fact that the market economy among enslaved people was substantially more developed and more important than historical records suggest has been the subject of a great deal of archaeological work. Jerome Handler and Frederick Lange (1978) touch on this issue in their landmark study of life under slavery in Barbados, citing primarily historical information to describe the internal market system there. Pulsipher and Goodwin (1999) use primarily historical evidence to describe the gardens of the enslaved and the selling of produce to others in slavery and passing traders alike, which took place at the margins of large sugar estates. In a sense, they suggest, this strategy allowed the enslaved "to prevail over the plantation system" and represents a "premier cultural feature" of their lives (Pulsipher and Goodwin 1999:24). In addition to being an economic exchange, this trading network, particularly as revealed through low-fired earthenware ceramics, also represents social exchange. Hauser and Armstrong (1999:89) discuss this process in their analysis of the free inhabitants of the East End, St. John, and their relationship with the rest of the island and the nearby Caribbean. Armstrong's extended study of the East End community of St. John goes beyond the material items traded and considers the whole maritime venture, suggesting that the market "afforded African Americans greater access to social and economic autonomy, and perhaps even freedom" (Armstrong 2003:12). In a similar vein, Hauser's work (2008) on the composition, production, and exchange of low-fired earthenwares in Jamaica demonstrates not only the complexity of the networks formed between enslaved individuals but also the integrated nature of plantation and market communities. Another example is the work of Heather Gibson

(2009), whose study of the market economy of Guadeloupe bridges the temporary emancipation of 1794–1802 and suggests that markets provided a measure of stability through the tumultuous revolutionary period.

A different perspective on this market economy is provided by Delle (2008), who sees it as part of the suite of practices used tacitly by white planters to oppress those they held in slavery. Markets provided access to manufactured goods but also bred dependence on these goods; after emancipation decreased access to provisioning grounds, the new oppression of wage labor was the only means to acquire these materials. Delle also discusses this transition from communal to individual, independence to more market dependence, in reference to religion and missionization, connecting wage labor and participation in the market economy with religious evangelization (Delle 2001). Laurie Wilkie and Paul Farnsworth also argue for alternative motives in whites' tolerance of these hidden markets, suggesting that at Clifton Plantation in the Bahamas, owner William Wylly attempted to minimize his overhead by granting his enslaved people more "free" time to work their own lands and encouraging their participation in the market, although they suggest that the attempt backfired (Wilkie 2001; Wilkie and Farnsworth 2005).

Landscapes of Trade, Community, and Control

The role of the Caribbean itself as an environment and a landscape has also been the subject of study, along with how this environment was manipulated by people for social ends. The Caribbean is a large area, and some parts are extremely remote from trading and population centers. Despite its present-day paradisiacal image, many areas are extremely harsh and difficult to farm. While not deterministic, the geography and environment of each island has had a role in how its occupants live, move around, and build their communities. An example is provided by the frequent discussions of potable water and the difficulties of obtaining it on small islands. Armstrong (2003) even sees water use as an issue that united the East End community of St. John, and both Barry Higman (1998) and Christopher Clement (1997) suggest that the availability of water sometimes determined many aspects of plantation development. Norman Barka's (2001) detailed history of landscape use on St. Eustatius highlights the role of environmental as well as social factors in determining how settlements were spread across the island at different time periods (see also Seiter, this volume).

Most authors, while not unaware of environmental factors, focus on the more human aspects of settlement. Armstrong and Matthew Reilly (2014) have recently considered an early version of the postcolonization Caribbean landscape with their study of a pre-sugar plantation in Barbados. One of the few studies that considers indentured Europeans as well as enslaved African laborers, this analysis also highlights the fact that the sugar landscapes that have received so much attention did not arise de novo but rather after a generation or more of Caribbean colonialism. Another version of these early landscapes is given by Hauser and Armstrong (2012), arguing that early settlers on some islands outside the mainstream of colonial process were actively avoiding formal government structures, creating in the process informal settlements quite different from expected models. In a study related to same authors' contributions to this volume, Krysta Ryzewski and John Cherry (2015) demonstrate that the complexity and diversity of plantation landscapes in the island of Montserrat can best be studied with a multiscalar approach to the whole island rather than a focus on individual plantations only (see also Bates, this volume; Delle, this volume.)

Spaces were also structured to create and constrain social relationships. Clement (1997) considers the spatial structure of Tobagan sugar plantations, describing the typical layout primarily as a function of practical needs of the white owners, such as power for mills and surveillance position for great houses. He also considers the "performance" value of plantation main houses, built to make statements to and foster a sense of community among the plantation owners. Delle analyzes the construction of landscape and how it was used in the negotiation of relationships between owners and enslaved people, arguing that "class structure was reified by the spaces reserved for members of these distinct classes; this class-stratified space was manifested most directly in the creation of the material spaces of overseers' houses and great houses" (1999:147; see also Smith and Bassett, this volume.)

Dan Hicks (2007) applied the long tradition of British landscape archaeology to St. Lucia and St. Kitts and argued for a shift from a seventeenth-century model of "feudal" landscapes, enforcing power directly—for instance, with walled enclosures and militaristic organization—to a later, more classical rhetoric of power created through organized and "improved" landscapes. The rhetoric of "improvement" included landscapes that acted as "theatres" or "machines," where "the material, ideational and transatlantic landscapes of the planter elite were imagined and worked out" (Hicks 2007:63). Control of nature (e.g., through the placement of the house), of time, and of the enslaved peoples' lifestyles through surveillance were central in this landscape (see Lenik and Beier, this volume, for a related postemancipation discussion). John M. Chenoweth (2014) connects plantation layout to the social processes of identification, as race and religion interacted on a small plantation in the British Virgin Islands. Here the landowners manipulated space and material culture in order to improve their social and financial lot, recast their religion (Quakerism) into a form compatible with the slavery-based economy, and differentiated themselves from the enslaved people they held.

The difficulties of long-distance transportation exacerbate differences between class groups. Joe Joseph and Stephen Bryne's (1992) work in Old San Juan, Puerto Rico, compares wealthier and poorer areas and notes a correlation between wealth (defined through historical documentation) and the source of trade materials, with the highest status people using non-Spanish imports, middling people relying on Spanish imports, and the poorest using locally produced items. Farnsworth (1996) also considers trade and exchange, comparing two Bahamian plantations' access to markets. He concludes that on isolated sites such as the Caicos Islands plantation of Wade's Green, the distance from the market and difficulty of transportation had more effect on the ceramics recovered than personal choice or social factors such as ethnicity or socioeconomic status. On the other end of the spectrum, Georgia L. Fox's (2002) analysis of tobacco pipes in Port Royal speaks to the huge volume of trade and commerce that went through that site before the 1692 earthquake. She sees them as a reflection of English society's growth from feudalism into mercantilism and industrialism, as they were one of the first disposable commodities (see also Fox 2015).

Cultural Continuity: Searches for African "Survivals"

Kofi Agorsah (1999:62) cites a substantial number of works that have made contributions toward the effort to "re-affirm Africa's vital enduring cultural contributions to the New World and global community." Some of the earliest Caribbean archaeology to focus on nonwhite populations was part of an effort to find traces of the African cultures the enslaved were forced to leave behind. Agorsah (1999) compared sites in Ghana and the Caribbean, looking for African settlement patterns in the African-descended communities in the Caribbean to tease out commonalities that speak to the patterns of social behavior, particularly the use of house yards, and has also tied resistance efforts to the cultural backgrounds of the African-descended enslaved people held in Caribbean plantations who escaped to form "maroon" communities in cooperation with remaining native groups (Agorsah 1993; Goucher and Agorsah 2011).

James B. Petersen and colleagues (1999:160) and Barbara J. Heath (1999:197) define an African-derived tradition of low-fired earthenware production based on modeled construction (rather than wheel throwing), open firing, and lack of glazing. Petersen and colleagues go so far as to suggest that there is a "pan-regional, Afro-Caribbean ceramic tradition" (1999:189). They also use ceramic temper to suggest interisland trade, with Antigua as a focal point of manufacture, and speculate that this trade may have had a "homogenizing" effect on ceramic production, although they ultimately pull back from a monolithic picture of Afro-Caribbean material culture traditions (1999: 188–193). On the other hand, Heath (1999), while still seeing the pottery as a panregional phenomenon, focuses on the creole nature of these ceramics. She highlights earthenware's historically documented use in foodways, for water, and even for spiritual and musical purposes, suggesting that these may also be used to recognize panregional Afro-Caribbean ceramic traditions along with vessel form.

One of the earliest substantial works in Caribbean plantation archaeology is that of Handler and Lange (1978) and their colleagues in various subsequent related publications that discuss evidence for a strong African influence on burial customs among the enslaved people of Barbados. In analyzing over 100 burials, Handler, Robert S. Corruccini, and Robert J. Mutaw (1982) encountered several remains with what they termed "tooth mutilation." They cite a number of sources connecting this practice to African religions and list a number of other circum-Caribbean examples. Handler also considers African cultures to aid his interpretation of an unusual burial in Barbados that was consistent with several African religions' treatment of witches or other ostracized persons (Handler 1996). Armstrong and Mark L. Fleischman consider burials of enslaved Africans in house yards in Jamaica, suggesting African origins in their choice of location close to the living (Armstrong and Fleischman 2003).

Creolization and Ethnogenesis

As productive as these searches for African backgrounds have been, some would now take exception to their focus on pan-Caribbean and pan-African generalities. Hauser and Armstrong (1999) argue that the search for "Africanisms" has substantial problems, characterizing some studies of low-fired earthenware ceramics as "all or nothing" views of both artifacts and the people who made them; there is a danger, they suggest, of homogenizing the very diverse set of ethnic affiliations of Africa. Wilkie and Farnsworth sum up similar critiques, noting that, "by focusing on individual cultural materials and practices, scholars may only serve to create essentialized, static, and fragmented portraits of Caribbean culture" (Wilkie and Farnsworth 2005:4). Theresa A. Singleton (1998) made a related argument: that enslaved Africans are sometimes depicted as "mere recipients of culture change" and that some studies do not adequately consider power relations.

Many studies have engaged deeply with this critique. Armstrong (1990) has argued that European-origin artifacts in Jamaica could have been used differently by those of different backgrounds and therefore can be analyzed to reveal African worldviews as they interacted with these new materials. Wilkie (1999, 2000) draws attention to how manufactured items selected by enslaved people can similarly speak to African symbolic systems. She suggests that, while little success has been found in the search for explicit "Africanisms," more progress might be made by considering how "African-Americans selectively appropriated those [mass produced] goods that best reflected their cultural sensibilities and enabled them to construct New World creolized identities through new material culture" (Wilkie 2000:11). In their study of a Bahamian plantation, Wilkie and Farnsworth (2005) highlight the diversity of the experience of the enslaved, some of whom were born in Africa and had presumably built lives and families there, while others were born into slavery. The study suggests that the Bahamian culture as it stands today was not created simply from a borrowing of generalized African and generalized European practices but that many components—cultural, historical, environmental—shaped how those on this site negotiated their way in the plantation system.

Higman (1998) combines historical sources and archaeology, aiming to provide a more complete story of one plantation, considering house structure and how it reveals social relationships, foodways, clothing, and ornamentation as well as reviewing considerations of the idea of "community" and arguing for its applicability for enslaved groups. Farnsworth (1999) identifies African roots for ethnomedical practices, consumer choices, and foodways reflected primarily in ceramic forms and decoration (even though the forms are European in origin) in his comparative study of life on Bahamian plantations, but he also considers the connections to modern Bahamian society. Candice Goucher's (1999) discussion of metalworking in African beliefs and Caribbean practice, though finding few direct connections beyond African-derived designs in New World metalwork-ing, considers the whole suite of associations that are part of the "cultural memory" of those transported to the Caribbean.

Cultural identifications were never static but were constantly in motion. Farnsworth considers typical Bahamian housing for the enslaved, suggest-ing that there were many influences from West Africa and also possibly from England, though the "execution was Bahamian, producing a truly creole house form"(2001:268). On a broader scale, Armstrong's major work (2003) on the creole community of St. John charts how, over time, a group of small planters and the people they held enslaved melded into a single community. Through the lenses of exchange, age and gender relations, and religion, he studies how "residents forged new paths and emerged as active participants in the broader regional community" (2003:319).

Stories of the Spaces in Between

Using this literature as a foundation, this volume explores alternate stories of empire through archaeological investigations of sites that fall outside the usual scope of large cash-crop plantations and their cores. To examine the diversity of Caribbean people who carved out lives under imperial control, these case studies examine communities that included enslaved Africans, free people of color, and Europeans within islands controlled by one or more European powers. The authors not only address communities whose contribution to broad narratives of Caribbean history is overlooked but also employ innovative analytical techniques to take a new look at those previously considered. Their analyses fall roughly into two primary themes. Authors in part 1 (chapters 2–7), "The Spaces Between and Within," dis-cuss the spheres of interaction of several social groups inhabiting sanc-tioned and illicit spaces outside the plantation core during the period of slavery. Incorporating new approaches to scale and landscape, several of these chapters also consider different kinds of plantation spaces and paths of movement between them. Authors in part 2 (chapters 8–13), "Transition and Postemancipation Analyses," take up the challenge noted earlier to in-vestigate Caribbean daily life directly prior to and following emancipation. These chapters range from the period of apprenticeship into the twentieth century. For reference, Figure 1.2 presents an overview of the Caribbean region with the islands of focus noted, along with the authors who discuss these places.

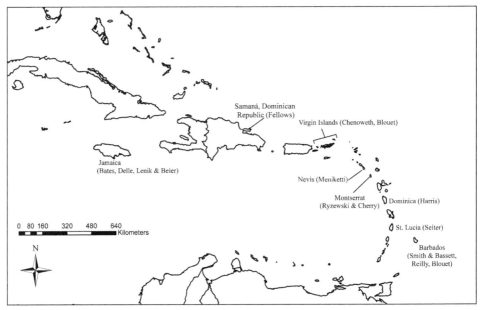

Figure 1.2. Map of the Caribbean with islands and sites discussed in the volume indicating the authors whose chapters focus on each. (Map by John M. Chenoweth based on data from the Pacific Disaster Center, ghin.pdc.org)

Part 1: The Spaces Between and Within

In chapter 2, Frederick H. Smith and Hayden F. Bassett discuss archaeological investigations of the caves and gullies surrounding the St. Nicholas Abbey sugar plantation in Barbados. While the layout of plantation villages demonstrates a great deal of planter control, the private landscapes of enslaved people offer insights into the activities and experiences where the reach of the planter was more limited. The caves, as liminal spaces on the landscape between adjoining plantations, appear to have served as meeting areas for enslaved people and, later, free workers. The privacy of these spaces afforded physical mobility and social interaction between enslaved people from surrounding villages and may have fostered activities that were not permitted in the public sphere, such as gaming and leisure. Gullies are thus viewed as conduits and corridors that connected communities in the plantation-dominated landscape of Barbados and offered a temporary respite from the challenges of plantation life.

Matthew C. Reilly explores socioeconomic interactions between "poor whites" or "Redlegs" and Afro-Barbadians in chapter 3, interpreting these through material culture and a particular reading of a Barbadian plantation landscape. The tenantry of Below Cliff, now shrouded in dense forest, is located on the "rab" land or marginal zone of Clifton Hall Plantation deemed unsuitable for large-scale agricultural production. Despite the marginality of the space in terms of plantation production and a perceived socioeconomic isolation of island "poor whites" in general, Below Cliff was a space of heightened interracial interaction. Reilly argues that such seemingly marginal spaces (as well as the people who inhabit them) are significant arenas through which to explore the dynamic and nuanced race relations that played out in everyday life on and around the plantation. While plantation slavery was crucial in the development of modern racial ideologies and hierarchies, including attempts to rigidly impose and police racial boundaries, archaeological evidence suggests that at the local level these boundaries were exceedingly porous.

In chapter 4, Lynsey A. Bates analyzes the relationship between plantation landscapes and the people who altered and maintained those landscapes in order to facilitate the understanding of slavery across different spatial and temporal contexts. The plantation system as embodied in Jamaican sugar estates required that estate owners create a suite of strategies that maximized labor, time, and space to make cash-crop production profitable. At the same time, enslaved people developed their own strategies to use the domestic and agricultural spaces of the plantation. To assess these sets of strategies, this chapter investigates the spatial organization of several estates by integrating modern topographic and historic map data. The results of this analysis suggest the conditions under which enslaved laborers cultivated basic foodstuffs and marketed surplus provisions.

Much of what we know archaeologically about the material realities of Caribbean plantation slavery is based on the interpretation of objects recovered from plantation village contexts. While a majority of those enslaved on plantations did in fact live in the village, not all did. In chapter 5, James A. Delle analyzes a previously unexamined material and spatial reality of Jamaican plantations: the existence and importance of extravillage localities in which people lived. Defined here as "field houses," these structures were dispersed across the plantation landscape, located within agricultural fields and provision grounds. The material considered comes from an early nineteenth-century plantation known as Marshall's Pen; excavations conducted on three field houses provide the data from which this interpretation is derived.

In chapter 6, Jane I. Seiter combines a program of landscape survey with a close analysis of maps and census records to reveal patterns of landscape development in St. Lucia very different from that on some other islands. Underneath the remains of vast sugar estates with their monumental architecture lies evidence of an earlier phase of small-scale plantations growing a surprising diversity of crops. Building on a legacy of subsistence agriculture inherited from the Amerindians, European settlers on St. Lucia carved out a patchwork of small holdings cultivating cotton, cocoa, coffee, tobacco, ginger, cassava, indigo, and bananas. The comparative absence of large sugar plantations allowed people without much capital to purchase and develop land, creating new opportunities for free people of color to amass wealth and gain political power. The emergence of a class of free black landowners had a profound impact on St. Lucian society, which in turn greatly affected the larger political struggles that rocked the Caribbean in the late eighteenth century.

Krysta Ryzewski and John F. Cherry demonstrate the advantages of a survey-centered approach for examining cultural landscapes on Montserrat in chapter 7. Their case study focuses on the multimethod survey of the Potato Hill landscape employed during the 2013 field season of the Survey and Landscape Archaeology on Montserrat Project. Potato Hill's artifact assemblage is the largest and among the earliest historic-period collections to be recovered on the island. The evidence suggests that Potato Hill was a non-elite settlement occupied by multiple communities and households between the late seventeenth and nineteenth centuries. Understandings of Potato Hill's changing use and inhabitants over the course of its long occupational history are situated within survey results from the surrounding landscape, especially historic-period sugar plantations and military structures. This case study also raises several questions concerning methodological approaches, temporal categories, scales of analysis, and material culture classification in Caribbean historical archaeology.

Part 2: Transition and Postemancipation Spaces

In chapter 8, Marco Meniketti describes survey work conducted on Nevis to locate one of three postemancipation African villages depicted in an 1871 map, the site of Morgan's Village. Artifacts at the site suggested a strong pre-emancipation component, so it represents an important period of Nevis' history: the transitional phase from slavery-based plantations to an economy with wage labor and a free citizenry experimenting in a mature, agro-industrial capitalist mode. This was a period that set the stage for emergent Nevisian identity. The village site and map promised insights into the period between 1838 when the "apprentice period" ended and the 1870s as new economic and social relationships coalesced and were mediated by global events. What was encountered instead was a village seemingly abandoned soon after emancipation, suggesting a dynamic not previously appreciated. Preliminary analysis suggests a pre-emancipation community that evolved with the changing times.

Helen C. Blouet's study in chapter 9 investigates Barbados's eighteenth- and nineteenth-century Moravian Christian burial sites to highlight processes of community building and culture change in mortuary contexts. These can be linked to larger political transformations across the island and Caribbean region, such as emancipation. Here she identifies historical variation in burial site materiality and spatiality to understand how burial grounds reflected and informed changes in policies and relationships within disparate congregations and the larger societies. Examining the periods before and after the end of slavery, this chapter highlights the significance of burial sites and commemorative practices in the context of dynamic processes of Moravian community building, maintenance, and transformation.

In some ways, little except a legal status changed for many enslaved Africans when slavery ended in the British colonies of the Caribbean as land and capital were held by their former enslavers. In the British Virgin Islands, however, personal effort and a series of historical contingencies led to the creation of many small freehold farms held by the newly free. In chapter 10, John M. Chenoweth considers initial archaeological work at one of these sites, highlighting the creative negotiation expressed by women and men who held their own land despite living in an oppressive empire. Although traded goods are found, Chenoweth suggests that the residents may have engaged quite selectively with the market economy controlled by whites and tied to imperial power structures.

After emancipation, land and the economic opportunities connected with landownership were important in individuals' decisions about where to go and what to do. For this reason, the postemancipation period is extraordinarily important for understanding how various territories in the Caribbean were reconstituted and became what they are today. In chapter 11, Khadene K. Harris uses archaeological data to examine changes that occurred on a Dominican plantation after 1838 and, by so doing, casts new light on the distinctive character of postemancipation life. She attempts to understand these shifts by focusing on the built environment and the changing use of space over time. Along with archaeological evidence, historical documents and ethnographic data illustrate the preoccupations of the planter class during the postemancipation period and the ways in which the newly freed Dominicans sought to exercise control over their own time and labor.

Previous research in British Caribbean colonies investigates the lives of free and enslaved military personnel during the period of Atlantic slavery within the context of each outpost's strategic significance. Less well known are militia infantry and artillery troops who were stationed at military sites from the late nineteenth to the mid-twentieth century. In Jamaica, Rocky Point Battery (later Fort Rocky) the subject of chapter 12, by Stephan Lenik and Zachary J. M. Beier, defended Kingston Harbor from the 1880s until the Second World War. Jamaican volunteer militia and enlisted men as well as European officers and engineers stationed at this battery chose a British military life that dictated a regime of rigid spatial and temporal segregation whereby imperial thinking was deployed as military strategy. This chapter examines ceramics, tobacco pipes, and uniform parts recovered from the fort as objects that reflect institutional material culture that strove for homogeneity. At the same time, these objects left room for the assertion of a complex set of affiliations and individuality in a setting structured by British imperialism and geographic isolation.

Fleeing a tremendous rise in racial tensions and an American nationality increasingly defined by whiteness, a small group of free blacks fled the United States for the island nation of Haiti in 1824, settling in what is now Samaná, Dominican Republic. The descendants of the original settlers continued to self-identify as both "American" and "black" until the most recent generations. In chapter 13, Kristen R. Fellows focuses on issues of communal identity within the globally connected Caribbean, with special attention paid to the intersection of race and nationality. Oral-historical and archival data reveals how the American community in Samaná continuously negotiated the "double consciousness" of their African American identity in a place influenced first by the black Republic of Haiti and later the white, Hispanic, and Catholic nationalism of the Dominican Republic. As with many Caribbean communities, the United States has also played an important role in the development, maintenance, and dissolution of this communal identity.

In the final chapter of the volume, Laurie A. Wilkie weaves together these themes and discusses the future of historical archaeology in the Caribbean region.

Conclusion

One of the great strengths of contemporary historical archaeology is the now widespread recognition that the physical remnants left behind by past generations, the elements of material culture that make up the archaeological record, have the power to reveal much about those who lived far from the seats of imperial power. Archaeologists are increasingly recognizing that "places" of structure and colonialism were manipulated and negotiated into "spaces" as they were lived in ways that are at once complex and constrained, empowering and enslaving, triumphant and tragic. By focusing on different times, places, and perspectives "in between" the traditional views of the plantation core, it is our hope that the chapters in this volume contribute to a deeper understanding of the experiences of those who lived in the historic Caribbean, who created, nurtured, and ultimately cut the roots of empire.

References Cited

Agorsah, E. Kofi
1993   Archaeology and Resistance History in the Caribbean. *African Archaeological Review* 11:175–195.
1999   Ethnoarchaeological Consideration of Social Relationship and Settlement Patterning among Africans in the Caribbean Diaspora. In *African Sites Archaeology in the Caribbean*, edited by Jay B. Haviser, pp. 38–64. Marcus Wiener Publishers, Princeton, New Jersey.
Armstrong, Douglas V.
1985   An Afro-Jamaican Slave Settlement: Archaeological Investigations at Drax Hall. In *The Archaeology of Slavery and Plantation Life*, edited by Theresa A. Singleton, pp. 261–287. Academic Press, Orlando, Florida.
1990   *The Old Village and the Great House: An Archaeological and Historical Examination of Drax Hall Plantation, St. Ann's Bay, Jamaica*. University of Illinois Press, Urbana.
2003   *Creole Transformation from Slavery to Freedom: Historical Archaeology of the East End Community, St. John, Virgin Islands*. University Press of Florida, Gainesville.
Armstrong, Douglas V., and Mark L. Fleischman
2003   House-Yard Burials of Enslaved Laborers in Eighteenth-Century Jamaica. *International Journal of Historical Archaeology* 7(1):33–65.
Armstrong, Douglas V., and Matthew C. Reilly
2014   The Archaeology of Settler Farms and Early Plantation Life in Seventeenth-Century Barbados. *Slavery & Abolition* 35(3):399–417.
Barka, Norman F.
2001   Time Lines: Changing Settlement Patterns on St. Eustatius. In *Island Lives: His-*

torical Archaeologies of the Caribbean, edited by Paul Farnsworth, pp. 103–141. University of Alabama Press, Tuscaloosa.

Barnes, Jodi A. (editor)

2011   *The Materiality of Freedom: Archaeologies of Postemancipation Life*. University of South Carolina Press, Columbia.

Battle-Baptiste, Whitney

2011   *Black Feminist Archaeology*. Left Coast Press, Walnut Creek, California.

Bell, Edward L.

1994   *Vestiges of Mortality & Remembrance: A Bibliography on the Historical Archaeology of Cemeteries*. Scarecrow Press, Metuchen, New Jersey.

Brill, Robert H., I. Lynus Barnes, Stephen S. C. Tong, and Emile C. Joel

1987   Laboratory Studies of Some European Artifacts Excavated on San Salvador Island. In *First San Salvador Conference: Columbus and His World*, edited by Donald T. Gerace, pp. 247–292. College Center Finger Lakes, Bahamaian Field Station, Bahamas.

Chenoweth, John M.

2011   Religion, Archaeology, and Social Relations: A Study of the Practice of Quakerism and Caribbean Slavery in the Eighteenth-Century British Virgin Islands. Ph.D. dissertation, Department of Anthropology, University of California, Berkeley.

2012   Quakerism and the Lack of "Things" in the Early Modern. In *Modern Materials: The Proceedings of CHAT Oxford, 2009*(BAR 2363), edited by Brent Fortenberry and Linda McAtackney, pp. 73–84. Archaeopress, Oxford.

2014   Practicing and Preaching: Creating a Religion of Peace on a Slave Plantation. *American Anthropologist* 116(1):94–109.

Clement, Christopher Ohm

1997   Settlement Patterning on the British Caribbean Island of Tobago. *Historical Archaeology* 31(2):93–106.

Courtaud, Patrice, André Delpuech, and Thomas Romon

1999   Archaeological Investigations at Colonial Cemeteries on Guadeloupe: African Slave Burial Sites or Not? In *African Sites Archaeology in the Caribbean*, edited by Jay B. Haviser, pp. 277–290. Marcus Wiener, Princeton, New Jersey.

Craton, Michael

1978   *Searching for the Invisible Man: Slaves and Plantation Life in Jamaica*. Harvard University Press, Cambridge, Massachusetts.

Curet, L. Antonio.

2011   Colonialism and the History of Archaeology in the Spanish Caribbean. In *Comparative Archaeologies*, edited by Ludomir R. Lozny, pp. 641–672. Springer, New York.

Deagan, Kathleen

1988   Archaeology of the Spanish Contact Period in the Caribbean. *Journal of World Prehistory* 2(2):187–233.

Deagan, Kathleen, and José María Cruxent

2002   *Columbus's Outpost among the Taínos: Spain and America at La Isabela, 1493–1498*. Yale University Press, New Haven, Connecticut.

de Certeau, Michel
1984   *The Practice of Everyday Life*. Translated by Steven F. Rendall. University of California Press, Berkeley.

Delle, James A.
1999   The Landscapes of Class Negotiation on Coffee Plantations in the Blue Mountains of Jamaica: 1790–1850. *Historical Archaeology* 33(1):136–158.
2001   Race, Missionaries, and the Struggle to Free Jamaica. In *Race and the Archaeology of Identity*, edited by Charles E. Orser Jr., pp. 177–195. University of Utah Press, Salt Lake City.
2008   An Archaeology of Modernity in Colonial Jamaica. *Archaeologies* 4(1):87–109.
2014   *The Colonial Caribbean: Landscapes of Power in the Plantation System*. Cambridge University Press, Cambridge.

Delle, James A., and Kristen R. Fellows
2014   Death and Burial at Marshall's Pen, a Jamaican Coffee Plantation, 1814–1839: Examining the End of Life at the End of Slavery. *Slavery & Abolition* 35(3):474–492.

Delle, James A., Mark W. Hauser, and Douglas V. Armstrong (editors)
2011   *Out of Many, One People: The Historical Archaeology of Jamaica*. University of Alabama Press, Tuscaloosa.

Delpuech, André
2001   Historical Archaeology of the French West Indies: Recent Research in Guadeloupe. In *Island Lives: Historical Archaeologies of the Caribbean*, edited by Paul Farnsworth, pp. 21–59. University of Alabama Press, Tuscaloosa.

Ewen, Charles R.
1990a   *The Archaeology of Spanish Colonialism in the Southeastern United States and the Caribbean*. Society for Historical Archaeology, Ann Arbor, Michigan.
1990b   *From Spaniard to Creole: The Archaeology of Cultural Formation in Puerto Real, Haiti*. University of Alabama Press, Tuscaloosa.
2001   Historical Archaeology in the Colonial Spanish Caribbean. In *Island Lives: Historical Archaeologies of the Caribbean*, edited by Paul Farnsworth, pp. 3–20. University of Alabama Press, Tuscaloosa.

Farnsworth, Paul
1996   The Influence of Trade on Bahamian Slave Culture. *Historical Archaeology* 30(4):1–23.
1999   From the Past to the Present: An Exploration of the Formation of African-Bahamian Identity during Enslavement. In *African Sites Archaeology in the Caribbean*, edited by Jay B. Haviser, pp. 94–130. Marcus Wiener, Princeton, New Jersey.
2001   "Negroe Houses Built of Stone Besides Others Watl'd + Plaistered": The Creation of a Bahamian Tradition. In *Island Lives: Historical Archaeologies of the Caribbean*, edited by Paul Farnsworth, pp. 234–271. University of Alabama Press, Tuscaloosa.

Fellows, Kristen R., and James A. Delle
2015   Marronage and the Dialectics of Spatial Sovereignty in Colonial Jamaica. In *Current Perspectives on the Archaeology of African Slavery in Latin America*, edited by Pedro P. A. Funari and Charles E. Orser Jr. Springer, New York.

Fox, Georgia L.
2002   Interpreting Socioeconomic Changes in 17th-Century England and Port Royal, Jamaica, through Analysis of the Port Royal Kaolin Clay Pipes. *International Journal of Historical Archaeology* 6(1):61–78.
2015   *The Archaeology of Smoking and Tobacco.* American Experience in Archaeological Perspective Series. University Press of Florida, Gainesville.

Gibson, Heather R.
2009   Domestic Economy and Daily Practice in Guadeloupe: Historical Archaeology at La Mahaudière Plantation. *International Journal of Historical Archaeology* 13(1):27–44.

Goucher, Candice
1999   African-Caribbean Metal Technology: Forging Cultural Survivals in the Atlantic World. In *African Sites Archaeology in the Caribbean,* edited by Jay B. Haviser, pp. 143–156. Marcus Wiener, Princeton, New Jersey.

Goucher, Candice, and E. Kofi Agorsah
2011   Excavating the Roots of Resistance: The Significance of Maroons in Jamaican Archaeology. In *Out of Many, One People: The Historical Archaeology of Colonial Jamaica,* edited by James A. Delle, Mark W. Hauser, and Douglas V. Armstrong, pp. 144–162. University of Alabama Press, Tuscaloosa.

Hamilton, Donny L.
1996   Historical Archaeology on British Sites in the Seventeenth-Century Caribbean. In *The Archaeology of Sixteenth- and Seventeenth-Century British Colonization in the Caribbean, United States, and Canada,* edited by H. M. Miller, Donny L. Hamilton, Nicholas Honerkamp, Steven R. Pendery, Peter E. Pope, and James A. Tuck, pp. 3–12. Guides to Historical Archaeological Literature. Society for Historical Archaeology, Ann Arbor, Michigan.

Handler, Jerome S.
1996   A Prone Burial from a Plantation Slave Cemetery in Barbados, West Indies: Possible Evidence for an African-Type Witch or other Negatively Viewed Person. *Historical Archaeology* 30(3):76–86.

Handler, Jerome S., Robert S. Corruccini, and Robert J. Mutaw
1982   Tooth Mutilation in the Caribbean: Evidence from a Slave Burial Population in Barbados. *Journal of Human Evolution* 11(4):297–313.

Handler, Jerome S., and Frederick W. Lange
1978   *Plantation Slavery in Barbados: An Archaeological and Historical Investigation.* Harvard University Press, Cambridge, Massachusetts.

Hardt, Michael, and Antonio Negri
2000   *Empire.* Harvard University Press, Cambridge, Massachusetts.

Hauser, Mark W.
2008   *The Archaeology of Black Markets: Local Ceramics and Economies in Eighteenth-Century Jamaica.* University Press of Florida, Gainesville.
2011   Routes and Roots of Empire: Pots, Power, and Slavery in the 18th-Century British Caribbean. *American Anthropologist* 113(3):431–447.

Hauser, Mark W., and Douglas V. Armstrong
1999   Embedded Identities: Piecing Together Relationships through Compositional

Analysis of Low-Fired Earthenwares. In *African Sites Archaeology in the Caribbean*, edited by Jay B. Haviser, pp. 65–93. Marcus Wiener, Princeton, New Jersey.

2012   The Archaeology of Not Being Governed: A Counterpoint to a History of Settlement of Two Colonies in the Eastern Caribbean. *Journal of Social Archaeology* 12(3):310–333.

Haviser, Jay B.

1999   Introduction. In *African Sites Archaeology in the Caribbean*, edited by Jay B. Haviser, pp. 1–8. Marcus Wiener, Princeton, New Jersey.

2001   Historical Archaeology in the Netherlands Antilles and Aruba. In *Island Lives: Historical Archaeologies of the Caribbean*, edited by Paul Farnsworth, pp. 60–82. University of Alabama Press, Tuscaloosa.

Heath, Barbara J.

1999   Yabbas, Monkeys, Jugs, and Jars: An Historical Context for African-Caribbean Pottery on St. Eustatius. In *African Sites Archaeology in the Caribbean*, edited by Jay B. Haviser, pp. 196–220. Marcus Wiener, Princeton, New Jersey.

Hicks, Dan

2007   *"The Garden of the World": An Historical Archaeology of Sugar Landscapes in the Eastern Caribbean*. British Archaeological Reports International Series 1632, Studies in Contemporary and Historical Archaeology 3. Archaeopress, Oxford.

Higman, Barry

1995   Thimbles and Thimble-Rings from the Circum-Caribbean Region, 1500–1800: Chronology and Identification. *Historical Archaeology* 29(1):84–92.

1998   *Montpelier, Jamaica: A Plantation Community in Slavery and Freedom, 1739–1912*. University of the West Indies Press, Kingston, Jamaica.

2014   Survival and Silence in the Material Record of Slavery and Abolition. *Slavery & Abolition* 35(3):527–535.

Hill, Erica

1995   Thimbles and Thimble Rings from the Circum-Caribbean Region, 1500–1800: Chronology and Identification. *Historical Archaeology* 29(1):84–92.

Hoffman, Charles A.

1987   Archaeological Investigations at the Long Bay Site, San Salvador, Bahamas. In *First San Salvador Conference: Columbus and His World*, edited by Donald T. Gerace, pp. 237–246. College Center Finger Lakes, Bahamian Field Station, Bahamas.

Jacobi, Keith P., Della C. Cook, Robert S. Corruccini, and Jerome S. Handler

1992   Congenital Syphilis in the Past: Slaves at Newton Plantation, Barbados, West Indies. *American Journal of Physical Anthropology* 89:145–158.

Joseph, J. W., and Stephen C. Bryne

1992   Socio-Economics and Trade in Viejo San Juan, Puerto Rico: Observations from the Ballaja Archaeological Project. *Historical Archaeology* 26(1):45–58.

Keegan, William F.

1992   *The People Who Discovered Columbus*. University Press of Florida, Gainesville.

1996   West Indian Archaeology 2: After Columbus. *Journal of Archaeological Research* 4(4):265–294.

Kelly, Kenneth G.

2008   Creole Cultures of the Caribbean: Historical Archaeology in the French West Indies. *International Journal of Historical Archaeology* 12(4):388–402.

2009   Where Is the Caribbean? French Colonial Archaeology in the English Lake. *International Journal of Historical Archaeology* 13(1):80–93.

2014   Archaeology, Plantations, and Slavery in the French West Indies. In *Bitasion: Archéologie des Habitations-Plantations des Petites Antilles*, edited by Kenneth Kelly and Benoit Bérard, pp. 17–31. Sidestone Press, Leiden.

Kelly, Kenneth G., Mark W. Hauser, and Douglas V. Armstrong

2011   Identity and Opportunity in Post-Slavery Jamaica. In *Out of Many, One People: The Historical Archaeology of Colonial Jamaica*, edited James A. Delle, Mark W. Hauser, and Douglas V. Armstrong, pp. 243–257. University of Alabama Press, Tuscaloosa.

Khudabux, Mohammed Rakieh

1999   Effects of Life Conditions on the Health of a Negro Slave Community in Suriname. In *African Sites Archaeology in the Caribbean*, edited by Jay B. Haviser, pp. 291–312. Marcus Wiener, Princeton, New Jersey.

McEwan, Bonnie G.

1986   Domestic Adaptation at Puerto Real, Haiti. *Historical Archaeology* 20(1):44–49.

Mann, Rob W., Lee Meadows, William M. Bass, and David R. Watters

1987   Description of Skeletal Remains from a Black Slave Cemetery from Montserrat, West Indies. *Annals of the Carnegie Museum* 56(19):319–336.

Orser, Charles E.

1992   Bibliography of Slave and Plantation Archaeology. *Slavery & Abolition* 13(3):316–337.

Petersen, James B., David R. Watters, and Desmond V. Nicholson

1999   Continuity and Syncretism in Afro-Caribbean Ceramics from the Northern Lesser Antilles. In *African Sites Archaeology in the Caribbean*, edited by Jay B. Haviser, pp. 157–195. Marcus Wiener, Princeton, New Jersey.

Pulsipher, Lydia M., and Conrad M. Goodwin

1999   "Here Where the Old Time People Be": Reconstructing the Landscapes of the Slavery and Post-Slavery Era in Montserrat, West Indies. In *African Sites Archaeology in the Caribbean*, edited by Jay B. Haviser, pp. 9–37. Marcus Wiener, Princeton, New Jersey.

Reitz, Elizabeth J.

1992   The Spanish Colonial Experience and Domestic Animals. *Historical Archaeology* 26(1):84–91.

Ryzewski, Krysta, and John Cherry

2015   Struggles of a Sugar Society: Surveying Plantation-Era Montserrat, 1650–1850. *International Journal of Historical Archaeology* 19(2):356–383.

Scott, Elizabeth M.

1994   *Those of Little Note: Gender, Race, and Class in Historical Archaeology*. University of Arizona Press, Tucson.

Singleton, Theresa A.

1998   Cultural Interaction and African American Identity in Plantation Archaeology. In *Studies in Culture Contact: Interaction, Culture Change, and Archaeology*, edited by James G. Cusick, pp. 172–190. Southern Illinois University, Carbondale.

2001   Slavery and Spatial Dialectics on Cuban Coffee Plantations. *World Archaeology* 33(1):98–114.

Thomas, David Hurst (editor)

1992   *Columbian Consequences*, Volume 2. Smithsonian Institution Press, Washington, D.C.

Watters, David R.

1987   Excavations at the Harney Site Slave Cemetery, Montserrat, West Indies. *Annals of the Carnegie Museum* 56(18):289–318.

1996   Mortuary Patterns at Harney Site Slave Cemetery, Montserrat, in Caribbean Perspective. *Historical Archaeology* 28(3):54–73.

2001   Historical Archaeology of the British Caribbean. In *Island Lives: Historical Archaeologies of the Caribbean*, edited by Paul Farnsworth, pp. 82–102. University of Alabama Press, Tuscaloosa.

Wilkie, Laurie A.

1999   Evidence of African Continuities in the Material Culture of Clifton Plantation, Bahamas. In *African Sites Archaeology in the Caribbean*, edited by Jay B. Haviser, pp. 264–276. Marcus Wiener, Princeton, New Jersey.

2000   Culture Bought: Evidence of Creolization in the Consumer Goods of an Enslaved Bahamian Family. *Historical Archaeology* 34(3):10–26.

2001   Methodist Intentions and African Sensibilities. In *Island Lives: Historical Archaeologies of the Caribbean*, edited by Paul Farnsworth, pp. 272–300. University of Alabama Press, Tuscaloosa.

Wilkie, Laurie A., and Paul Farnsworth

2005   *Sampling Many Pots: An Archaeology of Memory and Tradition at a Bahamian Plantation*. University Press of Florida, Gainesville.

2011   Living Not So Quietly, Not So on the Edge of Things. In *The Materiality of Freedom: Archaeologies of Postemancipation Life*, edited by Jodi A. Barnes, pp. 58–68. University of South Carolina Press, Columbia.

1

The Spaces Between and Within

2

The Role of Caves and Gullies in Escape, Mobility, and the Creation of Community Networks among Enslaved Peoples of Barbados

FREDERICK H. SMITH AND HAYDEN F. BASSETT

Historical archaeologists in the Caribbean have investigated the lives of enslaved peoples largely through the study of their domestic spaces and burial grounds in plantation contexts, which has helped shed light on many of the day-to-day activities, material conditions, and mortuary practices of enslaved peoples. Yet enslaved peoples also carved out lives in the more liminal spaces of plantation societies. These spaces are what Dell Upton (1984:70) might call the "private landscapes" of enslaved peoples. While the layouts of plantation villages demonstrate a great deal of planter control, the private landscapes of enslaved peoples offer insights into the activities and experiences where the reach of the planter was more limited.

Archaeological investigations of the caves and gullies surrounding St. Nicholas Abbey sugar plantation in St. Peter Parish, Barbados, shed light on the activities that some enslaved plantation workers pursued. The gullies winding between St. Nicholas Abbey, the tenantry of Moore Hill, Portland Plantation, and other estates in St. Peter contain a series of caves, many of which possess historic-period material culture, including ceramics, clay tobacco pipes, and black bottle glass. These caves, as liminal spaces on the landscape between adjoining plantations, appear to have served as meeting places for enslaved peoples and, later, free workers from St. Nicholas Abbey and other estates. The privacy these spaces afforded seems to have spurred physical mobility and social interaction between enslaved peoples from surrounding villages and may have fostered activities that were not permitted in the public sphere, such as gaming, alcohol drinking, and more generalized types of leisure. We thus interpret gullies as conduits and corridors that connected communities in the plantation-dominated landscape of Barbados, places that offered a temporary respite from the challenges of plantation life.

Caves in Barbados

Caves are common on limestone islands like Barbados. In the seventeenth and eighteenth centuries, colonists and visitors to Barbados were fascinated by the many caves that dotted the island's landscape, and they described the extensive cave systems. In the late 1640s, Richard Ligon (1673:93), an English Royalist who fled to Barbados during the English Civil War, noted, "Caves are very frequent in the Island, and of several dimensions, some small, others extremely large and Capacious." A century later, Griffith Hughes, a naturalist and the rector of St. Lucy Parish church, visited numerous caves during his time in Barbados and noted their beauty and complex calcareous formations. According to Hughes (1750: 294), some of these caves were "spacious enough to contain 500 People." Ligon, Hughes, and other writers also noted evidence for prehistoric human occupation of these caves.

Indeed, caves in Barbados were used extensively in prehistoric times, and archaeologists have investigated several cave sites on the island. As early as 1902 the famed ethnologist and archaeologist Jesse Walter Fewkes surveyed caves in Barbados where large collections of Amerindian conch shell tools, pottery, "idols" (clay figures, or *adornos*), and other materials were found. The evidence convinced Fewkes that the prehistoric peoples of Barbados made extensive use of caves and led him to boldly claim that the prehistoric peoples of Barbados, unlike Amerindians in the other islands, were "practically cave dwellers" and that "they were probably the only Antilleans who made artificial caverns for habitation and other purposes" (Fewkes 1915: 50). Cave studies have become a prominent theme in the scholarship of the prehistoric Caribbean. Alice Samson and others have recently used the term "cavescapes" for the systematic study of subterranean human activity in caves (Samson et al. 2013). The term has thus far been applied to cave sites associated with pre-Columbian peoples in the Caribbean where the primary focus has been on funerary practices and ritual activities as well as the study of rock art. But what about the human occupation and use of caves in historic times? The study of historical-period cave occupations in Barbados adds a new dimension to cavescape studies because caves served an important escapist function in these tightly controlled social environments driven by coercive systems of labor.

Historical archaeological interest in caves in Barbados began in the early 1970s when Frederick W. Lange and Jerome S. Handler, along with field supervisor Robert Riordan, conducted archaeological investigations at Mapps Cave in St. Philip. The study was part of a broader research project that included the collection of oral histories, archaeological excavations, and archival research aimed at gathering information on slavery and plantation life in Barbados. The massive program they initiated was one of the pioneering projects in the development of African diaspora studies in historical archaeology. After testing a number of sites, including Mapps Cave, the researchers settled in for a substantial excavation of the now famous seventeenth- through nineteenth-century enslaved persons' cemetery at Newton Plantation in the parish of Christ Church. The findings from the Newton excavations were published in a landmark volume *Plantation Slavery in Barbados: An Archaeological and Historical Investigation* (Handler and Lange 1978). While discoveries at Newton diverted their attention and precluded further study at Mapps Cave, Lange and Handler (1980) managed to publish a short article on the Amerindian materials recovered from Mapps Cave. Moreover, in that article, the authors noted the presence of historical-period "china, glass, crockery, roof tiles, conch shell fragments, and some white clay pipe fragments" on the ground surface in the cave and a surrounding sinkhole.

Archaeological interest in Mapps Cave was renewed in the late 1990s when L. Daniel Mouer and Frederick H. Smith joined Handler for a further study at Mapps Cave, which sought to revisit the use of the site during the early historical period. A study of the assemblage of white clay tobacco pipe stems from the site led Mouer and Smith (2001) to conclude that the historic occupation of Mapps Cave covered a long period and that stratified occupational deposits at the site were probably intact. Mouer and Smith also reviewed original field and laboratory records from the 1972 excavation, notes pertaining to subsequent artifact analyses, and Handler's, Lange's, and Riordan's correspondence about the site (Handler 1998). This review was sufficient to convince Mouer and Smith that the site warranted further study, and in 1998 they conducted additional archaeological tests at Mapps Cave. Five years later, in 2003, Smith (2008) once again returned to Mapps Cave to carry out further analysis of archaeological and architectural remains at the site.

Mapps Cave is a relatively large cave by Barbadian standards. The cave entrance and two rock shelters sit in a limestone sink roughly 15 m^2 and between 3 and 5 m below the ground surface. Upon entering the limestone sink and cavern, it quickly becomes clear that human activity at the site has been extensive. The ground surface is littered with sherds of historical-period course and refined ceramics, white clay tobacco pipes, and black bottle glass.

As Lange and Handler (1980) showed, Amerindian peoples used the cave and sinkhole long before the arrival of the English in Barbados in 1627. But who was using it during the early historical era? In the early years of settlement, some British colonists were known to dwell in caves. For example, James Drax, an Englishman who arrived with the first party of English colonists in 1627, was reported to have "sheltered in a cave in the rocks" with a half dozen or so other Englishmen during the early years of settlement (Father Antoine Biet in 1654, cited in Handler 1967: 69). Drax later became one of the wealthiest sugar planters in Barbados and built a magnificent great house, but in the early days of settlement, caves offered Drax and some of his comrades an alternative to the timber and stone houses being erected in the island at that time. Yet, while some colonists may have exploited the caves of Barbados for shelter, instances of cave-dwelling English colonists were no doubt rare and probably occurred only during the first few years of colonization near primary settlements along the southern and western coasts. In contrast, Mapps Cave, located in what was the isolated eastern fringe of the island in the early to mid-seventeenth century, probably served as a temporary hideout for individuals and small groups of runaway slaves seeking a short-term flight from bondage, otherwise known as *petite marronage.*

Oral traditions and historical accounts suggest that enslaved runaways hid out in Mapps Cave. In the late 1640s, for example, Ligon wrote that fugitive slaves on the island "harbour themselves in Woods and Caves, living upon pillage for many months together" (1673:98). According to Ligon, "The runaway Negres, often shelter themselves in these Coverts, for a long time, and in the night range abroad the Countrey, and steale Pigs, Plantins, Potatoes, and Pullin, and bring it there; and feast all day, upon what they stole the night before" (1673:98).

Some caves were large enough to hold hundreds of people, and in many cases a thick natural curtain of vines obscured cave entrances from the view of would-be slave catchers. As a result, whites employed trained lyam-hounds to flush out fugitive slaves who were holed up in caves in the out-of-the-way hills, gullies, and dense forests of Barbados. Ligon's map of the Barbados, for example, illustrates two fugitives being chased and fired upon by a man on horseback in these rugged and unsettled parts of the island

Figure 2.1. Section of "A Topographicall Description . . . of Barbados" illustrating two runaway slaves. Frontispiece of Richard Ligon, *A True and Exact History of the Island of Barbadoes*, 2nd ed. (London, 1673). (Image Courtesy of the John Carter Brown Library at Brown University)

(Figure 2.1). Nearly a decade later, in 1657, the Barbados Council and Assembly continued to receive complaints from frustrated planters about rebellious runaways "lurkeing in woods and secrett places" (cited in Gragg 2003:159 and Handler 1997:188).

Concerns about the use of caves by enslaved runaways continued into the eighteenth century. John Oldmixon (1741:105), for example, noted that some of the caves in Barbados are "so large . . . that they will hold above three hundred Men," further noting, "To these Caves the Negroes often fly from the Fury of their Masters, when they are conscious to themselves, that their Guilt deserves a sever Punishment. They hide themselves there sometimes for Weeks together, and never stir out but at Night." Two decades later an eighteenth-century historian similarly described the island's caves as "the lurking-holes of run-away negroes" (Sale et al. 1764:211). The use of caves by runaways continued into the nineteenth century. Theodore Easel (1840:24–29) visited Barbados during the late 1830s and recorded the story of Paul, a young enslaved man who had encountered a group of four male runaways living in a cave in the side of a gully in St. Thomas Parish. According to Paul's account, the cave was well stocked with food and drink, and the men may have launched robberies from their hideout. Although the small size and high population density of Barbados made it impossible for runaway slaves in the island to establish permanent maroon communities like those in Jamaica, Brazil, and Suriname, there is compelling documentary evidence for various forms of *marronage* in Barbados, including the use of caves as temporary hiding places for runaways (Handler 1997). Moreover, archaeologists in other parts of the Caribbean, especially in Cuba and the Dominican Republic, have identified caves that they believe were once used by enslaved runaways, and there is some evidence to suggest that Mapps may have served that purpose from time to time. The most compelling archaeological evidence for *marronage* at Mapps Cave is the presence of a few seventeenth-century ceramic types and white clay pipe stems with large bore diameters mixed with Amerindian pottery and shell tools. The Amerindian materials may have been recycled and reused by enslaved runaways to help them survive during their flight, as has been argued for other sites of *marronage* in North America and the Caribbean (Agorsah 1993; Funari 1995; García Arévelo 1986; La Rosa Corzo 2003; Nichols 1988; Orser 1993, 1994, 1996:41–55; Orser and Funari 2001; Sayers 2014; Sayers et al. 2007; Smith 2008).

While the archaeological evidence for *marronage* at Mapps is limited, enslaved peoples appear to have used the cave and sinkhole extensively in the late eighteenth and early nineteenth centuries. Sherds of eighteenth- and nineteenth-century ceramics and bottle glass are liberally scattered about the ground surface. Moreover, the cave and sinkhole were heavily modified. In the sinkhole, there is a cut-coral retaining wall and a collapsed set of cut-coral stairs that were constructed to facilitate the descent from the ground surface to the sinkhole and cave below. A low wall was built across the mouth of the cave entrance, and a retaining wall was built inside of the cave. A hole was also chiseled into the roof, probably to let light into the dark recesses of the cave or to allow smoke to exit from an interior fire. The cave's stratigraphy shows clear periods of deposition stretching from the pre-Columbian times to the present. The disproportionate amount of drinking-related materials, such as black glass bottles, found archaeologically in the cave indicate that alcohol drinking, and perhaps alcohol production, took place in Mapps Cave.

Caves by Way of Gullies

The findings at Mapps sparked further investigation of caves in the gullies around St. Nicholas Abbey sugar plantation when Smith began archaeological work there in 2007. Workers on the estate, coming from the nearby villages of Castle tenantry and Moore Hill, noted the presence of caves in the gullies around St. Nicholas Abbey. They were intimately familiar with them. Some workers noted that as children they played in the caves and had seen the same types of ceramic and glass materials there that we were finding in our archaeological excavations around the estate. Some areas of gullies wherein the caves lie are currently used to graze sheep and cattle.

In 2007 we began surveying, mapping, photographing, and surface collecting these caves. The gullies are somewhat difficult to traverse, and while it is not known whether they were more open in the past, historical references suggest that they were rugged areas rarely traversed by Europeans. Although English descriptions of the island's caves begin in the seventeenth century, Europeans appear to have only frequented a few of the more remarkable caverns and gullies for the leisurely naturalism of the nineteenth century. To the planters and the English travelers to Barbados, the uncleared gullies were dense thickets that represented holdouts from cultivation, "affording harbourage for trees, bushes, trailers, and creeping plants, which have been exterminated from the cultivated lands" (Chester 1869:39). The gullies around St. Nicholas Abbey are steep and rugged, which is why they were left wooded and not used for sugarcane cultivation. However, they probably served as sources for wood for fuel in the factory and in domestic contexts on the estate.

Among the more sizable caves in the gullies near St. Nicholas Abbey is the one pictured in Figure 2.2. It consists of two tiers. The lower tier poses a cave roughly 25 m wide, 15 m deep, and 3–4 m high. A large, uncovered, relatively flat platform or landing juts out about 10 m in front of the mouth of the cave. It is not clear if this is an entirely natural platform or whether a retaining wall was constructed to shore up a platform area at the cave entrance. The second tier consists of a series of smaller caves roughly 5 m in width, diameter, and height. One can easily stand up in all of these caves, and the floor surfaces are relatively flat. The caves themselves are situated

Figure 2.2. Cave in the gully of St. Nicholas Abbey plantation, St. Peter, Barbados. (Photograph by Hayden Bassett)

high in the gully wall, looking down upon the gully floor. As such, the presence and quantity of artifacts within the caves indicates their historical use, as colluvial deposits containing artifacts are largely confined to outer slopes and bottom of the gully. Pearlware and whiteware ceramics were found on the ground surface near the cave entrance. Surface finds in and around the caves also included fragments of stoneware and black glass bottles, suggesting that alcohol drinking may have been a common activity at the site, as at Mapps Cave.

James A. Delle's (1998) study of coffee estates in Jamaica highlights the way plantation landscapes reinforced planter controls and surveillance. As Delle shows, plantation landscapes were designed to limit the mobility and privacy of enslaved workers. Unlike Jamaica, with its vast undeveloped areas, Barbados was densely populated and extensively cultivated, leaving few areas beyond the sight of whites. As discussed in the introduction to this volume, however, such surveillance could be thwarted. At St. Nicholas Abbey, the caves and rock shelters along the walls of the gully drainage are all but invisible from the roads and sugarcane fields above and the gully floor below. A curtain of dense vegetation conceals many of the openings. Pockets of material culture extend far back into the caves' recesses.

Finding and traveling to and through these spaces would have required intimate knowledge of the local network of gullies, a subtle form of "way-finding" attainable only through recurrent use. "Wayfinding," according to archaeologist Tim Ingold (2000:237), differs from map using in that "knowing where you are lies not in the establishment of a point-to-point correspondence between the world and its representation, but in the re-membering of journeys previously made, and that brought you to the place along the same or different paths." Moving through familiar terrain, the wayfinder narrates past movements, retracing the perceptual experience of journeying to, through, and along itineraries of places. These places are known not only through the experiences within them but also in the comings and goings of getting there and, if need be, getting back. In this sense, finding one's way through the web of overgrown gullies to caves and other meeting points in St. Peter Parish involved a localized knowledge embodied in reoccurring movements to place.

These hidden trails served what sociologist Erving Goffman might call paths for circumventing information control. From the caves, inhabitants could see without being seen and could safely commune with those who likewise knew the way through and to the gullies to chosen enclaves. Even today some estate workers will note that they prefer to travel through the gullies rather than open roads to limit others' knowledge of their movements. Moreover, the presence of modern beer and liquor bottle fragments around the caves indicates that these caves have served as drinking spaces in relatively recent times.

Other similar caves were located further down the gully in an area known as "Adventure" by people from the villages in the surrounding area. These caves, equally as spacious, possessed the largest represented span of material culture, though none had sizable platforms at their entrances. As with the caves further east in the same gully, surface survey suggested extensive use of these spaces in the late eighteenth and early nineteenth centuries. Yet unlike the caves to the east, the material culture underneath the countless rock shelters of "Adventure" suggested perhaps both a more prolonged residential occupation as well as temporary use, from the eighteenth through the twentieth centuries and possibly into the twenty-first century.

The gully wherein these caves lie runs from the back of St. Nicholas Abbey great house to the nearby Portland Plantation. Since 2007 two plantation village sites have been identified at St. Nicholas Abbey, and both are located along the edge of this gully with households likely wrapping around a small protruding branch of the gully. An early village that dates from the seventeenth to the early nineteenth century sits across the gully from a later village, which dates from the late eighteenth through mid-nineteenth century (Bergman and Smith 2014). Recent archaeological testing in 2014 revealed that the later village continued to be occupied long after emancipation and perhaps well into the twentieth century.

From the site of the later village at St. Nicholas Abbey one can see directly to Portland estate. If the slave village at Portland was located near the factory, as it is at St. Nicholas Abbey and at other estates in Barbados, then the two villages would have been in sight of each other. Moreover, the gully connects with two other branches that run to the adjacent Welchtown Plantation in the south and Castle and Mt. Gay estates in the north. It is likely that these gullies served as conduits for people traveling between plantations and meeting spaces for people from surrounding estates from the earliest days of plantation slavery in the area.

*   *   *

It is probably no coincidence that today the rum shops at Diamond Corners sit at the confluence of these gullies near the caves that once served as clandestine meeting and drinking spaces for enslaved laborers. The connections between the enslaved and free communities of St. Nicholas Abbey and neighboring plantations therefore point to the need to understand gully throughways as liminal places integral to the experience of plantation workers, whether enslaved or free, in Barbados.

Connecting enslaved communities, the island's networks of gullies appear to have provided navigability and common ground to seemingly insular plantation villages. Caves, as discrete places connected in these gully systems, were made meaningful by enslaved people through movement, as they were used as paths. Locating and connecting caves in this way builds upon Ingold's (2000:219) conception of places as "bound together by the itineraries of their inhabitants, . . . exist[ing] not in space but as nodes in a matrix of movement." Defining place by movement follows a growing body of literature on mobility studies in the social sciences and humanities that recognizes the ontological primacy and investigative potential of information, objects, and the human body in motion (Clifford 1997; Marcus 1995; Sheller and Urry 2006). Moreover, recent contributions have demonstrated the need for archaeologists to consider the tenets of this "motilities paradigm" by theorizing and addressing past movement and motion (Beaudry and Parno 2013; Fowles 2011; Snead 2011, 2012). As explored here, a focus on the movement of enslaved people allows us to understand the enslaved condition on both a regional and localized scale and, perhaps more significantly, the connective relationship between the two scales.

Movement through these concealed and unassuming throughways geographically articulated the itineraries of what Upton (1984) describes as "black landscapes," a plantation experience distinct from the movement characterizing "white landscapes." To define the white and black experiences of plantation society in this way, Upton shifts the understanding of social divisions from distinct spaces to dynamic routes of race and class. In this way such divisions were not necessarily spatially segregated but occurred along conduits—both black and white—that intersected and overlapped one another within and beyond the plantation boundaries. In the routes traveled by the island's gentry and common planters, the proprietor was at the center of a constructed world experienced by social peers as a "processional" hierarchy (Upton 1984:66). They traveled the roadways in public view, to and through places of civic, ecclesiastical, and domestic visibility and interaction. In contrast, black landscapes centered on the home quarter, with routes radiating out near and far upon prescribed and clandestine paths, both seen and unseen by the planter class. Through these landscapes, as Upton (1984:70) suggests, "separation from white control allowed slaves to form communities that were held together by their mastery of the slave landscape of woods, fields, and waterways." In St. Peter, Barbados, the gullies were a central part of those clandestine paths.

Movement through the gullies afforded a degree of unseen mobility for those bound to the plantation landscape. Such routes paralleled, intersected, and in some cases deviated far from the roads upon which planters and overseers traveled and surveilled by carriage and horseback. Through the nineteenth century, Europeans viewed the gullies as an obstacle to their mode of movement and travel. As one Englishman described the gullies of Barbados, "They are often of great length. And their depth and steepness will frequently compel a horseman to make a long detour" (Chester 1869:29). These "detours" from the white landscape allowed the gully routes of enslaved laborers to largely go unwitnessed and the caves within to remain unknown to the planter class.

Arawak Temple: Caves beyond Prehistory

A short distance from the caves and gullies that intersect at Diamond Corners is a large cave that sits along a modern road in the village of Mile and a Quarter. Here a set of modern concrete stairs leads into a hollow shelter intricately carved from the bedrock. The people in the village refer to the cave as the "Arawak Temple," and it was saved by the Barbadian government during a road construction project and preserved as a tourist attraction in the 1950s. The cave is clearly the product of human modification, although it is difficult to determine exactly when it was carved. There is no soil to speak of inside the cave, although late-eighteenth and early-nineteenth-century ceramic and glass materials can be found scattered around the surface areas surrounding the site. A cherub-like feature was carved into the wall above the entrance to the cave, and slots were carved into some of the walls, possibly to hold floor joists. High above the cave's floor, a cryptic set of initials and what is perhaps a date of 1686 are carved into the wall in old script.

The Arawak Temple was described in great detail by Hughes in his *Natural History of Barbados* published in 1750. Hughes noted that during the time he was writing, the people from the surrounding areas called it "Indian Castle" because of the large amount of Amerindian material found at the site and the unique character of those artifacts. Hughes believed that Amerindians inhabited the cave, especially during storms and during the wet season months, and that they also dug a pond near the cave to hold rainwater. According to Hughes, "With part of the Clay, which they dug out, they made their Earthen-ware, such as Pots and Pans; and, like the Idolaters of old, out of the same Materials they made to themselves Gods, and worshiped them. Among several broken Fragments of Idols, said to be dug up in this place, I saw a Head of one, which alone weighed above sixty Pounds Weight. This, before it was broken off, stood upon an oval Pedestal above three Feet in Height" (1750:7). Fewkes (1915:49) embraced Hughes' interpretation of Indian Castle and used it to bolster his argument that prehistoric Barbadians were "cave dwellers" and that "Barbados is the only West Indian island where artificial cave dwellings were made." However, Fewkes ignored evidence that the cave may have been modified during the historic era. Clearly, there were modifications to the cave during the early historic period. Fewkes, believing this to be an Amerindian cave dwelling, described the cherub-like figure above the cave entrance as simply a "rude figure in relief" (see Figure 2.3). We, however, believe the figure to be a representation of a cherub in the Christian tradition and believe the cave may have served as a small church or some other specialized meeting area for Christians, perhaps poor whites, enslaved people, or freedmen, sometime during the seventeenth or eighteenth centuries. Burn marks and drains

Figure 2.3. Carving of a cherub-like image at the entrance to the Arawak Temple, St. Peter, Barbados. (Photograph by Hayden Bassett)

carved into the limestone floor and an adjoining cylindrical chamber also suggest that it may have also served as a limekiln at some point. Although Fewkes' initial reaction to the site was that it looked like a limekiln, he ultimately rejected that interpretation. Thus, this curious space, partially cavernous and partially carved, represents a landscape feature with a multitude of uses and meanings to different groups from the prehistoric Amerindians to Christians, laborers, naturalists, tourism boards, and even archaeologists. The Arawak Temple—like many caves on the island—tells a story of deeply layered meanings.

Conclusion

Amerindians were not the only people to exploit the caves and gullies of Barbados. Recent scholarship on cave use in the region has largely been limited to pre-Columbian inhabitants (e.g., Kambesis and Machel 2013). Yet cave use on the island, as illustrated through the Arawak Temple, Mapps Cave, and the caves that wind through the gullies around St. Nicholas Abbey, has a long history that extends through to the present. As unique fixtures in the landscape, caves and the materials left in them by passing generations speak to the changing world around them through their constant appropriation and reappropriation. The Arawak Temple was once likely integral to the routes of movement that defined the changing Amerindian landscape, with connections forged in strategic and meaningful ways. In more recent times, the use of gullies linked the Arawak Temple to a landscape of movement routed through a world unseen by the planters. By the mid-twentieth century, tourism enmeshed and redefined Arawak Temple in a different route, a route defined by curiosity and consumption of exotic place. As caves continue to be used throughout the island as tourist attractions, storage spaces, residences, animal pens, and subjects of archaeological discourse, our scholarship must see them not as discrete isolated spaces but as connected upon historically contingent and socially meaningful routes of movement.

Whites in Barbados believed that enslaved peoples hid out and took refuge in caves. In the Western imagination, caves were dark and dangerous places. They were the entrances to hell and the meeting places of dangerous people. Perhaps the best example of the place of caves in Western imagination comes from Shakespeare's *Macbeth*, wherein witches used a cave to perform their magic and chant spells such as "Double, double, toil, and trouble" (act 4, scene 1, line 10). Seeing the mouth of a cave deep in the gully network of Barbados, one English traveler likened the view to the "robber scenery" of Salvator Rosa's seventeenth-century painting *A Mountainous Landscape with Bandits Robbing Travellers* (Easel 1840:193). Perhaps this is why early English colonists in Barbados thought of caves as hideouts for runaways and why so many Barbadians today believe the slave revolt of 1816 was fomented and conjured in the dark recesses of Mapps Cave. However, the caves and gully systems in Barbados appear to have usually served a more mundane yet important function. As rugged and uncultivated areas, the gullies in St. Peter, and perhaps throughout Barbados, provided a private space where enslaved peoples could meet and travel with little restriction, and relationships between members of different villages could be established and maintained. As Upton points out in Virginia, enslaved workers could use these secretive spaces to temporarily quit the plantation without ever actually leaving the estates.

Caves and their connective gullies were actively incorporated into the lived experience of enslaved peoples by their routes of movement. Mobility was central to plantation operations. Whether localized or extending beyond the property, moving resources, commodities, and people in highly orchestrated ways was vital to production. Yet archaeological and historical evidence reveals that despite the visual strategies of control by the planter and managerial class, enslaved people appropriated and modified the island's unique environment to circumvent visibility and extend their physical mobility to spaces beyond the plantation.

Caves and gullies were indeed liminal spaces. While the sugarcane fields, quarters, factories, roads, and great houses were symbols of other people's power, the uncultivated caves and gullies were fluid sanctuaries from plantation life. While "cavescapes" may be an appropriate term for isolated caves, such as Mapps, "gullyscapes" might be more appropriate for the dynamic network of caves and gullies that run through St. Peter. The gullies surrounding St. Nicholas Abbey may have served as clandestine corridors between surrounding sugar estates. Through these corridors information was spread, regional community ties were reinforced, and a regional identity was forged. As with Mapps Cave, the caves situated in the gullies surrounding St. Nicholas Abbey appear to have provided extensive periods of social interaction and social integration among workers from regional estates. The presence of black glass fragments and pieces of stoneware drinking mugs hint at the likelihood that alcohol drinking was one of the main activities to occur at these sites. As a social performance, alcohol drinking would have helped strengthen community bonds and foster the expression of regional identities. And the presence of modern beer and liquor bottle glass at the cave sites demonstrates the ongoing use of gullies as corridors and meeting spaces for plantation workers today.

References Cited

Agorsah, E. Kofi
1993   Archaeology and Resistance History in the Caribbean. *African Archaeological Review* 11(1):175–195.
Beaudry, Mary C., and Travis G. Parno (editors)
2013   *Archaeologies of Mobility and Movement.* Springer Science & Business Media, New York.
Bergman, Stephanie, and Frederick H. Smith
2014   Blurring Disciplinary Boundaries: The Material Culture of Improvement during the Age of Abolition in Barbados. *Slavery & Abolition* 35(3):418–436.
Chester, Greville John
1869   *Transatlantic Sketches in the West Indies, South America, Canada, and the United States.* Smith, Elder & Company, New York.
Clifford, James
1997   *Routes: Travel and Translation in the Late Twentieth Century.* Harvard University Press, Cambridge.

Delle, James
1998   *An Archaeology of Social Space: Analyzing Coffee Plantations in Jamaica's Blue Mountains.* Plenum, New York.

Easel, Theodore (pseud.)
1840   *Desultory Sketches and Tales of Barbados.* London.

Fewkes, J. Walter
1915   Archaeology of Barbados. In *Proceedings of the National Academy of Sciences of the United States of America*, 1(1):47–51. Williams & Wilkins Company, Baltimore.

Fowles, Severin M.
2011   Movement and the Unsettling of the Pueblos. In *Rethinking Anthropological Perspectives on Migration*, edited by Graciela Cabana and Jeffrey Clark, pp. 45–67. University Press of Florida, Gainesville.

Funari, Pedro P. A.
1995   The Archaeology of Palmares and Its Contribution to the Understanding of the History of African-American Culture. *Historical Archaeology in Latin America* 7:1–41.

García Arévelo, Manuel A.
1986   El Maniel de José Leta: Evidencias arqueológicas de un posible asentamiento Cimarrón en la Región Sudoriental de la Isla de Santo Domingo. In *Cimarrón*, edited Jose J. Arrom and Manuel A. García Arévelo, pp. 33–76. Fundación García Arévelo, Santo Domingo, Dominican Republic.

Gragg, Larry Dale
2003   *Englishmen Transplanted: The English Colonization of Barbados, 1627–1660.* Oxford University Press, Oxford.

Handler, Jerome S.
1967   Father Antoine Biet's Visit to Barbados in 1654. *Journal of the Barbados Museum and Historical Society* 32:56–76.
1997   Escaping Slavery in a Caribbean Plantation Society: Marronage in Barbados, 1650s-1830s. *Nieuwe West-Indische Gids* 71:183–225.
1998   Research Notes and Related Materials Shipped to the Barbados Department of Archives, January 1998; Box1: Archaeology Projects (1971, 1972, 1973, 1987).

Handler, Jerome S., and Frederick W. Lange
1978   *Plantation Slavery in Barbados: An Archaeological and Historical Investigation.* Harvard University Press, Cambridge.

Hughes, Griffith
1750   *The Natural History of Barbados.* Printed for the author, London.

Ingold, Tim
2000   *Perception of the Environment: Essays in Livelihood, Dwelling and Skill.* Psychology Press, London.

Kambesis, Patricia N., and Hans G. Machel
2013   Caves and Karst of Barbados. In *Coastal Karst Landforms*, edited by Michael J. Lace and John E. Mylroie, pp. 227–244. Coastal Research Library 5. Springer, Netherlands.

Lange, Frederick W., and Jerome S. Handler

1980   The Archaeology of Mapp's Cave: A Contribution to the Prehistory of Barbados. *Journal of the Virgin Islands Archaeological Society* 9:3–17.

La Rosa Corzo, Gabino

2003   *Runaway Slave Settlements in Cuba: Resistance and Repression*. University of North Carolina Press, Chapel Hill.

Ligon, Richard

1673   *A True and Exact History of the Island of Barbadoes*. 2nd ed. Parker, London.

Marcus, George E.

1995   Ethnography in/of the World System: The Emergence of Multi-Sited Ethnography. *Annual Review of Anthropology* 24(1):95–117.

Mouer, Daniel L., and Frederick H. Smith

2001   Revisiting Mapps Cave: Amerindian and Probable Slave Occupation of a Sink-Hole and Cavern, St. Philip Parish, Barbados. In *Proceedings of the 18th International Conference for Caribbean Archaeology*, pp. 301–307. Guadeloupe, French West Indies.

Nichols, Elaine

1988   *No Easy Run to Freedom: Maroons in the Great Dismal Swamp of North Carolina, 1677–1850*. University of South Carolina Press, Columbia.

Oldmixon, John

1741   *The British Empire in America: Containing the History of the Discovery, Settlement, Progress and State of the British Colonies on the Continent and Islands of America*. Printed for J. Brotherton, J. Clarke, A. Ward, J. Clarke, C. Hitch, J. Osbourn, E. Wicksteed, C. Bathurst, Timothy Saunders, and T. Harris, London.

Orser, Charles E., Jr.

1993   *In Search of Zumbi: The 1993 Season*. Midwestern Archaeological Research Center, Normal, Illinois.

1994   The Archaeology of African-American Slave Religion in the Antebellum South. *Cambridge Archaeological Journal* 4(01):33–45.

1996   *A Historical Archaeology of the Modern World*. Springer, New York.

Orser, Charles E., Jr., and Pedro P. A. Funari

2001   Archaeology and Slave Resistance and Rebellion. *World Archaeology* 33:61–72.

Sale, George, George Psalmanazar, Archibald Bower, George Shelvocke, John Campbell, and John Swinton

1764   *An Universal History: From the Earliest Accounts to the Present Time*. Vol. 41. Printed for C. Bathurst, London.

Samson, Alice V. M., Jago Cooper, Miguel A. Nieves, Reniel Rodriguez-Ramos, Patricia N. Kambesis, and Michael J. Lace

2013   Cavescapes in the Pre-Columbian Caribbean. *Antiquity* 087(338).

Sayers, Daniel O.

2014   *A Desolate Place for Defiant People: The Archaeology of Maroons, Indigenous Americans, and Enslaved Laborers in the Great Dismal Swamp*. University Press of Florida, Gainesville.

Sayers, Daniel O., P. Brendan Burke, and Aaron M. Henry
2007   The Political Economy of Exile in the Great Dismal Swamp. *International Journal of Historical Archaeology* 11(1):60–97.
Sheller, Mimi, and John Urry
2006   The New Mobilities Paradigm. *Environment and Planning* A 38(2):207–226.
Smith, Frederick H.
2008   *The Archaeology of Alcohol and Drinking.* University Press of Florida, Gainesville.
Snead, James E.
2011   The "Secret and Bloody War Path": Movement, Place and Conflict in the Archaeological Landscape of North America. *World Archaeology* 43(3):478–492.
2012   Obliterated Itineraries: Pueblo Trails, Chaco Roads, and Archaeological Knowledge. In *Highways, Byways, and Road Systems in the Pre-Modern World*, edited by Susan E. Alcock, John Bodel, and Richard J. A. Talbert, pp. 106–127. Wiley-Blackwell, Oxford.
Upton, Dell
1984   White and Black Landscapes in Eighteenth-Century Virginia. *Places* 2(2):59–72.

3

"Poor Whites" on the Peripheries

"Poor White" and Afro-Barbadian Interaction on the Plantation

MATTHEW C. REILLY

In the early morning hours after a particularly rainy night, I follow Wilson Norris along a partially cleared path that marks the boundary between a sugarcane field to the west and the daunting escarpment of Hackleton's Cliff to the east. Boots caked in mud from the previous night's downpour, we come to an opening in the thick brush that lines the edge of the cliff. The opening reveals a well-manicured though steep and slippery path that meanders down the escarpment of the cliff into the dense forest below. Each morning Wilson, now in his early 70s, descends the narrow dirt pathway with a sharpened hoe and a large empty animal-feed sack to collect coconuts. Carefully walking through the woods, he makes stops at patches of coconut trees that had been planted by his father in decades past. As he effortlessly uses the hoe to husk the outer shell of a coconut, he quietly relays details of the individuals and families who had once lived in the now-abandoned community in which we are standing.

After a morning's work of husking and collecting 50 coconuts, which would later be sold to a local baker, we turn to begin our climb back to Wilson's home. Seemingly unaffected by the weight of the coconuts that rest atop his head, Wilson ascends the muddy pathway with calculated, consistent, and precise steps. Upon reaching the top of the cliff, we exit the cane field and casually walk down the road toward the tenantry, a parcel of land on which residents pay rent to construct their homes and reside to the south of Clifton Hall Plantation. Greeting neighbors as we pass, we come to Wilson's modest boarded home where he carefully tosses aside the sack of coconuts and calmly sits on a rusty metal chair to have a drink of water.

Exhausted from the morning's activities, particularly the hike back up the side of the cliff, we casually discuss the plantation landscape that

Wilson has called home all his life. Born and raised in the now-abandoned tenantry below the cliff (officially called Below Cliff), Wilson has witnessed the tremendous transformations that have affected the Clifton Hall area as well as its residents over the course of his lifetime. By the time Wilson was born, families had begun moving from the tenantry of Below Cliff to neighboring communities. Wilson recalls the dynamic community life he experienced in Below Cliff. In particular, he nostalgically speaks of late afternoons in the tenantry when he, along with the other children, would watch as the men (and, less regularly, women) would make their way down the cliff via one of three passageways after a day's work on the plantation. Others would return to the tenantry from the coast where they worked as fishermen, carrying their nets and hauls of flying fish, snapper, and sea eggs.

"Poor Whites" on the Plantation

Like his father before him, Wilson spent much of his adult life working on the plantation. His father was employed as a gardener at Clifton Hall while Wilson cut cane and worked in the factory at a number of different plantations. Like most Barbadians and those living in the Caribbean region more broadly, Wilson's family history is tethered to the plantation. He, along with his ancestors, is intimately aware of its seasons, sights, sounds, and contours. Those who walked and worked the grounds of the plantation were and are members of a diverse network of laboring residents. Their movements through plantation spaces brought them into close contact with one another on a regular basis; such encounters were integral components to plantation life and were instrumental in forging social networks and relationships. When such encounters are compounded by the presence of diverse racial identities, such networks and relationships take on new meanings as plantation residents navigate complex socioeconomic and racial hierarchies on the plantation landscape.

Wilson, who has a complex racial genealogy composed of African and European lineages, is of a rather pale complexion and would be locally and pejoratively referred to as a "poor white" or a "Redleg." His skin color, rather than his racially diverse ancestry, imposes an identity upon him that holds significance in the history of plantation labor on the island. The terms "poor white" and "Redleg" are reflective of socioeconomic status but also speak to an ancestry associated with seventeenth-century European indentured servants whose descendants have inhabited Barbados for over three centuries (for etymologies of the terms, see Lambert 2005:100–101; Sheppard 1977:2–3; see also Keagy 1972; Price 1957; Simmons 1976).[1] The tenantry of his childhood, Below Cliff, was inhabited by a community of poor whites from at least the mid-eighteenth century to the early 1960s. Throughout Below Cliff's occupation, poor whites had significant and regular interactions with free and enslaved Afro-Barbadians.

The labor history of Barbados is rather unique for the Caribbean given the persistent presence of significant numbers of European indentured servants (Beckles 1985, 1989). Despite small populations of poor whites on other Caribbean islands (see Akenson 1997; Brehony 2007; Johnson and Watson 1998; Watson 2000), Barbados was home to between 8,000 and 12,000 poor whites throughout the period of slavery and into the post-emancipation era (Sheppard 1977). Given the persistence of a working-class European-descendant population on the landscape, even following the decline in the use of indentured servitude, the plantation structure and landscape cannot be simply reduced to a binary model of white, male authority figures (planters, managers, overseers) and enslaved or free Africans and Afro-Barbadians. This chapter explores interactions between racially diverse plantation residents through an analysis of material culture recovered during the course of excavations of the Below Cliff tenantry, specifically coarse earthenwares. The plantation landscape is also analyzed to suggest how residents facilitated such interactions in a relatively harsh and unaccommodating environment beginning in the decades leading up to emancipation in 1834.

Fundamental to a nuanced analysis of the Barbadian plantation complex is the recognition that enslaved and formerly enslaved Afro-Barbadians were not alone on the landscape. Aside from planters, managers, and overseers with whom the enslaved would have had regular interaction (with the exception of absentee owners), the enslaved and formerly enslaved (following emancipation) would have encountered working-class "white" plantation residents or employees. In terms of socioeconomic status, poor whites and the enslaved had more in common with each other than either group did with the plantocracy (Watson 2000). In addition to serving as militia tenants and working as small farmers, fishermen, craftsmen, and hucksters, many poor whites were employed as wage laborers on the plantation. Although this phenomenon has been noted in passing (Handler 2002; Roberts 2011:249), the pronounced presence of these laborers on the plantation landscape has often gone entirely overlooked (Cateau 2006).

Analyses of the plantation must take seriously the complexities of cultural, racial, class, and gender identities that are not reductively dependent on dichotomies of white/black, enslaved/free, or European/African. Embedded in the binary model of planter/slave is the potent hierarchical structure in which the white plantocracy held considerable power over enslaved Africans or those of African descent. Despite ample evidence of the abilities of the enslaved to subvert, challenge, and resist planter control (for the Caribbean, see Armstrong 1990; Armstrong and Kelly 2000; Delle 1998, 2014; Hauser 2008; Haviser 1999; Singleton 2001, 2009), this model accurately encapsulates the fundamental principles of the race-based institution of slavery that plagued the Americas for roughly four centuries. Therefore, interpreting the diversity of those who coped with economic hardships in no way discounts the historical fact and significant implications of this system on the daily lives of those most affected. Rather, by considering the full spectrum of racial and class identities on the plantation landscape, it is possible to observe the existence, extent, and effects of interaction between individuals and groups who lacked substantial material means and experienced plantation power structures in diverse ways.

In what follows, I shed light on how a poor white presence on the Barbadian plantation landscape adds unique and significant dimensions to socioeconomic power hierarchies. Despite the substantial impact such power structures had on the lives of plantation residents as well as on how they viewed their own identities and those of others, such structures did not prohibit or significantly inhibit the frequent interactions between poor whites and Afro-Barbadians. Poor white tenants living in Below Cliff found employment at nearby plantations, including Clifton Hall. Here they served as general laborers, overseers, bookkeepers, factory workers, distillers, gardeners, seamstresses, and domestic servants, often working alongside the enslaved (albeit under a different legal status). While living in communities physically separated by an imposing geological feature, the roles of poor whites and the enslaved in plantation production processes facilitated direct interaction on a daily basis. The physical separation of poor white and Afro-Barbadian communities can be interpreted as an attempt by the plantocracy to establish, maintain, and make manifest cultural or racial group disparity (Epperson 1999; for a discussion of such boundaries in Barbados, see Jones 2007). Evidence of the transgression of such boundaries, however, illustrates the ability of laboring populations to define and develop their own social and economic networks across racial boundaries.

If the plantation landscape is the setting in which such interactions took place, its space needs to be reimagined in order to consider how poor whites manipulated and maneuvered through plantation spaces that were designed to circumscribe racial roles and identities. The plantation landscape was designed in particular and purposeful ways to maximize efficiency as well as control over the laboring population (Delle 1998, 2011, 2014; Lenik 2012; for how planters balanced the two, see Bates 2014). Surveillance and other control mechanisms were of the utmost importance for planters to effectively manage their estates. Given that the institution of slavery was dependent upon race-based hierarchies in addition to those of class, landscape surveillance and control were tantamount to maintenance and protection of racial boundaries and power divisions.

Scholars have suggested that poor whites in colonial contexts raised significant concerns among the plantocracy about the fortitude of racial and class boundaries (Stoler 2002; for Barbados, see Jones 2007; Lambert 2005). Ultimately, however, they were viewed as marginal and inconsequential to agro-industrial sugar production. The poor whites in Below Cliff, and those in similar plantation locales around the island, inhabited spaces deemed undesirable and marginal by those concerned with economic efficiency and plantation surveillance. Viewed archaeologically, however, the former vitality of such spaces receives new life. The spatial orientation of Clifton Hall Plantation discussed below reveals that how planters view, value, and allocate space often stands in stark contrast to the meanings that such spaces actually afford to non-elite residents.

The Sugar Revolution and the Rise of the Redlegs

The term "sugar revolution" has long been used to describe the dramatic economic, social, political, and geographic transformations that occurred in the mid-seventeenth century as colonial territories shifted to the large-scale production of sugar (for a discussion of the term, see Higman 2000; see also Beckles 1989; Dunn 1972; Menard 2006; Mintz 1985; Sheridan 1974; Williams 1994 [1944]). There is a general consensus among scholars of the period and region that Barbados was the focal point of these transformations in the English West Indies, transformations that would sweep across the Caribbean region and influence the development of the plantation infrastructure in many American contexts. While the use of enslaved African labor was already under way in the New World, including Barbados (Bridenbaugh and Bridenbaugh 1972; Menard 2006), the shift to sugar production sparked an exponential rise in the importation of Africans to serve the inaugural sugar island economy.

The effects of the sugar revolution in Barbados are particularly intriguing given the diversity of the labor pool in the years before, during, and after the initial boom in sugar production. From its establishment as an English colony in 1627 to the onset of the sugar revolution in the mid-to-late 1640s, Barbados' labor pool was primarily composed of European indentured servants, many of whom had willingly signed contracts of indentureship in search of opportunity in the New World. On the eve of the sugar revolution, Handler and Lange (1978:15) report that "by 1643–45, an estimated 5,680 to 6,400 slaves and 18,300 to 18,600 European males or 'effective men' lived on the island." In turn, the onset of large-scale sugar production drastically altered island demographics and the manner in which servants were recruited.

The insatiable need for field hands necessitated by the labor-intensive crop spurned an influx of coerced or involuntary European servants. Petty criminals, political prisoners, prisoners of war, and kidnapped children primarily from Ireland, England, and Scotland were transported across the Atlantic to fulfill the needs of Barbadian planters (Beckles 1989; Dunn 1972; Newman 2013; for the Irish, see Beckles 1990; Gwynn 1930, 1932; Shaw 2013). Additionally, Barbadian planters came to be increasingly involved in the purchase of enslaved Africans. By the early 1680s the population on the island had exploded to over 20,000 white residents and roughly 40,000 enslaved Africans (Dunn 1969:7–9; Handler and Lange 1978:16–17). By this time Barbados was the wealthiest of England's New World colonial territories, representing what Gov. William Willoughby in 1667 would call "that fair jewell of your Majesty's crown [which] yields her Prince the greatest income" (qtd. in Sainsbury 1880:382–383).

Despite the large influx in indentured servants as the sugar revolution overtook the island, as the seventeenth century progressed, planters increasingly favored the use of enslaved Africans (Beckles 1985, 1989; Dunn 1972). Barbadian officials took note of the evident decline in the white population and in 1680 Gov. Jonathan Atkins lamented that "people no longer come to Barbados," adding that "many having departed to Carolina, Jamaica, and the Leeward Islands in hope of settling the land which they cannot obtain here" (qtd. in Harlow 1926:308n1). Despite this noticeable decline, many white laborers remained on the island, many of whom had finished their periods of indenture. Many flocked to Bridgetown, the island's principal port and capital, where they came to constitute a large portion of the island's urban poor (Welch 2003:118–119).

Others remained in the rural districts, and poor white communities were soon established across the island in marginal zones deemed unfit for efficient sugar cultivation. Such communities included small plots that were independently owned by poor white small farmers or parcels were rented out to residents by planters. By the 1670s Barbadian law stipulated that planters had to provide small parcels for the poor white tenants who served in the island militia (Sheppard 1977:59). While evidence suggests that this practice persisted into the nineteenth century (Marshall 1977:72), it is unclear how many plantation tenants actually served as militia members. Regardless of militia status, documenting the number of pre-emancipation poor white plantation tenantries is challenging since planters infrequently mentioned their presence in wills or land transfer deeds. In most cases, however, such communities were established on the fringes of the plantation landscape, occupying what was and is referred to as "rab" land, or land deemed unprofitable for agricultural production.

Based on a Barbadian act that required planters to retain white tenants on their estates to serve in the island's militia, many poor white tenants were militia members and therefore spent the majority of their time maintaining subsistence lifestyles. As such, many worked as small farmers, raising livestock and poultry, producing provisioning food stuffs, and participating in cottage industries that included the cultivation and production of ginger, cotton, aloes, jams, jellies, arrowroot, and vegetables to sell locally and in Bridgetown markets (Handler 1971:72–73, 81; Watson 2000:132). Others in close proximity to the coast made a living as fishermen (Welch 2005).

Although they fleetingly appear in the historical record (for appearances in parish Vestry Minutes, see Marshall 2003; Jones 2007), by the late eighteenth to early nineteenth century it is evident that the Redlegs were viewed with derision by the island's elites and those visiting the colony. Multiple accounts by island visitors provide disparaging portrayals of the island's poor whites, describing them as idle, debauched, indolent, alcoholic, vulgar, degenerate, dirty, racially arrogant, and crude (see, for instance, Bayley 1833:62; Coleridge 1826:273; Dickson 1789:37; Pinckard 1806:132–133; Thome and Kimball 1838:229). Special Magistrate J. B. Colthurst provides a pointed summation of such sentiments; in an 1836 journal entry Colthurst comments that "the militia of Barbadoes (the private men) is chiefly composed of the very lowest order of whites, the greater number of whom were born in the colony, and are a most idle and good for nothing set—proud, lazy, and consequently miserably poor" (qtd. in Marshall 1977:72).

Such accounts and derisive commentary illustrate that the poor whites were viewed as an entirely distinct, if marginalized and derided, population. Descriptions of the Redlegs are also made in stark contrast to the enslaved or free Afro-Barbadians, with whom they are said to have never intermixed; such a perception has haphazardly seeped into recent scholarship (Browne 2012:16; Finneran 2013:327n49; Hoyos 1978; Keagy 1972; O'Callaghan 2000:207–226). The taboo nature, yet rampant occurrence, of interracial relations and intimacies in colonial contexts has long been a staple of scholarship on colonial control, discourse, and discrepancies (see, for instance, Jones 2007; McClintock 1995; Stoler 1995, 2002). But the implications of notions of isolation, distinction, and endogamy have more quotidian consequences. In situating this brief historical narrative of the Redlegs, it is necessary to consider how apparent isolation or insularity compares with evidence recovered during excavations of the Below Cliff tenantry at Clifton Hall Plantation.

Below Cliff, St. John, Barbados

Clifton Hall Plantation lies in the eastern parish of St. John (Figure 3.1). The majority of the estate lies on a flat plateau that is home to some of the flattest land and most fertile soil on the island. In fact, the area is one of the few remaining strongholds for the disintegrating sugar industry. The eastern acreage of the property abuts the ridge known as Hackleton's Cliff, a prominent geological feature that spans much of the island's east coast. Following a vertical drop from roughly 230 meters above sea level to the surface below, a steep landscape rolls to the rocky eastern coast. Nestled below the escarpment are the ruins of the former tenantry, Below Cliff. While the history of the early years of the associated parcels is largely unknown, by the early 1650s the estate was a fully functioning sugar plantation. In a 1653 deed, the plantation is described as consisting of 209 acres of land "above ye Cliffe" and 50 acres below, 40 of which being described as "leased land"(Barbados Department of Archives RB3/3:11). It is unclear if this is indicative of a tenantry home to multiple residences or an individual holding the lease for all 40 acres. Regardless, its status as leased land indicates that at a time when land prices were dear due to the high price of sugar, the plantation owner was willing to forgo attempts to cultivate sugar on the unaccommodating land below the cliff.

As mentioned in the vignette that begins this chapter, the former tenantry is now shrouded in forest. Confirmed by former tenantry residents,

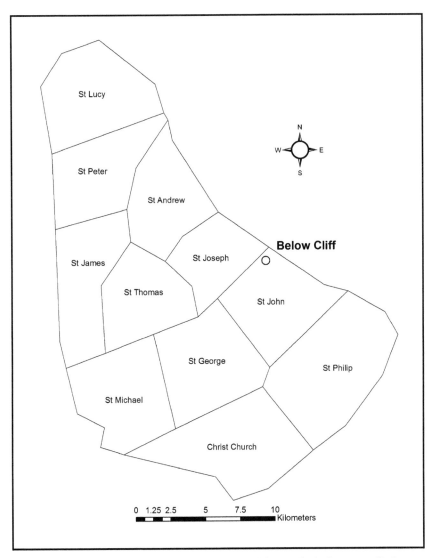

Figure 3.1. Map of Barbados with parish boundaries delineated. The location of Below Cliff is labeled in the parish of St. John. (Image by Matthew Reilly and Sarah Craft)

twentieth-century ethnographies (Davis 1978; Rosenberg 1962), and parish baptismal registries (St. Margaret's Registry Volumes, St. John Church, Barbados), residents began leaving the tenantry in the early 1940s until it was finally abandoned in the early 1960s. The inability of the parish doctor to access the tenantry as he entered old age, significant damage from hurricane Janet in 1955, and the availability of inexpensive land along the main road provided the impetus for residents to move their boarded homes (chattel houses) to new locales. While the recovery of white salt-glazed stoneware has only confirmed occupation dating back to the mid-eighteenth century, if the 1653 deed does in fact point to Below Cliff being a poor white tenantry, it suggests that the region was occupied by this community for roughly three centuries.

When reconnaissance began in the area in late 2012, it was first necessary to identify features on the landscape that had been hidden by the encroaching forest. With the assistance of Wilson and his cousin, Ainsley Norris, it was possible to locate and, in most cases, discern the last known occupants of over a dozen house sites through the use of oral histories. Despite the cumbersome forest, Wilson and Ainsley were also able to navigate the now nearly invisible pathways that had been used by tenantry residents to get from one household to another. They also pointed out places in which several narrow paths coalesced into larger thoroughfares that inevitably led toward the cliff—providing steep but manageable access to the top. Those living in Below Cliff would have used three named major points of entry/exit to the top of the cliff: the Gates, Monkey Jump, and the Ladders (Figure 3.2). The Gates is the only path of the three that is safely navigable today, largely due to Wilson's regular trips to collect coconuts. While the remaining two are deteriorating due to infrequent use, the expansion of the forest, and the damaging effects of heavy rainfall, the routes of each path are still fairly discernible on the ground.

With the landscape mapped in preliminary fashion, excavations commenced (following a sampling of 21 strategically placed shovel test pits) at the childhood home of Wilson Norris. The articulated ruins of the foundation, in addition to the insights provided by Wilson, made it possible to map the size and orientation of the 3.9 by 6.6 m rectangular structure prior to excavations. One by one meter excavation units were placed within the interior of the foundation (10 units) in addition to select units outside of the immediate foundation (11 units), including in the detached kitchen, trash pit, and walkway to the northeast of the foundation. Based on piles of limestone rubble to the northeast and northwest of the foundation as well as the visible raised platform upon which the foundation was constructed, it was evident that the site had gone through several episodes of (re)construction at the same location. In other words, episodes of rebuilding or renovations to existing structures took place on top of the previous architectural features.

Excavations within the limestone foundation proved challenging due to depths of roughly 2 m in multiple units as well as the ubiquity and

Figure 3.2. Satellite imagery of the Clifton Hall Plantation. The great house along with the cliff entrances/exits are plotted and labeled along with the site of Wilson Norris' childhood home, the principle site of ex-cavations. The three cliff entrances/exits also mark the edge of Hackleton's Cliff. (Image by Matthew Reilly)

instability of limestone fill. Despite methodological difficulties, material culture was recovered from all excavated levels, including several sherds of sponge-decorated whiteware found under large limestone boulders at depths of over 2 m. The recovery of imported wares dating to earlier periods (such as pearlware and white salt-glazed stoneware) in other contexts, in the same household as well as at neighboring house sites, indicates the complex stratigraphy found throughout the Below Cliff tenantry. An unstable environment susceptible to rockslides is a likely explanation for large layers of limestone fill and other disturbances.

In total, 3,590 artifacts were recovered. Based on dates associated with refined earthenwares and glass bottle shards, the assemblage encompasses materials from the mid-eighteenth century to the contemporary period with the majority of subsurface artifacts dating to the mid-nineteenth century. Significantly, for the purposes of exploring poor white and Afro-Barbadian interaction, coarse and refined earthenwares were recovered from all excavated levels, from 0–10 cm to depths in excess of 2 m.

(Re)Constructing the Plantation Landscape

In many ways, Clifton Hall fits the mold of a typical Barbadian sugar plantation. The great house sits along the main public north–south road. The works are centrally located, immediately to the southwest of the great house. Prior to emancipation, the village for the enslaved was situated to the east of the great house in what is now a cane field named Negro Yard. The field is to the east of the great house and is directly west of the edge of the cliff. The field directly south of Negro Yard is Monkey Jump, which shares its name with the cliff exit/entrance to the east. Field names were relayed by a Clifton Hall employee who had been working the cane fields for most of his adult life. In their own analyses of the plantation landscape and research on field names, Handler and Lange (1978:45) note that "the term [Negro Yard] was used for the area of plantations that contained the slave villages or settlements." Following emancipation, villages were relocated to the peripheries of the plantation, allowing the former village sites to be plowed and planted in cane (see also Handler 2002:124–127).

In reconstructing the landscape of Clifton Hall of decades and centuries past, it is necessary to focus not on the zones of the plantation that have traditionally received the most attention but on those spaces deemed marginal. The works served as the center of economic and laboring activity (Handler 2002). The great house (along with the residence of the overseer)

served as an imposing physical and symbolic reminder of the power structures and dynamics at play in plantation spaces and offered a vantage
point from which to observe, surveil, regulate, and control labor (Delle
1998, 2014; Lenik 2012). Archaeologically, the village for the enslaved has
long been a focal point of analysis in Caribbean contexts, demonstrating
cultural identities and transformations (Armstrong 1990, 1998, 1999; Kelly
2008), production and consumption practices (Hauser 2008, 2011a; Wilkie
1999, 2001; Wilkie and Farnsworth 2005), acts of resistance (Delle 1998,
2014; Singleton 2001), spatial organization (Armstrong and Kelly 2000),
economic activity (Gibson 2009; Handler and Wallman 2014), and burial
practices (Handler and Lange 1978; Handler et al. 1989). More specific to
Barbados, historical and archaeological studies have highlighted the nu-
ances of daily life within an enslaved village, including craft production,
provision cultivation, leisure time, religious beliefs, burial practices, social
networks with the enslaved on nearby plantations, architectural housing
techniques, material culture ownership, care for the sick, education, the effects of the amelioration process that sought to assuage the conditions under which the enslaved lived, and village organization (Bergman and Smith
2014; Handler 2002; Handler and Bergman 2009; Handler and Lange 1978;
Handler and Wallman 2014). Despite these detailed analyses, investigations
have yet to focus as much attention beyond the nucleus of the plantation,
which in turn effaces the poor white presence.

Hackleton's Cliff is an imposing barrier that starkly divides the Below
Cliff tenantry from the zones above. At first glance, such marked physical separation supports perceptions of poor white isolation and insularity. Given the size of the geological feature, it may seem logical for Below
Cliff residents to keep to themselves and be unconcerned with the everyday
functioning of the plantation and those who resided there. Physical separation can be used to the advantage of residents who experienced less surveillance and heightened autonomy (Armstrong 2003; Hauser and Armstrong 2012). Using James Scott (2009) in their analysis of similarly cast
spaces of marginality, Mark W. Hauser and Douglas V. Armstrong suggest
that "inhabitants had to take advantage of practical knowledge in order to
exploit these geographies of alternative possibility" (2012:316). Below Cliff
residents certainly fulfill this criterion by exploiting their geographies,
but, when warranted autonomy, some residents chose to be involved with
sugar agroindustry rather than lifestyles more compatible with "not being
governed."

As such, an understanding of Below Cliff's socioeconomic networks is wedded to the logics of plantation organization and responses to them. According to the logic of plantation organization, poor white tenants living below the cliff were perceived as marginal and inconsequential for the functioning of the sugar economy. Physically separated from the fields, works, great house, and village on top of the cliff, surveillance would have been difficult, if not impossible. Therefore, it is likely that planters viewed Below Cliff residents as out of sight and out of mind.

On the other hand, James A. Delle illustrates the dialectical nature of the landscape in offering a caveat to the idealistic planter vision of plantation design, functionality, and efficiency. He suggests that "those who were enslaved within these landscapes created social meanings of their own, sometimes quite different from those anticipated by the planters when they designed the landscapes" (2014:99; see also Armstrong and Kelly 2000; Delle this volume; Handler 2002). In addition to the enslaved, poor whites who lived and worked on the estate critically contributed to the production of space as well as its socioeconomic meaning, thus exemplifying tensions between space as conceived and space as perceived (Lefebvre 1991). Furthermore, the production of space by racially diverse plantation residents of the working class dramatically influenced how they experienced these spaces and each other. Evidence from the Clifton Hall landscape explicitly demonstrates that residents manipulated their environment in ways that subverted planter segregation attempts, and this manipulation calls into question notions of isolation. Additionally, it demonstrates the willingness of Below Cliff poor whites to be involved in the day-to-day functioning and happenings of the plantation.

Making specific choices that reflected their own affinities and preferences rather than the desires of planters, poor whites produced a landscape that facilitated interaction with Afro-Barbadians. The Gates, Monkey Jump, and the Ladders are three entryways through which individuals can climb up or down Hackleton's Cliff (Figure 3.2). The Gates marked the first and most southerly entryway. Monkey Jump was named after two large stones toward the top of the cliff separated by a distance of roughly 1 m—a gap across which monkeys would playfully jump. The Ladders was a reference to the steep and vertical climb necessary to reach the top of the cliff—the path had to be climbed hand over hand, as if climbing a ladder. All three were painstakingly carved into the limestone escarpment to facilitate relatively easy movement and all required regular maintenance.

It is certainly plausible that the pathways leading up and down the cliff were constructed solely to serve as conduits for poor white plantation employees to quickly travel to and from their place of employment. Thus, planters and managers would likely not take issue with employees traversing the paths they had constructed. If, however, we consider the location of the village for the enslaved, the specific routes chosen suggest that those using the pathways had other motivations. Monkey Jump and the Gates are located on either side of the field now named Negro Yard. If, as oral tradition holds, the field named Monkey Jump was a reference to the pathway to/from Below Cliff, it seems likely that the pathway predates the postemancipation period when the "Negro Yard" field would have received its name. Therefore, in imagining the landscape during the period of slavery, those ascending the cliff for a morning's work from either location in Below Cliff would arrive directly adjacent to the village for the enslaved. At the very least, enslaved Afro-Barbadians and poor white tenants would have been encountering each other on a daily basis. More likely, as suggested by the archaeological data presented below, they were mutually engaging in economic and social activities.

Furthermore, these designs, manipulations, and movements worked in both directions. In other words, the construction and use of these pathways could have easily allowed for enslaved Africans and Afro-Barbadians to comingle with poor whites in Below Cliff. Additionally, it is possible that they had a hand in the actual construction and maintenance of the pathways. The fact that the village and tenantry were part and parcel of the same estate raises significant questions concerning the legality and permissibility of such interactions. The 1661 "Act for the better ordering and governing of Negroes" explicates that slaves needed to receive written permission from their masters to leave the grounds of the plantation. Leaving the estate without the consent of their owner would warrant the culprit a "moderate whipping" (for more on this act, see Rugermer 2013; partially reprinted in Engerman et al. 2001). Since Below Cliff was technically part of the same estate, could planters legally punish a slave for descending into the poor white tenantry? Of course, planters may not have been concerned with the extent of the law and may have regularly acted upon their own assessment of permissible and impermissible behavior. Nonetheless, even if discouraged from engaging in activities with poor whites in general, the enslaved at Clifton Hall may have taken advantage of the inconspicuous locale of the tenantry. In short, interaction between enslaved Afro-Barbadians and poor whites was legal under island law and facilitated by physical alterations to the plantation landscape.

Poor White Pots and Market Encounters

The plantation landscape provides evidence that interaction took place between racially diverse inhabitants despite historical and contemporary claims of poor white isolation. Historical and archaeological data allow for a deeper reading of these interactions and attest to the nature and extent of some of the encounters. Furthermore, while the pre-emancipation landscape was the focus of the earlier discussion, interactions and exchanges persisted into the postemancipation era. In fact, based on information provided by the Norris family and by neighboring community members, many families of Afro-Barbadian descent lived in the Below Cliff tenantry before it was abandoned in the mid-twentieth century. Therefore, archaeological evidence of interracial interaction and exchange illustrates the effects of long-term contact between diverse plantation residents.

Interaction on the plantation landscape was manifest in everyday conversation, the passing of information, exchange of culture (in its complex and multiple forms), sexual relationships, and the circuitous routing of material goods. For the latter, Hauser's (2008, 2011a, 2011b) investigations into the manufacture, marketing, consumption, and use of locally produced ceramics have provided a useful framework through which to observe how material culture can simultaneously speak to identity as well as local and global economic networks. He argues that an analysis of domestic earthenwares "can make visible the complex networks of social relationships in which people engaged in everyday life" (2011a:443). Of particular significance in the context of the Barbadian plantation is that such networks involved enslaved and free Afro-Barbadians, poor whites, free people of color, merchants, and planters. Therefore, in addition to the pervasive racial hierarchies and power dynamics inherent in plantation societies, it is necessary to address how class is inextricably linked to the socioeconomic networks analyzed here.[2]

Coarse earthenwares are ubiquitous across the Barbadian landscape and form a substantial component of archaeological assemblages. Below Cliff is no exception. There are, however, significant disparities between those recovered from Below Cliff and other plantation site excavations. For instance, red earthenware assemblages from Trents Plantation (Armstrong and Reilly 2014) and Codrington Plantation (Loftfield 2001) were composed primarily of industrial sugar wares (cones and drip pots; see Handler 1963a:129), whereas the assemblage from Below Cliff is overwhelmingly utilitarian and domestic, consisting of 93.2 percent of the coarse earthenware assemblage.

The divergence may well be attributed to the physical distance between the tenantry and the works. Additionally, given that only certain members of the Below Cliff community were employed on the plantation, there was a certain level of detachment—physically, economically, and materially—between residents and the workings of the sugar industry.

Since the seminal ethnohistorical work on the island craft potting industry by Jerome Handler (1963a, 1963b, 1965), archaeologists working on the island have taken a keen interest in vessel production, consumption, use, and classification as well as the implications associated with the identities of those who made, acquired, and used them (Farmer 2011; Finch 2013; Handler and Lange 1978; Loftfield 1992, 2001; Scheid 2015; Siedow 2014; Stoner 2000, 2003). Handler (1963a:133–135) presents historical data illustrating the immigration of English potters to work on Barbadian plantations in the seventeenth century. Additionally, his ethnographic work (1963b) in the Chalky Mount potting village of the Scotland District notes that oral tradition suggests that "pottery was introduced in the area by whites" (142). While he explicitly highlights the indeterminate nature of these oral traditions, it is significant that Afro-Barbadian potters openly refer to the craft involving actors operating across racial lines despite the fact that it had become an exclusively Afro-Barbadian craft in the village of Chalky Mount at the time of Handler's ethnographic research.

In broader archaeological considerations of Caribbean pottery, however, scholars have largely been preoccupied with the Afro-Caribbean character of ceramic forms, production, consumption preferences, and use (see, for instance, Ahlman et al. 2009; Finch 2013; Gibson 2009; Handler and Wallman 2014; Hauser 2008; Hauser and Armstrong 1999; Heath 1988, 1999; Kelly 2008; Kelly and Norman 2006; Wilkie and Farnsworth 2005). While not inherently invalid in associating particular vessel forms or consumption practices with peoples of African descent, such assessments run the risk of "ethnic reductionism" (Siedow 2014) whereby ethnic diversity among Caribbean inhabitants is elided; such reductions omit the possibility of poor white involvement in addition to diminishing African cultural complexity and diversity (Finch 2013; Hauser and DeCorse 2003; Singleton 2006; Singleton and Bograd 2000).

The troubling dimensions of "ethnic reductionism" are well illustrated by the assemblage collected below the cliff. The diagnostic sherds of red earthenware recovered from Below Cliff represent vessels that have typically been associated with Afro-Barbadian production and usage. Handler (1963a) identifies three primary holloware vessel forms—the monkey (used

Figure 3.3. Contemporary example of a Barbadian monkey jar (*left*), coarse earthenware holloware base and body sherds (*top right*), and coarse earthenware holloware rim, body, and base sherds (*bottom right*). Sherds on the right are representative of the presence of vessels typically associated with Afro-Barbadians within contexts in the poor white tenantry. (Photographs by Matthew Reilly)

for the storage and cooling of water), a goglet or pitcher, and a *conneree* (used for the cooking, storage, or curing of meats). While the assemblage collected from Below Cliff lacks sherds that definitively correlate to individual specific vessel forms, the overwhelming majority of diagnostic sherds represented hollowares (92.2 percent) and distinguishable bases and rims illustrate that some or all of specific holloware vessel forms are represented (Figure 3.3).

From units excavated from three separate households, including Wilson Norris' childhood home, coarse earthenwares represented 29.1 percent of the total ceramic assemblage, or 307 of 1,055 (2.0 percent were industrial wares and 27.1 percent were determined to be domestic). The period of habitation, based on dates associated with imported ceramics, stretches from the mid-eighteenth century to the mid-twentieth century, with the majority of diagnostic materials dating to the mid-nineteenth century. The period of habitation and the high proportion of coarse earthenwares to imports stand in marked contrast to trends observed from households for the enslaved on Jamaican plantations. An analysis of ceramic ratios conducted at Drax Hall, Jamaica, by Armstrong (1990) illustrates that, for the six households considered, there was a direct correlation between average year of residency and proportion of refined imported earthenwares; as one moves from the mid-eighteenth century into the decades preceding emancipation, there is a noticeable increase in the presence of imported wares (overwhelmingly English in origin). Specifically, an increase in the percentage of imported wares was calculated from 14.4 percent to 17.4 percent for early-eighteenth-century contexts to 84.6 percent 88.9 percent for mid-nineteenth-century contexts (Armstrong 1990:136). Delle's data for ceramics collected during surface collections at Marshall's Pen, Jamaica (a coffee plantation roughly contemporaneous with the primary period of inhabitation for Below Cliff), coincide with Armstrong's findings. Delle (2014:158) reports that less than 20 percent of the assemblage was composed of coarse earthenwares. If we exclude stonewares and yellowware from these counts (which are included as coarse ceramics in Delle's analysis), the percentage drops to less than 2 percent. The ubiquity of refined imported wares by the end of the eighteenth century is also noted in Barbadian contexts, despite the heightened attention granted to coarse earthenwares (Agbe-Davies 2009; Armstrong and Reilly 2014; Handler and Lange 1978:135; Lange and Carlson 2009; Loftfield 2001).

The influx of European refined earthenwares during this period is often attributed to the general transformations in ceramic production outlined by the work of George Miller (1980), among many others. In short, the mass production, global availability, and affordability of English refined earthenware in the late eighteenth century correlates to the fact that by this time "locally produced bowls were partially supplanted by imported creamware and pearlware bowls" (Armstrong 1990:157). While English imported earthenwares make up 748 sherds of the 1,055 ceramic total in the Below Cliff assemblage, the percentage of coarse earthenwares is markedly higher than in the earlier and contemporaneous Jamaican contexts (for similar case studies, see Reeves 2011). The chemical compositions of the wares from the area have yet to be studied, but vessel forms, including the monkey jar and *conneree*, indicate that locally produced vessels are present. If such Afro-Caribbean wares were being supplanted by European imports by the nineteenth century in other Caribbean plantation contexts, to what can we attribute the heightened presence of coarse earthenwares below the cliff?

Even as affordable, mass-produced ceramics became increasingly available, Below Cliff residents demonstrated a dedication to the local ceramic industry. Historical and archaeological research has uncovered no evidence of a kiln in the immediate area, despite the presence of kilns in the parish at Pot House (Finch 2013) and Codrington Plantation. Therefore, unless residents were using open-air firing, it stands to reason that tenants were engaging in market activities with local hucksters rather than producing their own wares. The vessel forms present, such as monkeys and *connerees*, indicate that wares traditionally associated with Afro-Barbadian production methods and foodways (Handler 1963a; Loftfield 2001) were adopted by poor white tenants. Therefore, the quotidian forms of interaction between racially diverse plantation residents resulted in significant economic, material, and cultural exchange. This exchange simultaneously demonstrates the complex choices made by residents below the cliff in terms of their relationships to broader socioeconomic networks. Keeping in mind discourses of marginality and isolation, residents demonstrated a desire to participate in local markets and interact with their Afro-Barbadian neighbors while concomitantly opting to only partially succumb to the consumption transformations that were unfolding on a global scale. These ambiguities reveal an intentional and careful balance between socioeconomic scales that was mediated by Barbadian poor whites.

Poor white consumption and use of vessels traditionally referred to as Afro-Caribbean wares should come as no surprise when considering the limited economic means of poor whites and enslaved and free Afro-Barbadians as well as the dense population of the island (627 people per square mile in 1834 [Handler and Lange 1978: 13]); living in close proximity to racially diverse households of similar economic means certainly lends itself to exchange—material or otherwise. Documentary sources offer discriminatory accounts of the poor whites that profoundly deny their involvement in island economic spheres. Archaeological interpretations of locally produced coarse earthenwares that attribute ceramic production, consumption, and use solely to those of African descent similarly collapse the island landscape and deny the ability of economic networks that transcend racial boundaries. Studies of Montserrat's plantation landscape are recognizing similar ambiguities associated with coarse earthenwares, with Krysta Ryzewski and John F. Cherry (2015) noting that multiple and fluid island identities seriously hinder the direct association of coarse earthenwares to specific ethnic groups. Such reductions, however, are entirely contextually dependent. To what extent poor whites or other racially diverse demographics (Amerindians, East Asian indentured servants, free people of color, merchants, management, etc.) are present on the plantation landscape demands careful consideration.

This analysis in no way suggests that interactions and relationships across the color line were always amicable or without issue. In fact, historical evidence suggests that encounters between poor whites and Afro-Barbadians were often contentious and confrontational. During their six-month tour of the West Indies following emancipation in 1834, James Armstrong Thome and Joseph Horace Kimball (1838:229) illustrate the strained relationship between poor whites and Afro-Barbadians, noting that "they will beg of blacks more provident and industrious than themselves, or they will steal their poultry and rob their provision grounds at night," further adding that "they would disdain to associate with them." A similar observation is made a century earlier by A. Alleyne, the attorney for the Codrington estate in the parish of St. John. In a 1741 report on the progress made by the enslaved in receiving the gospel, Alleyne notes the bad example provided by the poor whites: "Besides the irreligion they [the enslaved] see every day among the poorer sorts of whites who in fact are often worse than the negroes, by receiving all stolen goods and trafficking with them on Sundays and cheating them of their corn by giving a leaf or two of tobacco for a pint of corn" (Society for the Propagation of the Gospel, Lambeth Palace Library, London Vol. B8, Item 51).

Interestingly, both accounts provide explicit evidence that poor whites and Afro-Barbadians, enslaved and free, were directly interacting with one another in market contexts. Additionally, it is evident that poor whites took advantage of Afro-Barbadians through uneven exchanges and direct theft. Despite bearing witness to such interaction, Thome and Kimball stridently deny interracial associations. Perhaps, then, there is truth to Thome and Kimball's (1838:230) assessment that the "high lineage" and "long line of their illustrious ancestry" (voiced sarcastically) associated with their white skin had developed a sentiment of racial superiority among the poor whites. We should not, however, overlook the possibility of amicable market relationships. While the archaeological evidence is silent as to the nature of the relationships between poor whites and Afro-Barbadians, poor whites nonetheless participated in island markets that potentially facilitated the passing of information and goods as well as developed relationships (Hauser 2008, 2011a).

Conclusion

Caribbean plantations were diverse spaces that drew racially diverse groups into intimate contact. They are characterized by harsh work regimes and crippling processes of dehumanization. Their survival throughout the Caribbean region as well as the persistence of structural inequalities are a physical reminder on the legacies of colonialism. These legacies are inherently tied to the race-based institution of slavery that made clear the power structures and hierarchies that stretched across the landscape. This chapter has suggested that marginal spaces on the plantation that were outside of the purview of planters and other figures of authority were spaces that facilitated behaviors that destabilized planter ideals of plantation organization.

Permitted heightened degrees of autonomy due to their legal status and skin complexion, poor whites manipulated their landscape to better serve the socioeconomic networks in which they took part. Of limited economic means and being defined as "white," they occupied a precarious position in Caribbean society. As such, they did not neatly fulfill specific roles within Barbadian society and economy. These ambiguities allowed poor whites to more routinely determine how they wanted to be involved in local, island, and global socioeconomic spheres. Tangible manifestations of interracial interactions are visible on the landscape of Clifton Hall Plantation. Furthermore, these interactions triggered material and cultural exchanges that included the mutually beneficial and the contentious. The significant presence of coarse earthenwares into the nineteenth century indicates that vessels traditionally associated with Afro-Barbadians were similarly consumed and used by Barbadian Redlegs. As such, a reimagining of the plantation landscape gives primacy to spaces deemed marginal and contests assumptions of isolation for those that lived and interacted within them.

Notes

1. The terms "poor white(s)" and "Redleg(s)" are initially provided with quotation marks to demonstrate their pejorative nature. They are used without the quotation marks throughout the chapter per convention. They remain problematic terms nonetheless.

2. Gender is also an essential component of this discussion, particularly when we consider who is producing goods brought to market (Farmer 2011) and the hucksters and higglers that operate in such spheres (Hauser 2008). For the purposes of this analysis, however, race and class are given primacy.

References Cited

Agbe-Davies, Anna S.
2009   Scales of Analysis, Scales of Value: Archaeology at Bush Hill House, Barbados. *International Journal of Historical Archaeology* 13(1):112–126.

Ahlman, Todd M., Gerald F. Schroedl, and Ashley H. McKeown
2009   The Afro-Caribbean Ware from the Brimstone Hill Fortress, St. Kitts, West Indies: A Study in Ceramic Production. *Historical Archaeology* 43(4):22–41.

Akenson, Donald H.
1997   *If the Irish Ran the World: Montserrat, 1630–1730.* McGill-Queen's University Press, Montreal.

Armstrong, Douglas V.
1990   *The Old Village and the Great House: An Archaeological and Historical Examination of Drax Hall Plantation, St. Ann's Bay, Jamaica.* University of Illinois Press, Urbana.
1998   Cultural Transformation within Enslaved Laborer Communities in the Caribbean. In *Studies in Culture Contact Interaction, Culture Change, and Archaeology*, edited by James G. Cusick, pp. 378–401. Center for Archaeological Investigations, Southern Illinois University Occasional Paper No. 25., Carbondale.
1999   Archaeology and Ethnohistory of the Caribbean Plantation. In *"I, too, am American": Archaeological Studies of African-American Life*, edited by Theresa A. Singleton, pp. 173–191. University Press of Virginia, Charlottesville.
2003   *Creole Transformations from Slavery to Freedom: Historical Archaeology of the East End Community, St. John, Virgin Islands.* University Press of Florida, Gainesville.

Armstrong, Douglas V., and Kenneth G. Kelly
2000   Settlement Patterns and the Origins of African Jamaican Society: Seville Plantation, St. Ann's Bay, Jamaica. *Ethnohistory* 47(2):369–397.

Armstrong, Douglas V., and Matthew C. Reilly
2014   Recovering Evidence of Initial Settler Farms and Early Plantation Life in Barbados. *Slavery & Abolition* 35(3):399–417.

Bates, Lynsey A.
2014   "The Landscape Cannot Be Said to Be Really Perfect": A Comparative Investigation of Plantation Spatial Organization on Two British Colonial Sugar Estates. In *The Archaeology of Slavery: A Comparative Approach to Captivity and Coercion*, edited by Lydia W. Marshall, pp. 116–142. Center for Archaeological Investigations, Southern Illinois University Occasional Paper No. 41, Carbondale.

Bayley, Frederic W. N.
1833   *Four Years' Residence in the West Indies.* London.

Beckles, Hilary McD.
1985   Plantation Production and White "Proto-Slavery": White Indentured Servants and the Colonisation of the English West Indies, 1624–1625. *Americas* 41(3): 21–45.
1989   *White Servitude and Black Slavery in Barbados, 1627–1715.* University of Tennessee Press, Knoxville.

1990   A "riotous and unruly lot": Irish Indentured Servants and Freemen in the English West Indies, 1644–1713. *William and Mary Quarterly* 47(4):503–522.

Bergman, Stephanie, and Frederick H. Smith
2014   Blurring Disciplinary Boundaries: The Material Culture of Improvement during the Age of Abolition in Barbados. *Slavery & Abolition* 35(3):418–436.

Brehony, Margaret
2007   Irish Railroad Workers in Cuba: Towards a Research Agenda. *Irish Migration Studies in Latin America* 5(3):183–188.

Bridenbaugh, Carl, and Roberta Bridenbaugh
1972   *No Peace beyond the Line: The English in the Caribbean 1624–1690.* Oxford University Press, New York.

Browne, David V. C.
2012   *Race, Class, Politics and the Struggle for Empowerment in Barbados, 1914–1937.* Ian Randle Publishers, Kingston.

Cateau, Heather
2006   Beyond Planters and Plantership. In *Beyond Tradition: Reinterpreting the Caribbean Historical Experience*, edited by Heather Cateau and Rita Pemberton, pp. 3–21. Ian Randle Publishers, Kingston.

Coleridge, Henry Nelson
1826   *Six Months in the West Indies in 1825.* London.

Davis, Karen Frances
1978   The Position of Poor Whites in a Color-Class Hierarchy: A Diachronic Study of Ethnic Boundaries in Barbados. Ph.D. dissertation, Wayne State University, Detroit, Michigan.

Delle, James A.
1998   *An Archaeology of Social Space: Analyzing Coffee Plantations in Jamaica's Blue Mountains.* New York: Plenum Press.
2011   The Habitus of Jamaican Plantation Landscapes. In *Out of Many, One People: The Historical Archaeology of Colonial Jamaica*, edited by James A. Delle, Mark W. Hauser, and Douglas V. Armstrong, pp. 122–143. University of Alabama Press, Tuscaloosa.
2014   *The Colonial Caribbean: Landscapes of Power in the Plantation System.* New York: Cambridge University Press.

Dickson, William
1789   *Letters on Slavery.* London.

Dunn, Richard
1969   The Barbados Census of 1680: Profile of the Richest Colony in English America. *William and Mary Quarterly* 26(1):3–30.
1972   *Sugar and Slaves: The Rise of the Planter Class in the English West Indies, 1624–1713.* University of North Carolina Press, Chapel Hill.

Engerman, Stanley, Seymour Drescher, and Robert Paquette (editors)
2001   *Slavery.* Oxford University Press, New York.

Epperson, Terrence W.
1999   Constructing Difference: The Social and Spatial Order of the Chesapeake Plantation. In *"I, too, am American": Archaeological Studies of African-American Life*,

edited by Theresa A. Singleton, pp. 159–172. University Press of Virginia, Charlottesville.

Farmer, Kevin
2011   Women Potters? A Preliminary Examination of Documentary and Material Culture Evidence from Barbados. *History in Action* 2(1):1–8.

Finch, Jonathan
2013   Inside the Pot House: Diaspora, Identity, and Locale in Barbadian Ceramics. *Journal of African Diaspora Archaeology and Heritage* 2(2):115–130.

Finneran, Niall
2013   "This Islande Is Inhabited with All Sortes": The Archaeology of Creolisation in Speightstown, Barbados, and Beyond, AD 1650–1900. *Antiquaries Journal* 93:319–351.

Gibson, Heather R.
2009   Domestic Economy and Daily Practice in Guadeloupe: Historical Archaeology at La Mahaudière Plantation. *International Journal of Historical Archaeology* 13(1):27–44.

Gwynn, Aubrey
1930   Cromwell's Policy of Transplantation. *Studies: An Irish Quarterly Review* 19(76):607–623.

1932   Documents Relating to the Irish in the West Indies. *Analecta Hibernica* No. 4:139–286.

Handler, Jerome S.
1963a   A Historical Sketch of Pottery Manufacture in Barbados. *Journal of the Barbados Museum and Historical Society* 30:129–153.

1963b   Pottery Making in Rural Barbados. *Southwestern Journal of Anthropology* 19(3):314–334.

1965   Land Exploitative Activities and Economic Patterns in a Barbados Village. Ph.D. dissertation, Department of Anthropology, Brandeis University.

1971   The History of Arrowroot and the Origin of Peasantries in the British West Indies. *Journal of Caribbean History* 2:46–93.

2002   Plantation Slave Settlements in Barbados, 1650s to 1834. In *In the Shadow of the Plantation: Caribbean History and Legacy*, edited by Alvin O. Thompson and Woodville K. Marshall, pp. 123–161. Ian Randle Publishers, Kingston.

Handler, Jerome S., and Stephanie Bergman
2009   Vernacular Houses and Domestic Material Culture on Barbadian Sugar Plantation, 1640–1838. *Journal of Caribbean History* 43:1–36.

Handler, Jerome S., Michael D. Conner, and Keith P. Jacobi
1989   *Searching for a Slave Cemetery in Barbados, West Indies: Bioarchaeological Ethnohistorical Investigations*. Center for Archaeological Investigations Research Paper Series, Issue No. 59, University of Southern Illinois, Carbondale.

Handler, Jerome S., and Frederick Lange
1978   *Plantation Slavery in Barbados: An Archaeological and Historical Investigation*. Harvard University Press, Cambridge.

Handler, Jerome S. and Diane Wallman
2014   Production Activities in the Household Economies of Plantation Slaves: Barba-

dos and Martinique, Mid-1600s to Mid-1800s. *International Journal of Historical Archaeology* 18(3):441–466.

Harlow, Vincent T.

1926   *A History of Barbados: 1625–1685*. Negro Universities Press, New York.

Hauser, Mark W.

2008   *An Archaeology of Black Markets: Local Ceramics and Economies in Eighteenth-Century Jamaica*. University Press of Florida, Gainesville.

2011a   Routes and Roots of Empire: Pots, Power, and Slavery in the 18th-Century British Caribbean. *American Anthropologist* 113(3):431–437.

2011b   Uneven Topographies: Archaeology of Plantations and Caribbean Slave Economies. In *The Archaeology of Capitalism in Colonial Contexts: Postcolonial Historical Archaeologies*, edited by Sarah K. Croucher and Lindsay Weiss, pp. 121–142. Springer Press, New York.

Hauser, Mark W., and Douglas V. Armstrong

1999   Embedded Identities: Piecing Together Relationships through Compositional Analysis of Low-Fired Earthenwares. In *African Sites: Archaeology in the Caribbean*, edited by Jay B. Haviser, pp. 65–93. Markus Wiener Publishers, Princeton, New Jersey.

2012   The Archaeology of Not Being Governed: A Counterpoint to a History of Settlement of Two Colonies in the Eastern Caribbean. *Journal of Social Archaeology* 12(3):310–333.

Hauser, Mark W., and Christopher R. DeCorse

2003   Low-Fired Earthenwares in the African Diaspora: Problems and Prospects. *International Journal of Historical Archaeology* 7(1):67–98.

Haviser, Jay B. (editor)

1999   *African Sites: Archaeology in the Caribbean*. Markus Wiener Press, Princeton, New Jersey.

Heath, Barbara

1988   Afro-Caribbean Ware: A Study of Ethnicity of St. Eustatius. Ph.D. dissertation, Department of Anthropology, University of Pennsylvania.

1999   Yabbas, Monkeys, Jugs, and Jars: An Historical Context for African-Caribbean Pottery on St. Eustatius. In *African Sites: Archaeology in the Caribbean*, edited by Jay B. Haviser, pp. 196–220. Markus Wiener Publishers, Princeton, New Jersey.

Higman, Barry W.

2000   The Sugar Revolution. *Economic History Review* 53(2):213–236.

Hoyos, F. A.

1978   *Barbados: A History from Amerindians to Independence*. MacMillan Caribbean, London.

Johnson, Howard and Karl S. Watson (editors)

1998   *The White Minority in the Caribbean*. Ian Randle Publishers, Kingston.

Jones, Cecily

2007   *Engendering Whiteness: White Women and Colonialism in Barbados and North Carolina, 1627–1865*. Manchester University Press, Manchester.

Keagy, Thomas J.
1972   The Poor Whites of Barbados. *Revista de historia de América* No. 73/74:9–52.
Kelly, Kenneth G.
2008   Creole Cultures of the Caribbean: Historical Archaeology in the French West Indies. *International Journal of Historical Archaeology* 12(4):388–402.
Kelly, Kenneth G. and Neil L. Norman
2006   Medium Vessels and the Longue Dureé: The Endurance of Ritual Ceramics and the Archaeology of the African Diaspora. In *African Re-Genesis: Confronting Social Issues in the Diaspora*, edited by Jay B. Haviser and Kevin C. MacDonald, pp. 223–33. University College London Press, London.
Lambert, David
2005   *White Creole Culture, Politics and Identity during the Age of Abolition.* Cambridge University Press, Cambridge.
Lange, Frederick W., and Shawn B. Carlson
2009   Distributions of European Earthenwares on Plantations on Barbados, West Indies. In *The Archaeology of Slavery and Plantation Life*, edited by Theresa A. Singleton, pp. 97–120. Left Coast Press, Walnut Creek, California.
Lefebvre, Henri
1991   *The Production of Space.* Blackwell Publishing, Malden.
Lenik, Stephan
2012   Mission Plantations, Space, and Social Control: Jesuits as Planters in French Caribbean Colonies and Frontiers. *Journal of Social Archaeology* 12(1):51–71.
Loftfield, Thomas C.
1992   Unglazed Red Earthenware from Barbados: A Preliminary Analysis. *Journal of the Barbados Museum and Historical Society* 40:19–36.
2001   Creolization in Seventeenth-Century Barbados: Two Case Studies. In *Island Lives: Historical Archaeologies of the Caribbean*, edited by Paul Farnsworth, pp. 207–233. University of Alabama Press, Tuscaloosa.
McClintock, Anne
1995   *Imperial Leather: Race, Gender and Sexuality in the Colonial Contest.* Routledge, New York.
Marshall, Woodville
1977   *The Colthurst Journal: Journal of a Special Magistrate in the Islands of Barbados and St. Vincent, July 1835–September 1838.* KTO Press, New York.
2003   Charity for the Undeserving? The Carpenter Trust and the Creation of the Parish Land Tenantry in St. Philip. *Journal of the Barbados Museum and Historical Society* 49:167–191.
Menard, Richard R.
2006   *Sweet Negotiations: Sugar, Slavery, and Plantation Agriculture in Early Barbados.* University Press of Virginia, Charlottesville.
Miller, George L.
1980   Classification and Scaling in 19th Century Ceramics. *Historical Archaeology* 14:1–40.
Mintz, Sidney W.
1985   *Sweetness and Power: The Place of Sugar in Modern History.* Penguin, New York.

Newman, Simon P.

2013   *A New World of Labor: The Development of Plantation Slavery in the British Atlantic*. University of Pennsylvania Press, Philadelphia.

O'Callaghan, Sean

2000   *To Hell or Barbados: The Ethnic Cleansing of Ireland*. Brandon Books, Dublin.

Pinckard, George

1806   *Notes on the West Indies*, Vol. 3. London.

Price, Edward T.

1957   The Redlegs of Barbados. *Yearbook of the Association of Pacific Coast Geographers* 10:35–39.

Reeves, Matthew

2011   Household Market Activities among Early Nineteenth-Century Jamaican Slaves: An Archaeological Case Study from Two Slave Settlements. In *Out of Many, One People: The Historical Archaeology of Colonial Jamaica*, edited by James A. Delle, Mark W. Hauser, and Douglas V. Armstrong, pp. 183–210. University of Alabama Press, Tuscaloosa.

Roberts, Justin

2011   Uncertain Business: A Case Study of Barbadian Plantation Management, 1770–93. *Slavery & Abolition* 32(2):247–268.

Rosenberg, Harry

1962   Social Mobility among the Rural White Population of Barbados. Unpublished Master's thesis, Brandeis University.

Rugermer, Edward

2013   The Development of Mastery and Race in the Comprehensive Slave Codes of the Greater Caribbean during the Seventeenth Century. *William and Mary Quarterly* 70(3):429–458.

Ryzewski, Krysta, and John F. Cherry

2015   Struggles of a Sugar Society: Surveying Plantation-Era Montserrat, 1650–1850. *International Journal of Historical Archaeology* 19(2):356–383.

Sainsbury, W. Noel (editor)

1880   *Calendar of State Papers, Colonial Series, America and West Indies, 1661–1668*. Longman, London.

Scheid, Dwayne L.

2015   The Political Economy of Ceramic Production in Barbados: From Ceramic Industry to Craft Production. Ph.D. dissertation, Department of Anthropology, Syracuse University, Syracuse, New York.

Scott, James C.

2009   *The Art of Not Being Governed: An Anarchist History of Upland Southeast Asia*. Yale University Press, New Haven, Connecticut.

Shaw, Jenny

2013   *Everyday Life in the Early English Caribbean: Irish, Africans, and the Construction of Difference*. University of Georgia Press, Athens.

Sheppard, Jill

1977   *The "Redlegs" of Barbados: Their Origins and History*. KTO Press, New York.

Sheridan, Richard
1974   *Sugar and Slavery: An Economic History of the British West Indies, 1623–1775.* Johns Hopkins University Press, Baltimore.

Siedow, Erik
2014   Reconfiguring Redware: Typological and Analytical Considerations of Barbadian Red Earthenware. *Journal of the Barbados Museum and Historical Society* 40:152–180.

Simmons, Peter
1976   "Red Legs": Class and Color Contradictions in Barbados. *Studies in Comparative International Development* 11(1):3–24.

Singleton, Theresa A.
2001   Slavery and Spatial Dialectics on Cuban Coffee Plantations. *World Archaeology* 33(1):98–114.

2006   African Diaspora Archaeology in Dialogue. In *Afro-Atlantic Dialogues: Anthropology in the Diaspora*, edited by Kevin A. Yelvington, pp. 249–287. School of American Research Seminar Series, Santa Fe, NM.

Singleton, Theresa A. (editor)
2009   *The Archaeology of Slavery and Plantation Life.* Left Coast Press, Walnut Creek, California.

Singleton, Theresa A., and Mark Bograd
2000   Breaking Typological Barriers: Looking for the Colono in Colonoware. In *Lines that Divide: Historical Archaeologies of Race, Class, and Gender*, edited by James A. Delle, Stephen A. Mrozowski, and Robert Paynter, pp. 3–21. University of Tennessee Press, Knoxville.

Stoler, Laura Ann
1995   *Race and the Education of Desire: Foucault's History of Sexuality and the Colonial Order of Things.* Duke University Press, Durham, North Carolina.

2002   *Carnal Knowledge and Imperial Power: Race and the Intimate in Colonial Rule.* University of California Press, Berkeley.

Stoner, Michael J.
2000   Codrington Plantation: A History of a Barbadian Ceramic Industry. Unpublished Master's thesis, Armstrong Atlantic State University, Savannah, Georgia.

2003   Material Culture in the City: Barbadian Redwares in Bridgetown. *Barbados Museum and Historical Society* 51:254–268.

Thome, James Armstrong, and Joseph Horace Kimball
1838   *Emancipation in the West Indies: A Six Months' Tour in Antigua, Barbados, and Jamaica, in the Year 1837.* The American Anti-Slavery Society, New York.

Watson, Karl Stewart
2000   "Walk and Nyam Buckras": Poor-White Emigration from Barbados, 1834–1900. *Journal of Caribbean History* 34(1&2):130–156.

Welch, Pedro L. V.
2003   *Slave Society in the City: Bridgetown, Barbados, 1680–1834.* Ian Randle Publishers, Kingston.

2005   Exploring the Marine Plantation: An Historical Investigation of the Barbados Fishing Industry. *Journal of Caribbean History* 39(1):19–37.

Wilkie, Laurie A.
1999   Evidence of African Continuities in the Material Culture of Clifton Plantation, Bahamas. In *African Sites: Archaeology in the Caribbean*, edited by Jay B. Haviser, pp. 264–275. Markus Wiener Press, Princeton, New Jersey.
2001   Methodist Intentions and African Sensibilities: The Victory of African Consumerism over Planter Paternalism at a Bahamian Plantation. In *Island Lives: Historical Archaeologies of the Caribbean*, edited by Paul Farnsworth, pp. 272–300. University of Alabama Press, Tuscaloosa.
Wilkie, Laurie A., and Paul Farnsworth
2005   *Sampling Many Pots: An Archaeology of Memory and Tradition at a Bahamian Plantation*. University Press of Florida, Gainesville.
Williams, Eric
1994 [1944]   *Capitalism and Slavery*. University of North Carolina Press, Chapel Hill.

4

Provisioning and Marketing

Surplus and Access on Jamaican Sugar Estates

LYNSEY A. BATES

Throughout the British Caribbean during the eighteenth and nineteenth centuries, enslaved people were required to procure their own subsistence crops in designated cultivation areas, often called provision grounds. Many planters considered this scheme as a beneficial cost-cutting measure that relieved their dependence on imported provisions and that used land unsuitable for cash-crop production. For enslaved people, this additional burden of time and labor to cultivate their daily subsistence necessarily added to the stresses of forced labor and limited resources that they experienced (Marshall 1991; Reeves 1997, 2011). Despite these expectations, enslaved people produced, controlled, and distributed the surplus foodstuffs that fueled the development of internal markets of many islands (Higman 1988; Mintz and Hall 1960; see also Delle, this volume). The provision grounds and house gardens were the literal spaces in which slaves generated their livelihood. As argued by Sidney W. Mintz and Douglas Hall (1960), it follows that surplus crop production facilitated slaves' engagement in local markets. In this chapter, I test the hypothesis that enslaved people, farming larger plots of land with favorable conditions, had the opportunity to produce a greater surplus and thereby exercised access to the market.

Analysis of the link that slaves established between the provision ground and the market includes two related concepts that characterize the connection between cultivation and marketing: surplus and access. I define surplus as the nonsubsistence foodstuffs grown by enslaved people for sale to traveling merchants or in local markets; on a broader level, it includes any marketable goods they produced, whether food or crafts, for barter or sale. Access refers to opportunities of slaves to purchase market goods with profits from the sale of surplus, a particular "deployment of surplus" as suggested by Mark W. Hauser (2014a). Access to the market in this case does not imply any particular motivation for participation in market activities but rather refers to the level of participation as represented by the remains of market goods.

The island of Jamaica is a useful source for studying the provisioning system, particularly on large sugar estates. In the early eighteenth century many Jamaican planters acquired mountainous terrain and demarcated provision ground plots after selling off the valuable logwood. Slaves across the island necessarily relied on their grounds to survive. Enslaved people in Jamaica were not immune to the food stresses experienced on the smaller islands of Barbados, Nevis, and St. Kitts, and during periods of drought and importation disruptions. During times of more advantageous conditions, they grew surplus crops in the hills and valleys unsuitable for sugarcane to the extent that many colonists outside the plantation relied on the sale of this fresh produce (Higman 2000; Simmonds 2002). The "spaces in between" that slaves managed for self-provisioning thus supported the system of bondage through additional labor, attachment to the land, and reliable internal supplies. At the same time, the market system established by enslaved people in the Caribbean also led to their "accumulation of liquid capital" to an extent "hardly to be expected under such circumstances" (Mintz 1983:113–114). This incongruity demonstrates that the provision ground system was a pivotal convergence of slave subordination and autonomy.

Testing the links between surplus and access requires detailed information about cultivated areas on historic estates and the goods purchased by enslaved people on those estates. To this end, I examine data from two Jamaican sugar estates, Stewart Castle and Papine. These estates have associated documentary and archaeological data, including a dated survey map with a legend and an associated archaeological assemblage recovered from the slave village. These two datasets allow for direct comparison of provisioning conditions, in the form of soil quality and acreage, and access, in the form of costly, imported goods recovered from the houses and yards of the enslaved. In addition, these two estates are nearly equivalent in the following characteristics: total estate size, 1006.16 acres at Stewart Castle and 1288.39 acres at Papine; the occupation periods of the villages, late eighteenth century through full emancipation in 1838; and proximity to large market centers, with the port town of Falmouth approximately 11 km from Stewart Castle and the economic hub of the island, Kingston, approximately 12 km from Papine. At the same time, distinctions between the two estates allow for comparison of several characteristics of sugar estates across the island, including cane processing power (in this case, water versus cattle), topographic variability, and the size of the enslaved workforce. I consider the second and third aspects as critical to mapping cultivation conditions in the provisioning areas of each estate.

To test the surplus and access hypothesis with measurable attribute data, a synthesis of historical and archaeological information is necessary. First I review the historical and archaeological evidence for provisioning and marketing by enslaved people in Jamaica and the Caribbean more broadly. To assess the cultivation conditions within the provision grounds that facilitated the production of surplus, I estimate soil quality and available acreage on Stewart Castle and Papine Estates. I then examine whether the relative inequality in provisioning areas corresponds to differences in the imported goods that enslaved people acquired. Cost and frequency of refined ceramic vessels according to form and decoration suggest the degree of access each community exercised over time. The material culture evidence suggests that the community of Papine purchased costly ceramics to a greater degree than the Stewart Castle community. While a larger sample of estates is necessary to further explore this pattern, the data presented here indicate observable variation in surplus and access between these communities, supporting the hypothesis outlined above.

Provisioning and Marketing Strategies in Jamaica during the Period of Slavery

Conquered by the Spanish in the early sixteenth century, the island of Jamaica became a British colony in 1655 and within 100 years became the primary producer of sugar in the region (Mintz 1985; Ward 1988). Disruptions stemming from war and violent weather, however, threatened the success of sugar in the last quarter of the eighteenth century, with heavy costs in the importation of food and supplies (Carrington 1988, 1996; O'Shaughnessy 1996; Ragatz 1928). The fall of St. Domingue as a competitor as well as the reopening of the European market with the defeat of Napoleon could not outweigh the rising costs of running a sugar estate and the increasing debts to London creditors (Burnard 2011; Sheridan 1974). These factors forced many estates into mortgage and assumed ownership by agents in the early nineteenth century (Higman 2005).

On large and small estates alike, planters had to provide materials to feed, clothe, and house an enslaved workforce. The provisioning of food to slaves in Jamaica primarily took two forms: rationed staples such as corn (maize) meal (or wheat flour) and salt fish (primarily imported from the New England colonies and then Canada following the American Revolution) and the cultivation of basic foodstuffs such as corn, yams, and plantains by enslaved people in house gardens and allotted "Negro grounds." The process of self-provisioning by enslaved people in these allotted spaces was one way in which planters and colonial officials attempted to stave off food shortages that accompanied climactic events and disruptions in trade. With the British loss of the North American colonies, the Jamaican Assembly encouraged this practice, and the metropolitan government drew on its widespread colonial network to transport food-bearing plants to the Caribbean holdings (Sheridan 1976). Despite these efforts, the tenuous sustainability of the large Jamaican enslaved workforce, nearly 162,000 people by 1754 (Burnard 2011; Ryden 2009), was a constant concern for owners and their agents throughout the period of slavery.

Drawing on previous colonial laws, the Consolidated Slave Act of 1792 stated that "every master, owner, or possessor . . . shall allot and appoint a sufficient quantity of land for every slave . . . in order to provide, him, her, or themselves, with sufficient provisions for his, her, or their, maintenance." An additional clause required planters to set aside "at least one acre of land for every ten negroes . . . over and above the negro-grounds aforesaid; which lands shall be kept up in a planter-like condition." The 1792 act included a new clause related to provision grounds—namely, that the planter, overseer, or manager "shall personally inspect into the condition of such negro-grounds once in every month at the least, in order to see that the same are cultivated and kept up in a proper manner" (Edwards 1793:II:146). Clearly, these prescriptions must be taken with a grain of salt as to whether Jamaican planters followed them. The addition of the new clause to the 1788 laws suggests that little oversight was being carried out to ensure that these areas were of the necessary size or were maintained as explicitly outlined. For example, regional variability in the presence or size of provisioning areas is exemplified in David Ryden's (2000) study of a St. Andrew parish survey. This document indicates that planters reserved on average 68 acres for growing provisions, although 8 of the 25 owners did not indicate that any portion of their property was devoted to food production. This evidence suggests the degree of differential management practices even at very small scales.

Historical accounts indicate that enslaved people focused their energy on the staple starches of bananas, plantains, yams, cassava, and potato, with occasional plantings of maize and sorghum (Edwards 1793:II:124; Parry 1955, 1962; Pulsipher 1991). Additional foods consisted of protein resources acquired through husbandry, market transactions, and fishing. It was a common practice for slaves to raise chickens, pigs, and goats to supplement their rations of salted fish. Others sold their salted herring ration in the market in order to purchase salted pork (Stewart 1823:268). The meat and eggs from these animals were often sold by women on market day (Bush 1990; Stewart 1823:99).

Enslaved laborers primarily grew root vegetables and starches in ground plots (Mintz and Hall 1960; Pulsipher 1984, 1990, 1991, 1994). Local root vegetables include arrowroot, cassava, dasheen (for its leaves), and sweet potato. Starchy root crops introduced by the Spanish include yams (one New World and one African), eddoes, and Irish potatoes. The Spanish also introduced several fruit-bearing trees, namely, citrus (orange and lemon), banana, and plantain. In similar fashion to the yam, the plantain became a staple food due to its starch-like quality and ability to grow in difficult terrain. Several local trees, including the star apple, guava, and papaw, likely supplemented slave diets in locales with standing forests (Parry 1955:8). While its exact origins remain vague, the coconut tree was also an integral part of the diet, providing much-needed oils and fats when meat was scarce.

With the surplus produce in hand, enslaved people traveled from the plantation, often weekly, to market their wares. Documentary evidence points to the role of slaves as both sellers and consumers in Jamaica and other islands. The markets that enslaved people frequented in Jamaica were primarily those of large port towns along the coast, including Kingston, a burgeoning city during the eighteenth century that served as the center of trade for the island by the turn of the century (Higman 1991; Simmonds 2002). A few inland markets also grew over time, with the foremost being the former capital of St. Iago de la Vega, later renamed Spanish Town (Robertson 2008). Enslaved people on estates across the island also sold food crops to traveling middlemen and women known as "higglers." While higglering was essential to the success of the internal markets, any material signature is difficult to trace since higglers' weekly set of goods varied considerably. A notable exception is Hauser's (2006, 2008, 2009, 2011) analysis of locally made coarse earthenwares that he argues were transported and sold by female higglers to plantation villagers. Other enslaved marketers who ran stalls in the market centers sold the produce, animal products, and crafts carried to market by higglers or individuals from estates.

The Sunday markets in urban centers served as the chief avenue by which slaves acquired cash (McDonald 1993:30; Senior 1835:41; Simmonds 2002:279). While bartering was still prevalent in the eighteenth century, payment in cash in exchange for goods was the primary transaction type by the nineteenth century (Higman 1996:228). Edward Long's (1774:I:537) now-famous assertion that slaves controlled a significant portion of the coin in circulation on the island, however exaggerated, indicates the extent of the market participation of slaves. Few references to this assertion discuss Long's additional comments on introducing a "small coin" minted in England, accommodated to the dealings between "Negroes, who supply the market with small stock, and other necessaries" and the "white families supplied from those markets" (Long 1774:I:571). These remarks on the marketing activity of the enslaved directly acknowledge the extent to which the enslaved and free people of color engaged in the economy.

Accounts of slaves as consumers emphasize that they not only supplemented their diet with imported foodstuffs but also purchased "little necessaries or comforts" (Cooper 1824:4; Marshall 1991). The former included any of the following: "salt pork and beef, cod fish, butcher's meat, rice, flour, bread, rum . . ." (Mathison 1811:2). The "comforts" generally consisted of clothing (Barclay 1826:27; Edwards 1793:II:124; McDonald 1993:126–128). Other goods included furniture, crockery, glass (De La Beche 1825), and, in some cases, "plates and dishes of Queen's or Staffordshire ware" (Edwards 1793:II:127). It is difficult to know how common these investments were for the average enslaved individual on a sugar estate. Historian Robert McDonald (1993:104) argues that individuals did not purchase "more than the bare essentials in household goods" until they had "sufficient food and clothing." Planters commenting on the practice of the sale of provisions remark that only the "industrious" among the enslaved community who worked their grounds efficiently profited from their additional labor (Beckford 1790:II:153). Archaeological evidence recovered from slave village contexts suggests that slaves invested in imported goods like "crockeryware" and other articles purchased in markets (Armstrong 1990; Delle et al. 2011; Hauser 2008).

Historian Richard Sheridan (1993) argued that the slaves' market activities created an "informal" economy parallel to the planters' control of cash-crop production and export that was completely dependent on the additional labor and time expended by enslaved people. Lorna E. Simmonds (2002:277) elaborates on this division in her discussion of Kingston markets. She notes the "formal" economy comprised "members of the white community and the Jewish mercantile group" supplying institutional demand, and the "informal" comprised marginal group members who supplied the "needs of lower orders" (see also Bickell 1825; Reeves 2011). Barry W. Higman (1996:228) argues that planter elites strove to keep these economies separate and distinct through commodity restrictions such that slaves were excluded from trading "in items of export production, imported goods, and status-linked commodities." Despite the attempts of owners and market competitors to restrict slaves' activities in the market, the archaeological record in Jamaican enslaved villages suggests their ability to acquire imported items such as ceramics, pharmaceutical bottles, and decorated tobacco pipes (Armstrong 1990; Delle et al. 2011; Hauser 2008).

The conditions that slaves exploited to produce a surplus thus are key to understanding the potential variability in market access between enslaved communities. As one of the few activities that can be viewed as a "breach in the slave system" (Mintz 1983:113), the participation by enslaved people within the internal market, and more broadly the provision ground system, reflects the transformation of self-provisioning from an expectation that placed a burden on enslaved individuals to an opportunity for market access.

Spaces of Provisioning on Sugar Estates

The location of provisioning areas, including domestic villages, was determined most often by the planter or manager. According to contemporary observers, the land allotted for "Negro grounds" was rocky; uneven; unsuitable for sugarcane, guinea grass, or other marketable crops; and physically peripheral to sugar-processing areas (Beckford 1790:II:153–155; Madden 1835:185; Stewart 1808:100). Since a majority of slaves relied upon their own labor to produce the greater part of their caloric intake, they were subject to the same overall environmental pressures as their owners, including soil quality, rainfall, disastrous weather events, and disruptions in trade with other British colonies. Planter treatises, often in answer to abolitionist sentiment, suggest that the "industrious" among the enslaved population could easily cultivate their grounds within the current sugar regime. The "sufficient quantity of land" called for in the Consolidated Slave Act of 1792 does not indicate any specifications for the overall area of the provision grounds or the size of the plot assigned to an individual. Whether he or she worked "a few square yards" (Collins 1803:36) or "a rood to an acre" (Senior 1835:41), these authors argue that the time and space to cultivate was only determined by an enslaved person's initiative. This point is illustrated by Bickell's (1825:11) assertion that members of the first gang, "upon large estates belonging to wealthy and humane proprietors," could influence other slaves to work the grounds for them and thereby produce a larger surplus. The general assumption in these treatises is that, on larger estates, slaves had access to a larger acreage of grounds, with the possibility of relocating for "fresh land, every year," if necessary (Edwards 1793:II:124).

As Theresa Singleton (2005, 2014) and others have suggested, examining how planters envisioned and developed the landscape is essential to reconstructing the use of space by enslaved people in those contexts. Previous plantation analyses (Delle 1998, 2014; Epperson 1999; Higman 1988; Orser and Nekola 1985) suggest that planters organized the landscape as a strategy to maintain the tenuous balance between profit and control. A planter's goal of maximum profit could not be achieved without consideration of the estate's topography and ecological zones, particularly growing conditions for cash crops and sources of processing power (Bates 2014; Higman 1988; Roughley 1823). In addition, they sought to locate centers of surveillance, such as the overseer's or manager's house, to maximize observation and policing of slaves within areas of manufacture and habitation (Beckford 1790:I; Mintz 1985). Previous analyses and the evidence in this chapter suggest that, for enslaved people living and working under a system of spatial control, their maintenance of spaces beyond the view or concern of the planter was a strategy that facilitated investment in other areas (Higman 1998; see also Delle this volume).

Prior to analysis, the idea of "maintenance" of space must be transformed into measurable attributes of historic plantation landscapes. Methodologically, following the approach of studies by Delle (2014), Hauser (2014b), and Singleton (2001, 2014), the most promising investigations of contested spaces within organized landscapes are those rooted in the comparison of properties managed by different owners and agents. Through quantitative analysis, spatial data does not merely provide information about an extractive labor system but rather sheds light on the landscape of slavery in a concrete way (Delle 1998; Higman 1988). Revisiting the central hypothesis, I consider data from two Jamaican sugar estates, Stewart Castle and Papine (see Figure 4.1), to test whether enslaved communities with larger provision grounds and more advantageous growing conditions gained greater access to market goods. I examine two related attributes that reflect an estate's provisioning resources: available acreage and soil quality, measured by slope and soil type. Available acreage is an estimate of acreage per enslaved

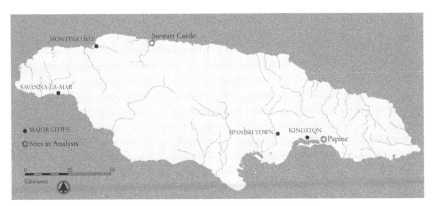

Figure 4.1. Location of Stewart Castle and Papine Estates, Jamaica. (Base Map Courtesy of DAACS)

individual based on the plat data and slave register data for each estate. To approximate relative soil quality, I integrate historic and modern cartographic data to characterize the growing conditions within provisioning areas noted on historic survey plats of the two estates. Using geographic information system software, I reference the historic plats to their current position on the landscape and generate digital elevation models and slope data within the former estate boundaries.

The Landscapes of Stewart Castle and Papine Estates

As noted earlier, Stewart Castle and Papine reflect topographic differences in north coast and south coast estates, the limestone hills and exposed bedrock of Stewart Castle contrasting with the flat, alluvial plain and foothills of Papine. While total acreage was nearly identical between the two estates, the potential provision ground acreage differed by more than 150 acres in favor of Papine (Table 4.1). These differences set the stage for examining the conditions of self-provisioning within each estate.

Stewart Castle Estate was established by James Stewart in 1754. His son was forced to mortgage the estate in 1797, although he later reclaimed possession of the property, under the management of Robert Shedden and Sons, in 1810. It is possible that this James Stewart is the same one who authored *An Account of Jamaica and Its Inhabitants*, first published in 1808 and later published in an edited form in 1823 (Panning 1995, 1996). Surveyed by Munro, Stevenson, and Innes, the Stewart Castle plat is dated 1799 and is identified at that time as the property of "the honorable James Stewart esquire" (National Library of Jamaica, Kingston, Jamaica, Estate

Table 4.1. Acreage, population, and soil data for Stewart Castle and Papine Estates, Jamaica

			Provisioning Attributes			
Estate (Date of Historic Plat)	Acreage identified on Plat	Acreage per Enslaved Individual (acres)	Slope and Standard Deviation (degrees)	Majority Soil Type[a]	Soil Fertility; Recommended Agriculture (modern)[a]	Number of Enslaved Individuals (Date of Population)
Stewart Castle (1799)	180.0	0.88	17.4 (6.2)	Bonnygate stony loam	Limited due to erosion; Woodland, food trees	258 (1817)
Papine (1834)	514.5	4.04	5.9 (2.4)	St Ann clay loam over Bonnygate stony loam	Limited due to erosion; Pasture, vegetables, food trees, food crops	134 (1832)

[a] Barker 1986:17–19.

Map, Trelawny #235, 1799). The only other extant depiction of the estate is a painting by J. B. Kidd that details the works complex and the castle itself. This image clearly shows the cattle mill that crushed the cane from the surrounding fields as well as the other sugar-processing buildings and the roads that crossed the estate. Historian Stephen Panning (1995, 1996) detailed the history of the estate and conducted a survey of its extant buildings in the 1990s. The Stewart main house was a fortified structure surrounded by a masonry wall topped with broken wine bottles. While most Jamaican great houses were open to the island breezes, the Stewarts chose to secure their house from possible raids by maroons or their own slaves.

Representative of the smaller, coastal plain estates along the south coast, Papine Estate was established in the 1750s by Alexander Grant, a Scotsman who inherited the property as a penn or cattle farm (Yates 1955). In the late eighteenth century, the estate was owned by J. B. Wildman (Francis-Brown 2004, 2005). It was Wildman's manager who Lady Mary Nugent met when she toured the estate in October of 1801 (Wright 1966). The Papine aqueduct, which diverted water from the Hope River and powered the sugar mill, was a shared venture between three neighboring planters, and to this day it supplies the city of Kingston with water. The plat is dated 1834, the first year of "apprenticeship" in Jamaica and other British colonies in the Caribbean (National Library of Jamaica, Kingston, Jamaica, Estate Map,

St Andrew #1135, 1834; Higman 2011). Another image of the Papine Estate depicts the jointly owned aqueduct's relationship to the Papine "Negroe Grounds," the "Negro Houses and Gardens," and the Papine works as well as the neighboring Mona estate works (National Library of Jamaica, Kingston, Jamaica, Estate Map, St Andrew #616, undated). Papine Estate reflects the trend of smaller estates that were established early in the period of exponential estate growth during the early to mid-eighteenth century near the coast (Ryden 2000). Although Papine's total cane acreage is only 130 acres less than Stewart Castle, cane fields represented only 27.7 percent of the total estate area compared to 43.9 percent at Stewart Castle.

In terms of provisioning areas, the 1799 plat of Stewart Castle denotes two areas marked "Negroe Grounds," both measuring 180 acres, with an additional 48.25 acres in the village. It is likely, however, that the 48.25 acres were not all available to the laborers for gardens and housing since the area is denoted as "Negro house & Guiney grass." In this case, areas around the houses drawn on the plat suggest an area closer to 35 acres.

At Papine, one area is listed in the 1834 plat's legend as "Woodland and Negro grounds," with two additional areas simply noted as "Woodland"; the inclusion of the latter sections increases the acreage more than 11 times (Table 4.1). Previous research suggests that woodland areas may have been open to provision cultivation based on the frequency of the "woodland" description with "negro grounds" on plats dating from 1750 to the 1840s (Bates 2014, 2015). Additional cartographic evidence indicates that, at one point in time, Papine slaves had access to an area to the northeast of the village along an aqueduct that carried water to the mill (National Library of Jamaica, Kingston, Jamaica, Estate Map, St. Andrew 616, undated). Finally, a modern topographic map of St. Andrew indicates that the far northeastern corner of Papine Estate includes part of the Dallas Mountains; this particular area is noted as "Papine Mountain" (National Land Agency, Kingston, Jamaica, Topographic Map, Sheet 105d, 1972). Higman (1988) has argued that the term "mountain" was often used to denote land associated with provisioning peripheral or beyond an estate's boundary. Referencing of the 1834 Papine plat to the modern landscape indicates that this area falls within one of the "woodland" parcels. Finally, the Papine village was estimated based on its location within the larger "works" area that included an aqueduct, wheelhouse, boiling, and other outbuildings. Archaeological survey evidence indicates that the village occupied the space noted in the survey plat (Galle 2009), with an approximate area of 27 acres.

Estimating the number of acres available on average to an enslaved individual or family to cultivate surplus remains a difficult task. In their analyses of account books from two neighboring Jamaican sugar estates, Higman (1976, 1998) and McDonald (1993) address the size of provision grounds and gardens per household at Old and New Montpelier, St. James. These sources provide approximate provision ground acreage per household of 2.34 acres and per individual of 0.738 acres. In addition, Higman (1998:195) discusses another account book that records 36 households that cultivated 102 separately listed provision ground plots, with an average of 2.83 plots per household. Unfortunately, this kind of detailed provision ground data is rare in the documentary record. Given this fact, I incorporate total population size to discuss the acreage available to enslaved people on the estates.

The number of enslaved individuals working and living at Stewart Castle and Papine Estates is recorded in the official registers conducted by the colonial administration beginning in 1817. An invaluable source of information on enslaved populations across the British Caribbean, the slave registers record the name, age, "color" and/or origin of each person owned by a given individual. For Stewart Castle and Papine Estates, I draw on the registries closest to the date of the plat to provide a closer approximation of the population at that time. The Stewart Castle data, reported by the lawyer for management firm Robert Shedden and Sons, indicates 169 men and women aged 18 to 61, 85 girls and boys 17 years old and younger, and three slaves older than 70. Since households cannot be reconstructed from this data, I consider each of these individuals as requiring some form of sustenance from the provision ground areas on the estate and thus do not exclude children and the elderly in estimating acreage available per enslaved individual. Even the meal cooked each day by one or more enslaved women for the "pot-gang" required food crops from the communal lands within the provision grounds (Collins 1803:93, 104; Senior 1835:57). In this way, small children, the infirm, the elderly, and newly arrived slaves received a daily meal. For Stewart Castle, including the village area, provisioning acreage available per individual was 0.88 acres, or 228.25 acres for 258 individuals.

In the case of Papine Estate, the date of the plat is 1834; I assume that this plat represents the estate's organization prior to the apprenticeship program, which was instituted in that year through 1838. There is no record of additional land purchased by J. B. Wildman near Papine during his ownership. For this reason, I incorporate data from the 1832 slave registry that lists the total population as 134 individuals. Between 1829 and 1832, 40 individuals were "removed" from Papine Estate to Wildman's estate Low Ground in the parish of Vere (Jamaica National Archives, Spanish Town, Jamaica, Registers of Returns of Slaves, 1B/11/7, Vere Parish, Register 1829 and Register 1832; Francis-Brown 2005). In addition, 11 births occurred and 5 male slaves aged 3 to 28 were brought to Papine from Low Ground and Salt Savannah, another estate owned by Wildman (Jamaica National Archives, Spanish Town, Jamaica, Registers of Returns of Slaves, 1B/11/7, Vere Parish, Register 1829 and Register 1832). Based on the plat and registry data, the provisioning acreage available per individual was 4.04 acres, or 541.34 acres for 134 individuals.

While the exact size of individual plots cannot be determined, this difference is clearly a significant one. Individuals at Stewart Castle may have needed to exploit less than favorable areas in order to cultivate provisions, while the Papine community had more choice in which areas to improve. With this data in hand, I examined soil profiles, compiled by the Department of Soil Science at the University of the West Indies (St. Augustine), and slope data calculated from modern topographic maps in the provisioning areas (Barker 1986). Although some denouement of the soil in these areas likely occurred due to continuous agriculture over the past 350 years, the locations of the main soil types remain roughly similar. Bonnygate stony loam is the primary or underlying soil type in the provisioning areas of both estates. This loam consists of a thin mantle present over white limestone and, when located on steeper slopes of greater than 10°, it is characterized by rapid drainage and limited fertility, and is suitable only for forest and food trees. The areas of Stewart Castle exhibit an average slope of 17.4° with a standard deviation of 6.2. In contrast, slope of the areas of Papine are on average 5.9° with a standard deviation of 3.9 (Table 4.1).

In combination, the soil quality data suggests that individuals at Stewart Castle had few opportunities available beyond the thin soils of Bonnygate stony loam. Enslaved people at Papine had access to Cuffy Gully gravelly sandy loam in the mountain land overlying Bonnygate stony loam, with a moderate risk of erosion in growing food crops and food trees. Generally, at either estate, it would have been difficult to cultivate food crops under the conditions of limited water retention, erodibility, and shallowness in the provisioning areas. Only the Papine village offered an opportunity for intensive cultivation, although this would be limited by low rainfall without additional irrigation. This data suggests that enslaved people seeking to produce subsistence and surplus crops needed to invest even more of their limited time and energy into this task. Evidence of this improvement is visible on the Stewart Castle landscape with terrace walls within the village house gardens and the planting of fruit-bearing trees (ackee and mango) within the Papine village. These conditions suggest that the Stewart Castle community was at a disadvantage in producing any surplus and in investing part of that surplus in market goods. I expect that this constraint resulted in a limited procurement of costly items by enslaved people at Stewart Castle, in contrast to their counterparts at Papine.

Marketing and the Acquisition of Imported Goods

The market system, which developed from the sale of surplus items by enslaved people in the Caribbean, also led to the acquisition of cash and goods by enslaved people (Mintz 1983). Despite the legal limitations imposed on slaves' marketing of commodities and the organization of the weekly markets, recognition of their economic activities underpinned their role as independent sellers and consumers in colonial markets (McDonald 1993:110). Historical research of slaves' economy, including market participation, suggests that these activities were one of the few independent (though sanctioned) avenues that slaves pursued "to make lives of their own" (Marshall 1991:60). As Mintz argued, the "historical facts 'on the ground' . . . stand as a violent exception to the intent of the plantation system and to the ideal status of the slaves" (1983:119).

With the limited historical accounts of what slaves purchased, archaeologists are uniquely positioned to provide evidence of the goods acquired by slaves since the remains of those goods are recovered in domestic contexts. Beginning with Robert Ascher and Charles H. Fairbanks' (1971) first foray into the archaeological evidence of slave life, subsequent excavations across North America and the Caribbean have yielded an abundance of imported manufactured goods, primarily ceramics. Explanations for this phenomenon include the taphonomic and economic factors involved in the deposition of different artifact materials over time. As James Deetz famously chronicled, many early colonial goods consisted of perishable materials such as plant fibers (wood, reeds, gourds) and metals like pewter that break down quickly under most conditions. When everyday items came to be made of iron, brass, ceramic, and glass, the amount of recoverable material increased (Deetz 1996 [1977]). An increase in frequency is also a function of availability since over time these items were produced in large quantities in European factories built with the profits of cash-crop production primarily in latter half of the eighteenth century.

At the same time, the material signature of consumption also signals some ability of the site's inhabitants to acquire these market items (Delle 1998, 2014; Galle 2010; Heath and Bennett 2000; Reeves 1997; Wilkie and Farnsworth 2005). In conjunction with the studies noted above, most archaeological examinations of slave economies are centered on the question of *why* enslaved people with limited resources would choose costlier items over locally available alternatives. In some cases, scholars argue that slaves on particular plantations received ceramics and other imported items from the master, whether for need or as an incentive for labor (e.g., Joseph 1993; Thomas 1995). In other studies, enslaved people made choices based on their position within the plantation hierarchy (Adams and Boling 1989; Drucker 1981; Otto 1984). These approaches, however, leave us with the question of the acquisition of everyday, imported items found in such large quantities across sites of slavery. Several studies of plantation Caribbean material address this question by examining imported (primarily English) ceramics as a medium through which power, ideals, and identities were communicated between social groups (Farnsworth 1996; Howson 1995; Reeves 1997; Wilkie 2000; Wilkie and Farnsworth 1999, 2005). Another line of inquiry interprets the strategies of enslaved people as responses to larger demographic and economic changes occurring within the Atlantic World (Galle 2006, 2011; Galle et al. 2010; Neiman 2008). In this approach, consumption and access are a function of costly signaling, a strategy in which males and females signal their fitness to potential mates and competitors.

As noted by Matthew Reeves (1997, 2011) and Jillian E. Galle (2011), I argue that understanding variability in an enslaved community's access to the market sheds light on the conditions of daily life as much as attempts to interpret the motivation or meaning behind their choices. Avoiding Jean Howson's (1990:90) caution that "the meaning of things somehow can be construed directly from frequency distributions," I examine how assemblages of discarded goods correlate to opportunities to purchase those goods and thereby the conditions of provision ground cultivation above. This method emphasizes that the opportunity to acquire and the practice of acquisition are moments in which responses to domination occurred, rather than merely the means to an end of status differentiation.

Measuring Access with Artifact Abundance Indices

One way to assess market access and participation is comparative, quantitative analysis of material culture distribution and attributes. Hauser's (2006, 2008) extensive study of market dynamics in Jamaica through the lens of the production and consumption of locally made coarse earthenwares (*yabbas*) illustrates how a single material culture class reflects the dynamic economic and social spheres of enslaved people. In similar fashion, I examine refined imported ceramics as a proxy for relative access to the market and acquisition of goods.[1] The consistent presence of these ceramics on domestic sites indicates that slaves living in different areas and under different working conditions were able to acquire market goods of this kind. This commonality makes it an ideal artifact category to examine market participation by enslaved people and any potential variability therein.

I assume that the purchase of individual vessels remained a significant expense to the enslaved person. George Miller and other scholars argue that the increasing mass production of these ceramics in England and Europe led to falling prices over time in American markets after 1750 (Miller 1980, 1984a, 1984b, 1988, 1991, 2000; Miller and Moodey 1986; Miller et al. 1994). Despite this trend, archaeological evidence suggests that increase in the consumption and discard of market goods, such as refined ceramics and buttons, by enslaved people outpaced the decreasing prices until the early nineteenth century (Galle 2011:242). Given that the archaeological record of slave village sites in the British Caribbean and throughout the American colonies includes not only "cheap" undecorated flatwares but also highly decorated, "costly" serving wares suggests that enslaved people sought out these items.

Furthermore, I assume that the assemblages recovered from each of these village sites reflect a cross-section of the enslaved community and a group-level consumption pattern. While previous work examined potential internal differentiation within enslaved communities (Higman 1998; McDonald 1993; Reeves 1997, 2011; Wilkie and Farnsworth 1999, 2005), the correlation of provision ground conditions and market access necessitates comparison of total assemblages. Ideally one could coordinate the rich historical record of an estate like Montpelier in St. James to determine which family groups cultivated particular provision ground plots as well as the occupations of each groups' members. Unfortunately, the documentary record pertaining to the estates in question does not allow for this type of detailed correlation.

The community-level comparison is also appropriate for these sites as they were excavated using a shovel-test-pit (STP) method that focused on expansive coverage of the village site, with additional 1 × 1 m units placed to capture structural features (Galle 2007, 2009). Neither Stewart Castle nor Papine village had significant above-ground evidence of house platforms; field programs were designed to gather chronological and spatial differentiation across the village space. STPs at both sites were 50 cm in diameter on 6 m centers. These measures were determined to best suit the analytical goals of broad spatial coverage while recovering suitable sample sizes and stratigraphic information from each pit. Unit excavations further explored depositional processes at the site and potential architectural features, such as terraces or cisterns. Temporal phasing within the village can be confirmed using stratigraphic evidence within these units (Cooper et al. 2008). Overall village patterns gleaned from this sampling strategy have informed several comparative analyses that include the Stewart Castle and Papine assemblages (Galle 2010, 2011; Galle et al. 2010; Neiman et al. 2010).

All recovered materials were cataloged according to protocols established by the Digital Archaeological Archive of Comparative Slavery, or DAACS (available on www.daacs.org). These detailed protocols ensure standardization of terminology, measurements, and identification across catalogers and assemblages from different locations and time periods. Within each assemblage, ceramic analysis was completed at the sherd level. Identifications of ware type, vessel category (hollow or flat), form, decorative genre, and individual decorative elements were attribute-based. For each recorded category of information, certain criteria for identification must be met. No attempt to mend or vesselize sherds was made except in cases where multiple sherds from the same context clearly mended together.[2] Data concerning form and decorative genre were aggregated due to the smaller sample sizes of individual identified forms. With this approach many sherds identified as either hollow or flat tewares, tablewares, and utilitarian vessels were included in the analysis, improving the reliability of form comparisons made between assemblages.

Time is a crucial factor to understanding intra- and intersite dynamics. Maintaining temporal control ensures that observed patterns reflect differences in access or choice within households or communities. Fraser D. Neiman and colleagues (2000) developed a technique for determining mean ceramic dates and occupational phases for sites excavated in STPs and units through the use of the frequency seriation method and correspondence analysis (see also Dunnell 1970; Galle 2006, 2010; Neiman and Smith 2005;

Smith and Neiman 2007). Each STP or unit level in a site is "phased" according to the ceramics found within it. This method thus groups contexts according to chronological phases that are directly comparable across sites. Previous research (Galle 2007, 2009) indicates that the primary occupational phases identified at Stewart Castle and Papine are contemporary, with peaks in the last quarter of the eighteenth century and the first quarter of the nineteenth century. This evidence supports investigation of the village assemblages as a whole rather than by separate occupational phases.

Following the approach of Neiman et al. (2000) and Galle (2006, 2010), I employ an artifact abundance index that estimates an artifact group's (Artifact Group 1) discard rate relative to the discard rate of a single baseline artifact group (Artifact Group 2). An abundance index is more reliable than relative frequencies since the baseline group either does not fluctuate with time or fluctuates in a predictable way (Neiman et al. 2000). This approach requires a denominator value that fits these criteria. Based on the available data, I selected total wine bottle glass as my baseline artifact group since the counts do not vary according to the occupational phases discussed above.[3] It is important to note that the perceived lack of correlation with time for a given Artifact Group 2 may be influenced by factors such as site formation processes or site occupation spans. Given this concern, I interpret the abundance indices as a measurement of relative investment by enslaved people in the given Artifact Group 1. This interpretation differs in that sense from the method employed by Galle (2006, 2010) wherein the calculated artifact index values are construed as discard rates.

Assemblages Recovered from the Stewart Castle and Papine Villages

The spatial data of the Papine and Stewart Castle provisioning areas indicates that the community of Stewart Castle may have been at a disadvantage in producing surplus and accessing the market compared to the Papine community. I test whether these differences correlate with unequal access to local markets by examining refined ceramics in each assemblage. To start, an abundance index of the total refined ceramic counts indicates variability between the two assemblages (Figure 4.2A). The results suggest that Papine residents invested to a greater extent in refined ceramics than the Stewart Castle residents. To potentially identify the underlying cause of the difference in total refined ceramic investment, I examine two attributes of refined ceramics, form and decoration, which varied by the known dimension of cost.

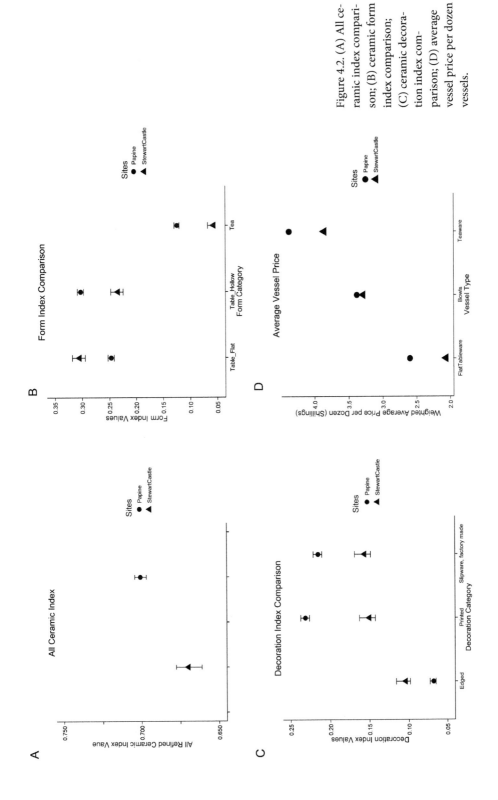

Figure 4.2. (A) All ceramic index comparison; (B) ceramic form index comparison; (C) ceramic decoration index comparison; (D) average vessel price per dozen vessels.

Miller's (1980, 1984b, 1991) work on ceramic price fixing by Staffordshire manufacturers in the nineteenth century provides some insight into the relative cost of vessels of different form and decoration. Based on his thorough documentary research, Miller focuses on plates, teacups and saucers, and bowls, although he provides prices of other vessels in English pence per dozen. Prices from the 1814 Staffordshire price-fixing list discussed by Miller (1984b) indicate that tablewares, including plates and soup tureens, were the least expensive refined earthenware forms, with increasing prices for bowls, chamber pots, and teawares. Clearly, the prices of each form also increase with added decoration. Howson's (1995:Table B.4) appendix of Jamaican merchant prices for ceramic vessels confirms the relative cost scaling by form. In addition, for each form, the Jamaican cost is consistently higher than those in the Staffordshire list, and undecorated plates exceed the cost of undecorated bowls.

The first aggregation approach draws on the common form categorization between teawares and tablewares. With the establishment of tea drinking across the British Empire in the eighteenth century, the cost of specialized vessels associated with serving tea and other hot beverages remained high (Edwards and Hampson 2005:55). As a broader form category, tableware incorporates dining and serving vessels, including plates, tureens, serving dishes, mugs, and bowls. The Staffordshire price list indicates that hollow versus flat attribute contributes to cost. In this sample, I incorporate hollow or flat sherds identified to the teaware and tableware form level. All of the teaware sherds are considered in one category since teacups and saucers, arguably the most common teaware forms recovered, were sold in sets. Therefore, more specific distinctions by form are subsumed under the larger categories of flat tableware, hollow tableware, and teaware.

* * *

Figure 4.2 includes the index values of form types between Stewart Castle and Papine (Figure 4.2B). As a measure of investment in different vessel types, these results suggest that the Papine community invested in the more costly hollow tableware and teaware forms to a greater degree relative to the Stewart Castle community. In contrast, the Stewart Castle investment focused on less expensive flat tablewares and hollow tablewares rather than teawares.

Miller's data clearly also addresses the cost differences between decorative techniques. Compared to undecorated versions of the same form, decorated vessels were consistently 33 percent more costly. For tableware forms such as plates and tureens, the least expensive decoration was edged wares, consisting of a combination of molded and painted elements (Miller 1991:5–6; Miller and Hunter 1990, 2001). Tablewares with simple hand-painted lines or plain bands were roughly equivalent to the edged wares cost. Transfer-printed tablewares in the common Blue Willow pattern or in other patterns were the most costly. Teawares, bowls, mugs, and other hollow forms were often painted, slipped, and rouletted in a variety of colors, a genre referred to historically as "dipped" or "dipt" wares and identified as Factory-Made Slipware in the DAACS system. Hand-painted vessels in overglaze and underglaze designs, primarily botanical and other bands, garnered 1.5 times the price of undecorated vessels. Finally, transfer-printed teawares were likely the most expensive, nonutilitarian vessels acquired by enslaved people in this sample.

The decoration data follows a similar trend as the form data (Figure 4.2C). The Stewart Castle assemblage reveals a greater investment in edge-decorated vessels compared to the Papine assemblage. However, investment in the other primary forms of decoration was greater than the edged wares, suggesting greater relative acquisition of slipped and transfer-printed vessels. With the form data in mind, it is possible that slaves in the Stewart Castle community selected slipped and printed hollow wares rather than more costly slipped and printed teawares. The greater investment in slipped and printed vessels at Papine suggests differential access to these kinds of vessels.

To further investigate the trends within these two sets of attribute data, I examine the average price of decorated vessel forms at each site. This approach provides a basic way to assess form and decoration within the sample. Average price estimations are based on the Staffordshire cost in shillings for decorated vessels and counts of identified sherds by form and decoration. Due to sample size limitations, I selected flat tableware, bowls, and teawares. A weighted average of all of the sherds with an identified form is calculated based on the number of sherds present in each decorative form category. This weighted average thus reflects the average price of the particular form, decorated and undecorated, within an assemblage (Figure 4.2D).

Average form price takes into account five decorative categories recorded in the Staffordshire lists: undecorated ("Cream Coloured"), dipped, painted, Willow pattern printed, and printed with another pattern (Miller 1984b:Figure 1). For bowls, the price for Willow and other patterns is equal at seven shillings per dozen. The results of the comparison indicate that the

Papine and Stewart Castle assemblages exhibit nearly identical investment in bowls but may had differential access to teawares and flat tablewares.

Discussion and Conclusions

For Stewart Castle, low values in serving vessels and teawares point to limited investment while the relatively comparable acquisition of slipped and printed vessels suggest greater investment. In this case, it is possible that the enslaved community at Stewart Castle selected according to decoration rather than form and function. The intersection of these lines of evidence, the average decorated price per dozen vessels, indicates that enslaved people at Stewart Castle spent less on plates than bowls and teawares. While they did not necessarily acquire the most expensive teawares relative to the Papine community, Stewart Castle community invested to the same extent in undecorated and decorated bowls, suggesting a preference for this form category.

The contrast between the two communities across these material attributes indicates that the hypothesis of surplus and access holds true. Papine residents with access to a greater amount of acres with favorable conditions consistently acquired costlier imported vessels, whether measured by form or decoration. In consideration of ceramic form, the data indicates that the Stewart Castle community invested in cheaper flat and hollow tablewares than expensive teawares compared to their counterparts.

The ceramic analysis thus contributes to an understanding of surplus and access by demonstrating variability in the acquisition of refined ceramic vessels. Consistently lower values in costly attributes suggest that enslaved people at Stewart Castle had more restricted access to the market, possibly based on provisioning constraints.

My approach to investigating how enslaved people capitalized on an exploitative system through spatial parameters and ceramic attributes is useful in its comparative examination of quantitative data. Compared to previous studies of Jamaican estates (Galle 2011; Reeves 1997, 2011), the spatial data hold labor expectations relatively constant; the labor and time expectations in cane planting, cutting, and processing were likely very similar at Stewart Castle and Papine. Given this controlled parameter, I focused on topographic variables to estimate conditions of cultivation based on a synthesis of historic and modern data. Extracting this data from comparable sources ensures that the correlations drawn between them are defensible. Similarly, relying on quantified archaeological data to evaluate hypotheses avoids the pitfalls associated with basic relative frequencies typically used by historical archaeologists. Since the total number of artifacts of an artifact type may fluctuate with time, using these counts as the basis of a ratio may introduce uncontrolled variability into the frequency estimates. By accounting for time with detailed chronologies and denominator values that do not vary with time, we can improve the analytical strategies we use to test variability within and between assemblages.

This analysis addresses the strategies that enslaved people developed to exploit a system designed to extract their energy and labor in all aspects of life. Following Mintz's (1983:113) assertion of the internal market as a "breach" in the slave system, I argue that the production of surplus and access to the market were primary points at which slaves asserted customary rights (McDonald 1993) to property in the form of land and goods. The series of actions encompassed in the provision ground system complicates restrictions related to slaves' "legal personality" and the lack of legal recognition of their "capacity for choice and action" (Klein 1971:83). The contradictory nature of slaves' assertion of rights exhibited in their daily choices and actions is a compelling impetus to examine the variability between the experiences of enslaved people. In the provision grounds, a very human aspect of a person's behavior—his desire to invest in the land and provide for his family—becomes construed by planters as a way to perpetuate his status as chattel property. At the same time, it is within these provision grounds that the customary property rights were most exercised (see Delle, this volume). These rights then extended to the acquisition of moveable property from the market. My approach to investigating how enslaved people capitalized on an exploitative system through spatial parameters and ceramic attributes is useful in its comparative examination of quantitative data. Compared to previous studies of Jamaican estates (Armstrong 1990, 2011; Armstrong and Kelly 2000; Galle 2011; Reeves 1997, 2011), within the spatial data, labor expectations are held relatively constant; the labor and time expectations in cane planting, cutting, and processing were likely very similar at Stewart Castle and Papine. Given this controlled parameter, I focused on topographic variables to estimate conditions of cultivation based on a synthesis of historic and modern data. Extracting this data from comparable sources ensures that the correlations drawn between them are defensible. Similarly, relying on quantified archaeological data to evaluate hypotheses avoids the pitfalls associated with basic relative frequencies typically used by historical archaeologists. Since the total number of artifacts of an artifact type may fluctuate with time, using these counts as the basis of a ratio may introduce uncontrolled variability into the frequency estimates. By accounting for time with detailed chronologies and denominator values that do not vary with time, we can improve the analytical strategies we use to test variability within and between assemblages.

Similar studies that address provisioning and market activity (Delle 2014; Galle 2011; Hauser 2014a, 2014b; Howson 1995; Reeves 1997, 2011) also analyze archaeological data from village areas. This project contributes to these interpretations of the provision ground system by testing hypotheses about spatial organization and goods acquisition in a comparative assessment of two estates in different regions of Jamaica.

Acknowledgments

This research was funded in part by the Wenner-Gren Foundation and the University of Pennsylvania's School of Arts and Sciences. Jillian E. Galle, Fraser D. Neiman, Elizabeth A. Bollwerk, Leslie Cooper, and two anonymous reviewers provided valuable feedback on earlier drafts of this chapter. Any errors are my own.

Notes

1. The term "refined" distinguishes these vessels according to the refining of the clay used to produce them. This process resulted in fewer impurities and a denser, consistently "clean" paste that could be thinly potted. This attribute applies to earthenwares, stonewares, and porcelains, although they were fired at different temperatures and covered with glazes of different composition.

2. Proponents of cross mending, vesselization, and minimum vessel counts argue that a sherd-based approach includes the danger of double-counting sherds that are part of the same vessel. However, by applying the same estimation technique to all of the samples involved, this approach produces a relative scale of price comparison. It also removes the often arbitrary and subjective identification of vessels from sherds that do not mend. In addition, this approach incorporates a larger sample of data rather than discounting sherds because they are not identifiable to a particular vessel. The arbitrariness of the vesselization process and the lack of agreed-upon standards upon which minimum vessel counts are calculated by different investigators complicate comparison across sites. An exception is the calculation of estimated vessel equivalencies that focus on identifiable sherds such as bases and rims (Orton et al. 1993). Small sample sizes for these completeness attributes in this sample precluded use of this approach.

3. The correlation test I employed is a Kendall's tau rank correlation; in this case, when the p value is greater than 0.1, then there is no significant correlation with time (Galle 2006:168). The p value for wine bottle glass in this sample was .945.

References Cited

Adams, William Hampton, and Sarah Jane Boling
1989   Status and Ceramics for Planters and Slaves on Three Georgia Coastal Planta-
        tions. *Historical Archaeology* 23(1):69–96.

Armstrong, Douglas V.
1990   *The Old Village and the Great House: An Archaeological and Historical Examina-
        tion of Drax Hall Plantation, St. Ann's Bay, Jamaica.* University of Illinois Press,
        Urbana.
2011   Reflections on Seville: Rediscovering the African Jamaican settlements at Seville
        Plantation, St. Ann's Bay. In *Out of Many, One People: The Historical Archaeol-
        ogy of Colonial Jamaica*, edited by James A. Delle, Mark W. Hauser, and Douglas
        Armstrong, pp. 77–101. University of Alabama Press, Tuscaloosa.

Armstrong, Douglas V., and Kenneth Kelly
2000   Settlement Patterns and the Origins of African Jamaican Society: Seville Planta-
        tion, St. Ann's Bay, Jamaica. *Ethnohistory* 47(2):369–397.

Ascher, Robert, and Charles H. Fairbanks
1971   Excavation of a Slave Cabin: Georgia, U.S.A. *Historical Archaeology* 5:3–17.

Barclay, Alexander
1826   *A Practical View of the Present State of Slavery in the West Indies.* Smith, Elder &
        Co., London.

Barker, G. H.
1986   *Soil and Land-Use Surveys No. 24 Jamaica, Parish of St. Ann.* University of the
        West Indies Regional Research Centre, Department of Soil Science, Trinidad.

Bates, Lynsey A.
2014   "The Landscape Cannot Be Said to Be Really Perfect": A Comparative Investiga-
        tion of Plantation Spatial Organization on Two British Colonial Sugar Estates. In
        The Archaeology of Slavery: A Comparative Approach to Captivity and Coercion,
        edited by Lydia W. Marshall, pp. 116–142. Center for Archaeological Investiga-
        tions, Southern Illinois University Occasional Paper No. 41, Carbondale.
2015   Surplus and Access: Provisioning and Market Participation by Enslaved Labor-
        ers on Jamaican Sugar Estates. Unpublished Ph.D. dissertation, Department of
        Anthropology, University of Pennsylvania, Philadelphia.

Beckford, William
1790   *A Descriptive Account of the Island of Jamaica: With Remarks upon the Cultiva-
        tion of the Sugar-Cane.* 2 vols. T. and J. Egerton, London.

Bickell, Richard
1825   *The West Indies as They Are; or, A Real Picture of Slavery: But More Particularly
        as It Exists in the Island of Jamaica.* Dotson and Palmer, London.

Burnard, Trevor G.
2011   Powerless Masters: The Curious Decline of Jamaican Sugar Planters in the Foun-
        dational Period of British Abolitionism. *Slavery & Abolition* 32(2):185–198.

Bush, Barbara
1990   *Slave Women in Caribbean Society, 1650–1838.* Heinemann, Kingston, Jamaica.

Carrington, Selwyn H. H.

1988   The State of the Debate on the Role of Capitalism in the Ending of the Slave System. *Journal of Caribbean History* 22(1–2):20–41.

1996   The United States and the British West Indian Trade, 1783–1807. In *West Indies Accounts: Essays on the History of the British Caribbean and the Atlantic Economy*, edited by Roderick A. McDonald, pp 149–151. University of the West Indies Press, Cave Hill, Barbados.

Collins, David

1803   *Practical Rules for the Management and Medical Treatment of Negro Slaves in the Sugar Colonies*. J. Barfield, London.

Cooper, Leslie, Jillian E. Galle, Fraser D. Neiman, Karen Hutchins, and Derek Wheeler

2008   Uncovering Jamaican Slave Villages through Spatial Survey: Methods and Results. Scientific Poster presented at the 73rd Annual Meeting of the Society of American Archaeology, Vancouver, B.C., March 26–30.

Cooper, Thomas

1824   *Facts Illustrative of the Condition of the Negro Slaves in Jamaica: With Notes and an Appendix*. J. Hatchard and Son, London.

Deetz, James

1996 [1977] *In Small Things Forgotten: The Georgian World View, Material Culture and the Consumer Revolution*. Cambridge University Press, Cambridge.

De La Beche, Henry Thomas

1825   *Notes on the Present Condition of the Negroes in Jamaica*. T. Cadell, London.

Delle, James A.

1998   *An Archaeology of Social Space: Analyzing Coffee Plantations in Jamaica's Blue Mountains*. Contributions to Global Historical Archaeology. Plenum Press, New York.

2014   *The Colonial Caribbean: Landscapes of Power in Plantation System*. Cambridge University Press, New York.

Delle, James A., Mark W. Hauser, and Douglas V. Armstrong

2011   *Out of Many, One People: The Historical Archaeology of Colonial Jamaica*. University of Alabama Press, Tuscaloosa.

Drucker, Lesley M.

1981   Socioeconomic Patterning at an Undocumented Late 18th Century Lowcountry Site: Spiers Landing, South Carolina. *Historical Archaeology* 15(2):58–68.

Dunnell, Robert C.

1970   Seriation Method and Its Evaluation. *American Antiquity* 35(3):305–319.

Edwards, Bryan

1793   *The History, Civil and Commercial, of the British Colonies in the West Indies*. 2 vols. Luke White, Dublin.

Edwards, Diana, and Rodney Hampson

2005   *White Salt-Glazed Stoneware of the British Isles*. Antique Collectors' Club Ltd, Suffolk, United Kingdom.

Epperson, Terrence W.

1999   Constructing Difference: The Social and Spatial Order of the Chesapeake Plantation. In *"I, Too, Am America": Archaeological Studies of African-American Life*, edited by Theresa A. Singleton, pp. 159–72. University Press of Virginia, Charlottesville.

Farnsworth, Paul
1996   The Influence of Trade on Bahamian Slave Culture. *Historical Archaeology* 30(4):1–23.

Francis-Brown, Suzanne
2004   *Mona Past and Present: The History and Heritage of the Mona Campus, University of the West Indies.* University of West Indies Press, Kingston.
2005   Finding Families within the Communities Enslaved on the Mona and Papine Estates, 1817–1832. *Caribbean Quarterly* 94–108.

Galle, Jillian E.
2006   Strategic Consumption: Archaeological Evidence for Costly Signaling Among Enslaved Men and Women in the Eighteenth-Century Chesapeake. Unpublished Ph.D. Dissertation, Department of Anthropology, University of Virginia.
2007   Background Information on Stewart Castle Village. Electronic document, http://www.daacs.org/sites/stewart-castle-village/. Accessed April 28, 2014.
2009   Background Information on Papine Village. Electronic document, http://www.daacs.org/sites/papine-village/. Accessed April 30, 2014.
2010   Costly Signaling and Gendered Social Strategies Among Slaves in the Eighteenth-Century Chesapeake: An Archaeological Perspective. *American Antiquity* 75(1):19–43.
2011   Assessing the Impacts of Time, Agricultural Cycles, and Demography on the Consumer Activities of Enslaved Men and Women in Eighteenth-Century Jamaica and Virginia. In *Out of Many, One People: The Historical Archaeology of Colonial Jamaica*, edited by James A. Delle, Mark W. Hauser, and Douglas V. Armstrong, pp. 211–242. University of Alabama Press, Tuscaloosa.

Galle, Jillian E., Leslie Cooper, Fraser D. Neiman, and Ivor Conolley
2010   Identifying Change in Household- and Specialist-Produced Coarse Earthenwares from 18th and 19th Century Jamaican Slave Villages. Scientific Poster Presented at the 75th Annual Meeting of the Society of American Archaeology, St. Louis, Missouri, April 14–18.

Gosse, David St. A.
2004   The Haitian Revolution Race & Plantation Management in Early Nineteenth Century Jamaica. *Caribbean Quarterly* 50(4):1–13.

Hauser, Mark W.
2006   Hawking Your Wares: Determining the Scale of Informal Economy through the Distribution of Local Coarse Earthenware in Eighteenth-Century Jamaica. In *African Re-Genesis: Confronting Social Issues in the Diaspora*, edited by Kevin C. McDonald, pp. 160–175. Left Coast Press, Walnut Creek, California.
2008   *The Archaeology of Black Markets, Local Economies, and Local Pottery in Eighteenth-Century Jamaica.* University Press of Florida, Gainesville.
2009   Linstead Market before Linstead? Eighteenth-century Yabbas and the Internal Market System of Jamaica. *Caribbean Quarterly* 55(2):89–111.
2011   Routes and Roots of Empire: Pots, Power, and Slavery in the 18th-Century British Caribbean. *American Anthropologist* 113(3): 431–447.

2014a   Land, Labor, and Things: Surplus in a New West Indian Colony (1763–1807). *Economic Anthropology* 1(1):49–65.

2014b   Blind Spots in Empire: Plantation Landscapes in Early Colonial Dominica (1763–1807). In *The Archaeology of Slavery: A Comparative Approach to Captivity and Coercion*, edited by Lydia W. Marshall, pp. 143–165. Center for Archaeological Investigations, Occasional Paper No. 41., Southern Illinois University Press, Carbondale.

Heath, Barbara J., and Amber Bennett

2000   "The little Spots allow'd them": The Archaeological Study of African-American Yards. *Historical Archaeology* 34(2):38–55.

Higman, Barry W.

1976   *Slave Population and Economy in Jamaica, 1807–1834.* Cambridge University Press, New York.

1986   Jamaican Coffee Plantations, 1780–1860: A Cartographic Analysis. *Caribbean Geography* 2(2):73–91.

1988   *Jamaica Surveyed: Plantation Maps and Plans of the 18th and 19th Centuries.* Institute of Jamaica, Kingston.

1991   Jamaican Port Towns in the Early Nineteenth Century. In *Atlantic Port Cities: Economy, Culture, and Society in the Atlantic World 1650–1850*, edited by Franklin W. Knight and Peggy K. Liss, pp. 117–148. University of Tennessee Press, Knoxville.

1996   Patterns of Exchange within a Plantation Economy: Jamaica at the Time of Emancipation. In *West Indies Accounts: Essays on the History of the British Caribbean and the Atlantic Economy in Honour of Richard Sheridan*, edited by Roderick A. McDonald, pp. 211–231. University of the West Indies Press, Kingston.

1998   *Montpelier, Jamaica: A Plantation Community in Slavery and Freedom, 1739–1912.* University of the West Indies Press, Kingston.

2000   The Sugar Revolution. *The Economic History Review* 53(2):213–236.

2005   *Plantation Jamaica 1750–1850: Capital and Control in a Colonial Economy.* University of the West Indies Press, Kingston.

2011   *A Concise History of the Caribbean.* Cambridge University Press, Cambridge.

Howson, Jean

1990   Social Relations and Material Culture: A Critique of Archaeology of Plantation Slavery. *Historical Archaeology* 24(4):78–91.

1995   Colonial Goods and the Plantation Village: Consumption and the Internal Economy in Montserrat from Slavery to Freedom. Unpublished Ph.D. dissertation, Department of Anthropology, New York University, New York.

Joseph, Joseph W.

1993   White Columns and Black Hands: Class and Classification in the Plantation Ideology of the Georgia and South Carolina Lowcountry. *Historical Archaeology* 27(3):57–73.

Klein, Herbert S.

1971   *Slavery in the Americas: A Comparative Study of Virginia and Cuba.* Quadrangle Books, Chicago.

Long, Edward
1774   *The History of Jamaica, In Three Volumes*. T. Lowndes, London.
Madden, Richard Robert
1835   *A Twelvemonth's Residence in the West Indies, during the Transition from Slavery to Apprenticeship*. J. Cochrane and Co., London.
Marshall, Woodville K.
1991   Provision Ground and Plantation Labour in Four Windward Islands: Competition for Resources during Slavery. In *The Slaves' Economy: Independent Production by Slaves in the Americas*, edited by Ira Berlin and Philip D. Morgan, pp. 48–67. Frank Cass, London.
Mathison, Gilbert Farquhar
1811   *Notices Respecting Jamaica, in 1808—1809—1810*. Printed for John Stockdale, Piccadilly, London.
McDonald, Roderick A.
1993   *The Economy and Material of Slaves: Goods and Chattels on the Sugar Plantations of Jamaica and Louisiana*. Louisiana State University Press, Baton Rouge.
Miller, George L.
1980   Classification and Economic Scaling of 19th Century Ceramics. *Historical Archaeology* 14:1–40.
1984a   Marketing Ceramics in North America: An Introduction. *Winterthur Portfolio* 19(1):1–5.
1984b   George M. Coates, Pottery Merchant of Philadelphia, 1817–1831. *Winterthur Portfolio* 19(1):37–49.
1988   Origins of Josiah Wedgwood's Pearlware. *Northeast Historical Archaeology* 16: 80–92.
1991   A Revised Set of CC Index Values for Classification and Economic Scaling of English Ceramics from 1787 to 1880. *Historical Archaeology* 25(1):1–25.
2000   Telling Time for Archaeologists. *Northeast Historical Archaeology* 29:1–22.
Miller, George L., and Robert Hunter
1990   English Shell Edged Earthenware: Alias Leeds Ware, Alias Feather Edge. In *The Consumer Revolution in 18th Century English Pottery*, Proceedings of the Wedgwood International Seminar, no. 35:107–136. Birmingham, Alabama.
2001   How Creamware Got the Blues: The Origins of China Glaze and Pearlware. In *Ceramics in America*, edited by Robert Hunter, pp. 135–161. Chipstone Foundation, University Press of New England, Lebanon, New Hampshire.
Miller, George L., Ann Smart Martin, and Nancy S. Dickinson
1994   Changing Consumption Patterns: English Ceramics and the American Market from 1770 to 1840. In *Everyday Life in the Early Republic*, edited by Catherine E. Hutchins, pp. 219–248. Winterthur Press, Delaware.
Miller, George L., and Meredith Moodey
1986   Of Fish and Sherds: A Model for Estimating Vessel Populations from Minimal Vessel Counts. *Historical Archaeology* 20(2):59–85.
Mintz, Sidney W.
1983   Caribbean Marketplaces and Caribbean History. *Radical History Review* 27:110–120.

1985   *Sweetness and Power: The Place of Sugar in Modern History.* Penguin, New York.

Mintz, Sidney W., and Douglas Hall

1960   The Origins of the Jamaican Internal Marketing System. *Yale University Publications in Anthropology* 57:3–26.

Neiman, Fraser D.

2008   The Lost World of Monticello: An Evolutionary Perspective. *Journal of Anthropological Research* 64(2):161–193.

Neiman, Fraser D., Jillian E. Galle, Leslie Cooper, and Ivor Conolley

2010   Building a Regional Chronology from Diverse Digital Data: An Example from Jamaica. Thomas Jefferson Foundation. Scientific Poster Presented at the 75th Annual Meeting of the Society of American Archaeology, St. Louis, Missouri, April 14–18.

Neiman, Fraser D., and Karen Y. Smith

2005   How Can Bayesian Smoothing Help Decipher the Occupational Histories of Late-Eighteenth-Century Slave Quarters at Monticello? Thomas Jefferson Foundation. Scientific Poster Presented at the 70th Annual Meeting of the Society of American Archaeology, Salt Lake City, Utah, March 30–April 3.

Neiman, Fraser D., Leslie McFaden, and Derek Wheeler

2000   Archaeological Investigation of the Elizabeth Hemmings Site (44AB438). Manuscript on file, Department of Archaeology, Thomas Jefferson Foundation, Charlottesville, Virginia.

Orser, Charles E., Jr., and Annette M. Nekola

1985   Plantation Settlement from Slavery to Tenancy: An Example from a Piedmont Plantation in South Carolina. In *The Archaeology of Slavery and Plantation Life*, edited by Theresa A. Singleton, pp. 67–94. Academic Press, Orlando.

Orton, Clive, Paul Tyers, and Alan Vince

1993   *Pottery in Archaeology.* Cambridge Manuals in Archaeology. Cambridge: Cambridge University Press.

O'Shaughnessy, Andrew

1996   West India Interest and the Crisis of American Independence. In *West Indies Accounts: Essays on the History of the British Caribbean and the Atlantic Economy*, edited by Roderick A. McDonald, pp. 126–148. University of the West Indies Press, Cave Hill, Barbados.

Otto, John Solomon

1984   *Cannon's Point Plantation 1794–1860: Living Conditions and Status Patterns in the Old South.* Academic Press, New York.

Parry, John H.

1955   Plantation and Provision Ground: An Historical Sketch of the Introduction of Food Crops into Jamaica. *Revista de Historia de América* 39:1–20.

1962   Salt Fish and Ackee: An Historical Sketch of the Introduction of Food Crops into Jamaica. *Caribbean Quarterly* 8(4):30–36.

Panning, Steven

1995   Exploring Stewart Castle Estate. *Jamaican Historical Society Bulletin* 10(14):172–180.

1996   Exploring Stewart Castle Estate. *Jamaican Historical Society Bulletin* 11(16):200–205.

Pulsipher, Lydia M.

1984   Discovering Water Management Strategies on an 18th Century Sugar Plantation. *Context* (Boston University Center for Archaeological Studies) 3(3):1–2.

1990   They Have Saturday and Sundays to Feed Themselves: Slave Gardens in the Caribbean. *Expedition* 32(2):24–33.

1991   Galways Plantation. In *Seeds of Change: A Quincentennial Commemoration*, edited by Herman J. Viola and Carolyn Margolis, pp. 138–159. Smithsonian Institution Press, Washington, D.C.

1994   The Landscapes and Ideational Roles of Caribbean Slave Gardens. In *The Archaeology of Garden and Field*, edited by Nicole F. Miller and Kathryn L. Gleason, pp. 202–221. University of Pennsylvania Press, Philadelphia.

Ragatz, Lowell J.

1928   *Fall of the Planter Class in the British Caribbean, 1763–1833*. Century Co., New York.

Reeves, Matthew

1997   "By their own labor": Enslaved Africans' Survival Strategies on Two Jamaican Plantations. Unpublished Ph.D. dissertation, Department of Anthropology, Syracuse University.

2011   Household Market Activities among Early Nineteenth-Century Jamaican Slaves: An Archaeological Case Study from Two Slave Settlements. In *Out of Many, One People: The Historical Archaeology of Colonial Jamaica*, edited by James A. Delle, Mark W. Hauser, and Douglas Armstrong, pp. 183–210. University of Alabama Press, Tuscaloosa.

Robertson, James

2008   Late Seventeenth-Century Spanish Town, Jamaica: Building an English City on Spanish Foundations. *Early American Studies* 6(2):346–390.

Roughley, Thomas

1823   *The Jamaica Planter's Guide; or, A System for Planting and Managing a Sugar Estate, or Other Plantations in that Island, and throughout the British West Indies in General*. Longman, Hurst, Rees, Orme, and Brown, London.

Ryden, David B.

2000   "One of the Fertilest Pleasentest Spotts": An Analysis of the Slave Economy in Jamaica's St Andrew Parish, 1753. *Slavery & Abolition* 21:32–55.

2009   *West Indian Slavery and British Abolition, 1783–1807*. Cambridge University Press, Cambridge.

Senior, Bernard M.

1835   *Jamaica, as It Was, as It Is, and as It May Be: Comprising Interesting Topics for Absent Proprietors, Merchants, &c*. T. Hurst, London.

Sheridan, Richard B.

1974   *Sugar and Slavery: An Economic History of the British West Indies, 1623–1775*. Johns Hopkins University Press, Baltimore.

1976   The Crisis of Slave Subsistence in the British West Indies during and after the American Revolution. *William and Mary Quarterly* 33(4):615–641.

1993   From Chattel to Wage Slavery in Jamaica, 1740–1860. *Slavery & Abolition* 14(1): 13–40.

Simmonds, Lorna E.

2002   The Afro-Jamaican and the Internal Marketing System: Kingston, 1780–1834. In *Jamaica in Slavery and Freedom: History, Heritage and Culture*, edited by Kathleen E. A. Monteith and Glen Richards, pp. 274–290. University of the West Indies Press, Kingston.

Singleton, Theresa A.

2001   Slavery and Spatial Dialectics on Cuban Coffee Plantations. *World Archaeology* 33:98–114.

2005   An Archaeological Study of Slavery at a Cuban Coffee Plantation. In *Dialogues in Cuban Archaeology*, edited by L. Antonio Curet, Shannon L. Dawdy, and Gabino La Rosa Corzo, pp. 181–199. University of Alabama Press, Tuscaloosa.

2014   Nineteenth-Century Built Landscape of Plantation Slavery in Comparative Perspective. In *The Archaeology of Slavery: A Comparative Approach to Captivity and Coercion*, edited by Lydia W. Marshall, pp. 93–115. Center for Archaeological Investigations, Occasional Paper No. 41, Southern Illinois University Press, Carbondale.

Smith, Karen Y., and Fraser D. Neiman

2007   Frequency Seriation, Correspondence Analysis, and Woodland Period Ceramic Assemblage Variation in the Deep South. *Southeastern Archaeology* 26(1):47–72.

Stewart, John

1808   *An Account of Jamaica, and Its Inhabitants*. Longman, Hurst, Rees, and Orme, London.

1823   *A View of the Past and Present State of the Island of Jamaica; with Remarks on the Moral and Physical Condition of the Slaves, and on the Abolition of Slavery in the Colonies*. Oliver and Boyd, Edinburgh.

Thomas, Brian W.

1995   *Community among Enslaved African Americans on the Hermitage Plantation, 1820s–1850s*. Ph.D. dissertation, Department of Anthropology, State University of New York at Binghamton, New York.

Ward, J. R.

1988   *British West Indian Slavery, 1750–1834: The Process of Amelioration*. Clarendon Press, Oxford.

Wilkie, Laurie A.

2000   Culture Bought: Evidence of Creolization in the Consumer Goods of an Enslaved Bahamian Family. Historical *Archaeology* 34(3):10–26.

Wilkie, Laurie, and Paul Farnsworth

1999   Trade and the Construction of Bahamian Identity: A Multiscalar Exploration. *International Journal of Historical Archaeology* 3(4):283–320.

2005   *Sampling Many Pots: An Archaeology of Memory and Tradition at a Bahamian Plantation*. University Press of Florida, Gainesville.

Wright, Philip (editor)

1966   Lady Nugent's Journal of Her Residence in Jamaica from 1801 to 1805. Institute of Jamaica, Kingston.

Yates, Geoffrey S.

1955   A Note on the Origins of the Names Papine and Mona. *Jamaica Historical Society Bulletin*, No. II.

5

Life beyond the Village

Field Houses and Liminal Space on a Jamaican Coffee Plantation

JAMES A. DELLE

The plantation system that characterized the British West Indies for most of their colonial history was a particularly violent and oppressive manifestation of colonial capitalism. Historians and archaeologists of the plantation system generally agree that the organization of production, which included the enslavement of millions of people over the course of time, was brutal and dehumanizing and created extremely difficult conditions for those so unfortunate as to be caught up in it. It is therefore easy to conclude, as many including myself have done (e.g. Delle 1998, 2014), that the landscapes of the plantation system were planned and developed to create and maintain a structure, order, and discipline that maximized the ability of the planter class to extract wealth at as low a monetary cost as possible, regardless of the human cost accrued, which, admittedly, was great (Orser 1994, 1996; Orser and Funari 2001).

With that said, scholars for generations (e.g., Mintz and Hall 1960) have recognized that the enslaved people of Jamaica, despite the harsh conditions of slavery, developed and maintained a social and economic system that was in many ways beyond the control of the plantation elite and that, eventually, even the planters came to depend upon (Armstrong 1990; Delle 2014; Hauser 2008; Wilkie 2001; Wilkie and Farnsworth 1999, 2005). While it has been well demonstrated that the industrial and domestic core of plantations were subject to intense surveillance (Delle 1998, 1999, 2014), Jamaican plantations were composed of hundreds—sometimes thousands—of acres that could not be simultaneously controlled by the handful of white estate staff managing the plantation. Theft and pilfering were common, not only of export crops grown on the estates but also of the provisions grown in plantain walks for the use of white plantation employees and in provision grounds for the use of the enslaved. Runaways hid, often for months, at the peripheries of estates, living on what they could gather from the wilderness and the provision grounds on the margins of plantation space. Maroons established permanent towns and villages in several parts of the island; although they were cooperating with the colonial government by the end of the eighteenth century, they were a constant reminder of the fragility of the system and its ultimate inability to control the entire landscape of the island of Jamaica, which is no larger in land mass than the state of Connecticut (Burnard 2004; Higman 1998, 2002, 2005; Sheridan 1985; Singleton 2010).

Just as the colonial government could not control the space of the entire island, individual planters could not control the entire space of the estates they had carved out. This was particularly true on large estates managed by attorneys for absentee, bankrupt, or deceased proprietors. Marshall's Pen, a coffee plantation that was part of a larger property owned by the absentee Earl of Balcarres, was such an estate. Archaeological and documentary research on the estate reveals that by the end of the 1820s, the plantation landscape of Marshall's Pen, which included two villages for enslaved workers, was characterized by a dispersed alternative settlement pattern of houses in the periphery in which the African Jamaican population of the estate, though still enslaved, created a sociospatial reality that coexisted with and contradicted that imposed by plantation managers. This chapter explores one manifestation of that alternative spatial reality, the existence of field houses away from the dominating gaze of the white plantation staff.

Marshall's Pen

Although Jamaica's plantation economy had been dominated by sugar since the end of the seventeenth century, in the opening years of the nineteenth century the colony experienced a boom in plantation-based coffee production. Record high prices for coffee, brought on by the collapse of coffee production in the French colony of St. Domingue in the wake of the Haitian Revolution, encouraged investors large and small to acquire and improve coffee lands in Jamaica's largely undeveloped interior. As the eighteenth century drew to a close, the mountains of eastern and central Jamaica, so long a hostile wilderness to the planter class, were teeming with hundreds of developing coffee plantations, from small 50-acre plots worked by leased ("jobbed") labor gangs to sprawling 1,000-acre estates worked by hundreds of slaves. Not one to miss the opportunity to gain from such a promising enterprise, the outgoing governor, Alexander Lindsay, the sixth Earl of

Balcarres, eagerly invested in vast coffee properties, leaving the island in 1801 to become one of Jamaica's wealthiest absentee coffee planters (Delle 2008, 2009; Smith 1996, 2002).

At the conclusion of his term as governor of Jamaica (1795–1801), Balcarres acquired coffee properties in the former parish of St. George (now in Portland) and a part of St. Elizabeth later incorporated as the parish of Manchester, including the eponymous Balcarres Plantation in St. George and Martins Hill and Shooters Hill in St. Elizabeth. In 1801 Balcarres returned to Britain, taking up residence in the ancestral home of his wife (and first cousin), Elizabeth Dalrymple Lindsay, in Wigan, Lancashire, where Balcarres had established a successful series of industrial businesses, including collieries and the Haigh Iron Works, which produced engines and pumps for the coal mining industry. From his seat at Haigh Hall, Balcarres maintained his estates in Jamaica as an absentee proprietor. An energetic businessman, the earl remained closely involved with the management of his estates through an extensive and detailed correspondence with Thomas Fowlis, his merchant factor in London, as well as with a Kingston merchant house, Atkinson, Bogle and Company (which changed names multiple times, as partners came and went, e.g., to Atkinson, Adams, and Robertson and to Adams, Robertson, and Co.); the various partners in this house served as his agents, or attorneys, in Jamaica. This correspondence, in its near entirety, has been kept by the Lindsay family and is preserved at the National Library of Scotland as part of a collection of family papers known as the Crawford Muniments. The papers relating to the Jamaican plantations of the sixth Earl of Balcarres and, following his death, relating to his son, the future 24th Earl of Crawford, are an unequaled source of information about the social and economic world of Jamaica's nascent coffee industry.

Although coal mining and the production of heavy machinery remained his primary business focus, the sixth Earl of Balcarres (hereafter Balcarres) was closely involved in the management of his estates and actively worked to maximize the value of his Jamaican interests. At various times his strategies for improving the Jamaica plantations included the acquisition of additional enslaved laborers, the segregation of creole from African people, the establishment of a gender balance on the estates through targeted purchases of women, and the expansion of his land holdings by acquiring underdeveloped properties. He kept close watch, through quarterly reports, of the efficiency of production and the overall value of his various estates.

Marshall's Pen, a property then in St. Elizabeth, was acquired by Balcarres

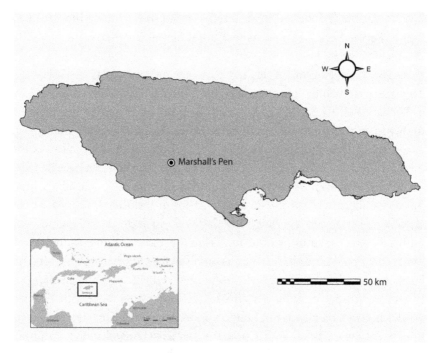

Figure 5.1. Location of Marshall's Pen, Jamaica. (Image courtesy of Mark Hauser)

as part of his attempt to increase the acreage he could put under productive cultivation (Figure 5.1). Whereas his estates known as Martins Hill and Balcarres Plantation were acquired as going concerns, Marshall's Pen was purchased by Balcarres as a largely undeveloped run of land. In 1812 40 acres of old-growth forest were cleared for the first coffee production on what was then called "Douglas Run"—eventually renamed Marshall's Pen. The first "negro houses" were constructed on the site the same year. It would appear that this initial site preparation was completed by laborers from Martins Hill; it was not until 1814 that a gang of enslaved laborers was purchased for Balcarres by his Jamaica attorneys and situated in the newly erected "negro houses" at Marshall's Pen.

In 1815 Marshall's Pen had the best prospect for coffee production of any of Balcarres' properties. That year his attorneys ordered the abandonment of coffee production on Martins Hill, which from that point forward functioned as a cattle pen. During these early years the enslaved population at Marshall's Pen was quite isolated, being managed by a man who lived at least three hours walk away through undisturbed forest. Although there were already 70 acres in coffee on the former Douglas Run by 1815, the

Jamaica attorneys felt it necessary to recommend that an overseer's house be constructed closer to the "important settlement of Marshall's Pen." It was not until 1819, however, that a bookkeeper was assigned to Marshall's Pen; the records indicate that Martins Hill remained the center of operation for Balcarres' St. Elizabeth estates, with a single overseer, Adam White, managing both plantations. White was an infrequent visitor to Marshall's Pen, and the initial development of the plantation went on with little daily supervision by a white estate staff. While a number of workers lived on the property at Marshall's Pen, many more remained at Martins Hill, trudging five miles to the fields and back each day; a second village was erected nearer to Marshall's Pen in 1821 to decrease this burden on the workers; this latter settlement became known as New Green (Crawford Muniments, National Library of Scotland, Edinburgh, 23/8/107).

From the middle of the 1810s, activities on Martins Hill centered on clear-cutting land and converting it to pasturage, exporting timber products as logwood, and the raising and selling of horned stock. At Marshall's Pen, between 20 and 40 acres of old-growth hardwood was felled annually and the land converted to provision grounds to feed the enslaved community and coffee fields for export production.

Alexander Lindsay died in March of 1825, at which time his son and heir, James Lindsay, the seventh Earl of Balcarres (later the 24th Earl of Crawford), took over the proprietorship of the Jamaican estates. Having, by his own account, "no knowledge in regard to West India property" (Crawford Muniments, National Library of Scotland, Edinburgh, 25/11/8), the younger earl (hereafter Crawford, to distinguish him from his father) secured the advice of Edward Hamlin Adams, a former partner in the Kingston merchant house of Adams, Robertson, and Co., which the elder earl had retained to manage local affairs in Jamaica. Adams had returned to England in April of 1823, having purchased the stately Bailbrook House near Bath, and lived in comfortable retirement on the income he was then making from the fortune he had accumulated as a Kingston merchant. Adams, a veteran West Indian estate attorney, recommended that James Lindsay cease investing in his Jamaica properties and focus on his interests at home. Despite having been born in Kingston, Adams had a very dark opinion of West India plantations: "at best their returns are precarious and when seemingly greatest are often rendered so at the cost of the vital interest of the place by the slave labourer being sacrificed" (Crawford Muniments, National Library of Scotland, Edinburgh, 25/11/8). Adams advised Crawford to be wary of his island agents (he, Adams, having been one himself!) as they were prone to mismanage funds, make large capital investments without the concurrence of the proprietor, and ignore the opinions of the absentees "who cannot have local knowledge." He further warned Crawford that, by their day in the 1820s, West India properties could only be sold at a loss: "if you get the value of the slaves and cattle, your land and works you are well contented to sacrifice." He advised against paying for jobbing gangs, as the practice of leasing other people's slaves was something that "no property can afford" (Crawford Muniments, National Library of Scotland, Edinburgh, 25/11/8).

Made apprehensive by this pessimistic attitude toward the prospect of plantation investments, Crawford must have been shocked to receive his first accounts from the Jamaican properties. He reported back to Adams that "operations now adopted with respect to these properties is dramatically opposite to the kind advice contained in your letter," as the agents had ordered between 90 and 100 acres of forest to be clear-cut by jobbing gangs, and a new population of 93 people had been purchased with "a very large outlay of money." Resigning himself to the idea that "by keeping the estates in a productive state, there is at least some hope of better times if it does no more at present than pay its own expenses," Crawford decided to take an active part in the management of the estates, both through his own correspondence with his attorneys in Jamaica and through the agency of Thomas Fowlis, his merchant factor in London, whom he trusted more than his Jamaica attorneys. By August of 1825, Adam White, the long-serving overseer of both Martins Hill and Marshall's Pen, was discharged, an action that Crawford criticized as having been too long in coming (Crawford Muniments, National Library of Scotland, Edinburgh, 25/11/7). He nearly accused one of the partners in the merchant house of dissembling concerning the White affair. Robert Robertson had remarked to Crawford that the house did not feel it had the discretion to dismiss White; Crawford replied that in searching through his father's correspondence, he could not "find in them anything that can bear such a construction" (Crawford Muniments, National Library of Scotland, Edinburgh, 25/11/11). Upon learning that Robertson was in England in February of 1826, Crawford requested an audience with the attorney, as he found the accounts "transmitted to me from Jamaica very unsatisfactory, there being many omissions of important pieces of information" (25/11/11). He scrutinized the plantation accounts, calling his attorneys to task when he felt they were in the wrong or when he suspected profiteering at his expense was ongoing. Of note, Crawford criticized Robertson for combining the accounts of Martins Hill and Marshall's Pen, particularly the slave lists.

Crawford remained in possession of Marshall's Pen during the transition away from slavery. As with many proprietors, his agents attempted to renegotiate the terms of plantation labor following the 1838 abolition of the apprenticeship system and the final end of compulsory labor in Jamaica. As the appointed date of liberation, August 1, 1838, drew nearer, Crawford explored a variety of options to keep the estates supplied with labor. Among the ideas he considered were the importation of contract laborers from Malta and the importation of European (likely Irish) farmers to work on indenture. As neither of these schemes proved practicable, the estate management attempted to negotiate annual labor contracts with the soon-to-be emancipated workers at Marshall's Pen. While the drivers (referred to as "headmen" after emancipation) and sawyers agreed to annual terms, the carpenters, coopers, wagon men, masons, blacksmiths, and field laborers demanded a daily wage of at least 3 shillings 4 pence and the free use of their houses and grounds. Eventually a compromise was worked out, and some members of the emancipated workforce remained employed on the estate throughout the 1840s, paying an annual rent on their houses and grounds. Although sections of the estate were sold in small lots to local laborers, and some larger sections to wealthier investors, Marshall's Pen was kept under coffee production using wage labor through 1850, at which point Crawford began divesting himself of the Jamaican properties. In 1853 Marshall's Pen was purchased by the Muirhead family of Mandeville, who kept the property until 1939, when the current owners of the property, the Sutton family, purchased the estate. Large-scale coffee production was abandoned by the Muirheads, and Marshall's Pen has been run as a cattle farm since the 1850s.

The People of Marshall's Pen

Although Jamaican coffee planters, including Balcarres, were able to find a ready market for their product in the years following the Haitian Revolution, they fell on hard times during the Napoleonic Wars. Because the largest market for Jamaican coffee was the European continent, when the Napoleonic government imposed a continent-wide blockade on British goods, Jamaican planters suffered a calamitous price decline brought on by an overproduction crisis. The warehouses of London and Liverpool were packed with Jamaican coffee that could not be sold at half the price it had received just a few years prior. Balcarres was among those with the capital and wherewithal to run their plantations at a loss during the economic crisis, waiting on what they hoped would be the opening of the European markets upon Napoleon's eventual defeat. Balcarres, a career military man and, by 1812, a general in the army, undoubtedly recognized the gravity of Napoleon's decision to invade Russia and the consequences of his ensuing retreat. Napoleon invaded Russia in late June 1812; a month later, on July 31, Balcarres contradicted an order he had given to his attorneys in May to abandon Balcarres Plantation, instructing them rather to make a significant investment in land and slaves for Martins Hill, at that time his primary coffee plantation (Crawford Muniments, National Library of Scotland, Edinburgh, 23/14/16, May 30, 1812 and July 31, 1812). Napoleon was forced to abandon Moscow on October 11, 1812, and began his disastrous retreat back to France. The remnant of Napoleon's Grande Armée was famously smashed by a combination of Russian harassment, severe winter conditions, and a plague of typhus-infected lice. By the end of November, the emperor had abandoned the shell of his once-mighty army to its fate in Lithuania and seemed little able to enforce the blockade. Perhaps not coincidentally, on November 29, 1812, Atkinson, Bogle, and Co. informed Lord Balcarres that they had begun clearing and planting a new coffee settlement on his property known as Douglas Run—the settlement that would soon come to be known as Marshall's Pen (Crawford Muniments, National Library of Scotland, Edinburgh, 23/8/67).

The first people to be settled on Marshall's Pen were purchased through a bill of sale secured by Mssrs. Barings Brothers and Co. for £4677. Atkinson and Bogle described the people as having previously been enslaved on a property they had managed, "about 60 in number . . . in families of the most prime, healthy people" (Crawford Muniments, National Library of Scotland, Edinburgh, 23/8/71). The valuation list they sent to Balcarres suggests that this first group of people at Marshall's Pen included 12 families with children, 2 apparently childless couples, 8 single men in their twenties, and a lone adolescent girl. The oldest member of the group was 36-year-old Jasper, described as the head driver (Crawford Muniments, National Library of Scotland, Edinburgh, 23/8/72). These people were "removed . . . to the new settlement of Marshall's Pen, where they are comfortably established, their grounds and houses having been previously put in perfect preparation for their reception" (Crawford Muniments, National Library of Scotland, Edinburgh, 23/8/72, April 3, 1814). The village was augmented by an additional purchase of 42 people in March of 1817 and, apparently, the transfer of a number of people from the previously established settlement at Martins Hill. The population of the first village at Marshall's Pen stood at 108 in June of 1816 and would remain consistently between 100 and 120 people throughout the period of slavery (Crawford Muniments, National Library of Scotland, Edinburgh, 23/8/39).

For the remainder of the Earl of Balcarres' life, Marshall's Pen and Martins Hill were managed as a single, large estate consisting of a settlement of people on the coffee-producing land of Marshall's Pen and another population of people living some five miles away at Martins Hill, which was run primarily as a cattle-breeding pen. Although the picking and processing of a coffee crop was not nearly as labor-intensive as the cultivation and production of sugar cane, the opening of a new coffee property required heavy labor to clear old-growth hardwood forests and prepare coffee fields for their initial crop. The relatively small population at Marshall's Pen was joined in their labor by gangs of workers from Martins Hill, who were forced to walk the five miles from their homes to the coffee fields at Marshall's Pen and back daily. After several years, a second village, known as New Green, was established approximately half way between the two settlements, though still at some distance from the coffee fields at Marshall's Pen. By 1822 there were at least three villages on the sprawling estate: the original village at Martins Hill, the village of Marshall's Pen, and New Green. The village at Marshall's Pen was located on a small landform known locally as "Negro House Hill," taking its name from the early-nineteenth-century term used to define people of African descent and the use to which the enslaved people of Marshall's Pen put the hill (Figure 5.2).

Archaeological investigations conducted at Marshall's Pen have revealed that the circa 1812 village on Negro House Hill was organized into a series of house compounds with shared access to yard space and pig pens, whereas the circa 1822 village at New Green was organized linearly, with houses flanking either side of a bisecting road (Delle 2009, 2011, 2014). This diversity in settlement forms for plantation villages seems to have been common in Jamaica in the early nineteenth century (Armstrong and Kelly 2000; Higman 1998). However, evidence exists to suggest that not all enslaved plantation workers lived in plantation villages, including a first-person description by Lady Maria Nugent of enslaved people sleeping inside the great house at Seville Plantation (Wright 2002) and various drawings of "negro" huts and houses made by various visitors to the island, including William Berryman, who sketched daily life in the early nineteenth century (Figure 5.3). Berryman's sketches include a depiction of an enslaved family who apparently did not live in a village.

Coffee plantations like Marshall's Pen, carved out of Jamaica's old-growth

Figure 5.2. Franklin and Marshall College students conducting a controlled surface collection on Negro House Hill. (Photograph by James A. Delle)

Figure 5.3. *Negro Hut with Figures in Plantain Walk*, sketch by William Berryman, ca. 1808. A plantain walk was a garden that produced the banana-like food crop for use by the white and enslaved residents of a plantation. The image appears to depict a visit by an estate book-keeper or overseer to one of the enslaved families who did not reside in a village. (Image in public domain via Wikimedia Commons)

hardwood forests, often had ambiguous boundaries, both in terms of where the legal property of one planter ended and another began and in terms of how intermediate spaces not yet developed as part of the plantation complex were used. As to the latter, runaways would often squat on the peripheries of plantations, filching crops from remote provision grounds or creating small garden plots in remote spots where they hoped they would not be detected. Boundary disputes between planters were apparently common in nineteenth-century Jamaica and were often resolved by the island's court system. Between 1803 and 1830, the Lindsays were involved in no fewer than three such lawsuits. In resolving the boundary suits, surveyors were engaged to measure the property boundaries in an effort to determine the extent of any trespasses over the lines. Two of the resulting survey maps survived in the Lindsay family papers, one of which clearly identifies the location of "negro" houses and huts dispersed across the plantation landscape, outside of the concentrated village settlements.

Archaeology at Marshall's Pen

In the late 1990s I began a project at Marshall's Pen to examine village life on a large Jamaican coffee estate. After three successful field seasons, the project was suspended when the landowner, Robert Sutton, died quite unexpectedly. After a hiatus of nearly a decade, research was resumed at the estate, this time concentrating on testing whether the houses that appeared on the surveying plats drawn during the land disputes of the early nineteenth century could be located and tested. Between 2011 and 2013, archaeological testing was conducted on three locations identified on the plats.

Fellows and Delle (2015) have argued that plantation space was multivalent and contested and that, at least in some cases, earlier models may overstate the degree to which space was controlled by the plantation elite. The nature of the plantation system in Jamaica was such that many plantations, including the larger estate of which Marshall's Pen was a constituent part, contained thousands of acres of undeveloped land; often more than half of an estate was defined as undeveloped woodland or ruinate or else was used by the enslaved population as what was commonly called "Negro Grounds" or "Provision Grounds" (Delle 1998, 1999; Fellows and Delle 2015). The landscape of early-nineteenth-century Jamaica, particularly in the interior where coffee plantations like Marshall's Pen were located, contained thousands of acres of land that was not in the direct control of the plantation elite. It was to these spaces that the maroons first removed to establish their sovereignty, and in which runaways not welcomed by the maroons would seek refuge (Bilby 2005; Campbell 1990; Goucher and Agorsah 2011).

Such intermediate spaces existed not only between plantations but within them. In Jamaica there is a spatial tradition of farmers occupying temporary field houses. Such small, temporary shelters are often located near pieces of land cultivated by farmers who may or may not have clear title to the land they are working, a tradition that may date back the era of colonial slavery (Fellows and Delle 2015). It has long been established that the slavery system in Jamaica was largely dependent on the cultivation of provision farms, the produce of which was used for local consumption and exchange by enslaved people (Hauser 2008) and for use by—and sale to—white plantation employees who created economic exchange networks with those enslaved on the plantations they managed (Delle 2014). Any surplus value generated through the sale of provisions would be kept by the enslaved workers who had grown and sold the produce and not the plantation that claimed ownership of both the land and the laborers (Fellows and Delle 2015). The field house tradition likely dates back to the establishment of the provision ground system, which was observed in Jamaica as early as the 1670s (Delle 2014).

The archaeological record of Marshall's Pen suggests that the use of such field houses predates emancipation in Jamaica. A plat of the estate drawn during the boundary disputes of the 1820s clearly indicates that a number of small structures, alternately referred to on the maps as "huts" or "negro houses," we scattered around the estate, including in areas defined as provision grounds. Archaeological field testing conducted in 2012 resulted in the location of five of these field houses.

Feature 3.1.1

One of the extravillage house sites excavated in 2012 was located on one of the nineteenth-century maps near a landscape feature identified on the map as a bridge; in the late 1990s the pasture in which the feature was located was still referred to as "Bridge Pasture," although this place name seems to have recently fallen out of use. An obvious house platform was pointed out to us by an employee working at Marshall's Pen near a piece of ground he currently is gardening to produce root crops and other vegetable products for sale in the Mandeville market; notably, he has built himself a small expedient shelter nearby that serves as a field house while he is tending his crops (Fellows and Delle 2015). Five 1 m × 1 m excavation units

Figure 5.4. "Bridge House," Feature 3.1.1, under the process of excavation. (Photograph by James A. Delle)

were excavated into the house platform, and a total of 190 artifacts were recovered, including fragments of undecorated creamware; annular and finger-painted slipped (mocha) ware; shell-edged, transfer-printed, and hand-painted polychrome pearlware; brown stoneware; fragments of kaolin pipe stems and bowls; green bottle glass; clear architectural glass; and several wrought iron nails. A single brass button was uncovered, as was a fragment of perforated copper sheeting, likely a piece of a copper coffee pulping mill that was recycled and used as a grater; two similar pieces were found in the context of the enslaved village at Marshall's Pen.

Although many of the recovered ceramics were small fragments, the form of several pieces could be identified, including fragments of six footrings from plates and the rim of a chamber pot. Utilitarian wares, including multiple pieces of brown stoneware with a jug handle, were also recovered. The glass assemblage included two fragments of a black glass wine bottle base and a fragment of a bottle neck. Together the assemblage clearly dates to the pre-emancipation era and, given the high density of domestic artifacts recovered from the excavation units, points to this feature being a domestic structure that was likely occupied for a significant time (Figure 5.4).

Features 6.1.1 and 6.2.1

In 2012 two additional field house locations, noted on the nineteenth-century survey maps, were tested at Marshall's Pen. Two house platforms were identified, which share an extended yard space. The first of these features a marl floor. Rather than destroy the feature to determine if any artifacts could be recovered from below the floor, two excavation units were excavated at the edge of the feature; only a single sherd of blue transfer-printed whiteware was recovered. Two units were also excavated at the second house platform, with negative results. A series of shovel test pits were dug in the shared yard space, with more promising results. Although only a light scatter of artifacts was recovered, these included wrought iron nails and fragments of several kaolin pipes. The evidence suggests that, unlike Feature 3.1.1, Features 6.1.1 and 6.2.1 were likely expedient houses occupied sporadically to provide shelter from sudden storms, likely located in or near provision grounds on the estate (Figure 5.5).

Feature 5.1.1

A fourth isolated house platform was excavated in 2012. Located in a pasture known as "Hanson," the house platform was more massive than the

Figure 5.5. Feature 6.1.1, in foreground with marl floor exposed, and Feature 6.2.1, house platform in background. (Photograph by James A. Delle)

other field houses tested. A total of eighteen 1 m × 1 m units were excavated, revealing a large 12 m × 18 m house platform. The material culture recovered dated primarily to the early or middle twentieth century and included wire nails and staples, clear bottle glass, and several crown bottle caps, suggesting that this structure was either constructed later, or was heavily reoccupied after the turn of the twentieth century.

Conclusion

Testing of locations of field houses at Marshall's Pen indicates that the settlement of the plantation was far more complex than a dichotomous division of space into white/black, overseer/slave, owner/worker. Although the majority of the population likely lived in one of two villages known to exist on the site, the number of field houses so far identified indicates that enslaved workers lived throughout the plantation. Although we know of no other similar maps indicating the locations of field houses for other plantations in Jamaica, it seems unlikely that Marshall's Pen was unique in this settlement pattern. The landscape of Jamaica would likely have featured hundreds if not thousands of these small, expedient, temporary houses. Workers on a given estate would have had the opportunity, whether sanctioned or not, to find some measure of privacy in these kinds of houses, located far from the bustle of the cramped plantation village and the watchful gaze of the plantation overseer. More significantly, perhaps, because some of these field houses are clearly associated with provision grounds, it seems more than likely that provision gardens located in the margins of estates and carved out of the forests between the industrial and residential cores of plantations would have featured houses like this, to which men and women could flee, either to escape conditions in which they found themselves enslaved or to create temporary sovereignty over their own movement through their ability to extract a living from the land of Jamaica in places in the landscape unknown to the white planters and their estate staffs.

Acknowledgments

I would like to thank all those colleagues and students, past and present, who made this research possible, especially Kristen Fellows and Jordan Pickerell. Much gratitude is owed to Ann Sutton, owner of Marshall's Pen, for allowing us long-term access to her property, as well as the staff of the

Jamaican National Heritage Trust for years of assistance in the field. I am very grateful to the Earl of Crawford and the Lindsay Trust for allowing me access to their family papers in the National Library of Scotland.

References Cited

Armstrong, Douglas V.
1990   *The Old Village and the Great House: An Archaeological and Historical Examina-tion of Drax Hall Plantation, St. Ann's Bay, Jamaica.* University of Illinois Press, Urbana.
Armstrong, Douglas V., and Kenneth Kelly
2000   Settlement Patterns and the Origins of African Jamaican Society: Seville Planta-tion, St. Ann's Bay, Jamaica. *Ethnohistory* 7(2):369–397.
Bilby, Kenneth M.
2005   *True-Born Maroons.* University Press of Florida, Gainesville.
Burnard, Trevor
2004   *Mastery, Tyranny, and Desire: Thomas Thistlewood and His Slaves in the Anglo-Jamaican World.* University of North Carolina Press, Chapel Hill.
Campbell, Mavis C.
1990   *Maroons of Jamaica: 1655–1796.* Africa World Press, Trenton, New Jersey.
Delle, James A.
1998   *An Archaeology of Social Space: Analyzing Coffee Plantations in Jamaica's Blue Mountains.* Plenum Press, New York.
1999   The Landscapes of Class Negotiation on Coffee Plantations in the Blue Moun-tains of Jamaica, 1790–1850. *Historical Archaeology* 33(1):136–158.
2008   An Archaeology of Modernity in Colonial Jamaica. *Archaeologies: The Journal of the World Archaeology Congress,* 4(1):87–109.
2009   The Governor and the Enslaved: Archaeology and Modernity at Marshall's Pen, Jamaica. *International Journal of Historical Archaeology* 12(4):488–512.
2011   The Habitus of Jamaican Plantation Landscapes. In *Out of Many, One People: The Historical Archaeology of Colonial Jamaica,* edited by James A. Delle, Mark W. Hauser, and Douglas V. Armstrong, pp. 122–143. University of Alabama Press, Tuscaloosa.
2014   *The Colonial Caribbean: Landscapes of Power in the Plantation System.* Cam-bridge University Press, Cambridge.
Fellows, Kristen R., and James A. Delle
2015   Marronage and the Dialectics of Spatial Sovereignty in Colonial Jamaica. In *Cur-rent Perspectives on the Archaeology of African Slavery in Latin America,* edited by Pedro P. A. Funari, and Charles E. Orser Jr., pp. 117–132. Springer, New York.
Goucher, Candice, and Kofi Agorsah
2011   Excavating the Roots of Resistance: The Significance of Maroons in Jamaican Archaeology. In *Out of Many, One People: The Historical Archaeology of Colonial*

Jamaica, edited by James A. Delle, Mark W. Hauser, and Douglas V. Armstrong, pp. 144–162. University of Alabama Press, Tuscaloosa.

Hauser, Mark W.

2008 *An Archaeology of Black Markets: Local Ceramics and Economies in Eighteenth-Century Jamaica*. University Press of Florida, Gainesville.

Higman, Barry W.

1998 *Montpelier, Jamaica: A Plantation Community in Slavery and Freedom, 1739–1912*. University Press of the West Indies, Mona, Jamaica.

2002 The Internal Economy of Jamaican Pens, 1760–1890. In *Slavery without Sugar: Diversity in Caribbean Economy and Society since the Seventeenth Century*, edited by Verene A. Shepherd, pp. 63–81. University Press of Florida, Gainesville.

2005 *Plantation Jamaica, 1750–1850: Capital and Control in a Colonial Economy*. University of the West Indies Press, Kingston, Jamaica.

Mintz, Sidney W., and Douglas Hall

1960 *The Origins of the Jamaican Internal Marketing System*. Yale University Publications in Anthropology, New Haven, Connecticut.

Orser, Charles E., Jr.

1994 Toward a Global Historical Archaeology: An Example from Brazil. *Historical Archaeology* 28(1):5–22.

1996 *A Historical Archaeology of the Modern World*. Plenum Press, New York.

Orser, Charles E., Jr., and Pedro P. A. Funari

2001 Archaeology and Slave Resistance and Rebellion. *World Archaeology*, 33(1): 61–72.

Sheridan, Richard B.

1985 The Maroons of Jamaica, 1730–1830: Livelihood, Demography and Health. *Slavery & Abolition* 6(3)152–172.

Singleton, Theresa A.

2010 African Diaspora in Archaeology. In *The African Diaspora and the Disciplines*, edited by Tejumola Olaniyan and James H. Sweet, pp. 119–141. Indiana University Press, Bloomington.

Smith, Simon D.

1996 Accounting for Taste: British Coffee Consumption in Historical Perspective. *Journal of International History* 27(2): 183–214.

2002 Coffee and the "Poorer Sort of People" in Jamaica During the Period of African Enslavement. In *Slavery without Sugar: Diversity in Caribbean Economy and Society since the Seventeenth Century*, edited by Verene A. Shepherd, pp. 102–128. University Press of Florida, Gainesville.

Wilkie, Laurie A.

2001 Methodist Intentions and African Sensibilities: The Victory of African Consumerism over Plantation Paternalism at a Bahamian Plantation. In *Island Lives: Historical Archaeologies of the Caribbean*, edited by Paul Farnsworth, pp. 272–300. University of Alabama Press, Tuscaloosa.

Wilkie, Laurie A., and Paul Farnsworth

1999 Trade and the Construction of Bahamian Identity: A Multiscalar Exploration. *International Journal of Historical Archaeology* 3(4): 283–320.

2005   *Sampling Many Pots: An Archaeology of Memory and Tradition at a Bahamian Plantation*. University Press of Florida, Gainesville.

Wright, Philip (editor)
2002   *Lady Nugent's Journal of Her Residency in Jamaica from 1801 to 1805*. University of the West Indies Press, Mona, Jamaica.

6

Beyond Sugar

Plantation Landscapes and the Rise of a Free Black Population on St. Lucia

JANE I. SEITER

Much has been written about the "sugar revolution" that swept the islands of the eastern Caribbean in the seventeenth century. Sugar cane cultivation was introduced into Barbados and Martinique in the early 1640s and quickly spread throughout the West Indies, becoming the basis for the regional economy within a few decades of its arrival (Mintz 1985:35–39). Successful sugar planters made enormous profits that allowed them to buy up smaller plantations and consolidate the land into immense sugar-producing estates, driving out settlers with less capital. The effects on the Caribbean were startling. In short order, tens of thousands of enslaved people were imported from Africa to work the land, and "a community of prosperous small farmers roughly equal in wealth and social status" was transformed into "the preserve of a few great landowners who reduced their white compatriots to poverty" (Stein 1979:6).

Recent work by archaeologists, however, has begun to question the accuracy of using the "sugar revolution" as a paradigm for this period of development on all of the islands of the West Indies. On St. Lucia, a program of landscape survey joined with a close analysis of historical maps and census records has revealed a very different pattern of landscape development for the seventeenth and eighteenth centuries. Underneath the later remains of sugar estates with their monumental surviving architecture, including the curing and boiling houses, lime kilns, windmills, and water wheels, lies evidence of a long-lasting phase of small-scale plantations that grew a surprising diversity of crops. Coffee, cocoa, cotton, and indigo were grown for export alongside ground provisions such as cassava and bananas. Plantations remained small compared to those on the other islands, and were worked by fewer enslaved Africans or sometimes the owner's family alone.

Natural disasters, challenging topography, and political instability all hampered sustained agricultural growth. St. Lucia's development as a colony was subsequently later, slower, and more sporadic than that of many of its neighbors. This tardiness to conform to an overarching narrative of historical "progress" is perhaps one of the main reasons that St. Lucia has consistently been left out of many overviews of Caribbean history and development. Seen as a "space in between" other more prosperous or more politically important islands, its history has often been ignored or relegated to a footnote.

In this chapter, however, it is argued that the very marginality of this space allowed for the growth of an unusually diverse community of plantation owners. Unlike on other islands, where the great estates were mostly in the hands of a few wealthy absentee owners, St. Lucia provided an opportunity for less prosperous owners to purchase smaller amounts of undeveloped property. This also permitted a surprising number of free people of color to own land and climb the economic ladder. Understanding how and why St. Lucia's agricultural system developed and the ways that it deviated from the systems of its neighboring islands is the key to understanding the rise of this class of landowners, who are underrepresented in the documentary record and consequently have been overlooked in most conventional historiography.

This chapter uses a landscape-based archaeological approach to chart long-term material changes to the island of St. Lucia. It employs interdisciplinary methods, weaving together data drawn from the fields of archaeology, economics, geography, and social history to explore the stories of the island and the people on it before large-scale sugar cultivation took hold. After an initial look at the early settlement history of the island, evidence for the development of the plantation system in the early to mid-eighteenth century is examined. Landscape surveys of two of the island's estates move the discussion from an island-wide perspective to a site-specific study of the ways that the shifting nature of colonialism and the expansion of the plantation system resulted in a particular set of modifications to individual landscapes. The chapter closes with a look at how a growing population of free black landowners was able to buy into this plantation system while learning to navigate the tricky shoals of a colonial society that depended on race-based slavery for its prosperity.

Early Settlement of St. Lucia

Part of the chain of smaller islands known as the Lesser Antilles, St. Lucia falls between Martinique, its neighbor 24 miles to the north, and St. Vincent, located 21 miles to the south (see Figure 1.2). Barbados lies just over 100 miles to the southeast. In contrast to low-lying, easily cultivated islands such as Barbados and Antigua, much of the interior of St. Lucia is mountainous, with dense, almost impenetrable forests. Since at least the early eighteenth century, the island has been divided into *quartiers* or quarters, equivalent to counties, which today number 11.

St. Lucia's early colonial history was turbulent. France and Great Britain battled for possession for almost 200 years, primarily because the island's fine harbors and proximity to Martinique made it an ideal staging post for attacks on Fort-de-France, the main French naval base in the eastern Caribbean. St. Lucia swung back and forth between colonial powers more times than any other Caribbean colony, changing hands fourteen times and enduring several prolonged periods of neutrality, including from 1722 to 1745 and again from 1748 to 1762, when all settlement was officially banned on the island. France controlled it for much of this time, but it was captured by the English during the American Revolution, ceded back to the French in 1784, then switched sides several times during the French Revolution and Napoleonic Wars, until the Treaty of Paris finally ceded it permanently to Britain in 1814. The high degree of political instability and the widespread destruction of many of the oldest administrative records on the island caused by four major fires striking the capital city, Castries, and by periodic earthquakes and hurricanes make it difficult to reconstruct St. Lucia's early economic and political development. As a result, the island's role in the history of the Caribbean as a whole has been largely neglected. Many previous studies have assumed that widespread colonization and development took place only after the island reached a stage of relative stability following the Treaty of Paris that ended the Seven Years' War in 1763 (e.g., Jesse 1962:20–28). However, a thorough reading of archaeological evidence and documentary sources in the French and English archives, including early maps, census records, and government correspondence, sheds light on the period predating the Treaty of Paris, revealing heretofore unknown details about the extent and character of landscape change and population fluctuation throughout the early period of St. Lucia's history.

Although settlement of the Lesser Antilles stretches back more than

2,000 years, the earliest archaeological evidence for the occupation of St. Lucia dates to approximately AD 200, when Saladoid series ceramics began to appear on sites throughout the island (Hofman et al. 2004; Rouse 1992). The Amerindian peoples of the Caribbean sustained themselves by hunting, fishing, and cultivating cassava, sweet potatoes, yams, and other tubers in cleared land within secondary-growth forest (Watts 1987:53–71). Within a century and a half of Christopher Columbus' arrival in the Caribbean, the Amerindians of the Lesser Antilles were growing a mixture of native and introduced crops, including the aforementioned tubers along with bananas, sugar cane, cotton, tobacco, ginger, peanuts, corn, pineapples, coconuts, and citrus fruits (Hoy 1961:31).

The first recorded European attempts to settle St. Lucia took place in the beginning of the seventeenth century. Early English efforts in 1605 and 1638 failed in the face of Amerindian resistance (Nicholl 1607; Calendar of State Papers Colonial [CSPC] 1574–1660:1:301, Petition of the Governor and Company of London, July 28, 1639). A French settlement in 1651 led by a resident of Martinique who was married to an Amerindian woman was initially more successful, building a fort and cultivating cotton, tobacco, and ginger under its protection (Anonymous 1764:216–218). After a few years, relations with the Amerindians deteriorated and this settlement collapsed as well. The coming of a large contingent of English colonists from Barbados in 1664 finished off the stragglers from the French settlement. The Barbadian attempt, in turn, failed spectacularly, with the eventual death of nearly a thousand would-be settlers through sickness and misfortune (Burns 1954:301–302; CSPC 1669–1674:7:277, Additional Propositions to the Privy Council, February 17, 1670).

At this point, the larger islands of the Caribbean had been European colonies for more than a century. Many of the smaller islands such as St. Kitts, Barbados, Martinique, and Guadeloupe had thriving European settlements that were decades old and were already experiencing population pressures. In contrast, although one of the largest islands in the Lesser Antilles, St. Lucia was considered by most Europeans to be something of a blank spot on the map, a place still largely controlled by Amerindians and lacking a colonial governor, legislature, judiciary system, tax or custom collectors, or any towns or official ports.

Over the next few decades, the French on Martinique and the English on Barbados stepped up their campaigns to claim possession of St. Lucia. Planters on these more extensively developed islands looked to St. Lucia's forests as a source of wood to construct forts, houses, and machinery for their plantations and to fashion barrels in which to store and ship their produce. The excellence of St. Lucia's two main harbors, Carénage and Marigot, was an additional attraction, as each could hold large numbers of ships that might interrupt the trade from either Martinique or Barbados. Both islands feared what would happen if St. Lucia were to fall into enemy hands.

The first documentary evidence of sustained settlement dates to 1686, when the governor of Barbados sent a delegation to investigate reports of French settlers (CSPC 1685–1686:12:541, Stede to the Earl of Sunderland, January 8, 1686). They were met by four white and seven black men who claimed the island for France. The threat was extensive enough to warrant the sending of a British sloop to sail around the island, burning down the houses and plantations (CSPC 1685–1688:12:871VI, Journal of Captain Temple's Voyage to St. Lucia and St. Vincent, July 25–August 5, 1686). It appears that there was enough development to keep the British occupied destroying it for five days. The fact that the majority of the settlers encountered were black is perhaps noteworthy, given later developments on the island.

France and England each backed a large-scale attempt at colonization between 1719 and 1722, but neither succeeded, and the issue of who owned the island continued to remain in flux. In fact, it was this inability by either side to establish clear-cut title to the island that made it attractive to a new breed of permanent settler. St. Lucia provided an easily reached haven for debtors from nearby islands hoping to evade their creditors, for enslaved Africans looking for liberty, and for servants wishing to escape their indentures as well as others keen to evade official authority such as tax avoiders, military deserters, pirates, and smugglers (CSPC 1696–1697:15:1174, Memorial of the Agents for Barbados to Council of Trade and Plantations, July 10, 1697; CSPC 1720–1721:32:463iii, News from Barbados, April 25, 1721; Voyages Database 2008:Voyage 70,020).

The absence of a stable government and effective administrative oversight, when coupled with the availability of land that could be cleared and worked without needing to obtain title to it, made St. Lucia particularly attractive to those on the margins of colonial West Indian society who were looking for a place to settle without too many questions asked. Instability in the region had only increased with the coming of the War of Spanish Succession in 1702. According to Jean-Baptiste Labat, a French clergyman and engineer who spent more than a decade in the West Indies beginning in 1694, St. Lucia in particular had become "the refuge of soldier and sailor deserters; they find abundantly there what they need to live on and have great safety from the hands of those sent to take them, because it has natural redoubts on the tops of steep hills" (Labat 1722:4:461). Military deserters were joined by resident families of Amerindians, English families who were settling on St. Lucia to set up cassava and tobacco plantations, younger sons from Martinique who were unable to access any cultivatable land on that island, and, later, victims of a 1727 hurricane that ruined many of the cocoa plantations on Martinique (Archives nationales d'outre-mer [ANOM] Fonds ministérielles [FM]/C/8A/22/55, La Varenne to Minister of Marine, March 17, 1717; Pares 1936:197).

Development of the Plantation System

In spite of a policy that held St. Lucia to be officially neutral between France and England, settlers were increasingly coming to St. Lucia in search of available land throughout the first half of the eighteenth century. Census records from this period give a detailed look at the changing demographics of the island. The earliest preserved census, dating from June 1730, shows 463 persons resident on the island (ANOM FM/Dépôt des papiers publics des colonies [DPPC]/G/1/506/1). The census recorded 100 free men, race unspecified, fit to carry arms; 60 free women, 8 of whom were white and 52 of whom were black or of mixed race; 91 children; 175 enslaved people; and 37 Amerindians.

The most striking feature of these figures is the absence of people inhabiting an island of 616 km^2 in the middle of a densely populated area such as the Caribbean. Martinique, roughly twice as large, housed 59,223 people in 1731 while Barbados, although smaller than St. Lucia, had a total population of 64,865 by 1712 (Watts 1987:311, 320). With less than 1 percent of the population of either of these islands, the low figures in St. Lucia point to an island with a dispersed settlement pattern just beginning to coalesce into a plantation system.

Map evidence from this period attests to the presence of numerous small plantations separated by much open space. The earliest cadastral map, which predates the laying out of the first towns in 1745, shows 199 estates spread along the coasts of the island and up the rivers (ANOM FM/DFC/xxx/49pga/481b). The estates were tiny, with fields marked in green and houses in red, and the road system was embryonic at best. No nucleated village or town settlements had appeared by this point, and the interior of the island was completely unsettled.

Even at this early stage, it is notable that the ratio of free black to free white settlers was extremely high. Although the race of the men is unknown, in the 1730 census cited earlier, nearly 90 percent of the women and more than 80 percent of the children were free persons of color. Together, free women and children made up more than a third of the population, suggesting that by this point, St. Lucia was settled by a growing population of families, not one composed primarily of military deserters and transient woodcutters from Martinique and Barbados.

Also noteworthy is the fact that enslaved people made up only 38 percent of the population. The low proportion of enslaved workers points to an economy dependent on a variety of agricultural crops that could be planted, harvested, and processed with minimal labor, rather than sugar monoculture. Contemporary reports suggest that cotton was the main crop, supplemented by smaller amounts of cocoa, coffee, tobacco, ginger, and sugar (CSPC 1735–1736:42:183ii, Duke to Reddish, November 29, 1735). One British ship that visited the north of the island in 1736 found 15 or 16 cotton plantations there, 12 of which were owned by French inhabitants and the rest by British residents (CSPC 1735–1736:42:378ii, Crauford to Dottin, July 24, 1736). Given the lack of a large work force to clear the land, it is probable that these early plantations remained limited in scope.

As the century progressed, the work force increased steadily. By 1744 the enslaved population outnumbered the free population by nearly 3:1, with a total of 2,261 enslaved men, women, and children compared to 822 free individuals, representing a 12-fold increase in the number of slaves over the previous 14 years (ANOM FM/DPPC/G/1/506/3). Agricultural products were listed on the census records for the first time that same year, providing a snapshot of which crops were grown where. Comparisons between the various crops can be difficult since the French colonists used units of length to record some crops and units of area for others. Rows of cocoa, coffee, and banana plants were measured by the *pied*, or French foot, which was equivalent to a modern measurement of 1.066 feet. The land used to grow cotton, cassava, indigo, sugar, and ground provisions, on the other hand, was measured by the *carré*, or square, which was equivalent to roughly 3.2 acres. More than a thousand acres of cassava were under cultivation in 1744, as well as 63,500 *pieds* of cocoa, 105,220 *pieds* of coffee, and 140,570 *pieds* of bananas, all of which represented a transition from the cotton, ginger, and tobacco plantations of the 1650s. Bananas and cassava were grown as a subsistence crop to feed both the colonists and the slaves, while coffee and cocoa were intended for export. Cotton, the main crop of the 1730s, was left off the 1744 census, perhaps inadvertently; when it appeared the following year, it took up more acres than cassava (ANOM FM/DPPC/G/1/506/4).

No sugar was grown on the island at this time. Small amounts were cultivated beginning in 1747, remaining an experimental crop at best throughout the 1750s (ANOM FM/DPPC/G/1/506/5–11). Fears that increased competition would adversely affect the established sugar industries in the rest of the French West Indies led the governor-general on Martinique to ban the creation of sugar processing works on St. Lucia in 1745, effectively strangling the new industry (ANOM C/8A/56/389 12 January 1745).

Over the next several decades, cocoa and banana production increased steadily and indigo was introduced as a new crop, but coffee quickly came to dominate the island economy. It was grown across the entire island, with the amount of land devoted to coffee trees jumping from 105,220 *pieds* in 1744 to 1.2 million *pieds* in 1756 (ANOM FM/DPPC/G/1/506/3–8). Coffee was first introduced in the West Indies at Martinique in the early 1720s. It was well suited to growing in St. Lucia's hilly mountains on land that was marginal for other crops, and it could be grown on much smaller estates using fewer slaves than were required by sugar. Setting oneself up as a coffee planter required far less of an initial outlay to purchase the land, clear the jungle, and propagate the plants, and far fewer ongoing operating costs, making it attractive to those settlers who could raise less capital than the wealthy sugar planters of other islands.

David Watts (1987:326–352) has described how all Caribbean plantation societies, whether French, British, or Spanish, distinguished between big, middling, or small planters. The definition of each category varied between islands and over time, and distinctions were based more on the number of slaves owned rather than the number of acres held, since sizable portions of plantations could be undesirable land left as standing timber or pasture. In general, though, a landowner had to have in the region of 10 working slaves and 10 acres to be considered one of the small planters; landowners with fewer than those holdings were considered freedmen rather than planters and were not allowed to vote. In Barbados in 1680, for example, the large planters were expected to own at least 60 slaves and 100 acres, oftentimes many more, while the middling planters owned between 20 and 59 slaves and between 30 and 100 acres, sufficient numbers for a sugar plantation of modest size (Watts 1987:331). As the sugar plantation system intensified on each island, the numbers of large planters holding 1,000 or more acres worked by several hundreds of slaves increased dramatically.

When compared to Barbados in 1680, it becomes clear just how small St. Lucia's estates still were in 1756. On the scale above, 203 of Barbados's planters, or 8 percent, were considered large planters while just 1 of St. Lucia's 358 establishments qualified 75 years later, a mere 0.3 percent of the total (ANOM FM/DPPC/G/1/506/31; Watts 1987:329). Only 3 percent of St. Lucia's plantations would have been considered middling size in Barbados (versus 8 percent in Barbados) while 22 percent were small estates (versus 40 percent in Barbados). The real difference can be seen at the bottom of the economic scale: 75 percent of St. Lucia's landowners in 1756 owned fewer than 10 slaves and would have been considered merely freedmen in Barbados, against only 45 percent in Barbados in 1680.

The French colonial governments placed a greater emphasis on a diversity of crops than the British. Although the British encouraged sugar production while they owned the island during the American Revolution, a series of hurricanes and the collapse of sugar prices meant that within a few years of the French recovering St. Lucia in 1784, only 45 estates were still producing sugar (Momsen 1996:xxi). The number of plantations producing solely coffee equaled those producing sugar, with a slightly smaller number cultivating cocoa. The return of cotton was seen as the new savior of the economy in the 1780s; 34 former sugar estates were in the process of converting to cotton, and the total number of estates growing cotton outnumbered sugar by a factor of five to one. However, more than 40 percent of all the estates were growing a mixture of crops, with much of the less desirable land devoted to ground provisions. Moreover, many of the plantations had been abandoned in the face of hurricane damage and credit problems caused by the war, leaving four-fifths of the island's land uncultivated.

At the end of the eighteenth century, then, while many of the Caribbean colonies were generating substantial profits from their mature sugar plantations, St. Lucia was still trying to find its feet in the world economy. The planters had pinned their hopes first to cotton, then coffee, then sugar, and back to cotton again, but were never reliant on any one crop, rejecting the monoculture model that prevailed on many of the neighboring islands. The size of the average estate was small, with a high percentage of the landowners owning fewer than 100 acres, and sometimes much less.

Landscape Survey: Balenbouche and Fond d'Or Estates

Archaeological work undertaken at several former estates in St. Lucia has provided further insight into agricultural development in the context of particular plantation landscapes.

The vast majority of the archaeology on St. Lucia has focused on pre-historic occupation. Beginning in 2001 the first comprehensive series of landscape surveys and excavations targeting the historical period were launched by archaeologists from the University of Bristol. Balenbouche Estate on the southwest coast and Fond d'Or Estate on the central east coast were among the sites chosen, in large part because their surviving buildings and landscapes represent some of the best preserved remains of sugar estates on the island (Devaux 1975:115–116). Both feature an inner core of buildings forming the industrial zone of the sugar works next to a domestic occupation site represented by the estate or "great" house.

The first plantation surveyed, Balenbouche Estate, was one of the larger sugar estates on the island during the nineteenth century. When it was sold by judicial decree in 1836, its 587 acres brought a sum of 6,640 pounds sterling, the highest amount for any of the 75 estates sold by this method between January 1833 and January 1844 (Breen 1844:317). The building remains at Balenbouche are remarkably well preserved and include an intact mid-nineteenth-century water wheel and crushing machine as well as large boiling and curing houses dating to the late eighteenth century. Underneath these impressive remains, however, the survey and its attendant excavation revealed a previously unknown pre–sugar estate landscape that had been designed in conjunction with an early-eighteenth-century coffee works (Hicks 2007; Hicks and Horton 2001).

During the primary phase of industrial activity on the site, a coffee works had been constructed on an artificial terrace built into the hillside of a river bank. The main component of the works was a 5 m × 12.5 m coffee-processing building comprising a wheel pit holding a wooden waterwheel that powered a pulping machine in an adjacent machine pit and a cobbled surface with gutters serving as a washing area for the pulped beans (Figure 6.1). The works building was surrounded by a relatively simple water system featuring a dam and two mill ponds designed to ensure a sufficient water supply to power the works.

Beginning in the 1770s a wholesale reorganization of the estate took place and a complex system of water management and a series of sugar processing buildings—both representing a massive investment of time and

Figure 6.1. The coffee works at Balenbouche Estate, showing the cobblestone floor of the washing area in the foreground and the machine and wheel pits in the background. (Photograph by Jane Seiter)

labor—were constructed directly adjacent to the coffee works, rendering the coffee works inoperable. Changes to the sugar works continued into the postemancipation period, with older machinery being replaced by a water-wheel and crushing machine from the 1850s or 1860s that survive today.

The pre-1745 cartographic depiction of Balenbouche reveals a modest-sized estate owned by a planter named L'Ecuyer. A map of the quarter of Islet à Caret (the modern-day quarter of Laborie), prepared in 1770 during the coffee-works period, shows the estate consisting of 36.5 *carrés* (approximately 117 acres) in the possession of a planter named Martin (ANOM FM / Dépôt des fortifications des colonies [DFC]/xxx/49pfa/404). The 1756 census records document that Martin, his wife, and their five children lived in Islet à Caret with 28 enslaved adults and 10 enslaved children (ANOM FM/ DPPC/G/1/506/31). By 1787, after the estate had been reconfigured for the first phase of sugar cultivation, the plantation had nearly doubled in size, to 68.5 *carrés* (219.2 acres) (ANOM FM/DFC/xxx/mémoires/122/464). By 1815 the number of slaves on the estate had ballooned to 203, and by 1838 the grounds had expanded to 587 acres, five times its coffee-period size (National Archives, London, T 71/379; Breen 1844:317).

As Balenbouche illustrates, sometimes in the "spaces in between" the more familiar stories of empire building can be hiding in plain sight. Underneath the more obvious remains from the sugar plantation was the archaeological evidence of a smaller, less ambitious and less costly phase of early eighteenth-century development that relied on coffee cultivation carried out by a small workforce. The subsequent switch to sugar in the latter part of the eighteenth century necessitated a very considerable increase in acreage and slaves, changing both the lives of the people associated with the estate, whether enslaved or free, and the concomitant pace and extent of landscape development.

*   *   *

The landscape survey of Fond d'Or Estate in the quarter of Dennery tells a similar story of expansion and adjustment. Currently a nature reserve and heritage park, during the nineteenth century Fond d'Or was one of St. Lucia's larger sugar plantations. Upon its sale in July 1836, it comprised 607 acres and changed hands for 6,240 pounds sterling, the sixth largest and second most expensive of the 75 sugar estates sold by judicial decree during this period—second in price only to Balenbouche, in fact (Breen 1844:317). Substantial building remains and landscape features survive on the grounds, which sit on a high bluff overlooking a broad bay where the Fond d'Or River empties into the Atlantic Ocean.

The survey revealed at least four separate phases of industrial production at the core of the estate (Seiter 2011:78–83). The earliest phase occurred in the northeast of the site, where a mound denoted the former site of a windmill (Figure 6.2). Next to the windmill were the remains of a 6.5 m by 7.8 m stone building, whose size and location suggest a small associated works building, possibly a coffee-processing area that was later converted into a boiling house or rum distillery.

The works eventually expanded westward with the erection of an extensive sugar production facility, starting with a large cattle mill, approximately 40 m in diameter, in the center of the site. The sugar cane juice produced by the cattle mill traveled to a large boiling and curing house via a stone canal with an overflow reservoir. The cattle mill was eventually converted to a windmill, which was augmented by a smaller cattle mill added onto its north side. A third circular structure nearby also superficially resembles a cattle mill, but extensive rebuilding during the twentieth century has obscured its original design. The use of several different types of mills on one site is less surprising than at first glance. Multiple mills were often required

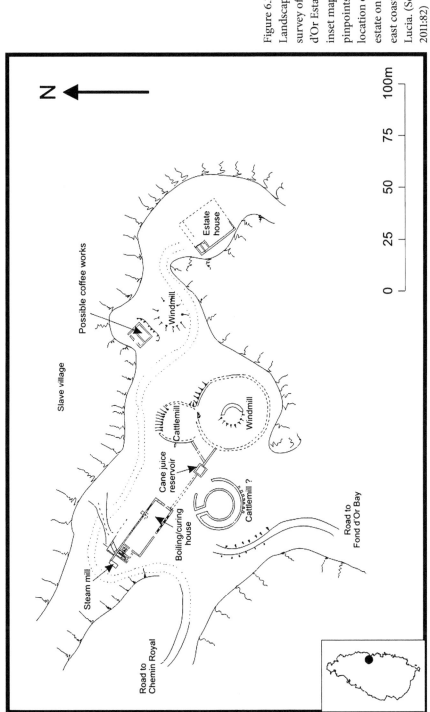

Figure 6.2. Landscape survey of Fond d'Or Estate; inset map pinpoints the location of the estate on the east coast of St. Lucia. (Seiter 2011:82)

N

Slave village

Possible coffee works

Windmill

Estate house

Cattlemill

Windmill

Cane juice reservoir

Cattlemill ?

Boiling/curing house

Steam mill

Road to Chemin Royal

Road to Fond d'Or Bay

0   25   50   75   100m

on estates with a large and efficient boiling system such as Fond d'Or. Both the windmill and cattle mill were supplanted by the final phase of production with a newer and more efficient steam-driven mill, parts of which still survive in situ within a later addition to the original boiling house.

By comparing the results of the landscape survey with the maps, plans, and census records available for the quarter of Dennery, it is possible to arrive at a tentative chronology for the Fond d'Or Estate. By 1732, 24 French inhabitants and 2 slaves resided in the present-day quarter of Dennery (ANOM FM/DPPC/G/1/506/2). The leading inhabitant of the quarter during the 1740s was a man named Dezinches, who is linked to Fond d'Or through the pre-1745 map of the island, which shows two small estates on either side of the Fond d'Or River, one belonging to "Desincheres" and the other to "l'Etang" (ANOM FM/DPPC/G/1/506/4–7; ANOM FM/DFC/xxx/49pfa/481b). Both are at the bottom of the bluff rather than on top, where the present-day estate lies.

The number of enslaved workers in Dennery increased dramatically during the mid-eighteenth century, jumping to 187 adults and 72 children by 1745, and to 319 adults and 157 children by 1756 (ANOM FM/DPPC/G/1/506/4, 8). By the latter year, 47 adults and 19 children were owned by "Veuve Dezincher," the widow of Dezinches/Desincheres, who lived on the estate with 1 child, while 8 adults and 5 children were owned by "Dubuq l'Etang fils," presumably the son of the original planter l'Etang (ANOM FM/DPPC/G/1/506/31). In fact, the widow of Dezinches, referred to as Dezincher in the 1756 census, held the third-largest number of enslaved individuals on the island at this time. The majority of the agricultural land in the quarter was devoted to growing bananas during the 1740s, but this had shifted by the 1756 census, which shows that more than three times as much coffee was grown in Dennery as cocoa and bananas, supplemented by smaller amounts of cassava and cotton. Given the available workforce, the size of the estates, and the dominance of the local economy by coffee cultivation, it is probable that, like the majority of the estates throughout the island, both of the estates at Fond d'Or were producing coffee supplemented by other crops by the mid-1750s.

Plans of each of the quarters were drawn up in 1770/1771. The Dennery plan shows that the two estates were owned jointly by "Demoiselle Dezinchere," probably the daughter of the widow Dezincher, although a cross next to her name suggests that she had passed away around the time of the survey (ANOM FM/DFC/xxx/49pfa/405 bis). Together they comprised 608 acres, making them the third largest of the 61 estates in the quarter.

Their land now stretched east all the way to the shores of Fond d'Or Bay and swept up from the flat of the river basin into the hills to the north and south. It is likely that the processing works for the estate were moved up onto the bluff when the two estates were consolidated, with the primary windmill-driven phase of works being constructed at this point.

During the late 1760s St. Lucia was taking its first tentative steps into sugar production. The restrictions on sugar were lifted in 1765, and by September 1773 34 estates were producing sugar, although the other 672 estates on the island were still growing coffee, cocoa, and cotton (ANOM FM/DPPC/G/1/506/19a). By 1787 the 608-acre estate at Fond d'Or was owned by "Hosten fils" (ANOM FM/DFC/xxx/mémoires/122/464, p. 46). Although it had previously been cultivating sugar, it was in the process of converting to cotton. The most likely interpretation is that the early cattle mill at Fond d'Or was constructed as part of the switch to sugar between 1775, when no cattle mills were listed in the Dennery census, and 1784, when five cattle mills were operating in the quarter.

As one of the 34 estates transitioning to cotton in 1787, Fond d'Or was not alone in attempting a remarkably quick conversion from coffee to sugar to cotton production. A depression in first coffee and then sugar prices combined with the damages caused by the British occupation of the island during the American Revolution and the disastrous hurricanes of 1780 and 1786 caused many of the estates to look elsewhere for profits. The turmoil brought by the French Revolutionary Wars of the 1790s further destabilized the plantation economy. St. Lucia was occupied twice by the British, recaptured again by the French, and finally ended up in British hands by the start of the Napoleonic Wars. Sugar production in many parts of the island was not sustained until the British were given permanent ownership by the 1814 Treaty of Paris. Even then it struggled, with the aforementioned 75 estates being sold off due to unpaid debts in the aftermath of the 1833 Slavery Abolition Act, which ushered in emancipation in the British West Indies.

Steam-powered mills first became widespread in the West Indies in the 1830s, with more than a dozen present on the island by the early 1840s (Breen 1844:292; Watts 1987:421). It is likely that the one at Fond d'Or was installed sometime after the estate's sale in 1836, when a new infusion of capital presumably allowed for the conversion to a more efficient but expensive technology.

Like Balenbouche, the story of Fond d'Or is one of adaptation to changing economic conditions. From coffee to sugar to cotton, and then back again to sugar, the owners of Fond d'Or were chasing prosperity in a time of uncertain prices and escalating production costs. Starting with small estates in the early eighteenth century growing crops that required less capital and fewer workers than sugar, the owners of both plantations increased their holdings and purchased ever greater numbers of slaves. By the late eighteenth century, both were experimenting with sugar, expanding their production under the British regime of the early nineteenth century. The sales caused by debt in the 1830s were followed by a period of considerable reinvestment that resulted in the emergence of the sizable sugar estates whose remains can be seen today.

Plantation owners were not the only people living through these times of change, of course. The workers on the estates were directly affected by the shifts in landscape development and society that transformed St. Lucia in the late eighteenth and early nineteenth century. On December 29, 1815, 143 enslaved individuals were living at Fond d'Or, including 27 families and 30 unrelated people, all of whom who were listed on the estate's "slave return" drawn up that year (National Archives, London, St. Lucia Plantation Slaves Register, T 71/379). Among the people in bondage on the estate were carpenters, masons, sugar refiners, cooks, domestic servants, a blacksmith, a cooper, and many field hands. Some, like Heureuse Bonne, whose age was given as 103, had been born in Africa and brought to the Caribbean. Others, like Heureuse's 64-year-old daughter Adélaide, had been born in St. Lucia, as had Adélaide's six daughters and three granddaughters. Adélaide was a nurse while her daughters worked in the fields. All of the Bonne women must have wondered what the future held for them and their descendants, particularly Heureuse and Adélaide, who had briefly tasted freedom in the 1790s and must have hoped that one day soon they and Adélaide's daughters would be able to live as free women again.

Growth of the Free Black Population

A significant outcome of the particular circumstances of landscape change on St. Lucia as documented above was the rise of a landowning population of free persons of color. By 1756 one-fifth of the estates on the island—68 in total—belonged to free black owners (ANOM FM/DPPC/G/1/506/31). Like the free white population, many of the free black landowners were also slaveholders, collectively owning 264 enslaved adults and 151 enslaved children, just over 10 percent of the enslaved population. In a land where wealth was based on controlling and marshaling the labor of others, free

Table 6.1. Number and size of estates owned by white and free black landowners in 1787

Quarter	Estates Owned by Whites	Average Size of White Estates (acreage)	Estates Owned by Free Blacks	Average Size of Free Black Estates (acreage)
Castries	68	256	29	107
Anse La Raye	72	143	32	69
Soufrière	98	145	6	72
Choiseul	52	108	11	45
Laborie	57	131	10	56
Vieux Fort	53	217	2	110
Micoud	70	198	20	28
Praslin	25	353	23	34
Dennery	66	237	0	N/A
Dauphin	49	76	27	50
Gros Islet	50	262	6	66
Total Estates	660		166	
Average Acres		197 acres[a]		61 acres[a]

Source: Archives nationales d'outre mer, Aix-en-Provence, France, Fonds ministérielles, Dépôt des fortifications des colonies, xxx/mémoires/122/464.

[a] The average acreage was calculated by summing the exact *carrés* of land for all the white- or black-owned estates on the island, converting from *carrés* to acres, and rounding to the nearest acre.

black landowners who wished to develop their property and increase their profits participated fully in the slave society. The largest slaveholder on the island at the time, in fact, was a free man of color named Nouës, who owned 81 adults and 60 children. A quarter of the free black landowners owned no enslaved individuals at all, however, a much higher percentage than that of the free white landowning population. The majority of the free people of color who owned land were on a lower economic footing than most of the white landowners, oftentimes working their plantations with no more than a handful of adult slaves.

As more and more land was brought under cultivation during the 1760s and 1770s, the proportion of estates owned by persons of color stayed constant. By 1787 blacks owned 166 of the 826 plantations, or 20 percent (Table 6.1). One difference between the estates owned by whites and estates owned by blacks was size. The average size of a black-owned estate on the island was 61 acres, while the average size of a white-owned estate was 197 acres,

Table 6.2. Free blacks in the West Indies during the late eighteenth century

Population	St. Lucia in 1789	Martinique in 1789	Guadeloupe in 1790	St.-Domingue in 1791	St. Vincent in 1787	Barbados in 1786	Jamaica in 1775
Free blacks as % of total population	7.4	5.3	2.9	4.5	2.2	1.1	2.1
Free blacks as % of free population	43	33	18	44	17	5	19

Sources: Archives nationales d'outre mer, Aix-en-Provence, France, G/1/506/30; Watts 1987:311–321.

more than three times greater. Overall, whites owned 93 percent of the land devoted to plantations while blacks owned 7 percent. Both sets of landowners primarily cultivated a mix of cotton, coffee, and cocoa, although more of the white landowners either grew sugar cane or had grown it in the past. The black-owned estates were often located in the marginal land on the slopes of hills. A free person of color named Loye even owned a 91-acre coffee estate on the site of the island's lone volcano.

Nevertheless, the achievement of land ownership by such a sizable number of free persons of color was a crucial step in the formation of a stable and relatively prosperous class of citizens. As the century progressed, the free black population on St. Lucia grew proportionally larger, following a general trend throughout the French West Indies. Between 1764 and 1789 the percentage of free blacks as a portion of the entire free population on St. Lucia increased from 29 percent to 43 percent. By the start of the French Revolution, the two groups of free individuals had achieved a rough parity, with whites barely outnumbering free blacks by a factor of 1.3:1. Throughout the Caribbean, only St. Domingue (later Haiti) equaled this demographic, with other islands having much smaller numbers of free blacks as a proportion of both their total population (including slaves) and their free population (Table 6.2).

Because of its considerable size and the comparative wealth and status that it had accrued, the free black population in St. Lucia had an outsized impact on regional events during the turbulent 1790s. They were among the most vociferous and loyal supporters of the French Revolution in the West Indies. On April 4, 1792, the National Assembly in France passed a landmark decree of racial equality. Although the decree applied only to free persons of color, the fear of it being extended to enslaved blacks on the islands split apart the colonial legislatures on Guadeloupe and Martinique, which ended up rejecting the ruling. St. Lucia, however, enthusiastically supported the decree and seated delegates from the free black community in the island's colonial legislature.

When the war between Britain and France came to the West Indies in 1794 in the form of the Brigands' War of the Lesser Antilles, the free black population used all of its resources to affect the outcome (Devaux 1997; Seiter 2011). Jean-Joseph Lambert, a free man of color, organized the resistance to the British invasion of St. Lucia during 1795. Although a tradesman and not a member of the landowning classes, he had served in the colonial legislature in the early 1790s and advanced £4,800 worth of rum and shoes to the French Republican government (Lambert 1799). Like Lambert, many of the officers in the French Republican forces were free men of color, such as the twelve officers from Guadeloupe and St. Lucia who were promoted during the battle of St. Lucia (Dubois 2004:239). The Republicans won that battle, driving out the British invaders and emancipating the slaves. St. Lucia then became the prime exporter of revolution throughout the Lesser Antilles, sending supplies and troops to Dominica, St. Vincent, and Grenada to resist the British and increase French territory.

In spite of its leading role in stirring up rebellion on the other Caribbean islands, the French Republican victory on St. Lucia was short lived. Two thousand combatants—a mix of previously enslaved people, free black landowners and tradesmen, and white French settlers who supported the Revolutionary cause—were captured when St. Lucia capitulated to a massive British army attack in 1796 (Seiter 2011). The prisoners were shipped back to prisons and prisoner of war camps in England. Lambert was one of those who endured years in British captivity, only to be released to France without the money to rejoin his wife and children back in the Caribbean.

Meanwhile, on St. Lucia the British reinstated slavery and attempted to remedy the destruction caused by the war. All cultivation of the land had stopped during the hostilities, with both sides employing widespread burning of fields as a military tactic, meaning no provision crops were harvested and no cotton, coffee, or sugar were produced to trade for imported food. As a consequence, more than two thousand enslaved people died of famine, and planters found themselves without the credit or labor to work their estates. The pace of reconstruction was slow, but by the end of 1799, 318 cotton, 118 coffee, 67 cocoa, and 41 sugar estates were functioning (National Archives, London, CO 253/2 Prevost to Portland no. 12, November 12, 1799).

After the war 20 percent of the prewar population of the island had died, been captured, or else simply fled (Breen 1844:165). The free black population, on the other hand, dramatically increased in the years after the war. At the turn of the century, free black residents were more numerous than white residents in 7 of the 11 quarters (compared to only 3 quarters a decade before). For the first time ever, free people of color outnumbered whites in the overall population, a demographic shift that had been almost unthinkable a decade previously. By 1805 there were more than twice as many free people of color as there were whites (Gaspar 1997:122).

Writing a decade after emancipation, Henry Breen, the great nineteenth-century historian of St. Lucia, reflected how the free people of color—as distinct from the newly emancipated people—had "rapidly progressed in numbers, wealth, and respectability" since the French Revolution: "Few as yet have become owners of the soil to any considerable extent; but much of the property in houses and land, both in Castries and Soufriere, is possessed by them. Some are opulent merchants, others respectable shopkeepers, and many are industrious tradesmen" (Breen 1844:166). Breen also noted that many of the public offices and professions, from the press to the bar to medicine, were filled by persons of color. The ownership of land that was pursued by their ancestors in the early days of the colony, although never reaching the heights of that enjoyed by the elites of the white population, had laid the foundations for the increased prosperity and social standing of the free black population over a century later, which continued to grow into the period after emancipation and beyond.

Conclusions

Recent archaeological surveys and documentary evidence located in the French and British archives point to a slowly developing plantation economy on St. Lucia in the late seventeenth and early eighteenth centuries. Building on a legacy of small-scale agriculture inherited from the Amerindians, the first European settlers on St. Lucia carved out a patchwork of small holdings cultivating cotton, ginger, and tobacco, later supplemented by cocoa, coffee, cassava, indigo, and bananas. The pattern of smaller estates growing a diversity of crops dominated St. Lucia throughout the eighteenth century. Such estates had lower start-up costs, required a smaller workforce, and could take advantage of more marginal land in higher elevations than the large sugar estates found on other Caribbean islands.

The absence of large sugar plantations and the corresponding availability of land allowed people without much capital to purchase and develop property, creating new opportunities for free people of color in particular to amass wealth, leading to the establishment of a relatively stable class of landowners and a consolidation of political power. This development in turn greatly affected the place of St. Lucia within the larger political struggles that rocked the Caribbean in the late eighteenth century. Free people of color on St. Lucia were strong supporters of the French and Haitian Revolutions and fought in large numbers across the Antilles in the conflicts of the 1790s. Thus, the particular path of landscape development in St. Lucia had a profound impact on the struggles for liberty and personal autonomy that took place not only on the island itself but also throughout the wider Caribbean.

As the other essays in this book make clear, sometimes the spaces in between the more well-known chronicles of colonialism in the Caribbean reveal unexpected information about the lives of the people who lived, worked, and died there. In this case, a landscape-based archaeological approach has helped to chart the materiality of changing plantation landscapes on St. Lucia, in the process exposing a plurality of individual colonial experiences within the broader rubric of slavery and empire building. As more attention is brought to bear on the people and places outside already familiar Caribbean contexts, it is hoped that a more nuanced view of development and an emphasis on telling stories that have not been told before will provide a useful counterpoint to the conventional narrative of the unstoppable rise of sugar.

References Cited

Anonymous
1764   *The Modern Part of an Universal History, from the Earliest Account of Time*, Vol. 41, *The History of America*. T. Osborne et al., London.
Breen, Henry H.
1844   *St. Lucia: Historical, Statistical, and Descriptive*. Longman, Brown, Green, and Longmans, London.
Burns, Alan
1954   *History of the British West Indies*. George Allen and Unwin, London.
Calendar of State Papers, Colonial, America and West Indies
1860–1994 *Calendar of State Papers, Colonial, America and West Indies 1574–1739*. 45 vols. Public Record Office, London. Available online at http://www.british-history. ac.uk/catalogue.aspx?gid=123.

Devaux, Robert J.
1975   *Saint Lucia Historic Sites, including Monuments, Buildings, Parks, Open Spaces.* Saint Lucia National Trust, Castries, St. Lucia.
1997   *They Called Us Brigands: The Saga of St. Lucia's Freedom Fighters.* Optimum, Castries, St. Lucia.

Dubois, Laurent
2004   *A Colony of Citizens: Revolution and Slave Emancipation in the French Caribbean, 1787–1804.* University of North Carolina Press, Chapel Hill.

Gaspar, David Barry
1997   La Guerre des Bois: Revolution, War, and Slavery in Saint Lucia, 1793–1838. In *A Turbulent Time: The French Revolution and the Greater Caribbean,* edited by David Barry Gaspar and David Patrick Geggus, pp. 102–130. Indiana University Press, Bloomington.

Hicks, Dan
2007   *"The Garden of the World": An Historical Archaeology of Sugar Landscapes in the Eastern Caribbean.* British Archaeological Report International Series 1632, Studies in Contemporary and Historical Archaeology 3. Archaeopress, Oxford.

Hicks, Dan, and Mark C. Horton
2001   *An Archaeological Landscape Survey, Building Survey and Evaluative Excavation at Balenbouche Estate, Saint Lucia, West Indies, Winter 2000–2001 Season.* University of Bristol, Bristol, United Kingdom.

Hofman, Corinne L., Menno L. P. Hoogland, and William F. Keegan
2004   *Archaeological Reconnaissance at Saint Lucia, West Indies, Preliminary Report.* Electronic document, http://media.leidenuniv.nl/legacy/st.luciareport2004.pdf, accessed March 1, 2016.

Hoy, Don R.
1961   *Agricultural Land Use of Guadeloupe,* Publication 884. National Academy of Sciences, National Research Council, Washington, D.C.

Jesse, Charles H.
1962   *Outlines of St. Lucia's History.* 2nd ed. St. Lucia Archaeological and Historical Society, Castries, St. Lucia.

Labat, Jean-Baptiste
1722   *Nouveau voyage aux isles de l'Amerique.* 6 vols. Paris.

Lambert, Jean-Joseph
1799   *Mémoire de Jean-Joseph Lambert.* Paris.

Mintz, Sidney W.
1985   *Sweetness and Power: The Place of Sugar in Modern History.* Penguin, New York.

Momsen, Janet H.
1996   *St. Lucia Bibliography.* ABC-CLIO, Oxford.

Nicholl, John
1607   *An Houre Glasse of Indian Newes.* Nathaniell Butter, London.

Pares, Richard
1936   *War and Trade in the West Indies 1739–1763.* Oxford University Press, Oxford.

Rouse, Irving
1992   *The Taínos: Rise and Decline of the People Who Greeted Columbus*. Yale University Press, New Haven, Connecticut.

Seiter, Jane I.
2011   The Archaeology of Resistance: The Brigands' War in St. Lucia 1794–1800. Unpublished PhD dissertation, Department of Archaeology, University of Bristol, Bristol, United Kingdom.

Stein, Robert Louis
1979   *The French Slave Trade in the Eighteenth Century: An Old Regime Business*. University of Wisconsin Press, Madison.

Voyages Database
2008   Voyages: The Trans-Atlantic Slave Trade Database. Available online at http://www.slavevoyages.org.

Watts, David
1987   *The West Indies: Patterns of Development, Culture and Environmental Change since 1492*. Cambridge University Press, Cambridge.

7

Surveying a Long-Term Settlement on Potato Hill, Montserrat

KRYSTA RYZEWSKI AND JOHN F. CHERRY

The starting points for plantation-era archaeology on the small Lesser Antillean island of Montserrat (see Figure 1.2) differ from those on islands where the physical evidence of plantations remains relatively intact and where estate plans, plat maps, and other types of documentation provide a wealth of information about the historic landscape. On Montserrat, surviving archival records are modest in quantity (there appear to be none, in fact, for Potato Hill, the focus of this chapter), and an active volcano has caused widespread damage to more than half of the island's built environment during the past two decades. As a result, other strategies for carrying out historical archaeological research become necessary, especially when the focus is on the "spaces in between" the industrial and domestic centers of plantation estates (Armstrong 2003; Delle 1998, 2014).

As an example of such strategies, in this chapter we present evidence from a systematic, gridded survey and modest test excavations conducted on Potato Hill, Montserrat, in 2013. Potato Hill is a prominent elongated knoll that runs east–west and divides Little Bay from Carr's Bay on the northwest coast of Montserrat (Figure 7.1). With its relatively flat summit, steep slopes, and (at the western end) vertical sea cliff, this location was both attractive for settlement and defensively advantageous; it also had access to water sources from the small ghauts (stream courses) that run down into the bays to north and south. Archaeological evidence indicates that Potato Hill was home to a small but long-term or repeatedly occupied settlement between the seventeenth and nineteenth centuries. Since it was nestled within the bounds of three modest plantation estates that were active during the peak of the island's eighteenth-century sugar economy and into the nineteenth century, understanding this site—as we aim to

Figure 7.1. The archaeological landscape of Potato Hill (A) includes the Little Bay Plantation (B), Little Bay (C), Carr's Bay (D), and the Gun Hill battery (E).

demonstrate—depends on setting it within a broader context and employing a multisited, multimethod strategy of inquiry.

The origin of the unusual toponym "Potato Hill" is not known. The hilltop settlement may have been home to an early community of Irish indentured servants who arrived from neighboring islands in the 1630s and composed the majority of Montserrat's labor force until the large-scale importation of African slaves replaced them by the turn of the eighteenth century (Akenson 1997; English 1930; McAtackney et al. 2014; Ryzewski and Cherry 2015; Zacek 2010). Local accounts recall a community atop Potato Hill during the nineteenth century populated by free and recently emancipated Afro-Caribbean residents. Neither of these suggestions, however, can be verified by firm historical evidence. A 1903 photograph of Potato Hill and its environs shows the hilltop unoccupied and overrun with vegetation, confirming that the settlement was abandoned by the turn of the twentieth century (Montserrat National Trust, Olveston, Montserrat, Sturge Family Papers). A primary aim of our discussion is to evaluate the archaeological evidence from Potato Hill in ways that might contribute to identifying the communities who lived there during the plantation era, about whom the historical records remain relatively silent. The material culture recovered from the 2013 survey informs a multiscalar interpretation that extends from individual dwellings, to the hilltop community, and to the wider northern region of Montserrat where the settlement was positioned within the island's plantation-dominated landscape.

Archaeology on Montserrat

Montserrat is a challenging and unusual setting in which to do archaeology. In comparison to others of the Leeward Islands, not much archaeology has happened there. Important work was conducted in the 1980s and 1990s by David Watters and colleagues at the site of Trants and several other prehistoric sites (Watters 1980, 1994; Watters and Scaglion 1980, 1994), and by Lydia Pulsipher and Conrad Mac Goodwin at Galways Plantation (Pulsipher 1982, 1991, 1994; Pulsipher and Goodwin 1982, 1999, 2001). A few short-term salvage excavations have also taken place since the 1970s (e.g., Bocancea et al. 2013; Miles and Munby 2006; Petersen and Watters 1988). The most recent sustained archaeological investigation is the excavation by Mary Beaudry and colleagues at the Little Bay Plantation (Beaudry and Pulsipher 2007; Beaudry et al. 2007; MacLean 2015), no more than a few hundred meters from Potato Hill, a point to which we return below.

There is no trained archaeologist resident on Montserrat, no official sites and monuments record exists, and a small national museum opened at Little Bay only in 2012. But more significant in shaping present-day conditions are the natural catastrophes that have struck Montserrat over the past three decades. Hurricane Hugo devastated the island in 1989 (Berke and Beatley 1997:82–116), and only six years later the Soufrière Hills volcano sprang to life, completely burying the capital town of Plymouth and forcing two-thirds of the island population to emigrate (Odbert et al. 2011; Pattullo 2000). It created a still-dangerous exclusion zone that encompasses more than half the island.

Life continues on a reduced scale in the north, where the Montserratian government, with British assistance, is engaged in the drawn-out process of establishing a new capital town in the Little Bay/Carr's Bay area, alongside ambitious plans to attract tourists. It is important to understand that our established archaeological research plans are in reality constantly in dialogue with the cultural resource management needs of the Montserrat National Trust, the small and underfunded agency responsible for all aspects of cultural heritage on the island, with whom we collaborate closely. Since the Trust lacks trained professionals in archaeology or heritage management, it often calls upon us during our field seasons to assist in the examination of sites that it feels are of particular significance to the island's history and that are usually also threatened by development. Such was the case in 2013, when—prompted by the convergence of research design, exigency, and serendipity—we were asked by the Trust to return to Potato Hill and conduct a full-scale, systematic archaeological survey of the cleared hilltop.

Survey and Landscape Archaeology on Montserrat

Recent development activities have inevitably overlapped with and become entangled in our own project, Survey and Landscape Archaeology on Montserrat (SLAM), under way since January 2010. This project adopts an explicitly diachronic, transconquest perspective that treats Montserrat's history as a continuum of transformative processes (cf. Armstrong 2003). With this scope, and in its equal involvement of both prehistorians and historical archaeologists, our work is in fact rather unusual for the Caribbean, a region in which the so-called Columbian divide has become entrenched in the framing of archaeological research questions. The project's specific goals include exploring the earliest human colonization of Montserrat, examining the island's long-term patterns of settlement, searching for evidence of interactions between Amerindian peoples and early European colonists, and gathering systematic knowledge about the island's multicultural landscape—both during and after the plantation era (Cherry et al. 2014; Cherry and Ryzewski 2014; Cherry, Ryzewski, and Leppard 2012; Cherry, Ryzewski, Leppard, and Bocancea 2012; Ryzewski and Cherry 2015).

In pursuit of these goals over the past six years, we have foregrounded the use of archaeological survey methods, including both large-scale (extensive) and intensive tract surveys; ground-truthing of LiDAR imagery; and gridded, total collection at specific sites, often accompanied by differential GPS mapping and sometimes by shovel test pitting or other modest types of exploratory excavation. This overall strategy can be characterized as a multisited, multiscale, multimethod approach (Ryzewski 2012). It has some definite advantages for our research goals on Montserrat, as we aim to illustrate in our Potato Hill case study. It should be understood from the outset, however, that in presenting our procedures on Montserrat, we do not wish to be prescriptive about appropriate methods for other islands or to conflate very different circumstances that exist elsewhere in the Caribbean.

Altogether, the SLAM archaeological survey has so far recorded 13 historic-period sites in the northern safe zone of Montserrat that are located beyond the central industrial or residential areas of known plantation estates. Some locations, including Potato Hill and Rendezvous Village, produced evidence of modest settlements apparently occupied for generations by non-elite communities whose members would doubtless have contributed to the plantation economy in various capacities, perhaps as laborers, servants, craftsmen, traders, farmers, militiamen, or mariners. As illustrated by Douglas Armstrong's (2003) investigation of the East End creole community on St. John (U.S. Virgin Islands), such settlements beyond the core of plantation estates existed and thrived for centuries—150 years in the case of East End. Residents of these communities beyond the plantation often performed valuable roles in the intra- and interisland socioeconomic networks in ways that continued to support and contribute to the plantation economy. Potato Hill's proximity to a range of other locales and sites of various types—the plantation estates of Little Bay, Rendezvous, Thatch Valley, Silver Hill, Drummonds, and Geralds, all within easy reach; the military installations at Gun Hill, Carr's Bay, and Valentine Ghaut; and the three bays in the near vicinity (Carr's, Little Bay, and Rendezvous)—inevitably shaped the daily lives of those who resided on this hilltop (Figure 7.1). In other words, Potato Hill was not a remote, unattached settlement, and the plantation estates in Montserrat's northernmost region did not exist in isolation. These sorts of contextual and multiscalar landscape perspectives, yielded by archaeological survey and coupled with historical research, move the focus of Montserrat's plantation history well beyond individual estates, extending the breadth and depth of understandings about the island's plantation system and its social and environmental contexts over time.

History of Survey at Potato Hill

Establishing what existed atop Potato Hill was an important priority for SLAM in light of the presence nearby of a prehistoric Late Ceramic Age site near the sea at Little Bay and the well-known Little Bay Plantation (an early historic-period site previously referred to as the William Carr Estate, situated between the new National Museum and the Montserrat Cultural Centre, under excavation, as noted above, since 2006). No archaeological exploration had taken place on Potato Hill prior to the inception of the SLAM Project in 2010. It sits squarely in the epicenter of planned development activities for the new capital town of Little Bay. Its role in this development has changed almost on a yearly basis, but the current plan is for the installation there of a gated luxury villa complex. SLAM made Potato Hill an early target for surface investigation in 2010 and subsequently conducted three limited, extensive-mode surveys of small portions of the hilltop while it was still covered by vegetation (in 2010, 2012, and 2014) as well as a more labor-intensive, gridded, systematic survey of the cleared western third of the hilltop (in 2013). These four survey operations have produced a total of 4,960 artifacts, the vast majority of which can be dated to the historic period on Montserrat (i.e., post-1632, the date of initial European settlement).

Extensive surveys faced a hilltop choked with a dense tangle of poisonous manchineel trees and areas in between trees obscured by knee-high grasses. These conditions made archaeological survey both dangerous and very difficult; nonetheless, by inspecting a number of areas of erosion, especially at the edges of the summit, it was possible to make an artifact collection that provided some sense of the occupational history of the hill, with abundant early historic materials present. By crawling among the manchineel trees, literally on hands and knees, the survey team was able to locate a rock-cut cistern, a waterstone (a natural rock hollowed out to trap water), and the foundations of a rectangular, stone-built structure toward the eastern end of the hill associated with pottery, glass, and other artifacts that date to the seventeenth through nineteenth centuries, confirming the presence of a modest settlement atop Potato Hill (designated Site 6 by SLAM; Ryzewski et al. 2010).

Initial development work on the hill began during the first two weeks of December 2012, when a bulldozer road was driven up the southern slope and onto its central summit, with another cut running from it to the northern and eastern areas (as seen in Figure 7.1). At this time the western portion of the hilltop, together with its northern and southern slopes, were stripped of all vegetation; careful inspection showed that the bulldozer had removed vegetation but not cut into the topsoil, and on the whole we have reason to believe that any lateral displacement of soil and artifacts was minimal. Construction activities had paused by the time the SLAM team arrived for the 2013 field season, at which point we and the Montserrat National Trust agreed to prioritize the documentation of archaeological remains across the now-accessible, cleared western third of Potato Hill.

When survey began in May 2013, the hilltop was in excellent condition for archaeological surface survey work, owing to a dry winter: ground visibility conditions were good and—importantly—fairly uniform across the whole western hilltop. This condition, plus the recent clearance of the manchineel growth, suggested the opportunity for an intensive, gridded, surface survey of all available cleared areas on the hill. The objectives of this gridded survey were twofold: (1) to collect as large and as representative a sample of surface artifacts as possible in order to establish the full range of periods of use and/or settlement on Potato Hill; and (2) to control this collection spatially, in order (for example) to be able to map areas of the hill most intensively used in different period of the past so as to examine the differential distributions of specific categories of find (e.g., clay tobacco pipe fragments), or to associate artifacts closely with any structural remains encountered (Ryzewski and Cherry 2013).

The survey laid out a systematic grid of 103 survey squares measuring 10 m × 10 m, covering the entirety of the cleared area. Grid squares were numbered A–K (east to west) and 0–10 (north to south). This grid encompassed the entire western half of Potato Hill, from the sea cliff on the west to the central area that had not yet been cleared of manchineel, and including the gently sloping summit and the upper parts of the northern and southern slopes. We chose to focus our work on the western portion of the hill not only because of the superior visibility conditions there but also because preliminary inspection had indicated high densities of material, some of it clearly early seventeenth century—in contrast to the eastern end, which so far has produced predominantly eighteenth- and nineteenth-century finds.

With our small team and a few local volunteers, a 100 percent collection of all surface artifacts was conducted. We note here that this type of spatially controlled, nonintrusive, systematic surface collection has become standard practice in several parts of the world, such as the Mediterranean (e.g., Johnson and Millett 2013), as a means for the detailed spatial and temporal characterization of the plow zone archaeology of large sites. It is still extremely rare in the Caribbean, however, where shovel test pitting has generally been preferred. Among the very few comparable examples of which we are aware is a 2011 survey at the Mount Plantation on Barbados (Finch et al. 2013; although see Meniketti 2009 and Watters 1980 for other approaches involving pedestrian survey in the Lesser Antilles). We do not claim that our methodology is novel, but it is one that has produced prolific results that we do not think could have been achieved using other types of procedures.

Following the survey of these 103 units (covering an area of 1.03 ha), we placed six 50 cm × 50 cm shovel test pits (STP) atop the hill at strategically chosen locations (i.e., spots where survey indicated very fragmentary structural remains). Although these did confirm the existence of built structures, now razed to ground level, they produced only 26 artifacts in total, all of them historic, representing less than half of one percent of the

4,160 artifacts recovered by the gridded survey. Such efforts faced a familiar challenge we have experienced during shovel test pitting at several other sites on the island (Thatch Valley, Valentine Ghaut, Rocklands, and Glendon Hospital)—namely, that the region's pyroclastic soil deposits are shallow, largely composed of very hard-compacted clay, with most artifacts on or very near the surface (although stratigraphic layers are present). It is not our intention to assert the superiority of surface collection to STP excavation as a survey technique; in fact, we argue that multimethod survey strategies are essential for understanding patterns of diachronic landscape transformation in both vertical and horizontal spatial dimensions. In the case of Potato Hill, we owe our findings—the recovery of a very large artifact sample from the gridded survey, with excellent spatial and chronological structure—to the use of efficient surface collection *and* STP survey techniques.

Potato Hill in Context: The Silver Hill Region, Carr's Bay, and Little Bay

Our 2014–2015 search of the Montserrat historical archives (now held in the Montserrat Public Library in Brades), as well as research in several government and university archival repositories in Great Britain and the United States, has not yet located any detailed inventories, maps, or deeds relating to Potato Hill during the plantation era. More thorough archival research is ongoing, but even at this stage it is interesting to note that Potato Hill remains elusive in the otherwise exhaustive descriptions of its surrounding landscape, which appear in multiple eighteenth-century accounts of property transfers and disputes within the records of the King's Bench and Court of Common Pleas Records. Potato Hill is not mentioned in the 1739 division of the island's northern estates of Silver Hill and Little Bay among the Piper family (Montserrat Public Library Archive, Deed of Covenant between Christopher Piper, Robert Piper, William Piper, and John Piper. August 12, 1746, Court of King's Bench and Common Pleas, Pleas, 1771–1774, Box 82–50, pp. 82–50). Nor is it mentioned in the 1765 property transfer of the Little Bay Plantation to Robert Piper, which contains an illustrative description of the trees, woods, watercourses, and pastures of the hill's immediate setting (Montserrat Public Library Archive, Richard Roe v. John Doe, Court of King's Bench and Common Pleas, 1771–1774, Box 82–50, pp. 400). Later, in the records of a 1783 trespass case, the adjacent 450-acre sugar- and cotton-producing Carr Plantation is described, along with an extensive account of the boundaries of other northern properties (Montserrat Public Library Archive, Richard Roe v. John Doe, Court King's Bench and Common Pleas, 1778–1783. Box 82–105, p. 351). In this description, all of the known northern estates are mentioned, as are topographic landmarks and various landscape features, including place-names such as Indian Creek; yet Potato Hill goes unmentioned. The only possible reference to Potato Hill appears in a 1756 inventory attached to the last will and testament of Joseph Gerald, in which a description of his lands in the immediate area surrounding the hilltop include an itemization for a small crop of sugar grown on "Potato Piece" (Lamont Library Archives, Harvard University, Cambridge, Massachusetts, microfilm, Indenture between Mary Gerald and Edmund Akers, guardians of the Last Will and Testament of Joseph Herald. March 1, 1756. Record 169, Reel 3). Nevertheless, the 2013 archaeological survey produced a preponderance of eighteenth-century material culture, confirming that the hill was certainly occupied during the periods when the aforementioned records were entered. Why this hilltop community eluded generations of documentation is a question that our current historical research seeks to answer.

Although individual maps and plat drawings detailing plantation estates in the seventeenth or eighteenth centuries have yet to be located, a most unusual document, the 1673 map of Montserrat included as part of the Blathwayt Atlas (John Carter Brown Library, Brown University, Manuscript Map, accession number 8981–30, *Montserrat Island*), provides a critical resource for understanding Potato Hill within the context of the island's northernmost Silver Hill region. This extraordinary map depicts the island not in a standard Cartesian view from above but rather as an oval with a hole in the middle, since it is composed of a series of connected views of the island as seen from a vessel offshore (Pulsipher 1987). It illustrates the Montserratian landscape as it had been radically transformed during just four decades since European colonial settlers first set foot on the island in 1632. Large-scale clearance of the mature neotropical forest is apparent around and especially above newly established estates—the large, open fields necessary for sugarcane cultivation, made possible only by the large-scale arrival of enslaved Africans beginning in the 1650s and 1660s. The map's detail is remarkable, showing not only the new capital town of Plymouth and its bustling harbor but also individual named estates and buildings evidently visible from out at sea, including estate owners' houses and industrial structures such as windmills and sugar refineries (Pulsipher 1986). In addition, the Blathwayt map shows several estates, identified by their owners' names, along the northwest coast of the island: these include the plantations and "works" owned by Capt. William Carr, Maj. Thomas Caines, John Ely, Capt. Pieter Cove, Theodor Lowring, and Pieter Schaama. Potato Hill is clearly visible as a topographic feature on the 1673 map, but it is unlabeled. It is nonetheless clear that Potato Hill was nestled in close proximity to nearby estates, especially the Little Bay Plantation.

Currently Potato Hill is separated by, literally, the width of a cricket pitch from the Little Bay Plantation estate (Figure 7.1). This proximity inevitably raises the question of the relationship between these two sites and their relative status as well as poses an interesting problem in resolving archaeological, archival, and cartographic evidence. The few records that are available for the northern estates show that in the seventeenth century Capt. William Carr owned 300 acres in the Little Bay / Carr's Bay area (Beaudry et al. 2007; MacLean 2015). Carr's Estate would predate the 1667 French attacks (Pulsipher 1986:67) since his ownership of these lands was restored by the 1668 Act of Montserrat, and the lands must surely have included Potato Hill, which separates the two bays. In fact, the 1673 map appears at first glance to place Carr's house and plantation on top of Potato Hill, but there are major problems of scale and perspective in this most unusual map that, coupled with a lack of substantial mid-seventeenth-century archaeological evidence from our surveys and excavations, make such an identification unlikely.

Immediately east of Potato Hill, the Little Bay Plantation excavations have revealed evidence of a great house, a cattle mill, a boiling house, a village of enslaved laborers, and several other structures whose function is not yet clear. Archaeology has shown that the plantation house burned at the end of the eighteenth century, possibly ending residential occupation at the site, although following emancipation the estate apparently transitioned to cotton and lime juice production in the nineteenth century, and to a cattle estate in the early twentieth century (MacLean 2015). Useful as these site-specific data from Little Bay are, they are difficult to understand without putting them in their regional context in a way that accounts for the estate's interactions with the community on Potato Hill and at other nearby sites and estates. This work has revealed the diverse historic landscape of northern Montserrat. For example, along the lower flanks of Silver Hill (the highest point in the north) there existed the Thatch Valley and Valentine Ghaut estates. These small estates of about 100–250 acres indicate that the northern region's arid climate and dry soils were not well suited for sugar and cotton production, and the landscape was instead developed to serve as pasture and grounds for growing provisions to be used on Montserrat's larger, southern estates or perhaps for export (Reports to the Secretary of State on the Past and Present State of Her Majesty's Colonial Possessions, transmitted with the Blue Books for 1855, Vol. XLII:100).

More subtle clues to the occupation and uses of Potato Hill and its surrounding plantation-era landscapes are also visible in the hundreds of isolated manmade features that exist beyond the industrial and residential cores of sugar estate sites. To date, the SLAM Project has recorded over 300 such features. While often not easily datable, the majority clearly relate to plantation-era landscape modifications, resource management, property limits, and access routes between settlements (e.g., terracing, boundary walls and other landscape divisions, water collection or irrigation features, tracks and pathways, rock-cut ovens, pottery scatters, etc.).

As Pulsipher similarly observed in her work at Galways Plantation in the island's south, some of these less prominent landscape features dotting the Little Bay / Carr's Bay landscape speak to planters' abilities to organize production and domestic activities effectively within generally inhospitable environmental constraints (Pulsipher 1990). Dozens of such archaeological features have been discovered by survey in the Carr's Bay / Little Bay / Rendezvous Bay area, such as extensive terracing systems between Drummonds and Little Bay, water catchment stones along the slopes of Gun Hill and the Little Bay estates, and irrigation systems across the Rendezvous and Silver Hill estate landscapes (Cherry, Ryzewski, and Leppard 2012: 290–297, fig. 5). While dating such features is certainly challenging, we are inclined to regard most, if not virtually all of them, as belonging to the historic era, since on Montserrat—as on most of the islands of the Lesser Antilles—the majority of prehistoric settlements appear to be confined to locations on or very close to the coast (Cherry et al. 2014).

About one feature within the immediate ambit of Potato Hill and the Little Bay Plantation it is now possible to provide more detailed information. Gun Hill was, until 2013, located at the southern extremity of the Little Bay / Carr's Bay development area (Figure 7.1). In 2010 we located and mapped a few modest structural remains protruding from the tall grass atop this hill, speculatively identifying the isolated feature as a modest signal-beacon station (following suggestions in Crandall 2000). SLAM archaeologists returned to Gun Hill in 2013 to conduct rescue archaeology in advance of the hill's demolition to accommodate a projected new berth for large cruise ships. Clearance of the vegetation and subsequent excavation revealed that what we had earlier thought to be a signal station was in fact a remarkably well-preserved, D-shaped gun platform (Cherry and Ryzewski 2013). A very small number of diagnostic artifacts was recovered during the excavation, including white salt-glazed stoneware, coarseware, Staffordshire slipware, and creamware, dating the use of this gun platform to the mid- to late eighteenth century. The military structure on Gun Hill is closely paralleled by the Bransby Point Battery (Crandall 2000: 343–346), farther to the south on the west coast, completed sometime between 1667 and 1693 and part of the same defensive coastal artillery system installed by order of the British in response to attacks, or threats of attack, by the French, Dutch, Carib Indians, and privateers. These attacks spanned the seventeenth and eighteenth centuries, culminating in the French occupation of Montserrat between 1782 and 1784. Unfortunately, Gun Hill—both the site and the entire hill on which it sat—was demolished in September 2013, despite efforts by the Montserrat National Trust and the SLAM Project to encourage its preservation.

In summary, our archaeological landscape survey of the Silver Hill region of northern Montserrat has shown that plantation-era sites of different functions (e.g., industrial, residential, agricultural, military) operated more or less side by side. The Drummonds, Rendezvous, Silver Hill, Geralds, and Little Bay plantations coexisted in fairly close proximity to each other. There were also British military installations in the vicinity, such as the 1693 Carr's Bay Battery (Crandall 2000: 341–342) and the newly discovered substantial eighteenth-century cannon platform atop Gun Hill, overlooking Carr's Bay (Cherry and Ryzewski 2013). Although it does not receive attention in the historical records, Potato Hill sat squarely in the center of these residential, industrial, and defensive activities. It is within and with comparative reference to this dynamic landscape setting that we interpret the findings from our 2013 survey.

2013 Potato Hill Survey Findings

The gridded survey of Potato Hill yielded 4,160 artifacts over an area of 1.03 ha. Artifact density was not random but rather correlated with at least four domestic structures whose locations we identified during the survey. The overall artifact assemblage recovered from the survey is a rich and diverse array of material culture dominated by early historic ceramics, which comprise 71 percent (n = 2,938) of the assemblage. The 2,414 temporally diagnostic historic ceramics in the assemblage, coupled with supporting evidence from other artifacts, suggest that this westernmost area of Potato

Hill was inhabited from the seventeenth century through at least the first third of the nineteenth century, although the majority of diagnostic ceramics and tobacco pipe stems have manufacturing dates within the eighteenth century (Ryzewski and Cherry 2013). No diagnostic prehistoric pottery was recovered during the 2013 survey. It may be noted that 17.8 percent (n = 524) of the ceramic assemblage was composed of undecorated coarseware sherds, most of which are visually indistinguishable from comparable materials found on prehistoric sites of the Late Ceramic period across Montserrat (Bocancea et al. 2013). Nonetheless, further excavation of the A4 structure in 2015 has now produced hundreds of coarseware sherds in sealed stratigraphic contexts of later seventeenth- to eighteenth-century date, and we think it most likely that all of the coarsewares from the survey similarly belong to the historical era.

Distributional Patterns

Notable clusters of artifacts were identified in several different areas of the survey grid (Figure 7.2). These artifact concentrations do not necessarily indicate the precise location of past structures but rather occur close to and downslope of observed structural remains (e.g., the A4 structure is located near the B1–B3/C1–C2 concentration, and the D7 structure next to the C7–C8/D8 cluster). The largest concentration of artifacts was collected from C8, and it included materials ranging in date from the late seventeenth to early nineteenth century. The fact that these artifact clusters roughly correlated with discrete settlement areas (i.e., households) and with artifacts from particular time periods suggests the possibility that the proximate structures were inhabited at different times during the hilltop settlement's history. The densest concentration of artifacts occurred in only 18 survey squares (approximately 17.5 percent of the survey area) but contained 43 percent of all ceramics collected from the survey. Notable differences among these assemblages included the presence of two beads (one blue glass and one pink carnelian) and a reworked ceramic token in the cluster surrounding A4, the highest concentration of metal objects (n = 8) and a large quantity of lithics (n = 16) in the H4 cluster, and the presence of seventeenth- to early-eighteenth-century ceramics in J3–J5 and the immediate vicinity (e.g., two sherds of sgraffito, two of borderware, one of Bellarmine, and one of North Devon gravel-tempered ware). Temporal distinctions between some of the settlement areas are apparent. For example, the cluster surrounding the A4 structure contained the highest proportion of whiteware and pearlware ceramics on the site; by contrast, the materials in

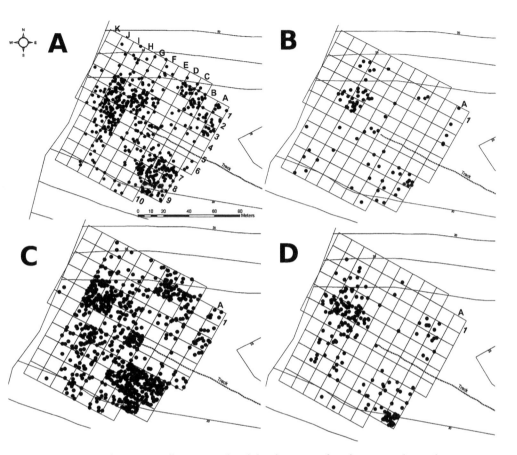

Figure 7.2. The Potato Hill survey grid and the clustering of artifact material types by density and quantity recovered. Corresponding alphanumerical labels for the survey grid squares are provided in Figure 7.1. (A) coarseware pottery, (B) lithics, (C) glass, (D) tobacco pipes.

I3/I4 and J3–J5 have predominantly seventeenth- to mid-eighteenth-century manufacturing dates. This latter cluster hints at the possible presence of a seventeenth-century settlement on Potato Hill belonging to some of the first generations of settlers on Montserrat, and it is also significant as the largest seventeenth- to early-eighteenth-century assemblage yet recovered on the island.

Structural Remains

Two grid squares, A4 and D7, revealed intact, aboveground, stone-built structural foundations. Faced stone and mortar rubble concentrations in

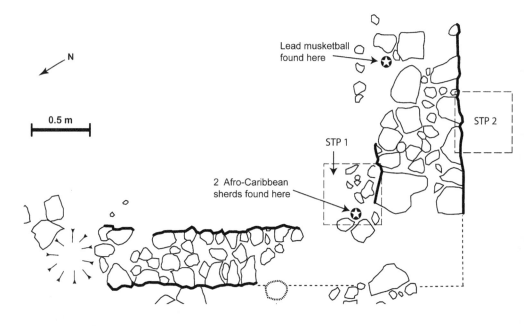

Figure 7.3. Plan of the structural remains in D7. (Image by Emanuela Bocancea)

two additional areas, H4 and B2, also suggested structures that have not survived. All four locations were further examined via six 50 cm × 50 cm STPs. Those in H4 and B2 did not locate belowground structural remains.

The structure in square D7 had a stone foundation consisting of exterior and interior faced, rubble-filled, mortared walls (Figure 7.3). The south and west walls of the structure's foundation were well preserved at ground level, but the north and east walls are now gone. It measured about 3 m (N-S) by 2.2 m (E-W)—dimensions consistent with those of a small domestic dwelling. The construction, use of space, and age of the D7 structure were examined by digging one STP in the interior of the southwest corner and another against the west wall's exterior face. These produced a piece of glass, several large coarseware (Afro-Caribbean) sherds in the corner where the two walls met, and a lead musket ball lodged in the south wall. The STPs revealed that the square, faced, and mortared foundation stones of the west wall began 20 cm below the surface and were not set directly on the bedrock but rather on a shallow deposit of clay; no foundation trenches dug into the bedrock or clay were present. In the area downslope of the structure (especially in grid squares C7 and C8), a substantial quantity of artifacts was recovered, suggesting a possible area of use or refuse-disposal associated with the house. Wider excavation here in 2015 produced no further architectural remains, but an enlarged artifact sample places this structure's occupation in the period from the late seventeenth to late eighteenth centuries.

Remains of a second stone foundation were located in the A4 grid square, consisting of a single course of faced stones with rubble packing and intermittent mortar; this structure probably measured about 5.3 m (west wall) by 2 m (south wall). At the southeast and southwest corners, piles of stones are positioned around hollow circular openings, possibly suggesting the former location of posts to support part of a wooden superstructure. In the areas downslope and to the northwest of A4 (especially in grid squares B1–B3), a substantial quantity of artifacts was recovered dating primarily to the early to mid-nineteenth century but with some earlier materials present. Two STPs were excavated in this structure: one in the interior of the structure, in order to investigate the flat interior space of the building, and another against the exterior west wall. These excavations uncovered a clay deposit interspersed with charcoal, mortar, and brick in the interior of the structure and also determined that the stone foundation of the structure sat directly on top of the underlying bedrock. The combination of the architectural elements, the artifacts found, and the clay soil mixed with architectural debris inside the walls confirm that this was the former location of a durable structure. In 2015 further excavations were undertaken in an area hitherto obscured by dense manchineel scrub immediately adjacent to the structure to its east. These revealed a large stone platform, bounded by well-constructed walls set directly on bedrock, measuring about 4 m (N–S) by 6 m (E–W); this may have served as some kind of courtyard area. Of the abundant ceramic finds, the earliest are later seventeenth century but the majority eighteenth century; over 200 sherds of handmade coarsewares were also found (Brace 2015).

In keeping with the predominant vernacular architectural practices across plantation-era Montserrat, the materials recovered from the STPs (e.g., nail fragments, mortar, brick) suggest that the structures in both A4 and D7 were probably wooden buildings set atop rubble-filled stone foundations.

Artifact Summary

The assemblage from the 2013 Potato Hill gridded survey consists of a diverse array of historic material culture. A total of 2,938 ceramics was collected, with historic-period ceramics in general (n = 2,414) and creamware

Table 7.1. Artifact quantities, minimum vessel count, and proportion of assemblage for the 2013 Potato Hill survey collection

Ware Type	Minimum vessel count	Sherd count	Proportion ceramic assemblage (n = 2,938)	Proportion overall assemblage (n = 4,160)
Agateware	2	11	0.4	0.2
Bellarmine	1	5	0.2	0.1
Borderware	1	5	0.2	0.1
Coarseware	21	524	17.8	12.6
Creamware	39	1295	44.0	31.0
Pearlware	39	212	7.2	5.1
Porcelain	13	153	5.2	3.7
Redware	10	48	1.6	1.2
Sgraffito	2	9	0.3	0.2
Staffordshire Slipware	13	27	0.9	0.7
Stoneware—British Brown	see varieties	53	1.8	1.3
Stoneware—Nottingham	see varieties	4	0.1	0.1
Stoneware—Other	see varieties	12	0.4	0.3
Stoneware—Red	see varieties	2	0.1	0.1
Stoneware—varieties combined	22	n/a	n/a	n/a
Stoneware—White Salt Glazed	19	149	5.1	3.4
Tin-Glazed	14	97	3.3	2.3
Westerwald	2	21	0.7	0.5
Whiteware	25	300	10.2	7.2
Yellowware	1	11	0.4	0.2

in particular (n = 1,295) being the most frequently occurring artifact types (Table 7.1).

The earliest historic ceramics were found in the vicinity of the J3–J5 cluster and include sgraffito (1650–1740), North Devon gravel-tempered ware (1680–1750), and borderware (seventeenth to early-eighteenth century) (Miller 1983; Noel Hume 1970). Significantly, Potato Hill is the only site among the 50 we have surveyed throughout the northern half of the island where any of these three pottery types have been located. Of equal importance is the fact that survey on the west side of Potato Hill produced very few examples of transfer print, industrial slipware, or hand-painted whiteware, three of the most frequently occurring ceramics found at nearby postemancipation settlements in Drummonds, Rendezvous Bluff, and Rendezvous Village as well as on the east side of Potato Hill. These ceramic varieties and their mid- to late-nineteenth-century production dates may suggest a shift in settlement location from Potato Hill and other enclaves to proximate inland, inward-facing, and upland locales in the postemancipation period, including the nearby settlements of Rendezvous, Drummonds, and Geralds.

In addition to ceramics, we recovered a sizable quantity of bottle glass (20 percent of the assemblage) and tobacco pipe fragments (5 percent of the assemblage) across the entire survey area. Although tobacco pipe stem bore-sizes do not always provide a reliable index of the date of manufacture, bore diameters of recovered pipe stems were measured to obtain a general sense of the average date of manufacture of materials present in the assemblage (see Agbe-Davies 2006; Bradley 2000; Heighton and Deagan 1971). The most frequently occurring bore size was 7/64", equivalent to a manufacturing date range of 1650–1680. This provides only a very rough estimate but one that is useful in the absence of diagnostic makers' marks or decorations on the majority (93 percent) of the 188 pipe fragments.

Iron nails and architectural materials (e.g., brick, mortar, plaster) were not widespread across the survey area and tended to be concentrated close to the structures in D7 and A4. Additional concentrations of architectural materials in the proximity of the artifact clusters in grid squares J3–J5 and B1–B3 support the artifactual data in suggesting that other structures were also present on the hill.

Lithic materials compose 2.5 percent of the assemblage (n = 104), a fact that at first sight might be taken as a sign of Amerindian activity. But, in fact, chert flakes and other débitage have been encountered on many of the historic-era sites we have investigated in northern Montserrat. The absence on Potato Hill of diagnostic prehistoric pottery suggests either that it was not the location of substantial settlement before the arrival of Europeans on Montserrat or, much less likely, that historic-period European and Afro-Caribbean settlement on the hill has eradicated traces of past Amerindian settlement. We have already noted that a substantial quantity of coarseware pottery was recovered (17.8 percent of the assemblage), which only future analyses can determine to be of local or nonlocal manufacture but which we currently think is most likely to have been used in tandem with the historic-era decorated ceramics of European origin.

Material Culture Interpretations

Viewing Potato Hill's material culture within the context of its environs and in light of comparable settlements from other islands in the region may assist in understanding the identities of the communities that lived on Potato Hill and the intra-island and regional economies in which they participated over the course of some two centuries.

Several special finds recovered during the 2013 survey provide insights into the material world of the Potato Hill residents (Figure 7.4). They include three triangular lead wedges, three lead coattail weights, at least one tool refashioned from a glass bottle as well as five lead shot, two lead net weights, four blue glass and pink carnelian beads, three reworked ceramic tokens made from tin-glazed and white salt-glazed stoneware pottery, two drilled creamware ceramic fragments, and two sherds from a Bidston Lighthouse pitcher of ca. 1790. Two additional tin-glazed pottery tokens, one drilled creamware sherd, a chert core, a blue glass decorative jewel, and additional lead net weights were recovered during SLAM's other surveys of Potato Hill before and after 2013. Taken together, these finds signal that the Potato Hill settlement's residents during the eighteenth and early nineteenth centuries acted resourcefully and strategically in refashioning broken objects into objects of personal adornment and trade, and by participating in local economies (e.g., fishing, processing meats, manufacturing objects).

These special finds are remarkable, but they are not unique to the Potato Hill settlement. Similarly refashioned ceramic tokens (sometimes also referred to as "gaming pieces") have been collected from the flanks of Gun Hill and excavated from the nearby Little Bay Plantation (MacLean 2015). Reworked, knapped bottle glass has been recovered during our surveys at several sites, including the Blakes and Thatch Valley estates (Ryzewski and Cherry 2015). These special finds were symbolic material expressions that facilitated residents' participation within a larger informal economy and system of socioeconomic value across at least the northern region of the island (see Hauser 2011:435). Regionally, refashioned objects were not altogether uncommon within non-elite house sites of free or enslaved residents elsewhere in the Caribbean, as Armstrong (2010:153) has illustrated in connection with the carved ceramics from the slave settlement at the Seville Plantation in Jamaica and as Jerome Handler and Diane Wallman (2014) discuss in reference to the Crève Coeur settlement on Martinique. In daily practice, these objects were part of the adaptive strategies that residents

Figure 7.4. Special finds recovered from surveys on Potato Hill, 2010–2014. *Clockwise from top left*: pottery fragments modified into tokens and drilled pendants; lead coattail weights, musket balls, net weights and triangular tokens; blue glass and pink carnelian beads.

employed to mediate the economic hardships and scarcity of materials they faced.

Coupled with information about the small size of residential structures on Potato Hill, the predominance of unmatched, undecorated ceramic wares and the absence of luxury items in the survey assemblage indicate that this site was a non-elite settlement. Across the survey area, we recovered a minimum of 226 individual vessels, with creamware (n = 39), pearlware (n = 39), whiteware (n = 25), stoneware (n = 22), and coarseware (n = 21) represented in the largest quantities (see Table 7.1). One noteworthy trend is that, of the 226 vessels recorded, 39 percent are flatware (e.g., serving plates, saucers), with a notable amount of white salt-glazed flatware (n = 19) represented in the assemblage. Overall, the diversity of ceramic types and morphologies in the minimum vessel count indicate a shift over time from a variety of imported European ceramics in the seventeenth and eighteenth centuries to a predominance of pearlware and whiteware in the nineteenth century. Similar trends have been documented in excavations of multiperiod household deposits at the Green Castle Estate on Antigua (Rebovich 2011).

A comparison of the Potato Hill assemblage with those recovered from two other village settlements within the British Caribbean—the slave villages of Seville Estate (Jamaica) and Bois Cotlette Estate (Dominica)—does not immediately reveal the identity of the Potato Hill residents in terms of their ethnicity, occupations, or status as free or enslaved. At the Seville Estate (SE), creamware composed 28.88 percent of the overall assemblage (n = 5,474) excavated from an enslaved settlement area, while at Bois Cotlette Estate (BC), it accounted for 19.3 percent of the total assemblage from the estate's slave village (n = 204) (Hauser 2011:436); creamware sherds represent 31 percent of the total survey assemblage from Potato Hill (PH) (n = 4,160), a proportion slightly higher but generally consistent with the artifact patterning at these two enslaved sites on Jamaica and Dominica.

While some of the similarities that emerge from these intersite comparisons demonstrate that Potato Hill's assemblage was similar to known settlements of enslaved laborers, others show some notable divergences. This requires more attention to the possibility that Potato Hill may have been home to a Euro-Caribbean, Afro-Caribbean, or creole population, potential community compositions that have received little previous attention in archaeological research on Montserrat. For example, 82 percent of the sherds recovered on Potato Hill, representing the vessels used by its residents, were made in Europe (SE = 74 percent, BC = 57 percent). Ceramics originating from non-English European manufacturers at Potato Hill are sparse, even if the 1.6 percent of the assemblage composed of redware were to be counted as potentially of French, Dutch, or Spanish manufacture (SE = 16 percent, BC = 31 percent). The greatest contrast is apparent in the proportion of coarse earthenware in the Potato Hill assemblage—17.8 percent—which suggests that the residents were active consumers of locally produced or traded pottery in addition to imported pottery (SE = 8.08 percent, BC = 5.8 percent).

In analyzing the finds from survey on Potato Hill (and from many other places on Montserrat), the most notable challenges involve making reliable distinctions between late prehistoric Amerindian coarsewares and historic-era Afro-Caribbean pottery, and discerning the differences between the prehistoric and historic manufacture of lithics. This quandary is not often confronted in projects that are either solely prehistoric or solely historic in emphasis, but it is an issue that will certainly demand closer inspection within the scope of our work on Montserrat. With regard to lithics, for example, the majority of artifacts found on Montserrat are fashioned from chert, very probably imported from the closest and most abundant source on Long Island, Antigua. The presence on Potato Hill of more than a hundred lithic artifacts might, taken in isolation, automatically be regarded as indicating a prehistoric activity area, but finds of scrapers fashioned from reworked bottle glass at Potato Hill and at several other nearby historic-era sites demonstrate continuity of knapping techniques after the time of European settlement and undermine easy temporal distinctions. Likewise, coarseware ceramics from Potato Hill demonstrate the chronologically confusing but potential ongoing employment of pre-European decorative practices (red ochre slip) and vessel morphologies (in the remains of two separate griddles for processing cassava and other tubers). These sorts of continuities are fascinating and puzzling. It is our intention in the next phase of the project to address potential technological and temporal differences in coarseware pottery via a systematic program of geochemical and petrographic analysis (Ryzewski and Cherry 2015:376–378).

The Potato Hill survey finds raise intriguing questions about the mixtures of people who may have inhabited the settlement, simultaneously or successively. As is evident from the special finds recovered from the site (along with similar items found throughout the Silver Hill region) and from the overall consumption practices involving pottery procurement and usage on the part of those who lived on Potato Hill, it is apparent that the estate boundaries surrounding and perhaps enveloping the site did not constrain movement of ideas, people, and commodities across northern Montserrat's colonial terrain (cf. Hauser 2011:431–432). Instead, its residents maintained identities, mediated by the objects they used and crafted, to engage intra-island transactions that operated outside the boundaries of estates but still within the bounds of the limits and inequalities perpetuated by the plantation economy.

Conclusion

As the results of the Potato Hill survey demonstrate, plantation landscapes on Montserrat cannot be fully understood by focusing solely on estate centers and their sugar mills, boiling houses, great houses, and other appurtenances.

Given the dearth of archival records and the ambiguity of the cartographic evidence, understanding Potato Hill's position within the historic, plantation-dominated landscape comes primarily from archaeological investigation. Systematic, gridded survey in 2013 produced 84 percent (n = 4,160) of all artifacts (n = 4,960) collected from Potato Hill since the SLAM

Project began to investigate the settlement in 2010. It is worth emphasizing that this large and historically significant sample—carefully quantified, spatially controlled, and revealing meaningful distributional patterns—was the result of just three days of survey followed by three days devoted to test excavations (although of course a year was subsequently expended on artifact analysis). Where conditions are appropriate, in other words, this type of rapid but thorough surface survey can generate robust, interpretable data with greater efficiency than the excavation of a large number of small STPs; we believe the procedure, though hardly novel, has the potential for far wider adoption within Caribbean historical archaeology. At the same time, the example discussed in this chapter makes it obvious that understanding diversity in settlement systems, social dynamics, and region-wide spheres of interaction (see Hofman et al. 2007) depends on acquiring high-quality data by means of multisited, multiperiod survey methods—ones that attend not only to "sites" in the traditional sense but also to the many other sorts of features, often quite ephemeral, that exist in the landscape and speak to past patterns of landscape use. Our preceding discussion of the evidence from Potato Hill would not have been possible in the absence of this wider data background.

Overall, the Potato Hill assemblage is among the most substantial and earliest historic-period collections of artifacts yet to be recovered systematically on Montserrat. The combination of locally made coarseware pottery, European-produced material culture, modified special finds, and small but sturdily built structural remains suggests that this was a non-elite settlement occupied by multiple groups of inhabitants, quite possibly of mixed ethnicity and ancestry, between the late seventeenth century and middle or late nineteenth century. While analysis of the 2013 survey assemblage has been productive in determining the spatial layout and discrete areas of the settlement, more archival research is necessary to identify who the strategic, resourceful, non-elite residents were on Potato Hill; how they fit into the plantation estates that were all around them; and how they responded to the changing conditions of colonialism and the island's plantation economy over the span of two centuries.

Acknowledgments

We wish to acknowledge our gratitude for the support and encouragement of Lady Eudora Fergus and Mrs. Sarita Francis, OBE, past and current directors of the Montserrat National Trust, under whose aegis we conduct our research on the island. Participants on the SLAM Project over the course of seven periods of fieldwork since January 2010 also deserve our thanks; in relation to the fieldwork reported in this chapter, we should mention especially Thomas P. Leppard, Emanuela Bocancea, and Douglas C. Anderson. Analysis of historic-era materials from Potato Hill in the archaeological laboratory at Wayne State University was greatly assisted by Athena Zissis, Samantha Malette, and Brenna Moloney. Fieldwork has been made possible through funding from the National Endowment of the Humanities (Grant #RZ51674-14), Joukowsky Institute for Archaeology and the Ancient World at Brown University, National Geographic Society Waitt Family Foundation (Grant W86–10), and Wayne State University.

References Cited

Agbe-Davies, Anna S.
2006   Alternatives to Traditional Models for the Classifications and Analysis of Pipes of the Early Colonial Chesapeake. In *Between Dirt and Discussion: Methods, Methodology and Interpretation in Historical Archaeology*, edited by Steven N. Archer and Kevin M. Bartoy, pp. 115–140. Springer-Science and Business Media, New York.

Akenson, Donald H.
1997   *If the Irish Ran the World: Montserrat 1630–1730.* Queens University Press, Montreal.

Armstrong, Douglas V.
2003   *Creole Transformation from Slavery to Freedom: Historical Archaeology of the East End Community, St. John, Virgin Islands.* University Press of Florida, Gainesville.
2010   Degrees of Freedom in the Caribbean: Archaeological Explorations of Transitions from Slavery. *Antiquity* 84(32):146–160.

Beaudry, Mary C., and Lydia M. Pulsipher
2007   *Narrative Report of March 2007 Archaeological Investigations at the Montserrat National Trust Heritage Site at Little Bay.* Report submitted to the Montserrat National Trust, Olveston, Montserrat, (April 14, 2007).

Beaudry, Mary C., Lydia M. Pulsipher, and Conrad M. Goodwin
2007   Legacy of the Volcano: Archaeology and Heritage at William Carr's Little Bay Estate, Montserrat, WI. Paper presented at the annual meetings of the Society for Historical Archaeology, Williamsburg, Virginia.

Berke, Phillip R., and Timothy Beatley
1997   *After the Hurricane: Linking Recovery to Sustainable Development in the Caribbean.* Johns Hopkins University Press, Baltimore.

Bocancea, Emanuela, Krysta Ryzewski, and John F. Cherry
2013   *Report on the Archaeological Excavations at the Valentine Ghaut Site, Rendezvous Bay, Montserrat, Conducted by the Survey and Landscape Archaeology on Montserrat Project (SLAM) from 2010–2013.* Report submitted to the Montserrat National Trust, Olveston, Montserrat.

Brace, C. Lorin, VI

2015   *Archaeological Excavations on Potato Hill, Montserrat, May–June 2015.* Report submitted to the Montserrat National Trust, Olveston, Montserrat.

Bradley, Charles S.

2000   Smoking Pipes for the Archaeologist. In *Studies in Material Culture Research*, edited by Karlis Karklins, pp. 105–133. Society for Historical Archaeology, Tucson.

Cherry, John F., Thomas P. Leppard, and Krysta Ryzewski

2014   The Prehistory of Montserrat: A Synthesis and an Update. In *Proceedings of the 24th Congress of the International Association of Caribbean Archaeologists, Martinique, W.I., July 23–30, 2011*, edited by B. Bérard, pp. 266–276. Université des Antilles et de la Guyane, Fort de France, Martinique.

Cherry, John F., and Krysta Ryzewski

2013   *Archaeological Excavations on Gun Hill, Montserrat, 2010–2013.* Report submitted to the Montserrat National Trust, Olveston, Montserrat.

2014   Archaeology at Risk, Archaeology of Risk: Diachronic Land-Use, Settlement, and Volcanic Activity on Montserrat. *Proceedings of the 24th Congress of the International Association of Caribbean Archaeologists*, edited by B. Bérard, pp. 408–420. Université des Antilles et de la Guyane, Fort de France, Martinique.

Cherry, John F., Krysta Ryzewski, and Thomas P. Leppard

2012   Multi-Period Landscape Survey and Site Risk Assessment on Montserrat, West Indies. *Journal of Island and Coastal Archaeology* 7(2): 282–302.

Cherry, John F., Krysta Ryzewski, Thomas P. Leppard, and Emanuela Bocancea

2012   The Earliest Phase of Settlement in the Eastern Caribbean: New Evidence from Montserrat. *Antiquity* 86 (333): Project Gallery. http://antiquity.ac.uk/projgall/cherry333/

Crandall, D. R.

2000   *A Military History of Montserrat, W.I.: Attacks, Fortifications, Cannons, Defenders, 1632–1815.* Privately Published, Montserrat.

Delle, James A.

1998   *An Archaeology of Social Space: Analyzing Coffee Plantations in Jamaica's Blue Mountains.* Plenum, New York.

2014   *The Colonial Caribbean: Landscapes of Power in Jamaica's Plantation System.* Cambridge University Press, Cambridge.

English, T. S.

1930   *Ireland's Only Colony: Records of Montserrat, 1632 to the End of the Nineteenth Century.* West India Committee Library, London.

Finch, J., Douglas V. Armstrong, E. Blinkhorn, and David Barker

2013   Surveying Caribbean Cultural Landscapes: Mount Plantation, Barbados, and Its Global Connections. *Internet Archaeology* 35 (doi:10.11141/ia.35.5).

Handler, Jerome S., and Diane Wallman

2014   Production Activities in the Household Economies of Plantation Slaves: Barbados and Martinique, Mid-1600s to Mid-1800s. *International Journal of Historical Archaeology* 18:441–466.

Hauser, Mark W.

2011   Routes and Roots of Empire: Pots, Power, and Slavery in the 18th-Century British Caribbean. *American Anthropologist* 113(3):431–447.

Heighton, Robert F., and Kathleen A. Deagan
1971   A New Formula for Dating Kaolin Clay Pipestems. *Conference on Historic Site Archaeology Papers* 6:220–229.

Hofman, Corinne L., Alistair J. Bright, Arie Boomert, and Sebastiaan Knippenberg
2007   Island Rhythms: The Web of Social Relationships and Interaction Networks in the Lesser Antillean Archipelago between 400 B.C. and A.D. 1492. *Latin American Antiquity* 18(3):243–268.

Johnson, Paul, and Martin Millett (editors)
2013   *Archaeological Survey and the City*. University of Cambridge Museum of Classical Archaeology Monograph 2. Oxbow Books, Oxford.

McAtackney, Linda, Krysta Ryzewski, and John F. Cherry
2014   Contemporary "Irish" Identity on the Emerald Island of the Caribbean: St Patrick's Day on Montserrat and the Invention of Tradition. In *Movements in Irish Landscapes: Diaspora, Identity, and Globalization at Home and Away*, edited by Rebecca Boyd and Diane Sabenacio Nititham-Tunney, pp. 113–134. Ashgate Press, Farnham.

MacLean, Jessica S.
2015   Sheltering Colonialism: The Archaeology of a House, Household, and White Creole Masculinity at the 18th-Century Little Bay Plantation, Montserrat, West Indies. Unpublished Ph.D. dissertation, Department of Archaeology, Boston University.

Meniketti, Marco
2009   Boundaries, Borders, and Reference Points: The Caribbean Defined as Geographic Region and Social Reality. *International Journal of Historical Archaeology* 13(1):45–62.

Miles, David, and Julian Munby
2006   Montserrat before the Volcano: A Survey of the Plantations Prior to the 1995 Eruptions. *Landscapes* 2:48–69.

Miller, Henry M.
1983   *A Search for the "City of Saint Maries." Report on the 1981 Excavations in St. Mary's City, Maryland*. St. Mary's City Archaeology Series, No. 1. Historic St. Mary's City Commission, St Mary's City, Maryland.

Noel Hume, Ivor
1970   *A Guide to Artifacts of Colonial America*. Knopf, New York.

Odbert, Henry, Paul Cole, and Adam Stinton (editors)
2011   *Island of Fire: The Natural Spectacle of the Soufrière Hills Volcano, Montserrat*. Seismic Research Centre, The University of the West Indies, St. Augustine, Trinidad and Tobago.

Pattullo, Polly
2000   *Fire from the Mountain: The Tragedy of Montserrat and the Betrayal of its People*. Constable, London.

Petersen, James B., and David R. Watters
1988   Afro-Montserratian Ceramics from the Harney Site Cemetery, Montserrat, West Indies. *Annals of Carnegie Museum* 57:167–187.

Pulsipher, Lydia M.

1982   Resource Management Strategies on an Eighteenth Century Caribbean Sugar Plantation: Interpreting the Physical, Archaeological and Archival Records. *Florida Anthropologist* 35(4):243–250.

1986   *Seventeenth Century Montserrat: An Environmental Impact Statement.* Historical Geography Research Series 17. Geo Books, Norwich.

1987   Assessing the Usefulness of a Cartographic Curiosity: The 1673 Map of a Sugar Island. *Annals of the Association of American Geographers* 77(3):408–422.

1990   They Have Saturdays and Sundays to Feed Themselves. *Expedition* 32(2):24–33.

1991   Galways Plantation, Montserrat. In *Seeds of Change: A Quincentennial Commemoration*, edited by Herman Viola and Carolyn Margolis, pp. 139–159. Smithsonian Institute Press, Washington.

1994   The Landscapes and Ideational Roles of Caribbean Slave Gardens. In *The Archaeology of Garden and Field*, edited by Naomi F. Miller and Kathryn L. Gleason, pp. 202–222. University of Pennsylvania Press, Philadelphia.

Pulsipher, Lydia M., and Conrad M. Goodwin

1982   Galways: An Irish Sugar Plantation in Montserrat, West Indies. *Postmedieval Archaeology* 16:21–27.

1999   Here Where the Old-time People Be: Reconstructing the Landscapes of the Slavery and Post-Slavery Era in Montserrat, West Indies. In *African Sites Archaeology in the Caribbean*, edited by Jay B. Haviser, pp. 9–37. Markus Wiener, Princeton, New Jersey.

2001   "Getting the Essence of It": Galways Plantation, Montserrat, West Indies. In *Island Lives: Historical Archaeologies in the Caribbean*, edited by Paul Farnsworth, pp. 165–203. University of Alabama Press, Tuscaloosa.

Rebovich, Samantha A.

2011   "From Africans to Antiguans": The Material Culture of Enslaved and Wage Labourers. In *Proceedings of the XXIII Congress of the International Association for Caribbean Archaeology, June 29–July 3, 2009, Antigua*, edited by Samantha A. Rebovich, pp. 460–465. Dockyard Museum, English Harbour, Antigua.

Ryzewski, Krysta

2012   Multiply Situated Strategies? Multi-Sited Ethnography and Archaeology. *Journal of Archaeological Method and Theory* 19(2):241–268.

Ryzewski, Krysta, and John F. Cherry

2013   *Report on the Survey and Excavations at Potato Hill, Montserrat, May 2013.* Report submitted to the Montserrat National Trust, Olveston, Montserrat.

2015   Struggles of a Sugar Society: Surveying Plantation-Era Montserrat, 1650–1850. *International Journal of Historical Archaeology* 19(2):356–383.

Ryzewski, Krysta, John F. Cherry, E. Z. Faro, Thomas P. Leppard, and E. Murphy

2010   *Survey and Landscape Archaeology on Montserrat: Report on the Pilot Season, January 2010.* Report submitted to the Montserrat National Trust, Olveston, Montserrat.

Watters, David R.

1980   Transect Surveying and Prehistoric Site Locations on Barbuda and Montserrat, Leeward Islands, West Indies. Unpublished Ph.D. dissertation, University of Pittsburgh.

1994   Archaeology of Trants, Montserrat. Part I: Field Methods and Artifact Density Distributions. *Annals of Carnegie Museum* 63:265–295.

Watters, David R., and Richard Scaglion

1980   Utility of a Transect Survey Technique in Caribbean Prehistoric Studies: Applications on Barbuda and Montserrat. In *Proceedings of the Eighth International Congress for the Study of the Pre-Columbian Cultures of the Lesser Antilles*, edited by Suzanne M. Lewenstein, pp. 338–347. Arizona State University Anthropological Research Papers No. 22. Arizona State University, Tempe, Arizona.

1994   Beads and Pendants from Trants, Montserrat: Implications for the Prehistoric Lapidary Industry of the Caribbean. *Annals of Carnegie Museum* 63:215–237.

Zacek, Natalie A.

2010   *Settler Society in the English Leeward Islands, 1670–1776*. Cambridge University Press, Cambridge.

2

Transition and Postemancipation Spaces

8

Dimensions of Space and Identity in an Emancipation-Era Village

Analysis of Material Culture and Site Abandonment at Morgan's Village, Nevis, West Indies

MARCO MENIKETTI

In this chapter I examine a lost and forgotten village, once part of a Caribbean plantation landscape, to shed light on the meaning and materiality of place and space as they were transformed during the first decades of emancipation. Villages as a unit of analysis can provide a different perspective from the plantation as a whole. Within the context of a village, social, economic, and cultural relations between members of a similar caste within the hierarchy of the colonial system emerged distinct from the relations defined by the broader plantation system.

Study of the African diaspora has often been framed by analysis of the plantation as a unit (Wilkie 2004: 110). Understanding the lives of the enslaved in contexts distinct from plantations gained traction in historical archaeology when the focus shifted to the community and household in African American and Caribbean studies (Singleton 1991). Approaches to diaspora studies have matured even further to examine the many hidden facets of society and space (Orser 1988, 1990, 1996a) to include class, identity, creolization, consumerism, labor consciousness, and materialism (Armstrong 2003; Battle-Baptiste 2011; Delle 1999; Hauser 2011; Meniketti 2000; Schloss 2009; Wilkie 2000, 2001; Wood 2012). Plantation studies have also expanded to encompass various site types and discourses, from plantation systems writ large to household-scale consumption (Franklin and McKee 2004).

The objective of this chapter is to investigate the context and potential meanings of space and social identity, and to understand individual and collective agency by considering the material culture and spatial dimensions of an abandoned plantation village that appears to straddle the historical divide from pre- to postemancipation. Integral to the analysis is the concept that landscape and spaces have been materially shaped by those who inhabit them, consciously and contextually. Landscapes and spaces are constructed as "people recognize, inscribe and collectively maintain certain places in ritual, symbolic, or ceremonial terms," and thereby become reference points (Ashmore and Knapp 1999: 14). The use of landscape as an organizing principle has developed over the past two decades as a powerful heuristic tool as well as a tool for extracting meaning from built environments (Ashmore and Knapp 1999; Murphy and Douglas 2000).

Historical Context

The English established their first Caribbean colony on the island of St. Christopher (St. Kitts) in 1625 under Capt. Thomas Warner. Not long afterward, in 1627, a band of settlers disaffected by Warner's leadership founded a colony on Nevis, a mere two miles away across a narrow strait (Hilton 1675). The island of Nevis rises steeply from the sea at the northern end of the Lesser Antilles (see Figure 1.2), its dormant volcanic mountain dominating the landscape. This former British colony was once a central nexus of the Atlantic economy and Caribbean sugar trade. The Nevis colony prospered for more than two centuries with an economy initially built on the production of luxury commodities, such as ginger, indigo, and tobacco, yielding after 1655 to near complete reliance on sugar. The second economic force driving agroindustrialism throughout the seventeenth and eighteenth centuries was the trade in enslaved Africans. For more than a century the colony was also the epicenter of this lucrative trade. The Royal African Company established its headquarters on Nevis in 1675 to be close to its principal clientele—the plantation owners of the West Indies, a favored position bitterly contested by neighboring colonies (Higham 1921:151).

Declining markets and competition from East Indian sugar imported into Britain at the dawn of the nineteenth century undercut the sugar-based economy, dragging Caribbean colonial prosperity down with it (Williams 1994). The end of the slave trade in 1807 and eventual emancipation in 1838 fundamentally restructured the character of plantation economies and the social relations on which they were based. While a few planters embraced industrial capitalism by introducing steam engines to power the mills and diversifying to cotton or other commodity production, many others simply abandoned operations while holding firmly to the land in absentia.

Sugar estates were first built along the western coast of Nevis, in view of St. Kitts, and spread north and south as quickly as the rainforest covering the island could be cleared (Hilton 1675; Sloane 1707). By 1675 plantations were operating around the island at various scales and had crept up Mt. Nevis as high as was suitable for the production of sugar cane (Sloane 1707). The steep rise of Mt. Nevis and its varied exposures gives Nevis seven distinct biomes or ecozones. Archaeological investigations corroborate the exploitation of upper elevations for plantations, first commented on by Sloane (1707), most of which employed animal mills (Meniketti 2006, 2015). By 1700 nearly all of the island's seven ecozones had been developed for sugar plantations although not with equal success.

Project Background

In 1871 former governor of Nevis Alexander Burke Iles produced a map attempting to show the colony as it stood during his tenure. Although somewhat distorted, it depicts with reasonable accuracy the spatial relationships of numerous plantations, road systems, townsites, and significant geographic features on the landscape. Coastal roads, built in the previous century before the map was drawn, are shown as already eroded or having fallen into the sea—a dramatic statement of environmental transformation.

Three locations on the map provide named villages of emancipated Africans. None of the villages appear on modern maps. Two of these locations, Vaughn's and Morgan's, had previously been villages for enslaved Africans and bordered on eponymous plantations. Only Morgan's sugar works appears on a modern map. A third village, named Harpies, was situated close to the capital of Charlestown and was not associated with any specific plantation and has no evident pre-emancipation component, although the Clarke, Pinney, and Parris estates are in the general vicinity. These village sites represent a tangible link to the historic period immediately following emancipation, when newly free populations of Africans and creole blacks were beginning to establish new social and economic identities and transitioning to wage labor.

Covered in dense vines at an elevation of 305 m are the ruins of Morgan's sugar works. The ruined mill complex stands adjacent to a historic road that once connected numerous estates along upper elevation contours, appropriately named Upper Round Road. The Morgan's sugar works face the west with a clear view of the roadstead at Charlestown, and, while not in the best location to fully capture the strong trade winds that buffet Nevis from the southeast, its windmill was suitably placed to provide at least intermittent power for crushing cane and was well situated for transporting product to the port at Charlestown. This particular estate, while neither at the highest elevation nor among the oldest on Nevis, has an associated laborers' village.

Ongoing government and private development beginning in the early 2000s impacted both the Vaughn's and Harpies sites. The Morgan's Village site, however, remained unidentified and uninvestigated. As late as 2005, Morgan's Village was simply a place on Governor Iles' map.

During field seasons in 2004 and 2005, I directed landscape surveys that included the Vaughn's location and, by chance, an area I tentatively identified as Morgan's Village. Terraced platforms, rock walls, and artifact scatters suggested a densely occupied area with extant pre-eighteenth-century components. Surface finds included pipe stems, fragments of Bellarmine, Rhenish stoneware, and even the lip of a reddish-yellow marbled costrel of Italian manufacture datable to the early seventeenth century. All of these artifacts suggested an early occupation of the area.

The site suspected as being Morgan's Village is located on steep, marginal land bordered by drainage ghauts. Millennia of rain have cut these natural runoff channels through the volcanic matrix composing much of Mt. Nevis. The land is defined here as marginal in that it is unsuited for sugar cane production and is extremely rocky, steep, and rapidly drained. While terraced cane plots higher on the mountain have been recorded, here the ground is strewn with massive boulders. Some of the boulders were put to use in constructing platforms or enclosures, possibly as animal pens, with appended rock walls.

During a brief interlude from another project in 2011, it was brought to my attention that the likely site of the Morgan's Village was being developed for a luxury villa and was therefore endangered (Meniketti 2011a). Working closely with the Nevis Historical and Conservation Society (NHCS), a plan for survey and documentation was developed. It was proposed to the NHCS that the site deserved to be studied as an important link between the period of slavery and postemancipation life on Nevis. This is a period little understood or investigated, and only a few studies on Nevis have addressed this period with any degree of significance (Galle et al. 2009). In 2013 we initiated the Morgan's Village project on behalf of the NHCS as an archaeological field school for San Jose State University with an eye toward rescue documentation.

Historically, aside from estate homes, house forms on Nevis were mostly wood-sided with thatched roofs and are shown in some estate maps as square wooden structures. The Clarke estate map in the NHCS archives in Charlestown (date unknown) depicts a row of wood-framed houses with thatched roofs alongside small furrowed provision plots. Even if these are generic representations, they are nonetheless informative about common types to be found in the Nevisian plantation landscape. Thatched roofs on both wooden and brick buildings are mentioned in the Laws of Nevis in the context of fire hazards, along with a requirement that they be replaced with shingles or be located more than 60 m from the main streets (NHCS, Hamilton Museum Archives, Charlestown, Nevis, An Act for Suppressing Thatch Houses and Erecting Brick or Stone Chimnies in all Towns. Laws of Nevis, 1700 Acts of Nevis Council). Houses were one room and were propped up on stone platforms (as can be found today) to allow air circulation beneath them. These houses are considered traditional on the island. The footprint of such ephemeral structures is rarely more than 11.2 m² and frequently less, somewhat at the small end of the spectrum for housing described for plantations in general (Ferguson 1992:68; Orser 1990:126). However, the rectangular pattern of large stones and leveling of the landscape is unmistakable. No other documentary record mentions housing aside from estate homes.

The village shown on the 1871 map suggests orderly rows of houses or huts built downslope from the sugar works, spread over several acres beginning at the edge of the Upper Round Road. This representation may be generic. To accompany his map, Governor Iles wrote a book about the general history of Nevis, much of it borrowed from earlier works, which provides an industrial inventory of operational mills and estates (Iles 1871). The Morgan's Village works are described as operational with a windmill. The windmill today is in a collapsed state.

By combining evidence of early occupation with the nineteenth-century map, the implications were clear that the Morgan's Village site could potentially provide insights into both pre- and postemancipation use of space, conceptions of place, and the material culture of an emergent society—one that was forming within a new colonial context of wage-labor capitalism as opposed to bondage.

The slave trade ended in 1807, and a phase referred to as the "apprenticeship period" was instituted in 1834. The rationale of colonial authorities and the British Parliament behind apprenticeship was that freedom could not be thrust on a people so long in bondage and that enslaved populations would need a period of adjustment to their new, unfamiliar condition. Furthermore, the formerly enslaved should be trained in useful skills from which they could make a living, suited to the colonies in which they lived. Such an arrangement should not be viewed as altruistic. In reality, the skill sets imparted during the apprenticeship era were principally best suited to the continuation of an agricultural labor force still serving the interests of the plantocracy (Bolland 1981; Williams 1994:135). Allowing emancipated Africans to fill other niches of colonial life was not part of the plan, nor was complete autonomy. Indeed, efforts were made to divest the newly emancipated from activities and trades that would lead to a decline in the labor force. It should be noted that in the French areas of the Caribbean, emancipated Africans were highly successful at fulfilling numerous roles beyond agricultural labor.

Freedom, when it came, had different meanings for the newly emancipated than for the plantocracy, who continued to consider the formerly enslaved as "their" labor (Delle 1999:140). Historically, this reaction to emancipation took many forms, with a greater or lesser degree of severity. Writing in 1861, William Sewell remarked that in Jamaica, where slavery was the very foundation of social and political structure, emancipation was "resolutely and systematically opposed," while elsewhere it was met with relative "cordiality" and resignation (qtd. in Comitas and Lowenthal 1973:137). This cannot be said to be true throughout the Lesser Antilles. Oppressive legislation was enacted to restrict labor opportunities in a blatant effort to preserve the status quo. However, there is a hint in Sewell's analysis of the postemancipation Caribbean that opportunity for freed people was uneven. In examining the scope of liberty emerging in this juncture, Thomas Holt notes that the "freedom that emancipation proffered was neither natural nor indigenous, but a historically particular and socially constructed phenomenon" (Holt 1992:xxii). The tension resulting between conflicting conceptions of freedom meant that there would be no escaping a contestation of identity, and some of this would take place in the context of landscape, which "invariably includes the concept of boundary" (Orser 1996b:139).

Bondage and Space

Physical landscapes such as industrial or plantation sites, where social relations are both synergistically enacted and conflicted, can be used to interpret place-based intersections of identity. Enslaved populations are subject to boundaries in various forms. Boundaries can be physical, mental, or both at the same time. In overcoming boundaries, transformation occurs through occupation or recognition of new spaces. In some instances, boundaries can be temporarily transcended through spiritual means, such as through enactment of traditional religious practices (Olmos and Paravisini-Gebert 2003:15). Colonial authorities perceived traditional and creolized religions as subversive and dangerous. Laws not only forbade the practice of these religions but also sought to disrupt the places of enactment as these places on the landscape came to be associated with resistance.

Whether conceived as landscapes of resistance, landscapes of capitalism, or landscapes of transformation, at the core of these frameworks is an awareness of interstitial places of contestation for identity of the now and genesis of the new—activities subversive to the politically dominant society. The challenge for archaeologists is to find material correlates in the ground that substantiate the realities of these metaphorical spaces and the behaviors that manifest from this tension.

The concept that space and place transcend mundane geographical context to embody distinct arenas wherein identity formation, resistance, cultural continuity, or transformation are realized has been integral to discourse in historical archaeology for more than two decades. Landscape orientations have become an important avenue of inquiry in historical archaeology (Brandon and Davidson 2005:113). The lens this perspective provides opens new vistas of understanding agency and interpreting unanticipated behaviors in confined or oppressive landscapes, an approach well suited for the analysis of industrial labor.

The materiality of space as posited by Henri Lefebvre (1979, 1993) has been a critical tool for archaeologists, offering a structure of analysis for the dialectics of landscapes and the way conceptions of "place" color social interactions (Symanski 2012:124). Ultimately, Lefebvre's insights create avenues for archaeologists to explore agency from the material record (Armstrong 2003; Delle 1999; Orser 1990, 1996b; Pulsipher and Goodwin 2001).

Given that enslaved populations were both physically and metaphorically bounded within controlled landscapes, it would seem reasonable to wonder to what degree or in what recesses of the landscape such populations could find meaningful agency or autonomy. However, descriptions of daily life, elaborate or otherwise, are rare. Few "have come to light," according to Michel-Rolph Trouillot (1996:306), "with which to flesh out the history of what ex-slaves and their immediate descendants did in specific circumstances and locales." That the events of emancipation occurred in the historical context of a maturing capitalist paradigm adds yet another layer of materiality to space and identity that makes analysis possible. Houses, consumable artifacts such as ceramics, and the partitioning and use of space observable in the archaeological record each offer avenues for analysis (Delle 2000b). Examining household assemblages in the context of post-slavery landscapes has been effectively carried out on other islands (Armstrong 2003; Kelly et al. 2011).

Compelling arguments have been made that the houses of enslaved people were emblematic of slavery and as vernacular forms might reasonably be expected to become extinct following emancipation (Farnsworth 2001:237). However, an opposing viewpoint could be advanced that homes represented a space detached and distinct from enslavement, a domain of semiautonomous behaviors—islands within oppressive landscapes where individuality and social identity could be expressed, displayed, enacted, and understood among enslaved, creolized, or ethnically similar peers. Home to enslaved Africans in the "functional plantation model," as Whitney Battle-Baptiste (2011:87) has phrased it, is a captive domestic realm, never completely their own yet "one of the few places men and women could gain their humanity and nurture their families." It follows from such a perspective that housing associated with enslaved populations was actively if not consciously appropriated by the residents and represents material expressions of self. Thus, such "homespace" offered a measure of self-expression and a place where thoughts of resistance might also be nurtured (Battle-Baptiste 2011:95). Such actions are all the more subversive or clandestine by being in view of the estate and may have served a similar role following emancipation in the context of new labor relations. The term "self" is applied here as opposed to "individuality" for a reason; self speaks more to group identity than does individuality, which may set one apart, even within a group.

Field Testing

The first objective of fieldwork during the 2013 season was to locate the Morgan's Village site and correlate it with the 1871 map. In the summer of

2013 such dense vegetation was encountered that it caused some alarm and safety issues, particularly because the site is flanked by steep drainages. More alarming still was yet another luxury villa under construction atop the very location we had surface collected back in 2005.

The site investigated stretches steeply downslope beginning 10 m from the ruins of the Morgan's Village sugar works. The slope drops about 3 m for every 10–20 m of distance, for a slope of 15–20 percent. However, the slope is regularly interrupted by terraced platforms. The uppermost boundary of the site is the historic Upper Round Road, and it is split perpendicularly by a historic road that meets Upper Round Road, forming a T. This road is also shown on the 1871 map, likely serving the Morgan's Village estate directly and no doubt the nearby Hermitage estate as well. It is still in use by foot traffic.

Transects in 2013 were conducted perpendicular to the survey of 2005 employing a larger crew at tighter intervals to ensure thorough coverage. Survey above the Morgan's Village sugar works and beyond it along two roads were also conducted, primarily for evidence of alternative habitations and also to confirm that the artifacts being found at the site were not just washing down onto the slopes over time from some unknown refuse dump. These outcomes could be ruled out. The evidence from these transects above the road detected no trace of habitations or refuse middens.

Working with a survey interval of 5 m, the field team gradually began to encounter dry-stacked stone walls, rectangular dry-stone foundations, house platforms, regular-interval terracing, and longitudinal wall constructions that turned out to be the borders of historic roads. In all, 32 above-surface structures were documented, along with two cobbled roadbeds that linked areas further downslope with current areas of habitation. Several water catchments dug out from the hillside and lined with stone and two substantial boundary walls were also recorded. There was also evidence of a number of nonnative plants of domestic value. The presence of tamarind (*Tamarindus indica*) and other fruit bearing trees such as mango (*Mangifera indica*) in association with households is not uncommon in the historic record—many were introduced during the era of slavery—and serve as important dietary supplements till this day (Barlow 1993). Evidence of additional agriculturally useful plants were noted, such as soursop (*Annona muricata*) and screw pine (*Pandanus utilis*), a nonnative plant from which thatch can be manufactured.

The recovery of a wrought iron cane hoe, detected by a metal detector next to one of the house platforms, and handfuls of square-head wrought iron nails further underscored the character of the village. The hoe matches best with the Type III tool categorized by William Kelso at Kingsmill plantation (Kelso 1984:193; see also Evans 2012; Ferguson 1992:43). A use-trail (common right-of-way path) was also recorded traversing the lower tract of the site. The trail led to a clearing where traditional charcoal manufacture was carried out.

The area of the site investigated measured 100 m in the downslope direction by 100 m along the contours. House platforms were not evenly distributed over the space but tended to cluster on the terraced sections. House platforms in the clusters averaged 3 m apart, but averages do not tell the story, as some were elevated relative to others owing to slope. If a conservative assumption of 3 persons per household is assigned, a density of 60 residents for the sample fraction can be derived.

Testing House Platforms

Nine standard 1 × 1 m test units were excavated. Placement of these units was strategic rather than random. Four were intended to test house platforms, three to examine specific structures, and others intended to yield information about the terracing. The purpose of these test units was to determine site depth and stratigraphic history. Stratigraphic profiles proved to be essential for site interpretation. It was also hoped that artifact evidence would show that these were, in fact, house platforms and not random stone piles resulting from clearing.

Raised houses afford air circulation beneath structures but also provide a convenient space for storage or trash disposal. We further anticipated finding artifacts of mid- to late-nineteenth-century manufacturing dates with which we might confirm our supposition that the site was Morgan's Village based on the 1871 date of the Iles map.

The upper strata of the units were composed of a rich, dark mix of forest litter and organic material, as one might expect under a forest canopy. This organic deposit varied from 10 to 20 cm in depth and exhibited variable stages of decomposition. Beneath this layer the soil attained a uniform texture, density, and color for minimally 30 cm. The upper 20 cm were almost devoid of artifacts other than a very occasional ceramic sherd and fragmentary bottle glass and may be explained by bioturbation alone. In the strata beneath 30 cm artifacts became more frequent, the majority of which were ceramics.

Types identified included a wide variety of lead-glazed yellow-and-brown slipped and combed Staffordshire wares, gray stoneware, sherds of

Rhenish stoneware, and blue shell-edged whiteware with deeply incised edge work. Pipe stems were also recovered from most of the units, although not uniformly. Blue decorated Delft bowl fragments and hand-painted polychromes were also recovered from two of the units.

Units at Specific Structures

Three of the excavated units were positioned to investigate specific structures found on the site. Unit 4 was sunk at the apparent threshold to a large rectangular dry-masonry foundation. The interior measurements of this structure were 5.75 m × 2.63 m. The exterior dimensions were less certain owing to collapsing walls. The interior was dug out deeper than the surrounding land. The wall averaged .65 m in thickness in places where it could be reliably measured. Large stones positioned at the center of the enclosure built up to the level of the walls hint that the structure once supported a floor and would have been a prominent building. Unit 4 was set immediately adjacent to the evident doorway and yielded ceramic and glass fragments.

Unit 3 was excavated at the corner of the tallest stone buttress wall (designated as Feature 22) on the site and adjacent to a low boundary wall. Unit 7 was set 2 m away. Bioturbation was extensive from tree roots in these units, yet artifact patterns were consistent with the other units.

Unit 5 was excavated within a space defined by a rectangular arrangement of stacked stones and boulders. The flattened space was bordered upslope by stacked dry-masonry standing walls 1.5 m high. The stone arrangement sits alongside a drop off to a ghaut on its north side, and to the south is a gentle slope leading to another rectangular stone cluster. Here, as elsewhere across the site, space between platforms averaged 5 m. This unit produced a significant fraction of Afro-Nevisian coarse, low-fired earthenware; pipe stems; charcoal; and square nails.

Two units were excavated in areas hypothesized to represent exposed terracing or pathways exterior to house platforms rather than lived-in spaces. The character of these units differed significantly from the house platform units or the units excavated in specific structures. Beneath the organic layer making up the upper 20 cm, the units were generally filled with cobble rubble or larger stones mixed with gravels. The units did not contain artifacts; however, nodules of iron oxide were found. Similar nodules are used today by traditional Nevisian potters, who pulverize it into a powder and add it to clays to give local pottery a distinctive reddish color.[1] Traditional Afro-Nevisian pottery is widely used for utilitarian purposes

(Meniketti 2011b; Wilkie 2000). The presence of dense clays as well as iron oxide suggests the possibility of on-site production of Afro-Nevisian wares (on analysis of social meaning for local pottery production, see Hauser 2011).

Over the entire area surveyed, platforms are regularly spaced on flat terraces, giving the slope the appearance of a broad staircase. Two throughways or alleys are evident in the distribution of the platforms over the topographic contours, one of which is clearly in current intermittent use.

Artifacts

The majority of the assemblage is composed of three classes of artifacts: ceramic, glass bottle, and smoking pipe fragments—mostly stems (see Table 8.1). Metal artifacts, few in number, were almost entirely nails of various types and a single cane hoe fragment. No other metal items or hardware typically associated with houses or sugar works were detected, nor was there any household hardware. It is as if entire houses were removed from the site rather than simply abandoned to the elements.

While a few artifacts can be demonstrated to be common to the mid-nineteenth century, ceramics in the assemblage are overwhelmingly eighteenth and even seventeenth century in character. For instance, a high percentage of ceramics were various forms of yellow-and-brown lead-glazed slipwares, Staffordshire wares, delft, and other types of early colonial import. Represented were dot patterns, combed or marbled types, and edge-notched forms (see Figure 8.1). Our expectation had been to find nineteenth-century types in the upper layers, such as decorated whitewares or transfer printed styles. These were present in very small numbers and were overshadowed by the number of Afro-Nevisian wares. Rhenish stoneware with cobalt blue (Westerwald type) and several pale-blue Delft sherds suggested a range of early colonial wares not typical of assemblages associated with African households on Nevis. However, nearly all types could be considered usual for the colonial trade in ceramics in the seventeenth- and eighteenth-century Caribbean and North America generally (Majewski and Noble 1999).

The artifacts point compellingly to an earlier occupation than previously expected, with hardly any representing the period in which historical documents suggest the site was occupied. This evidence hints at two probable scenarios: the population residing at Morgan's Village lacked access to contemporary middling ceramics as a result of economic conditions or, more likely, the population was for the most part no longer residing at the site

Table 8.1. List of ceramics from the assemblage representing finds from all units and surface collected materials

Type	Manufacturing Count (n = 401)	Date Range[a]
Afro-Nevisian ware	217	1690–1900
Delft		
Blue patterned/floral	8	1640–1800
Staffordshire ware		
Combed	30	1670–1790
Dotted	3	1670–1790
Marbled	3	1670–1790
General Stoneware		
Saltglazed grey	5	1720–1805
Rhenish Westerwald	6	1700–1775
Brown mottled	5	1690–1775
Bead and reel rim (Queen's pattern creamware)	1	1740–1800
Transfer printed (blue)	1	1775–1810
Shell-edged rim (blue)	1	1760–1785
Polychrome hand painted		
Red and green floral	6	1820–1840
Pearlware plain	8	1760–1820
Undecorated whiteware	53	1820–1900
Creamware plain	31	1730–1835
Mocha annular	2	1790–1890
Unidentified redware	4	?
Unknown	15	?
Bellarmine medallion	1	1650–1760
Costrel lip/neck	1	1620–1640

[a] The general manufacturing date range suggests a pre-emancipation-era occupation of the site.

soon after emancipation and therefore not depositing nineteenth-century refuse.

Afro-Nevisian wares do not come to prominent numbers until the middle levels between 20–40 cm depth. Levels beneath, down to 50 cm, contain a mix of coarse earthenware and Staffordshire types. A third possibility for which the data is limited, but one deserving mention, is that the earliest phase at the village may have initially had only a limited African component. To further test this proposition would require more historical knowledge of the Morgan's estate than is currently available. However, the Hermitage estate, less than half a mile along the road, was in operation as

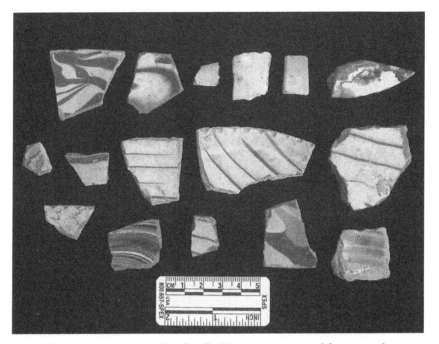

Figure 8.1. A representative sample of Staffordshire wares recovered from several units.

early as 1675 (Leech 2005) and may be a source of the pottery. While Afro-Nevisian ware came to be used in many households on Nevis, European or African, it is generally absent from the earliest sites on the island. Every unit contained dark green glass at each level below surface, and several contained onion bottle fragments in the lower levels.

Another pattern of some significance was the diminishing number of Afro-Nevisian wares in levels where undecorated whiteware and cream-ware appear. Afro-Nevisian wares return in greater numbers in the upper levels as imported wares wane in numbers. When we compare the patterns from multiple units, it is evident that local earthenware and common whiteware are the principal components of these later assemblages. If ware types can be equated with economic status and prosperity, then a cycle of economic adjustments is evident. In other words, there were periods when imported wares were in greater use compared to locally manufactured types, suggesting both a preference for such ware and the capacity to acquire them. However, economic status assessment is not that simple, with many intervening factors to account for (Ferguson 1992:22; Orser 1990:125).

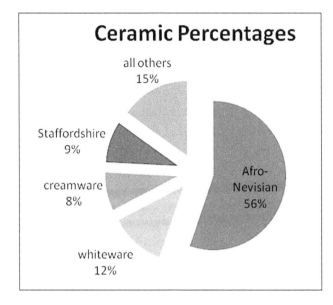

Figure 8.2. Comparative percentages of the principal ceramics recovered from the excavated units revealing the strong reliance on traditional Afro-Nevisian wares and low-cost import wares.

Afro-Nevisian earthenware dominated the assemblage. Plain whiteware and creamware were found in two of the units. The single house platform represented by Unit 4 contained a full array of colonial import wares with a decreasing presence of coarse earthenware in levels containing whiteware and pearlware types. Overall, only twenty sherds in the assemblage from all nine units are unmistakably plates, and the majority of these are early lead-glazed yellow slipware from deeper levels. Whitewares were highly fragmentary, but curvatures suggest mainly bowls and cup forms as opposed to plate or saucer forms. There are too few to speak definitively about foodways (see Figure 8.2).

Analysis and Interpretation

Artifacts come to the archaeological record by myriad routes—purposeful discard, breakage, or loss. They represent pieces of a household. Yet artifacts are recognized as the "result of expressions reflective of individual and community" (Armstrong 2003:68). Artifacts can be shown to embody values, traditions, and spiritual beliefs in addition to revealing foodways (Ferguson 1992; Galle 2011; Hauser 2011; Orser 1990; Schroedl and Allman 2002). The fragmentary ceramic evidence suggests acceptance of a wide range of colonial wares but primary reliance on traditional Afro-Nevisian ware and plain, low-cost imports. It can be surmised that the residents were economically stressed before and on the eve of emancipation, sharing a common material culture reflecting their common economic and social status.

As artifacts were recovered, unanticipated patterns emerged. In the end, we are left trying to explicate three unexpected findings. First, although the map of Governor Iles depicts a village in 1871, only a negligible number of artifacts on the surface dated to the mid-nineteenth century. Nearly all of what was recovered was datable between 1725 and 1825. This finding was further substantiated by the majority of excavation units across the site. In all classes of artifacts—ceramics, glass, pipe stems, nails—the trend was for earlier rather than later occupation. While this would not be unexpected for a site with a pre-nineteenth-century component, the general absence of artifacts dating later than 1825 was unexpected considering the village's presence on the 1871 map.

A second finding of note is the absence of household architectural debris. In comparison to other sites investigated across Nevis, there is a lack of hardware, hearth material, or construction material and a relatively low nail count, insufficient to account for dwellings that must have been at the site. The third intriguing finding was the pattern of ceramic acquisition and distribution across the site, suggesting changing economic circumstances and a depression in the later phases until immediately after emancipation, when acquisition of new ceramics ceases altogether. Even allowing for the most conservative date ranges, the evidence points to the site being vacant at the time Iles produced his map.

Several questions immediately suggested themselves: Why is the site so devoid of nineteenth-century material? Had the proprietors of the Morgan's estate provided housing in another area of the plantation after emancipation? This explanation seems unlikely as the village site is immediately adjacent to the factory works and would have been an equally efficient placement for surveillance over wage laborers as it had been for enslaved labor. Was the village abandoned? Indeed, moving away from surveillance might have served as sufficient motivation to the newly emancipated. If so, was the move motivated by economic instability, social transformation, or eviction? Did the inhabitants relocate elsewhere in the immediate aftermath of emancipation owing to a desire to distance themselves from a place perceived as linked with bondage? Unlike larger islands under British sovereignty, however, there was very little Crown land on Nevis on which the former enslaved could reside.

As early as 1838, on the cusp of full emancipation, laws on Nevis were enacted to prevent off-island migration (Thomas-Hope 1995:165). It was foreseen by the plantocracy that freed people may not desire to engage in agroindustrial labor, and, in many cases throughout the British Leewards, efforts were made to prevent freedmen from acquiring land or engaging in any activity not tethered to sugar (Mintz 1985:176). Indeed, "for capitalism to succeed craft production must cease" (Mrozowski 1991:96). Colonial policy did not end with emancipation; efforts to confine self-determination continued after emancipation (Holt 1992).

The practice of off-island migration with intent to return at a future time to buy land became a well-established pattern in the first decades after emancipation (Frucht 1968; Olwig 1987, 1995:116). This pattern continues and in no small part functions as an important feature of Nevisian economy today. Historically, many Nevisians, following emancipation, relocated to Jamaica and other British holdings where more Crown land was available on which to homestead. On an island of barely 35 square miles, the majority of the habitable land on Nevis was owned by absentee landlords, with very little land available for the newly free to acquire. Labor competition arose as colonial authorities sought to make up for shortfalls and to undercut workers organizing to improve wages by importing labor from elsewhere in the British Empire.

An important feature of capitalism is the commodification of time—one of the few leverage points available to labor. The capacity to offer one's labor in exchange for a wage is equivalent to offering one's time. The use of time, like the use of space or movement across landscape, is an assertion of self and can be deemed subversive in the minds of the capitalists whose interests are threatened. In the use of time or in spatial movement, we can see the vital elements of asserting identity. These elements may be affirmed by community and given legitimacy through enactment. In the immediacy of emancipation, the formerly enslaved found they had to navigate a new legislative and labor-focused landscape. While opportunities for making a living are limited by decree, opportunities to express self-definition are not. Although subtle, finding new places to live, new occupations, or lifeways distinct from those that are institutionally proscribed can serve as ways in which identity can be derived or asserted. On Nevis, as elsewhere in the British Caribbean, finding employment away from plantation work was a difficult but not insurmountable task.

In an effort to understand the phenomenon of village abandonment, it has been necessary to look elsewhere for examples, such as Jamaica or

Dominica. In a provocative analysis of population movement following emancipation, Trouillot (1996: 310) examined the myriad motivations spurring migration from Dominica, stating that "flight" from estates in the early days of emancipation is not mono-causal, resulting also from such issues as land–labor ratios, wages, the memory of slavery, and social relations.

The archaeological evidence also suggests that the site had a long occupancy prior to the nineteenth century and that, following emancipation, the residents actively disassociated themselves from the estate. In essence, while many may have continued to work on the estate, the population did not feel bound to live near it or elected to sell their labor to competing estates. This conscious move away from the village and what it represented likely began immediately after full emancipation as the newly enfranchised initiated a new phase of negotiated identity, both social and economic in scope. In essence, the village no longer represented a home place. The break appears to have been rapid, spanning only a few years. Relocation to a new space to begin afresh, even if only a half a mile away, can be construed as part of a new and emergent collective agency in the process of identity construction. For some formerly enslaved people, "freedom meant the ability to move" (Trouillot 1996:312). If an exodus from the Morgan's site had occurred, why, then, was it indicated on the 1871 map? It is likely that the societal shift went unrecognized on the landscape by colonial authorities.

The event of emancipation cannot be divorced from the economic realities in which the plantation system was enmeshed. Capitalism as a social system was maturing and gaining strength. Relations between labor and factory-estate owners were evolving. Stephen Mrozowski (1991:96) cogently frames the issue in terms of wage consciousness, stating that there developed "different views of what labor meant to those who labored vis-a-vis those offering wage based-labor." The Morgan's Village residents were changing their economic role, creating new relations, and asserting latent autonomy.

Trouillot has suggested a lack of integration of the capitalist consumer mentality as linked to wage labor (Trouillot 1996: 309). However, archaeological studies of consumer patterns on Nevis (Meniketti 2015), Jamaica (Armstrong 2003; Delle 2000a; Hauser 2011), and the Bahamas (Wilkie and Farnsworth 2005) suggest instead that capitalist consumer mentality was not absent among the enslaved population. Rather, it was manifesting in a different context in which the symbols and meanings of consumer practices differed from Euro-creole value systems that were more intimately wedded to those of the dominant society. Indeed, in order to implement a new paradigm, "materiality incentives for wage labor had to be instituted, along with material aspirations" (Holt 1992:xxii). Nevisians were buying into the material aspirations, but this manifested most in distancing themselves from social spaces of the old order.

Although place and space are distinct concepts, they intersect. Spaces and places are both domains of negotiation between different sectors of societies. In linking identity with space, Orser (1996b:137) invoked Lefebvre's (1979, 1993) insightful recognition of the dual character of space as concrete in place but also as shaping the cognitive landscape in the plantation context. Consider places of worship as focal points for ideologies. The spaces within such places may be reserved or partitioned for particular functions and rituals or to demarcate special roles for actors during worship. The meanings of these niche domains become internalized by those who participate in the behaviors deemed appropriate to the place.

However, no longer being enslaved did not free one from pervasive economic systems. As Holt frames the conundrum, in Jamaica "slavery as a system and ideology was supplanted by free labor, which ushered in its own embedded coercive forms" (Holt 1992: xxii). In addition to coercive labor practices, the act of production acquired new meanings that were imbued with capitalist materiality (Lefebvre 1979:287, 290). It follows that the character of productive space or lived-in space would change to conform to new ideologies.

While a few residents of the village may have continued to live at Morgan's for a time, and some may have been loath to quit their small plots, for others moving to a new location or migrating elsewhere in the British colonies would have been an attractive option and an overt display of collective agency asserting new conceptions of self. To Governor Iles, placing the village on his map in its historical location may have been an effort to maintain an ordered landscape, but a landscape that, nonetheless, the plantocracy no longer completely controlled.

Acknowledgments

I would like to express my gratitude to Evelyn Henville, executive director of the NHCS, and to Mr. Noel Williams of Hamilton estate and his family for their assistance on the site. I also wish to thank San Jose State University and the Department of Anthropology for supporting this research. Special thanks must be extended to the field school students and to our field supervisor, Chis Keith, and collections manager, Joanna Monaco. I note with appreciation the comments of reviewers of earlier versions of this chapter that helped shape its final form.

Note

1. One student from the project spent several days documenting traditional pottery manufacture with a renowned local potter and witnessed the preparation and use of the iron-oxide nodules in the fabric of the ceramics.

References Cited

Armstrong, Douglas
2003   *Creole Transformations*. University Press of Florida, Gainesville.
Ashmore, Wendy and A. Bernard Knapp
1999   Archaeological Landscapes: Constructed, Conceptualized, Ideational. In *Archaeologies of Landscape*, edited by Wendy Ashmore and A. Bernard Knapp, pp. 1–30. Wiley-Blackwell, Oxford.
Battle-Baptiste, Whitney
2011   *Black Feminist Archaeology*. Left Coast Press, Walnut Creek, California.
Barlow, Virginia
1993   *The Nature of the Islands*. Chris Doyle Publishing, Dunedin, Florida.
Bolland, O. Nigel
1981   Systems of Domination after Slavery: The Control of Land and Labor in the British West Indies after 1838. *Comparative Studies in Society and History* 23(4):591–619.
Brandon, Jamie, and James Davidson
2005   The Landscapes of Van Winkle's Mill: Identity, Myth, and Modernity in the Ozark Upland South. *Historical Archaeology* 39(3):113–131.
Comitas, Lambros, and David Lowenthal
1973   *Slaves, Free Men, Citizens: West Indian Perspectives*. Anchor Books, New York.
Delle, James A.
1999   The Landscapes of Class Negotiation on Coffee Plantations in the Blue Mountains of Jamaica, 1790–1850. *Historical Archaeology* 33(1):136–158.
2000a   The Material and Cognitive Dimensions of Creolization in Nineteenth-Century Jamaica. *Historical Archaeology* 34(3):56–72.
2000b   Negotiating Social Relations under Slavery on Coffee Plantations in Jamaica, 1790–1834. In *Lines that Divide: Historical Archaeology of Race, Class, and Gender*, edited by James A. Delle, Stephen A. Mrozowski, and Robert Paynter, pp. 168–201. University of Tennessee Press, Knoxville.
Evans, Chris
2012   The Plantation Hoe: The Rise and Fall of an Atlantic Commodity, 1650–1850. *William and Mary Quarterly* 69(1):71–100.
Farnsworth, Paul
2001   "Negroe Houses Built of Stone besides Others of Watl'd + Plastered": The Cre-

ation of Bahamian Tradition. In *Island Lives: Historical Archaeologies of the Caribbean*, edited by Paul Farnsworth, pp. 234–271. University of Alabama Press, Tuscaloosa.

Ferguson, Leland
1992   *Uncommon Ground: Archaeology and Early African America, 1650–1800.* Smithsonian Institution Press, Washington, D.C.

Franklin, Maria, and Larry McKee
2004   Introduction. African Diaspora Archaeologies: Present Insights and Expanding Discourses. *Historical Archaeology* 38(1):1–9.

Frucht, Richard
1968   Emigration, Remitteances and Social Change: Aspects of the Social Field of Nevis, West Indies. *Anthropologica* 10(2): 193–208.

Galle, Jillian E.
2011   Assessing the Impacts of Time, Agricultural Cycles, and Demographics on the Consumer Activities of Enslaved Men and Women in Eighteenth-Century Jamaica and Virginia. In *Out of Many, One People: The Historical Archaeology of Jamaica*, edited by James A. Delle, Mark W. Hauser, and Douglas V. Armstrong, pp. 211–257. University of Alabama Press, Tuscaloosa.

Galle, Jillian E., Fraser D. Neiman, Leslie Cooper, Derek Wheeler, Roger Leech, and Robert Philpott
2009   Sugar, Slaves, and Shovel-Test-Pits: Preliminary Results from Nevis. Thomas Jefferson Foundation, University of Southampton, National Museums Liverpool/ The International Slavery Museum. Scientific Poster presented at the Annual Meeting of the Society of American Archaeology, Atlanta, Georgia.

Hauser, Mark W.
2011   Of Earth and Clay: Locating Colonial Economies and Local Ceramics. In *Out of Many, One People. The Historical Archaeology of Jamaica*, edited by James A. Delle, Mark W. Hauser, and Douglas V. Armstrong, pp. 163–182. University of Alabama Press, Tuscaloosa.

Higham, Charles S. S.
1921   *The Development of the Leeward Islands under the Restoration 1660–1688: A Study in the Foundations of the Old Colonial System.* Cambridge University Press, Cambridge.

Hilton, John
1675   Relation of the First Settlement of St. Christophers and Nevis, By John Hilton, Storekeeper and First Gunner of Nevis. In *Colonising Expeditions to the West Indies and Guianas, 1623–1667*, edited by J. Harlow. Haklyut Society, London.

Holt, Thomas
1992   *The Problem of Freedom: Race, Labor, and Politics in Jamaica and Britain 1832–1938.* Johns Hopkins University Press, Baltimore.

Iles, John Alexander Burke
1871   *An Account Descriptive of the Island of Nevis.* Fletcher and Son, Norwich.

Kelly, Kenneth, Mark W. Hauser, and Douglas V. Armstrong
2011   Identity and Opportunity in Post-Slavery Jamaica. In *Out of Many, One People: The Historical Archaeology of Jamaica*, edited by James A. Delle, Mark W. Hauser,

and Douglas V. Armstrong, pp. 243–257. University of Alabama Press, Tusca-loosa.

Kelso, William

1984   *Kingsmill Plantations 1690–1800: Archaeology of Country Life in Colonial Virginia.* Academic Press, San Diego, California.

Leech, Roger

2005   Impermanent Architecture in the English Colonies of the Eastern Caribbean: New Contexts for Architectural Innovation in the Early Modern Atlantic World. In *Perspectives in Vernacular Architecture X*, edited by K. Breisch and K. Hoagland, pp. 153–168. University of Tennessee Press, Knoxville.

Lefebvre, Henri

1979   Space: Social Product and Use Value. In *Critical Sociology: European Perspectives*, edited J. Friedberg, pp. 285–295. Irvington, New York.

1993   *The Production of Space.* Donald Nicholson-Smith, Translator. Blackwell, Oxford.

Majewski, Teresita, and Virgil Noble

1999   British Ceramics on the American Colonial Frontier 1760–1800. In *Old and New Worlds*, edited by Geoff Egan and R. L. Michael, pp. 299–309. Oxbow, Oxford.

Meniketti, Marco

2000   Post-Colonial Transformation and Invention of Cultural Identity on Nevis, West Indies. *Journal of Post-Colonial Historic Studies* 1(1):139–163.

2006   Sugar Mills, Technology, and Environmental Change: A Case Study of Colonial Agro-Industrial Development in the Caribbean. *Journal of the Society for Industrial Archeology* 32(1):53–80.

2011a   The Bush Hill Estate and Landscapes of Capitalism: A Case Study in Economic and Social Transition at Bush Hill Estate, Nevis. *Proceedings of the XXIII Congress of the International Association for Caribbean Archaeology, 2009*, edited by A. Rebovich, pp. 331–341. English Harbour, Antigua.

2011b   Preliminary Comparative pXRF Analyses of Indigenous Saladoid Wares and Colonoware from Nevis, West Indies. *Caribbean Connections*, February 1(1). Field Research Centre, Antigua.

2015   *Sugar Cane Capitalism and Environmental Transformation: An Archaeology of Colonial Nevis.* University of Alabama Press, Tuscaloosa.

Mintz, Sidney W.

1985   *Sweetness and Power: The Place of Sugar in Modern History.* Penguin, New York.

Mrozowski, Stephen A.

1991   Landscapes of Inequality. In *The Archaeology of Inequality*, edited by Randall H. McGuire and Robert Paynter, pp. 79–101. Basil Blackwell, Oxford.

Murphy, Alexander, and Douglas Johnson

2000   Encounters with Environment and Place. In *Cultural Encounters with Environment: Enduring and Evolving Geographic Themes*, edited by Alexander Murphy and Douglas Johnson, pp. 1–13. Rowman and Littlefield, Lanham, Maryland.

Olmos, Margarite Fernandez, and Lizabeth Paravisini-Gebert

2003   *Creole Religions of the Caribbean: An Introduction from Vodou and Santeria to Obeah and Espiritismo.* New York University Press, New York.

Olwig, Karen Fog
1987   Out Migration on Nevis. In *Land and Development in the Caribbean*, edited by Jean Besson and Janet Momson, pp. 153–170. MacMillan, London.
1995   Cultural Complexity after Freedom: Nevis and Beyond. In *Small Islands, Large Questions*, pp. 100–120. Frank Cass, London.
Orser, Charles E., Jr.
1988   The Archaeological Analysis of Plantation Society: Replacing Status and Caste with Economics and Power. *American Antiquity* 53(4):735–751.
1990   Archaeological Approaches to New World Plantation Slavery. In *Archaeological Method and Theory*, Vol. 2, edited by Michael Schiffer, pp. 111–154. University of Arizona Press, Tucson.
1996a   Artifacts, Networks, and Plantations: Toward a Further Understanding of the Social Aspects of Material Culture. In *Historical Archaeology and the Study of American Culture*, edited by Lu Ann De Cunzo and Bernard L. Herman, pp. 233–256. Winterthur Museum. University of Tennessee Press, Knoxville.
1996b   *A Historical Archaeology of the Modern World*. Plenum, New York.
Pulsipher, Lydia, and Conrad Goodwin
2001   "Getting the essences of it": Galway Plantation, Montserrat, West Indies. In *Island Lives: Historical Archaeologies of the Caribbean*, edited by Paul Farnsworth, pp. 165–203. University of Alabama Press, Tuscaloosa.
Schloss, Rebecca Hartkoph
2009   *Sweet Liberty: The Final Days of Slavery in Martinique*. University of Pennsylvania Press, Philadelphia.
Schroedl, Gerald, and Todd Allman
2002   The Maintenance of Cultural and Personal Identities of Enslaved African and British Soldiers at the Brimstone Hill Fortress, St. Kitts, West Indies. *Historical Archaeology* 36(4):38–49.
Singleton, Theresa A.
1991   The Archaeology of Slave Life. In *Before Freedom Came: African American Life in the Antebellum South*, edited by Edward Cambell Jr. and Kym Rice, pp. 155–191. University Press of Virginia, Charlottesville.
Sloane, Hans
1707   *A Voyage to the Islands of Madera, Barbados, Nieves, St. Christophers and Jamaica, with the Natural History of the Herbs and Trees, Four-Footed Beasts, Fishes, Birds, Insects, and Reptiles of the Last of Those Islands*. London.
Symanski, Luis Claudio
2012   The Place of Strategy and the Spaces of Tactics: Structures, Artifacts, and Power Relations on Sugar Plantations of West Brazil. *Historical Archaeology* 46(3):124–147.
Thomas-Hope, Elizabeth
1995   Island Systems and the Paradox of Freedom: Migration in the Post-Emancipation Leeward Islands. In *Small Islands, Large Questions*, pp. 161–178. Frank Cass, London.
Trouillot, Michel-Rolph
1996   Beyond and Below the Merivale Paradigm: Dominica's First 100 days of Free-

dom. In *The Lesser Antilles in the Age of European Expansion*, edited by Robert Paquette and Stanley Engermann, pp. 305–323. University Press of Florida, Gainesville.

Wilkie, Laurie A.

2000   Culture Bought: Evidence of Creolization in the Consumer goods of an Enslaved Bahamian Family. *Historical Archaeology* 34(3):10–26.

2001   Methodist Intentions and African Sensibilities: The Victory of African Consumerism over Planter Paternalism at a Bahamian Plantation. In *Island Lives: Historical Archaeologies of the Caribbean*, edited by Paul Farnsworth, pp. 272–300. University of Alabama Press, Tuscaloosa.

2004   Commentary: Considering the Future of African American Archaeology. *Historical Archaeology* 38(1):109–123.

Wilkie, Laurie A., and Paul Farnsworth

2005   *Sampling Many Pots: An Archaeology of Memory and Tradition at a Bahamian Plantation*. University Press of Florida, Gainesville.

Williams, Eric

1994   *Capitalism and Slavery*. University of North Carolina Press, Chapel Hill.

Wood, Margaret

2012   Mapping the Complexities of Race on the Landscape of the Colonial Caribbean, United States Virgin Islands, 1770–1917. *Historical Archaeology* 46(4):112–134.

9

African Moravian Burial Sites on St. John and Barbados

A Comparison of Spaces within Lived Experiences and Social Transformations from Slavery to Freedom

HELEN C. BLOUET

Scholars of Moravian history in the Caribbean and North America have produced valuable information concerning social changes within African diaspora communities at local, regional, and transatlantic levels. Important lines of study include the manipulation of Moravian Christian theology and the influence of Moravian missions on race and class relations (Gillespie and Beachy 2007; Richards 2007; Roeber 2007; Sensbach 2000, 2007). Research also illuminates how African Moravians, a group composed of enslaved and free people of African descent who became the focus of Caribbean Moravian mission work, used the missions to their advantage (Klinkers 2007; Sensbach 1998, 2005). In all such research areas, historians have highlighted the effects of slavery and emancipation on the development and transformation of spiritual communities in American and Caribbean colonial societies. Surprisingly, few archaeologists or anthropologists have contributed to this African diaspora and colonial research despite the presence of material evidence (for exceptions, see Armstrong 2003; Blouet 2010, 2013; Ferguson 2011; Lenik 2009; South 1999; Wood 2012).

Moving forward, there is great potential for anthropologically informed interpretations of behavioral and material shifts across Caribbean, Moravian, and African diaspora spaces linked to political transformations from enslavement to freedom. One area of note concerns mortuary sites and funerary practices, a topic anthropologists and archaeologists commonly examine in order to interpret linkages between individual people and communities in life, death, and social change (Parker Pearson 1993). In the context of transformations from slavery to emancipation, significant sociopolitical actions occurred that influenced and were therefore informed by commemorative practices honoring the deceased (Baxter and Marshall 2009; Brown 2008; Jamieson 1995; Rainville 2009a, 2009b; Reis 2007; Seeman 2010).

In this chapter, I present archaeological and historical evidence from St. John and Barbados cemeteries to highlight varied and even unexpected actions and meanings behind the placement of burials in the landscape. In particular, I compare data for the frequency of nineteenth-century church cemetery burials versus estate and household interments among African Caribbean peoples affiliated with Moravian missions. Drawing from the concept of materiality, or the idea that living individuals, decedents, social structures, spaces, and objects engage in relationships of influence that create multiple meanings and reference points for lived communities (Fahlander and Oestigaard 2008; Meskell 2005; Mullins 2012; Renfrew et al. 2004), I place the burial data in the context of sociopolitical structures and transformations before and after the end of slavery in the nineteenth century (Brown 2008; Reis 2007; Seeman 2010; Terrell 2005; Verdery 1999), and I demonstrate that mortuary sites and spaces reflected and contributed to community building, maintenance, and social change triggered through the end of slavery.

The Establishment and Rooting of African Moravian Communities in the Caribbean

The study of Moravian history in the Caribbean complements the study of the African Caribbean past because the Moravian mission played an important role in the development and transformation of African Caribbean communities throughout the region. Having been kidnapped from western and central regions of Africa and then transported to the Caribbean, the enslaved labored under bondage on rural estates and in urban economic centers. As a form of control, they were treated inhumanely by their owners, and many died as a result of overwork, corporal punishment, inadequate food and water, tropical diseases, and poor protection from the elements. Moravian missions emerged on the islands of St. John, Barbados, and elsewhere, in part to assist the enslaved in the mitigation of these terrible social conditions. Moravian churches became integral parts of African Caribbean communities, and they remained after slavery into the present day (Furley 1965; Hall 1992; Sensbach 2005). The missions had important implications for the transformation of sociopolitical structures, even in the context of burial sites and practices.

Moravian missionaries were inspired by an interpretation of Protestantism that developed in Eastern Europe and Germany, whose adherents strove to live lives of service, prayer, and love for Jesus Christ (Atwood 1997; Fries 1973; Sawyer 1990; Smaby 1988; Wood 2012). In the eighteenth century, backed by the support of German count Nicholas Ludwig von Zinzendorf, the Moravian Church established a missionary movement of "international ambassadors for evangelical Protestantism" (Sensbach 1998:19; Weinlick 1956:93). Zinzendorf and his evangelical ambassadors commenced mission work in the Caribbean in the 1730s, specifically the Danish West Indies (St. John, St. Thomas, and St. Croix). From there they spread to the British West Indies and opened stations in Jamaica, Antigua, and Barbados by the 1760s.

The Moravian stories on St. John and Barbados are interesting to compare because they took place in very different geographic and cultural contexts. St. John was a Danish colony that struggled to make a profit from sugarcane and provision agriculture due to the island's small size, rocky and uneven topography, inconsistent rainfall, and unrelenting vegetation. Denmark commenced colonizing the Caribbean after Spain, England, France, and Holland possessed much of the arable real estate. The Danes acquired St. John and St. Thomas in the late seventeenth century and St. Croix in 1733. The Danish West India Company used an open settlement policy that allowed people from different cultural and socioeconomic backgrounds to establish homes, plantations, and businesses. Danish authorities established Lutheran churches for their colonists, but the open settlement policy necessitated the tolerance of other European (though not African) religious establishments, such as Dutch Reformed and Catholic churches as well as Jewish synagogues. Funding allotted to the varied religious institutions on St. John was rather limited, and the Lutheran Church itself could not afford to missionize to large numbers of enslaved Africans and their descendants. Therefore, they permitted Moravian missionaries to take on this responsibility, although those holding enslaved Africans opposed this because they saw the Moravians as a threat to the institution of slavery (Hall 1992).

According to contemporary thought, if the enslaved people became Christians, they could not be slaves and they would become free. This system equated "black" with "heathen" and "slave" and "white" with "Christian" and "free" (Carstens 1997:1; Haagensen 1994; Hall 1992:41–44; Wood 2012:117). Given this scheme, early Moravian missionaries were imprisoned and attacked for their endeavors in the early eighteenth century in the Danish West Indies, but in 1747 the Danish government passed an ordinance that granted protection to all Moravian missionaries in its Caribbean possessions. The Moravian Church helped bring about this action because it did not object to the institution of slavery. According to its doctrine, God created the social hierarchy in which slavery existed. Devout Moravians should practice obedience and accept God's worldly order. Instead of challenging this order, missionaries instructed the enslaved to accept their status and to live moral lives. By doing so, anyone, regardless of race or class, could achieve salvation in the afterlife (Armstrong 2003:296; Furley 1965; Richards 2007:55; Sensbach 2000, 2005:71).

This perspective persuaded those holding enslaved people to modify their views on the relationship between slavery and Christianity. They accepted that slaves could be Christians—in other words, upstanding, compliant laborers. As a result, racial difference became rooted more in physical or biological distinctions of whiteness and blackness rather than cultural behaviors such as religion (Wood 2012:128). By the late eighteenth century, it grew acceptable for enslaved peoples to join the Moravian missions. In the 1790s on St. John, most of the nearly two thousand enslaved people became members of St. John's Bethany and Emmaus mission churches (Moravian Church 1789–1794:1:60; 152–153), and the proportion of Moravians remained high well after emancipation in 1848. Moravian churches on St. John still exist as vital parts of many communities on the island today (Hall 1992).

On the other hand, though relatively small, Barbados was an agriculturally successful British colony that developed monumental wealth for the English Crown and private investors (Beckles 2007). "Little England," or "Bimshire," as Barbados came to be known, received considerable oversight and influence from the Crown, government, and Anglican Church (Beckles 2007). Despite the close control from Britain, the Moravians found opportunities to develop missions to the enslaved on Barbados. Due to similar social climates found in the Danish West Indies, Britain would not allow the Anglican Church to include African-descended peoples in its congregations. However, after Moravians presented their views on the relationship between slavery and Christianity, the British colony allowed them to open formal missions, four of which opened between the late eighteenth and the mid-nineteenth centuries (Beckles 2007:120; Holmes 1818).

The Barbados colony tolerated Moravians, but missionaries faced disease, death, and financial difficulties, and thus African Moravian communities remained small (Moravian Church 1811:5:239–240). In 1817, the year in which the first comprehensive census of the enslaved population was taken (Richardson 1985:86), 214 African-descent peoples, or less than 1 percent, out of the recorded 77,493 enslaved individuals and over 3,000 free people of color were registered as Moravians (Moravian Church 1811–1814:6:436–437). By 1830, with the enslaved population numbering 82,000, about 1,030 people, or just over 1 percent of the population, were associated with the Moravian Church (Blouet 1980:129; Moravian Church 1831:12:43). Once Anglican churches allowed African Barbadian membership in the early nineteenth century, Moravian churches lost some of their constituents to Anglican congregations because they had fewer resources to retain members (Beckles 2007:203–204). Still, Moravian communities persisted after emancipation in 1838 and continue to contribute to Barbados's contemporary island society.

Did the enslaved join the Moravian missions of their own accord? It is difficult to say for sure, but it is important to consider the following. Some slaves were probably forced to become members by their owners because it was believed that the missions would instill more obedience in and control over the enslaved. At the same time, enslaved people may have also chosen to develop relationships with and become part of the Moravian religious community because they saw benefits in mission relationships, such as learning how to read and write. They may have also found advantages to incorporating Moravian religious and burial practices into their existing customs to help protect their minds, bodies, and souls in the torturous world of slavery. Gradually the social spaces, networks, and resources that enslaved and free people of African descent developed through the missions contributed to the hunt for freedom (Sensbach 2005).

Mortuary Materialities and Spaces as Receptors of and Contributors to Social and Political Structures and Transformations

In the remainder of this chapter, I refer to historic mortuary practices and landscapes to demonstrate how enslaved and free Moravian community members socially and politically transformed their mortuary sites in ways that reflected and therefore informed broader social trends in their lives before and after the end of slavery. Work in mortuary archaeology indicates that people regularly transform their mortuary practices and funerary customs, and these shifts are impacted by both independent ingenuity and a community's sociocultural experiences, political circumstances, physical surroundings, available resources, and ideas of commemoration (Berggren and Nilsson Stutz 2010; Chesson 2001; Childe 1945; Durkheim 1915; Francis et al. 2005; Frazer 1922; Hertz 2008; Kroeber 1927; Mauss 1990; Moore 2010; Mytum 2004; Parker Pearson 1999; Peterson 2013; Rakita et al. 2005; Robben 2004; Tylor 1871; Williams 2003). Differences in group affiliation and social status influence but do not predetermine how people create mortuary practices (Binford 1971; Brown 1971; Chapman and Randsborg 1981; Charles and Buikstra 1983; Goldstein 1976, 1981; Hodder 1982; McGuire 1988; O'Shea 1984; Parker Pearson 1982; Peebles and Kus 1977; Saxe 1970, 1971; Silverman 2002; Tainter 1978).

To illuminate people's social and political motivations in the creation, use, and transformation of mortuary sites and objects, I examine relevant burial sites on the two islands from a materiality perspective that claims that "material objects and things . . . are involved in and variously influence social development" (Fahlander and Oestigaard 2008:4; see also Ingold 2007; Meskell 2005; Miller 2005; Renfrew et al. 2004; Tilley 2004; Tilley et al. 2006). This perspective contends that human development and use of objects and spaces create complex social meanings and identities influenced by fields of uniformity and individuality, empowerment and enslavement, positivity and negativity. In this chapter, I compare this process before and after the end of slavery in the nineteenth century.

Plantation and postemancipation research has shown how the organization of landscape and space by people of different socioeconomic groups created opportunities for the elite to naturalize their power and discipline subaltern groups through surveillance (Brandon and Davidson 2005; Delle 1998, 2001; Epperson 2000; Shackel 1994; Wood 2012) as well as for the non-elite to negotiate, resist, and transform power structures (Delle 2014; Delle et al. 2011; Gibson 2009; Hauser 2008; Jamieson 1995; Norton and Espenshade 2007; Singleton 2015). For elites and holders of authority, the use of space echoed and informed their social position. As they claimed the land best suited to their houses, modes of transport, economic networks, and social circles, they signified their personal or institutional authority. The elites, based on their position in and use of the land, created real possibilities of control, domination, and violence (Delle 2001; Wood 2012).

For those being controlled, dominated, and violated, several kinds of material remains from daily life reflect various senses of agency, compromise, and resistance against those in power. Examples come from diverse contexts such as foodways and economic practices (Brunache 2011; Gibson 2009; Hauser 2008), housing and village space (Armstrong 1990; Kellar 2004; Singleton 2015), and burial practices (Blouet 2013, 2014; Brown 2008; Delle and Fellows 2014; Saunders 2015; Turner 2013). Such remains show that enslaved lives could not be completely controlled by their captors. Acts of agency, compromise, and resistance contributed to the development of local social contexts for the enslaved, contexts symbolized and transformed in the social and built landscapes through daily practice, sites, and objects. On St. John and Barbados, the enslaved took opportunities to carry out burial and commemorative practices derived from those they used before being taken from their diverse homelands on the African continent. They combined what they knew in dynamic ways with European and Caribbean social and cultural influences to create new mortuary spaces and practices that played important roles in the development and transformation of local societies. Over time, material and spatial evidence for burial practices both reflected and informed contexts of slavery and freedom as well as transitions from pre- to postemancipation.

The ways in which people use and transform mortuary sites and practices as part of their dynamic social experiences and histories are linked to important connections with the dead manipulated by the living through material culture and the built environment (Hodder 1982; Parker Pearson 1993; Silverman 2002:4). Charles and Buikstra (2001) affirm that the living know and remember where ancestors are placed in the landscape through acts of "referencing" and long-term placement of the dead that create "living identity and [contribute] to the production of locality" (Silverman 2002:4). As Silverman quotes (2002:4), Arthur Saxe (1971) and Lynn Goldstein (1981) claim that burial sites are "disposal facilities [that] reflect a mapping onto the land by claimants to its resources." In the same study, Silverman reminds us that resources include not only physical materials but also social, cultural, spiritual, and ancestral forms. Indeed, Charles Leedecker (2009:155) reminds us that "it is impossible to understand the changes in mortuary behavior . . . without appealing to . . . notions of how material culture is actively used in a symbolic sense as a means for individuals and groups to actively negotiate their social position." Following Vincent Brown's (2008) study on nineteenth-century funerary practices in pre- and postemancipation Jamaica, I argue that St. John's and Barbados's Moravian congregations created, maintained, and modified mortuary sites and objects that socially and politically impacted the living because real and imagined linkages between the living and the dead, symbolized in objects, spaces, and kinship, remained "integral to both social organization and political mobilization, and therefore vital to historical transformation" (Brown 2008:6; see also Bender et al. 1997; Parker Pearson 1993, 1999; Rainville 2009a, 2009b; Rakita et al. 2005; Seeman 2010; Silverman 2002;

Silverman and Small 2002; Verdery 1999; Williams 2003). In other words, much like what scholars have identified regarding the roles of landscape in the development, perpetuation, and transformation of power, cultural capital, and symbolic violence (Brandon and Davidson 2005; Delle 1998, 2014; Epperson 2000; Orser 2001, 2006; Shackel 1994; Singleton 2015; Wood 2012), material relationships between the living and the dead on St. John and Barbados echoed and influenced broad social contexts, such as distinctions between and transformations in race, class, economic, and religious identities before and after the end of slavery. Furthermore, depending on the context, mortuary transformations from slavery to freedom represented empowering social change as well as social constraints for individuals and communities.

Slavery, racism, classism, and religious control on St. John and Barbados restricted funerary expressions practiced by enslaved African Moravian communities. Despite such barriers, the customs developed by enslaved communities became important cultural practices that failed to die under bondage (Beckles 2007; Hall 1992). While funerary expressions increased in variety leading up to and after emancipation in some cases, in other instances they also reflected new restrictions encountered by freed African Moravians. Therefore, an investigation of complex meanings behind mortuary transformations before and after the end of slavery allows us to reexamine battles over equality and access to opportunity that remained after the fall of slavery.

Methods for Identifying Social and Political Structures and Transformations through Mortuary Materialities and Spaces

Evidence for influential relationships between the materiality of death and broader social change exist in a variety of burial sites and documentary data sets across St. John and Barbados in both residential and nonresidential contexts. Residential sites appear within or near homes and living spaces while nonresidential sites refer to places removed from daily household living, such as church cemeteries (Adams and King 2011:3).

This study focuses on the two Moravian church cemeteries on St. John and the five Moravian cemeteries on Barbados, relating them to documentary records and in some cases material remains of relevant residential burial sites. Concerning the church cemeteries and household burial sites, I analyzed Moravian missionary burial records, including trends over time regarding who most often received interment within them. To identify any information regarding connections between death, politics, and social change, I also examined pre- and postemancipation entries in the *Moravian Periodical Accounts* (Moravian Church), a missionary publication that published information recorded in missionary letters and reports written by both European and African Caribbean peoples. For physical data, I visited the 7 Moravian church cemeteries and 60 residential burial sites to record any evidence of changes in mortuary or funerary material culture related to politics and social change. To capture structural, stylistic, and locational information, I took photographs, wrote field notes, collected GPS coordinates, and digitized field maps. The combined analysis of documentary records, material remains, and historic landscapes allowed me to identify multiple ways in which the materiality of death mirrored and contributed to broad social change within disparate Moravian congregations, African diaspora communities, and the broader societies in which they existed from the eighteenth to the early twentieth century.

It is important to note here that the material remains discussed in this manuscript are not great in number due to the fact that the subsurface excavation of residential burial sites is intentionally not part of this study because the local communities prefer that such sites remain unexcavated out of respect for the deceased. In addition, most former residential burial sites are difficult to identify today because they are not easily visible on the ground surface due to their impermanent physical nature. As research increasingly reveals, most grave markers created for Africans and African Caribbeans in the eighteenth and nineteenth centuries, if they were constructed at all, were built of cemented or free-standing fieldstone that over time grew displaced by overgrowth, activity, and development (Blouet 2013; Delle and Fellows 2014; Saunders 2015).

Material remains for the islands' combined seven Moravian cemeteries are more numerous because these sites contain larger numbers of durable cemented masonry markers. In addition, site overgrowth and development were regularly monitored and restricted over time. Collectively, forms and locations of grave markers created over the last 260 years provide evidence of how interrelationships between death, politics, and social change manifested in burial practices and mortuary landscapes. In particular, among historic grave markers and cemeteries, it is possible to identify diverse and changing power relationships between Moravian missions, Danish and British colonial settlements, and enslaved and free Africans and African

Caribbean peoples. It is evident that social circumstances for living and deceased African Caribbean peoples differed from pre- to postemancipation St. John and Barbados.

Analysis

There are two important trends where death and burial mimicked and influenced social contexts related to race and class relations in St. John and Barbados. These pertain to the role of burial customs in segregation practices and in changes from slavery-based to free societies.

Burial Sites and Practices as Spaces and Customs of Segregation

The first trend is that overwhelmingly, before the end of slavery, European Moravians received burial in St. John's and Barbados's Moravian churchyards more often than African Moravians. This evidence is supported by surviving burial registers that catalogue church cemetery burials for most European missionaries and their families and plantation burials for most African Moravians and their families. Although the majority of African Moravians were buried outside the Moravian cemeteries, Margaret Wood (2012:126–127) finds that small numbers of African Moravians may have received interment at Emmaus before the end of slavery by arguing that African Moravians were buried in the churchyards in rows near, but separate from, white Moravians. In comparison, Leland Ferguson (2011:87–88) also found in Moravian settlements of the Wachovia region of North Carolina that in the eighteenth and early nineteenth centuries, the enslaved were buried in the same cemetery as white missionaries and at times segregated from them. The Emmaus burial rows evaluated by Wood (2012) exhibited evidence for burial practices used in other cemeteries associated with enslaved African Caribbean communities, such as the clustered organization of the burials; the presence of fieldstone, earth mounds, shell, lilies, and Christmas bushes (*Comocladia dodonaea*) for grave markers; and the remains of annular and sponge-decorated pearlware vessels from 1785–1840 as grave offerings or objects used in commemorative rituals (Wood 2012:126–127).

Accounts from the same era also suggest that some individuals of African descent were buried in Moravian cemeteries (Brady 1994 [1829]:168; Oldendorp 1987:418). Due to the absence of inscribed names and dates of death associated with the grave markers in question at Emmaus, it is difficult to identify an accurate number of African Moravian individuals. To be sure, an overwhelming majority of the African Moravian burials recorded in St. John's and Barbados's burial registers before the end of slavery reveal that burials outside the churchyards were the norm for enslaved Moravians.

Despite the restrictions from churchyard burials before the end of slavery, African Moravians created significant burial practices near their homes and villages that equally maintained sacred and secular connections between the living and the dead. Although these burial practices were created under slavery's social, political, and cultural constraints, they contributed to a sociocultural foundation that fueled enslaved communities' self-awareness and drive to maintain humanity and achieve freedom. To identify potential insight on how people created and used plantation burials for African Moravians, we can look to written accounts that describe burial sites and practices used by African-descended peoples. Although the accounts were not written by African Moravians, are not specific to African Moravian plantation burial practices, and are only glimpses into practices used by people from African-derived Caribbean cultures, they provide some insight on how the burials and associated practices may have been created, placed, and performed near homes and villages.

In the mid-eighteenth century, Moravian missionary C.G.A. Oldendorp (1987:264) wrote, "There are designated places on the plantations for the burial of Blacks. Some of them, however, are also buried not far from their houses." Most accounts lack specificity, but in the mid-eighteenth century Johan Carstens (1997:15) remarked that enslaved and free Africans in the Danish West Indies interred respected individuals under their homes: "When they have carried the body through all their streets, they take him back to his own house, where they have dug a grave in the middle of the floor. They lower the deceased into it, humming and singing mournful songs. Then they throw a handful of all the fruits of the island down on the coffin, along with containers full of all sorts of drinks that are prepared there. These things will he have to feed on, as well as . . . all his good friends, whom they believe to live and assemble together in the valley in the kingdom of the dead. Then they cover the grave." As on St. John, Barbadian burial registers and written records reveal that the majority of Africans and their descendants in the Moravian Church received interment on the plantations where they lived and worked, while most European Moravians received burial in the church cemeteries. The enslaved were buried "in the ground of the plantation where they die" (Jonathan Atkins, *An Account of His Majesty's Island of Barbadoes and the Government Thereof*, February 1676, Colonial Office Group, Public Records Office, London, 1/36, No.

20),and according to various accounts from the Society for the Conversion in 1829, identified by Handler and Lange (1978:173), "in their usual burying places on the estates," "on the plantations to which they belong," and "in places set apart for that purpose on each plantation."

Although most passages lack specific detail, David Parry (1789:17) provides a description of house-floor burials: "[The enslaved] . . . are superstitiously attached to the burial places of their ancestors and friends. These are generally as near as can be to the houses in which they live. It is frequent to inter a near relation under the bed-place on which they sleep, an unwholesome and dangerous practice which they would think it the utmost tyranny to alter." This same degree of importance placed on burials among African Barbadians was also felt among African St. Johnians. In fact, after emancipation, those who had formerly held enslaved people on St. John hoped that connections to plantation burial sites and landmarks would influence the free, wage-earning labor force to remain living and working on or near the estates that formerly enslaved them (Olwig 1985:41), a strategy also employed on other islands, such as Jamaica (Delle and Fellows 2014:488).

Archaeological evidence for contemporary burial locations exists on St. John and Barbados. This evidence, too, is not directly attached to specific African Moravians, but it does provide useful context to consider. Elizabeth Kellar (2004) identified graves under house-floor remains in an enslaved laborer residence on the former Adrian Estate in central St. John, an estate recorded to have had enslaved African Moravians in residence. Douglas Armstrong (2003) recorded contemporary historic house yard burials near African St. Johnian residences on the East End peninsula, a region historically known for its African Moravian community and attachment to the Emmaus Moravian Church in Coral Bay. In addition to Bethany and Emmaus cemeteries on St. John, I identified 28 contemporary African St. Johnian household and community burial sites, many of which were attached to homes of African Moravians.

The most well-known examples of Barbadian burials of enslaved people on plantation grounds come from the former Newton Plantation. Jerome Handler and Frederick Lange (1978) identified a large burial ground that they archaeologically and historically determined to be the site of the plantation's cemetery for the enslaved. They identified and excavated over 90 burials, and although the identification of African Moravians was not their focus, they concluded that the majority of slaves on Newton Plantation, and possibly other Barbados plantations, were buried in defined, communal cemeteries throughout the slavery era. Over time, people increasingly practiced Christian-derived burial customs as they laid people to rest in the Newton Plantation slave cemetery. Christopher Crain and colleagues (2004) analyzed an urban cemetery in the Pierhead section of Bridgetown, Barbados, that also indicates the extended use of a common cemetery ground by diverse enslaved peoples, including those who performed African- and Christian-derived burial practices. Evidence for Christian- and African-derived customs was also encountered in the investigation of a cemetery for the enslaved in the Fontabelle section of Bridgetown (Farmer et al. 2005). The archaeological evidence from Barbados reveals the social diversity embodied over time by the enslaved who were laid to rest in these cemeteries, and they point to opportunities to investigate contributions in burial and commemorative practices as well as in social change made by many people, including African Moravians.

Meanwhile, the majority of European Moravian missionaries on St. John and Barbados received interment in the islands' Moravian church cemeteries. Moravian congregations on St. John established cemeteries that followed a typical eighteenth-century Moravian pattern (Wood 2012:125–126). Referring to North Carolina communities, Ferguson (2011:81) notes that faithful Moravians received burial in "God's Fields," which represented land "sown with the perishable bodies of . . . loved ones, with whom they will be reunited in spiritual glory on the day of resurrection." Moravians buried bodies in straight rows, as if they were seeds sown into a field for God. Burial rows grouped in square lots reinforced "this sense of God's field sown with seeds of the sleeping faithful" (Ferguson 2011:80; see also Atwood 1997). On Judgment Day, it was believed bodies would rise like growing plants out of the cemetery ground, the space between living humans and living spirits. They would ascend to Jesus Christ in Heaven and reunite with their souls.

Eighteenth- and early-nineteenth-century Moravians routinely interred members in rows by age and status. For example, children were typically placed in rows separate from adults. Wood (2012:126) points out that "this practice was an extension of a social practice called the 'choir system,' whereby church members associated with those who were most like themselves" (see also Fries 1973:53; Smaby 1988:10; Smith 1978). Moravians did not typically erect large monuments or upright gravestones. Rather, grave markers consisted of small square headstones or, in some cases, ledgers and tombs constructed of available stone, brick, mortar, and marble. Ledgers were predominantly flat, rectangular slabs that lay flush with the ground. They averaged 2 m in length, 70 cm in width, and 20 cm in height. The slabs could be one continuous piece of stone, or they could be made of brick, stone, and mortar. They were erected on the ground surface above the buried body. Tombs were mostly three-dimensional rectangular monuments that on average stood 2 m in length, 1 m in width, and 60 cm in height above the ground surface. Tombs could contain bodies in their lower half buried in the ground, or they could stand on the surface above buried bodies.

Survivors of the decedents commissioned short inscriptions on the markers that included the deceased's name, age, and years and places of birth and death. The decorum of the graveyards and the simplicity of the gravestones symbolized the unity of the Moravian church members and the "so-called democracy of death . . . the spiritual equality of all Christians. With white recumbent stones at the heads, the layout of graves resembles rows of beds with white pillows at their heads—the dead asleep in the garden" (Ferguson 2011:80–81).

Emmaus and Bethany cemeteries retain evidence for this Moravian pattern in some of the earliest burial rows referred to as "B" through "E" at both burial sites. Row A at both burial sites contains modern grave markers that commemorate the lives and deaths of those who passed away in the last few decades. Any remains of earlier markers, if indeed they initially existed there, are not discernible on the ground surface.

At Emmaus, row B's earliest markers include whitewashed square gravestones that memorialize subadult individuals (Figure 9.1). There are 16 markers present in row B, including 4 nineteenth-century markers with inscriptions that commemorate girls and 2 that represent boys. Inscriptions on 6 grave markers reveal that the oldest portion of Emmaus's row C, containing a total of 14 markers, contains adult white women. In her analysis of Emmaus cemetery, Wood (2012:126) strongly argues that these graves "marked with the name, place of birth, date of birth, place of death and date of death . . . [make it] possible to trace most individuals to a northern European birthplace or to European-born parents. While this does not prove absolutely that these individuals would have been considered white in the Danish West Indian context, it is highly likely that they were." Emmaus's row D contains 8 burials, but they possess no diagnostic evidence for the row's time of creation or the row's organization by the social choir burial pattern. This row may have been created after the early nineteenth century when the choir organization system ceased to be popular as a result of the global Moravian Church shifting its focus from the nurturing of social

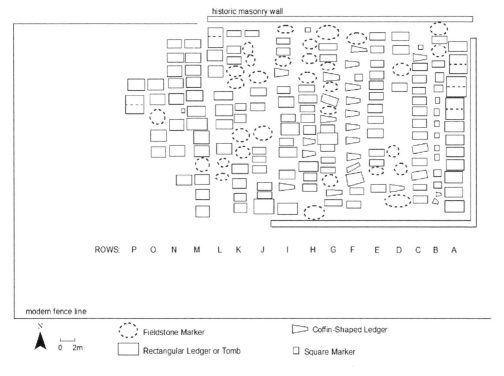

Figure 9.1. Emmaus cemetery, St. John. (Image by Helen Blouet)

choirs to the support of nuclear, biological families (Atwood 1997). In row E, with a total of 13 markers, 5 inscriptions reveal that adult white men rest in the earliest portion of the row.

Bethany's Row B includes 14 grave markers, 11 of which are the eighteenth- and early-nineteenth-century small, square, masonry markers with whitewashed facades. Eight of the square markers have inscriptions, six of which retain enough detail to identify the names and/or ages of the deceased. Of these, five commemorate a boy or girl who died before the age of five, four of which died before the end of slavery in 1848. Based on this evidence, row B was originally created to contain burials and markers that commemorated juvenile white individuals (Figure 9.2). Row C contains seven burials, but they possess no diagnostic evidence for time period or the influence of the social choir system. Their overall appearance also suggests they were created after the shift from social choir networks to biological family networks in the mid-nineteenth century.

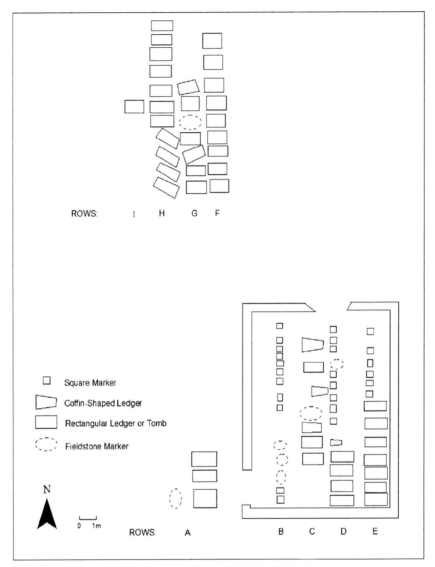

Figure 9.2. Bethany cemetery, St. John. (Image by Helen Blouet)

Row D has 14 markers, the earliest of which include 8 square markers, 3 of which possess legible names and ages at death. These surviving inscriptions indicate that adult men were first buried in row D during the eighteenth and early nineteenth centuries. Again, the names and dates on the markers suggest the men's white, European background. Row E's early grave stones stand as 6 square, whitewashed markers, 5 of which bear remains of inscriptions, 2 of which identify the commemorated as adult women. This evidence suggests that row E was first used for the burial and commemoration of adult women, and, like the previous rows, they contained the burials of white Europeans.

Unfortunately, no clear aboveground evidence for a choir burial plan exists for any of the five Moravian cemeteries on Barbados. In fact, the only remaining markers within the original section of the Sharon church cemetery, the earliest Moravian church cemetery to appear in Barbados at the end of the eighteenth century, are two rectangular tombs commemorating missionaries Adam Haman and David Lichtenthaeler, who died in 1799 and 1826, respectively. In fact, these two tombs, conjoined and sitting within a grassy opening that was the first cemetery space on the church property (Dorothea Rohde, personal communication, June 12, 2011), may not be the original tombs, but the inscribed stones placed on their surfaces probably once lay on top of the original tombs or markers.

Interactions between Social Transitions from Slavery to Freedom, Burial Spaces, and Mortuary Practices

The second way in which politics influenced burial location occurred in the years leading up to and after emancipation in 1838 on Barbados and in 1848 on St. John. It is evident in Moravian burial records that shortly before and just after emancipation on both islands the use of the Moravian burial grounds increased, although the rise was much more significant in Barbados. This was a complex product of emancipation and shifting social structures that defined who had particular land access, property ownership, and organizational memberships. For example, the Moravian Sharon church burial register reveals that in the 1820s, 57 percent of the 37 recorded burials for people of African descent occurred in the Sharon church cemetery, and the remaining 43 percent of the recorded burials were placed on plantation estates (Barbados National Archives, Black Rock, microfilm, Sharon Moravian Church Book, St. Thomas Parish 1767–1854). A similar frequency occurred in the Mount Tabor Moravian cemetery (Barbados National Archives, Black Rock, microfilm, Mount Tabor Moravian Church Book, St. John Parish 1828–1860).

On St. John however, the use of either Bethany or Emmaus Moravian churchyards for African Moravian burials in the 1820s was intermittent (Moravian Archives, Bethlehem, Pennsylvania, microfilm, Emmaus Church Register, 1833–1881. Moravian Church in the Eastern West Indies Record Group). In the 1830s a significant majority of African Moravians were buried in Barbados's Moravian cemeteries (Barbados National

Archives, Black Rock, microfilm, Mount Tabor Moravian Church Book, St. John's Parish 1828–1860; Barbados National Archives, Black Rock, microfilm, Sharon Moravian Church Book, St. Thomas 1767–1854, Black Rock, Barbados). For instance, the Sharon cemetery records show the frequency of African Moravian churchyard burials was 74 percent while estate burials composed 21 percent. Locations of the remaining 5 percent are unknown due to incomplete records. St. John's Bethany and Emmaus records from the 1830s again mark these cemeteries as uncommon places for African Moravian burials. In fact, St. John's African Moravians were not buried in Moravian cemeteries the majority of the time until the early to mid-twentieth century.

The written records for Barbados are important to rely on because very few markers from this period are identifiable in the Barbados Moravian churchyards. This evidence is a common occurrence for most contemporary Caribbean burials, suggesting that few people received markers or the markers did not survive over time. Yet there is some evidence that reveals material transformations in Barbados's pre- to postemancipation Moravian burial grounds. Unlike eighteenth- and early-nineteenth-century congregations in St. John that created traditional square Moravian markers, contemporary Moravians in Barbados used ledger and tomb styles. In addition, as the number of interred African Moravians increased in the churchyards in the years just before and after the end of slavery, the prevalence of less durable but affordable markers, few of which survived, also increased. It is likely that this popularity in less durable markers existed because people found them affordable and appropriate to use in the commemoration of community members.

Grave marker designs on St. John also transformed during the islands' transition to the postemancipation era. In St. John's Moravian churchyards after 1848, ledgers and tombs eclipsed the eighteenth- and early-nineteenth-century small, square grave markers as the predominant forms. Ledgers and tombs also stood alongside slowly rising numbers of more affordable markers, such as loose fieldstone, into the twentieth century. During the early twentieth century on both St. John and Barbados, grave marker creators also incorporated what are locally referred to as Moravian "bed markers." Over time, bed markers have not been restricted to use in Moravian cemeteries only. Diverse forms of bed markers are found in a multitude of cemeteries across the Caribbean. Bed markers resemble beds because each consists of a rectangular ledger base and on top of one end sits a three-dimensional triangular, square, or rectangular headstone resembling a pillow.

They stand atop terrestrial burials and outwardly convey the Moravian image of peaceful rest. On both St. John and Barbados, bed markers, tombs, and ledgers retained popularity through the twentieth century and into the present.

Discursive Spaces within Imperial Influence and Local Interaction: Social Reflections and Contributions from Pre- and Postemancipation Burial Sites on St. John and Barbados

Although an increase in the use of Moravian cemeteries occurred in both St. John and Barbados leading up to and after emancipation, it is important to emphasize that a significant increase occurred much earlier on Barbados than on St. John. Mid- to late-nineteenth-century church burial registers for Emmaus Church on St. John indicate that the majority of the church's African Moravian burials were placed near homes and in yards until the early 1880s, the last decade for which the historic African Moravian burial register is available for study due to poor preservation (Moravian Archives, Bethlehem, Pennsylvania, microfilm, Emmaus Church Register, 1833–1881. Moravian Church in the Eastern West Indies Record Group). Oral histories indicate that for much of the island, including members of Bethany Church, this trend continued well into the middle of the twentieth century (Blouet 2010; Olwig 1994), when most burials were, according to law (Title 19 Virgin Island Rules and Regulations. Part VI: Regulatory Provisions Concerning Public Health. Chapter 59b: Cemeteries. Sub-Chapter I: Public Cemeteries, 19 Virgin Islands Code § 2002), supposed to be placed in a defined community or church cemetery. This evidence is surprising, given the overwhelming use of Moravian cemeteries by African Moravians in postemancipation Barbados as well as St. Thomas (Wood 2012). On St. John we might expect higher rates of African Moravian burial in Moravian cemeteries since, as Wood (2012:120) notes, late-nineteenth-century African Moravian interments in Emmaus cemetery indicate the breaking down of racial segregation employed in the space. She writes,

> The community at Emmaus did not maintain spatially segregated burial patterns. Beginning in the 1880s burials of people with some degree of African heritage begin to populate spaces previously reserved for whites. The burial of William George is the first to break the pattern of segregation. George died in 1881 and was placed in a row that had previously been reserved for white men. The George

family was one of the original white families that settled on the East End of St. John in the late eighteenth century. By the 1880s generations of the George family had intermarried with free people of color and enslaved people (Armstrong 2003). William George's burial is next to the grave of Henrietta Andrew, a mulatto woman born in St. Thomas. Her inclusion in a row reserved for men further suggests a breakdown of the rigid social and spatial organization that European Moravians had imposed. Other burials marked by mounds, rings, shells, and plants were added to the landscape as time went on, many occupying the zone previously reserved for white missionaries. (Wood 2012:130)

The reasons for this and other differences in African Moravian burials on St. John and Barbados reflect the islands' social contexts and indicate the variable contributions of burial and commemorative practices to the islands' social changes from the pre- to postemancipation eras.

From the colonial regime's perspective in the pre-emancipation period, separate burials and grave markers for free European and enslaved African Moravians maintained social hierarchies and racial segregation. Burial sites created by the enslaved under early colonial social restrictions reflected and perpetuated political power relationships and tensions between enslaved blacks and free whites. For instance, for most of the slavery period on the two islands, the majority of the enslaved could not be buried in Moravian churchyards or other Christian cemeteries because of their enslaved and race status. Their social restrictions also affected their access to economic resources, and many could not afford durable masonry grave markers. Such constraints were echoed in Danish West Indian laws that limited the number of enslaved attendees at funerals for the enslaved (Hall 1992:63–64). This law is consistent with what Brown (2008), Reis (2007), and Seeman (2010:196–201) identified in Portuguese and British colonial contexts, that leaders of the colonies' free white populations, the actors of imperial rule, viewed funerary and mortuary controls as necessary pieces of their regimes, vehicles through which to exploit the lives of the enslaved.

In the face of limited control over burial practices, in this context the enslaved imbued their burial sites with emotions and remembrances. These were modes of agency, compromise, and resistance through which they connected with each other and the deceased in the face of imperial domination. Burial sites near households and villages effectively allowed enslaved individuals, families, and communities to oversee burials, protect the bodies and spirits of the deceased, and create social and ancestral attachment to the land (Armstrong 2003; Brown 2008:120–123; Delle and Fellows 2014; Gomez 1998; Jamieson 1995; Oldendorp 1987:183–84; Olwig 1994; Pulsipher and Goodwin 1999, 2001; Saunders 2015). The proximity of burials to homes and villages created a space of legacy between the living and the dead founded on localized attachments to burial sites. Such opportunities to bury group members in part contributed to the creation of senses of community and heritage, fortifying senses of togetherness among the enslaved amidst colonial pressures. These senses likely developed as enslaved people reflected on their relationships with the deceased and engaged in vigils, funerals, and the formation of burials, grave sites, and commemorative objects (Saunders 2015). Furthermore, this form of heritage that the enslaved developed, maintained, and transformed over time contributed to their group identity, voice, and strength that empowered them to resist slavery and achieve freedom.

From a Moravian missionary perspective, the concentration of European Moravian burials in the church cemeteries established a Moravian missionary identity, an identity that in part relied on distinctions between white European missionaries and black African and African Caribbean enslaved people, an interesting situation given that the first missionaries originally wanted to become slaves to gain solidarity with the enslaved African population (Wood 2012:120). Churches, mission great houses, and juxtaposing cemeteries stood as centers or spaces from which Moravian missionaries traveled out across the island to convert "heathen" Africans to Christianity and make them docile, hard-working, and God-fearing enslaved laborers in the colonial social hierarchy.

Separate burial sites for missionaries and African Moravians affected the use and transformation of grave markers in the Moravian church cemeteries. The predominant use of the cemeteries by white missionaries and their families in the early period influenced the kinds of grave markers that initially appeared. St. John's Moravian missionaries established cemeteries organized according to traditional Moravian patterns that incorporated customary square markers. Together the markers and cemeteries contributed to eighteenth- and early-nineteenth-century Moravian missionary senses of identity and belonging in the Danish colony. Cemeteries and markers often served this purpose throughout most Moravian Caribbean missions. This system differed from conventional practices used by other white colonists, who, depending on their economic class, might create fieldstone or rubble markers or purchase different masonry styles such as rectangular tombs and ledgers with varying accents and designs. Distinctions between Moravian mortuary practices and those used by other colonists maintained Moravian identity and community, connecting Caribbean Moravian outposts to European home churches. These mortuary differences, however, did not reflect a complete separation between Moravian missionaries and other white colonists such as elite planters and business people, for the missionaries moved in the same social, economic, and political circles as white elites (Wood 2012:124–125).

On fewer occasions in eighteenth- and early-nineteenth-century Moravian cemeteries, burials were marked in ways that differed from the standard Moravian square marker patterns. We see this by the lack of contemporary square markers and instead the presence of tombs and ledgers on Barbados. The lack of common square markers in Barbados, while possibly a product of deterioration or minimal building material availability, could also reflect Moravian efforts to blend in to their English colonial setting by adopting mortuary as well as social and economic practices. The colonial setting on Barbados was perhaps a more difficult place in which to create a respected niche than the Danish colony of St. John because it was a wealthy possession heavily structured and controlled by the English Crown, government, and Anglican Church whereas St. John's poorer colony was eager to attract people who could develop and maintain trade and society. In fact, Moravians on Barbados connected with Barbados's Anglican or Episcopalian heritage by referring to themselves with a former moniker, the Ancient Episcopalian Church (Gale 1953). This assimilative approach influenced the absence of traditional square Moravian markers and contributed to similarities seen across eighteenth- and early-nineteenth-century rectangular ledgers and tombs in both Moravian and Anglican cemeteries.

The increase in African Moravian burials in Moravian churchyards in the years leading up to and after emancipation indicated decreasing pressures within the local churches to segregate white and black interments, especially as more of the missions' local directors were of African descent. It also marked changes regarding what constituted appropriate and available burial locations within African Moravian communities. In effect, the increased use of Moravian burial grounds on St. John and Barbados gradually marked another viable option for freed communities. The time at which African Moravian communities integrated church burial grounds differed from Barbados to St. John. Moravian burial registers from Barbados indicate that the majority of documented African Moravians received interment in Moravian cemeteries by the 1830s while most African Moravians on St. John continued to use house yard and village burial sites into the early twentieth century (Barbados National Archives, Black Rock, microfilm, Emmaus Moravian Church Book, Coral Bay 1833–1881; Barbados National Archives, Black Rock, microfilm, Mount Tabor Moravian Church Book, St. John's Parish 1828–1860; Olwig 1994; Barbados National Archives, Black Rock, microfilm, Sharon Moravian Church Book, St. Thomas Parish 1767–1854).

African Barbadians used Moravian cemeteries earlier than African St. Johnians because they faced stricter laws that reduced their residential land access and use during transitions from slavery to freedom from the 1820s to the 1840s (Beckles 2007:204–205; Blouet 1980:126). Even after emancipation in 1838, plantation owners barred land ownership for the newly freed population, and significant increases in African Barbadian proprietorship did not occur until the late 1920s (Beckles 2007:211). Between the transitional period and the early twentieth century, the majority of the African Barbadian population rented property and lacked full control over their living situations, so they did not bury the dead on the land where they lived. Instead they interred deceased family and community members in sanctified Moravian grounds, cemetery spaces that afforded some sense of social and material stability within a web of weak links to land and property.

On St. John, however, although most African St. Johnians both before and after emancipation aligned themselves with the Moravian Church, the number of African St. Johnian burials in the Moravian cemeteries from the early nineteenth to the early twentieth century remained small. This absence was a product of at least two factors—one geographical, the other economical.

First, St. John was and is a hillier and more rugged island than Barbados, and this hindered the transport of dead bodies to the cemeteries. Second, despite people participating in the island's Moravian congregations, they had more opportunity than those on Barbados to secure family land on which to bury household members and create autonomous social and economic space. Although Danish West Indian authorities passed regulations from 1848 to the 1860s that barred St. John's newly freed laborers from land ownership, independent agricultural or mercantile endeavors, and work outside plantation labor, significant numbers of African St. Johnians migrated to St. Thomas for better jobs and wages, and there were fewer migrants to the British Virgin Islands (Olwig 1985:41). By the 1860s population decline crippled St. John's estate profits, and many prominent owners sold their lands (Olwig 1985:90–91). Gradually, former slavery-based plantations came under the control of African St. Johnians and African Caribbean transplants (Olwig 1985:93), and they created burial sites where they lived (Armstrong 2003; Blouet 2013; Kellar 2004).

Burial sites often contained fieldstone markers. On occasion, people created affordable brick-and-mortar markers. Since many African St. Johnians fulfilled their desire to acquire and control property, burial sites on residential land played important symbolic and material roles in establishing and maintaining land ownership and community heritage in the broader social space and landscape (Olwig 1994). Until the mid-twentieth century on St. John, if one had no family land on which to be buried, one was interred in a churchyard or public cemetery (Olwig 1985:152). In a sense, such cemetery burials and spaces on St. John represented social and economic instability at the family level, the opposite of the firm social footing their counterparts signified on Barbados.

Conclusion

The multiple implications of burial sites over time and space reveal complex relationships between mortuary space and material, people, and the social contexts in which they met. Through an anthropological materiality synthesis of diverse data sets, I conclude that mortuary contexts played important roles in society because they reflected and therefore informed social change and historical transformation from slavery to freedom. In addition, transitions in burial practices influenced by enslaved and free people of African descent, Moravian missions, and the colonial settings in which such groups interacted were not uniform across St. John and Barbados. Rather, to varying degrees, they both mirrored and shaped social changes, benefits, and challenges. The ways in which burial and commemorative practices changed following emancipation varied in perhaps unexpected ways depending on the kinds of social, economic, and political opportunities that were available to freed people and their descendants. When freedom came, lasting physical attachments continued in varying degrees, especially for freed people who gained legal claim to the land on which burial sites existed. Freed St. Johnians legally possessed land earlier than freed Barbadians, most of whom bore little chance of gaining full control of land until the early to mid-twentieth century. As a result, freed Barbadians created new, important legacies within Moravian church cemeteries, histories that reinforced their long-standing spiritual community commitment. On the other hand, many of St. John's African Moravians maintained the practice of burying near one's home or in a house yard.

While St. John's postemancipation house yard burials might reflect in part the retention of restrictions barring African Moravians from burying in the church cemeteries, the combined analysis of material, spatial, and documentary evidence demonstrates that the continued use of house yard burial sites also influenced and contributed to land access and ownership practices. Collectively, freed St. Johnians emphasized identities as land occupants and owners, or household members who were empowered by their experiences in an African Moravian spiritual community. In fact, residential burial sites are still recognized on St. John in the identification of land ownership histories (Blouet 2010; Olwig 1994). Conversely on Barbados, the increased number of churchyard burials, though demonstrating social connections to and community building within the Moravian churches, also indicates Barbadian African Moravians' lack of land access and ownership.

Finally, it is imperative to consider that a relatively high or low Moravian cemetery use rate did not determine outright the influence of the Moravian Church in the lives of many African Moravians on Barbados and St. John. Rather, people created social networks through Moravian churches, and in some cases they used the church cemeteries. In others, congregation members placed burials in house yards, village sites, and municipal grounds. In other words, African Moravian communities and identities were created and defined by more than burial spaces, let alone those in Moravian churchyards. In reality, African Moravians relied on diverse relationships with living and deceased community members in household, village, church, and island social and material contexts. Burial spaces are but one vital facet of that dynamic legacy.

Acknowledgments

The research presented in this article would not have been possible without the support of the following: on St. John and St. Thomas, the Virgin Islands National Park, the Friends of the National Park, the Virgin Islands Department of Natural Resources, the St. John local community and Moravian congregations, and the Enid M. Baa Public Library; on Barbados, the Moravian congregations at Calvary, Clifton Hill, Mount Tabor, and Sharon churches, the Barbados National Archives, the University of the West

Indies, Cave Hill; at Syracuse University, the Anthropology Department, the Program on Latin America and the Caribbean, the Maxwell School of Citizenship and Public Affairs, and the Graduate School; at Utica College, the Sociology and Anthropology Department, the School of Arts and Sciences, the Faculty Resource Committee, and the Office of Academic Affairs. Archivists at the Moravian Archives in Bethlehem, Pennsylvania, and at Moravian Church House, Muswell Hill, London, England, also helped me identify pertinent historic records. Any errors are my own.

References Cited

Adams, Ron L., and Stacie M. King
2011   Residential Burial in Global Perspective. In *Residential Burial: A Multiregional Exploration*, edited by Ron L. Adams and Stacie M. King, pp. 1–16. American Anthropological Association, Washington, D.C.

Armstrong, Douglas V.
1990   *The Old Village and the Great House: An Archaeological and Historical Examination of Drax Hall Plantation, St. Ann's Bay, Jamaica.* University of Illinois, Urbana.
2003   *Creole Transformation from Slavery to Freedom: Historical Archaeology of the East End Community, St. John, Virgin Islands.* University Press of Florida, Gainesville.

Atwood, Craig
1997   The Joyfulness of Death in Eighteenth Century Moravian Communities. *Communal Societies* 17:39–58.

Baxter, Jane, and Michael Steven Marshall
2009   Cemeteries, Histories, and Communities on a Bahamian Family Island: Historical Archaeology and Cemeteries on San Salvador. *Journal of the Bahamas Historical Society* 31:17–30.

Beckles, Hilary
2007   *A History of Barbados: From Amerindian Settlement to Caribbean Single Market.* Cambridge University Press, Cambridge.

Bender, Barbara, Sue Hamilton, and Christopher Tilley.
1997   Leskernick: Stone Worlds, Alternative Narratives, Nested Landscapes. *Proceedings of the Prehistoric Society* 63:147–178.

Berggren, Asa, and Liv Nilsson Stutz
2010   From Spectator to Critic and Participant: A New Role for Archaeology in Ritual Studies. *Journal of Social Archaeology* 10:171–197.

Binford, Lewis
1971   Mortuary Practices: Their Study and Their Potential. In *Approaches to the Social Dimensions of Mortuary Practices*, Memoir 25, edited by James Brown, pp. 6–29. Society for American Archaeology, Washington, D.C.

Blouet, Helen
2010   Marking Life and Death on St. John, Virgin Islands, 1718–1950: An Historical

Archaeology of Commemoration through Objects, Space, and Transformation. Unpublished Ph.D. dissertation. Department of Anthropology, Syracuse University.

2013   Interpretations of Burial and Commemoration in Moravian and African Diasporas on St. John, Virgin Islands. *International Journal of Historical Archaeology* 17:731–781.

2014   Spatial and Material Transformations in Commemoration on St. John, U.S. Virgin Islands. In *Materialities of Ritual in the Black Atlantic*, edited by Akin Ogundiran and Paula Saunders, pp. 280–295. Indiana University Press, Bloomington.

Blouet, Olwyn

1980   To Make Society Safe for Freedom: Slave Education in Barbados, 1823–1833. *Journal of Negro History* 65(2):126–134.

Brady, Lieutenant

1994 [1829]   Observations on the State of Negro Slavery in the Island of St. Croix. In *Kamina Folk: Slavery and Slave Life in the Danish West Indies*, edited by George Tyson and Arnold Highfield, pp. 159–180. Virgin Islands Humanities Council, St. Croix.

Brandon, Jamie C., and James M. Davidson

2005   The Landscape of Van Winkle's Mill: Identity, Myth, and Modernity in the Ozark Upland South. *Historical Archaeology* 39(3):113–131.

Brown, James

1971   The Dimensions of Status in the Burials at Spiro. In *Approaches to the Social Dimensions of Mortuary Practices*, Memoir 25, edited by James Brown, pp. 92–112. Society for American Archaeology, Washington, D.C.

Brown, Vincent

2008   *The Reaper's Garden: Death and Power in the World of Atlantic Slavery*. Harvard University Press, Cambridge.

Brunache, Peggy

2011   Enslaved Women, Foodways, and Identity Formation: The Archaeology of Habitation La Mahaudiere, Guadeloupe, circa Late-18th Century to Mid-19th Century. Ph.D. dissertation, Department of Anthropology, University of Texas, Austin.

Carstens, Johan Lorenz

1997   *St. Thomas in Early Danish Times: A General Description of All Danish, American, or West Indian Islands*. Translated by A. R. Highfield. Virgin Islands Humanities Council, Charlotte Amalie, St. Thomas.

Chapman, Robert, and Klavs Randsborg

1981   Approaches to the Archaeology of Death. In *The Archaeology of Death*, edited by Robert Chapman, Ian Kinnes, and Klavs Randsborg, pp. 1–24. Cambridge University Press, Cambridge.

Charles, Douglas and Jane Buikstra

1983   Archaic Mortuary Sites in the Central Mississippi Drainage: Distribution, Structure, and Behavioral Implications. In *Archaic Hunters and Gatherers in the American Midwest*, edited by James Phillips and James Brown, pp. 117–145. Academic Press, New York.

2001   Siting, Sighting, and Citing the Dead. In *Social Memory, Identity and Death: Ethnographic and Archaeological Perspectives on Mortuary Rituals*, edited by Meredith Chesson, pp. 13–25. American Anthropological Association, Arlington, Virginia.

Chesson, Meredith

2001   Embodied Memories of Place and People: Death and Society in an Early Urban Community. In *Social Memory, Identity and Death: Ethnographic and Archaeological Perspectives on Mortuary Rituals*, edited by Meredith Chesson, pp. 100–113. American Anthropological Association, Arlington, Virginia.

Childe, Vere Gordon

1945   Directional Changes in Funerary Practices during 50,000 Years. *Man* 45:13–19.

Crain, Christopher, Kevin Farmer, Frederick H. Smith, and Karl Watson

2004   Human Skeletal Remains from an Unmarked African Burial Ground in the Pierhead Section of Bridgetown, Barbados. *Journal of the Barbados Museum and Historical Society* 50:66–83.

Delle, James A.

1998   *An Archaeology of Social Space: Analyzing Coffee Plantations in Jamaica's Blue Mountains.* Plenum, New York.

2001   Race, Missionaries, and the Struggle to Free Jamaica. In *Race and the Archaeology of Identity*, edited by Charles E. Orser Jr., pp. 177–195. University of Utah, Salt Lake City.

2014   *The Colonial Caribbean: Landscapes of Power in Jamaica's Plantation System.* Cambridge University, Cambridge.

Delle, James A., and Kristen Fellows

2014   Death and Burial at Marshall's Pen, A Jamaican Coffee Plantation, 1814–1839: Examining the End of Life at the End of Slavery. *Slavery & Abolition* 35(3):474–492.

Delle, James A., Mark W. Hauser, and Douglas V. Armstrong (editors)

2011   *Out of Many, One People: The Historical Archaeology of Colonial Jamaica.* University of Alabama, Tuscaloosa.

Durkheim, Emile

1915   *The Elementary Forms of Religious Life.* Translated by J. W. Swain. George Allen & Unwin, London.

Epperson, Terrence W.

2000   Panoptic Plantations: The Garden Sights of Thomas Jefferson and George Mason. In *Lines that Divide: Historical Archaeologies of Race, Class, and Gender*, edited by James A. Delle, Stephen Mrozowski, and Robert Paynter, pp. 58–77. University of Tennessee, Knoxville.

Fahlander, Fredrik, and Terje Oestigaard (editors)

2008   *The Materiality of Death: Bodies, Burials, Beliefs.* British Archaeological Reports International Series, Oxford.

Farmer, Kevin, Frederick H. Smith, and Karl Watson

2005   The Urban Context of Slavery: An Archaeological Perspective from Two Afro-Barbadian Slave Cemeteries in Bridgetown, Barbados. *Proceedings of the Twenty-First Congress of the International Association of Caribbean Archaeology, St. Au-*

gustine, Trinidad, pp. 677–685. University of the West Indies, School of Continuing Education, St Augustine, Trinidad.

Ferguson, Leland

2011   *God's Fields: Landscape, Religion, and Race in Moravian Wachovia.* University Press of Florida, Gainesville.

Francis, Doris, Leonie Kellaher, and Georgina Neophytu

2005   *The Secret Cemetery.* Berg, Oxford.

Frazer, James

1922   *The Golden Bough: A Study in Magic and Religion.* Macmillan, New York.

Fries, Adelaide

1973   *Customs and Practices of the Moravian Church.* Board of Christian Education and Evangelism, Winston-Salem, North Carolina.

Furley, Oliver

1965   Moravian Missionaries and Slaves in the West Indies. *Caribbean Studies* 5(2): 3–16.

Gale, C.A.L.

1946–1947   The Lucas Manuscript Volumes in the Barbados Public Library. *Journal of the Barbados Museum and Historical Society* 14.

Gibson, Heather

2009   Domestic Economy and Daily Practice in Guadeloupe: Historical Archaeology at La Mahaudiere Plantation. *International Journal of Historical Archaeology* 13: 27–44.

Gillespie, Michelle, and Robert Beachy (editors)

2007   *German Moravians in the Atlantic World.* Berghahn Books, London.

Goldstein, Lynn

1976   *Spatial Structure and Social Organization: Regional Manifestations of Mississippian Society.* Unpublished Ph.D. dissertation, Department of Anthropology, Northwestern University.

1981   One-Dimensional Archaeology and Multi-Dimensional People: Spatial Organization and Mortuary Analysis. In *The Archaeology of Death,* edited by Robert Chapman, Ian Kinnes, and Klavs Randsborg, pp. 53–69. Cambridge University, Cambridge.

Gomez, Michael

1998   *Exchanging Our Country Marks: The Transformation of African Identities in the Colonial and Antebellum South.* University of North Carolina Press, Chapel Hill.

Haagensen, Reimert

1994   Description of the Island of St. Croix. In *Kamina Folk: Slavery and Slave Life in the Danish West Indies,* edited by George Tyson and Arnold Highfield, pp. 29–46. Virgin Islands Humanities Council, Charlotte Amalie, St. Thomas.

Hall, Neville

1992   *Slave Society in the Danish West Indies.* Johns Hopkins University Press, Baltimore.

Handler, Jerome S., and Frederick Lange

1978   *Plantation Slavery in Barbados: An Archaeological and Historical Investigation.* Harvard University Press, Cambridge.

Hauser, Mark W.

2008   *An Archaeology of Black Markets: Local Ceramics and Economies in Eighteenth-Century Jamaica.* University Press of Florida, Gainesville.

Hertz, Robert

2008   *Death and the Right Hand.* Translated by Rodney and Claudia Needham. Routledge, London.

Hodder, Ian

1982   The Identification and Interpretation of Ranking in Prehistory: A Contextual Perspective. In *Ranking, Resource and Exchange: Aspects of the Archaeology of Early European Society,* edited by Colin Renfrew and Steven Shennen, pp. 150–154. Cambridge University, Cambridge.

Holmes, John

1818   Historical Sketches of the Missions of the United Brethren. *Journal of the Barbados Museum and Historical Society* 33:3–13.

Ingold, Tim

2007   Materials against Materiality. *Archaeological Dialogues* 14(1):1–16.

Jamieson, Ross

1995   Material Culture and Social Death: African-American Burial Practices. *Historical Archaeology* 29(4):39–58.

Kellar, Elizabeth

2004   *The Construction and Expression of Identity: An Archaeological Investigation of the Laborer Villages at Adrian Estate, St. John, USVI.* Unpublished Ph.D. dissertation, Department of Anthropology, Syracuse University.

Klinkers, Ellen

2007   Moravian Missions in Times of Emancipation: Conversion of Slaves in Suriname during the Nineteenth Century. In *Pious Pursuits: German Moravians in the Atlantic World,* edited by Michelle Gillespie and Robert Beachy. Berghahn Books, London.

Kroeber, Alfred

1927   Disposal of the Dead. *American Anthropologist* 29(3):308–315.

Leedecker, Charles

2009   Preparing for an Afterlife on Earth: The Transformation of Mortuary Behavior in Nineteenth-Century North America. In *International Handbook of Historical Archaeology,* edited by Teresita Majewski and David Gaimster, pp. 140–157. Springer, New York.

Lenik, Stephan

2009   Considering Multiscalar Approaches to Creolization among Enslaved Laborers at Estate Bethlehem, St. Croix, U.S. Virgin Islands. *International Journal of Historical Archaeology* 13:12–26.

Mauss, Marcel

1990   *The Gift: The Form and Reason for Exchange in Archaic Societies.* Routledge, London.

McGuire, Randall

1988   Dialogues with the Dead: Ideology and the Cemetery. In *The Recovery of Meaning: Historical Archaeology in the Eastern United States,* edited by Mark P. Leone and Parker B. Potter, pp. 435–480. Smithsonian Institution Press, Washington, D.C.

Meskell, Lynn

2005   *Archaeologies of Materiality*. Wiley-Blackwell, Oxford.

Miller, Daniel (editor)

2005   *Materiality: Politics, History, and Culture*. Duke University Press, Durham.

Moore, Jerry

2010   Making a Huaca: Memory and Practice in Prehispanic Far Northern Peru. *Journal of Social Archaeology* 10:398–422.

Moravian Church

1789–1794   *Periodical Accounts Relating to the Mission of the Church of the United Brethren, Established among the Heathen*, Vol. 1. W. McDowall, London.

1814–1817   *Periodical Accounts Relating to the Mission of the Church of the United Brethren, Established among the Heathen*, Vol. 6. W. McDowall, London.

1831   *Periodical Accounts Relating to the Mission of the Church of the United Brethren, Established among the Heathen*, Vol. 12. W. McDowall, London.

Mullins, Paul

2012   The Importance of Innocuous Things. In *Historical Archaeology and the Importance of Material Things II*, edited by Julie Schablitsky and Mark P. Leone, pp. 31–44. *Historical Archaeology* special publication No. 9.

Mytum, Harold

2004   *Mortuary Monuments and Burial Grounds of the Historic Period*. Plenum, London.

Norton, Holly, and Christopher Espenshade

2007   The Challenge in Locating Maroon Refuge Sites at Maroon Ridge, St. Croix. *Journal of Caribbean Archaeology* 7:1–17.

Oldendorp, Christian G. A.

1987   *History of the Mission of the Evangelical Brethren on the Caribbean Islands of St. Thomas, St. Croix, and St. John*, edited by Johann Jakob Bossart, Arnold Highfield, and Vladimir Barac, and translated by Johann Jakob Bossard. Karoma, Ann Arbor, Michigan.

Olwig, Karen Fog

1985   *Cultural Adaptation and Resistance on St. John: Three Centuries of Afro-Caribbean Life*. University Press of Florida, Gainesville.

1994   *The Land Is the Heritage: Land and Community on St. John*. St. John Oral History Association, Cruz Bay, St. John.

Orser, Charles E., Jr.

2001   Race and the Archaeology of Identity in the Modern World. In *Race and the Archaeology of Identity*, edited by Charles E. Orser Jr., pp. 1–13. University of Utah, Salt Lake City.

2006   Symbolic Violence and Landscape Pedagogy: An Example from the Irish Countryside. *Historical Archaeology* 40(2):28–44.

O'Shea, John

1984   *Mortuary Variability: An Archaeological Investigation*. Academic Press, New York.

Parker Pearson, Michael
1982   Mortuary Practices, Society and Ideology: An Ethnoarchaeological Study. In *Symbolic and Structural Archaeology,* edited by Ian Hodder, pp. 99–113. Cambridge University, Cambridge.
1993   The Powerful Dead: Archaeological Relationships between the Living and the Dead. *Cambridge Archaeological Journal* 3(2):203–229.
1999   *The Archaeology of Death and Burial.* Texas A&M University Press, College Station.

Parry, David
1789   Extract of a Letter from Governor Parry to the Right Honorable Lord Sydney. August 18, 1788. *Parliamentary Papers 1789,* Vol. 26:13–24.

Peebles, Christopher, and Susan Kus
1977   Some Archaeological Correlates of Ranked Societies. *American Antiquity* 42(3): 421–448.

Peterson, Rick
2013   Social Memory and Ritual Performance. *Journal of Social Archaeology* 13:266–283.

Pulsipher, Lydia M., and Conrad M. Goodwin
1999   Here Where the Old Time People Be: Reconstructing the Landscape of the Slavery and Post-Slavery Era in Montserrat, West Indies. In *African Sites Archaeology in the Caribbean*, edited by Jay B. Haviser, pp. 9–37. Markus Weiner, Princeton, New Jersey.
2001   "Getting the Essence of It": Galways Plantation, Montserrat, West Indies. In *Island Lives: Historical Archaeologies of the Caribbean*, edited by Paul Farnsworth, pp. 165–203. University of Alabama, Tuscaloosa.

Rainville, Lynn
2009a   Savings the Remains of the Day: The Cultural Heritage of Historic American Cemeteries. *Journal of Field Archaeology* 34(2):195–206.
2009b   Home at Last: Mortuary Commemoration in Virginian Slave Cemeteries. *Markers: Annual Journal of the Association for Gravestone Studies* 26:54–83.

Rakita, Gordon, Jane Buikstra, Lane Beck, and Sloan Williams
2005   *Interacting with the Dead: Perspectives on Mortuary Archaeology for the New Millennium.* University Press of Florida, Gainesville.

Reis, João José
2007   *Death Is a Festival: Funeral Rites and Rebellion in Nineteenth Century Brazil.* Translated by H. Sabrina Gledhill. University of North Carolina Press, Chapel Hill.

Renfrew, Colin, Chris Gosden, and Elizabeth DeMarrais
2004   *Substance, Memory and Display: Archaeology and Art.* McDonald Institute for Archaeological Research, Cambridge.

Richards, Helen
2007   Distant Garden: Moravian Missions and the Culture of Slavery in the Danish West Indies, 1732–1848. *Journal of Moravian History* 2:55–74.

Richardson, David (editor)

1985 *Abolition and Its Aftermath: The Historical Context, 1790–1916.* Frank Cass, New York.

Robben, Antonius

2004 *Death, Mourning, and Burial: A Cross-Cultural Reader.* Wiley-Blackwell, Oxford.

Roeber, A. G.

2007 Moravians and the Challenge of Writing Global History of Diasporic Christianity. In *Pious Pursuits: German Moravians in the Atlantic World*, edited by Michelle Gillespie and Robert Beachy, pp. 239–244. Berghahn Books, London.

Saunders, Paula

2015 Analysis of an African Burial Ground in Nineteenth-Century Jamaica. *Journal of African Diaspora Archaeology and Heritage* 4(2):143–171.

Sawyer, Edward

1990 *All about Moravians: History, Beliefs, and Practices of a Worldwide Church.* Moravian Church of America, Bethlehem, Pennsylvania.

Saxe, Arthur

1970 *Social Dimensions of Mortuary Practices.* Unpublished Ph.D. dissertation, Department of Anthropology, University of Michigan.

1971 Social Dimensions of Mortuary Practices in a Mesolithic Population from Wadi Halfa, Sudan. In *Approaches to the Social Dimensions of Mortuary Practices*, Memoir 25, edited by James Brown, pp. 39–57. Society for American Archaeology, Washington, D.C.

Seeman, Erik

2010 *Death in the New World: Cross-Cultural Encounters, 1492–1800.* University of Pennsylvania Press, Philadelphia.

Sensbach, Jon

1998 *A Separate Canaan: The Making of an Afro-Moravian World in North Carolina, 1763–1840.* University of North Carolina Press, Chapel Hill.

2000 Race and the Early Moravian Church: A Comparative Perspective. *Transactions of the Moravian Historical Society* 31:1–10.

2005 *Rebecca's Revival: Creating Black Christianity in the Atlantic World.* Harvard University Press, Cambridge.

2007 Slavery, Race, and the Global Fellowship: Religious Radicals Confront the Modern Age. In *Pious Pursuits: German Moravians in the Atlantic World*, edited by Michelle Gillespie and Robert Beachy, pp. 223–238. Berghahn Books, London.

Shackel, Paul A.

1994 Town Plans and Everyday Material Culture: An Archaeology of Social Relations in Colonial Maryland's Capital Cities. In *Historical Archaeology of the Chesapeake*, edited by Paul A. Shackel and Barbara J. Little, pp. 85–96. Smithsonian Institution, Washington, D.C.

Silverman, Helaine

2002 Mortuary Narratives of Identity and History in Modern Cemeteries of Lima, Peru. In *The Space and Place of Death*, edited by Helaine Silverman and David B. Small, pp. 167–190. American Anthropological Association, Washington, D.C.

Silverman, Helaine, and David Small
2002   *The Space and Place of Death*. American Anthropological Association, Washington, D.C.
Singleton, Theresa A.
2015   *Slavery behind the Wall: An Archaeology of A Cuban Coffee Plantation*. University Press of Florida, Gainesville.
Smaby, Beverly
1988   *The Transformation of Moravian Bethlehem: From Communal Mission to Family Economy*. University of Pennsylvania, Philadelphia.
Smith, Rosamond
1978   The Choir System in Salem. In *Three Forks of Muddy Creek*, Vol. 5, edited by Francis Griffin, pp. 12–25. Old Salem, Salem, North Carolina.
Society for the Conversion and Religious Instruction and Education of the Negro Slaves in the British West India Islands
1829   Returns to Questions Addressed to the Clergy of the Diocese of Barbados and the Leeward Islands, up to December 31, 1828: Island of Barbados. *Report for the Year 1828*. London.
South, Stanley
1999   *Historical Archaeology in Wachovia: Excavating Eighteenth-Century Bethabara and Moravian Pottery*. Springer, New York.
Tainter, Joseph
1978   Mortuary Practices and the Study of Prehistoric Social Systems. *Advances in Archaeological Method and Theory* 1:105–141.
Terrell, Michelle
2005   *The Jewish Community of Early Colonial Nevis: A Historical Archaeological Study*. University Press of Florida, Gainesville.
Tilley, Christopher
2004   *The Materiality of Stone: Explorations in Landscape Phenomenology*. Berg, Oxford.
Tilley, Christopher, Webb Keane, Susanne Kuchler, Mike Rowlands, and Patricia Spyer (editors)
2006   *Handbook of Material Culture*. Sage, London.
Turner, Grace
2013   An Allegory for Life: An Eighteenth-Century African-Influenced Cemetery Landscape, Nassau, Bahamas. Unpublished Ph.D. dissertation, Department of Anthropology, College of William and Mary.
Tylor, Edward B.
1871   *Primitive Culture: Researches into the Development of Mythology, Philosophy, Religion, Language, Art, and Custom*. Murray, London.
Verdery, Katherine
1999   *The Political Lives of Dead Bodies*. Columbia University Press, New York.
Weinlick, John
1956   *Count Zinzendorf: The Story of His Life and Leadership in the Renewed Moravian Church*. Abingdon, New York.

Williams, Howard (editor)

2003   *Archaeologies of Remembrance: Death and Memory in Past Societies*. Kluwer Academic/Plenum, New York.

Wood, Margaret

2012   Mapping the Complexities of Race on the Landscape of the Colonial Caribbean, United States Virgin Islands, 1770–1917. *Historical Archaeology* 46(4):112–134.

10

The Archaeology of a Postemancipation Smallholder
in the British Virgin Islands

JOHN M. CHENOWETH

August 1, 1834, was in some ways only a stepping-stone toward actual freedom (Kelly et al. 2011:243). For many enslaved Africans, little except their
legal status changed when slavery ended in the British colonies, as land
and capital were still held by their former enslavers. In some islands such
as Jamaica, available land allowed some to extricate themselves from the
new kind of oppressions of a post-slavery plantation system, but many "former enslaved laborers remained caught in the social and economic web
of servitude, repressive wage labor, and an inability to gain access to land
and resources" (Kelly et al. 2011:257). In the British Virgin Islands (BVI),
however, the circumstances of emancipation were somewhat different. Personal effort and a series of historical events led to the creation of many
small farms wholly owned by the newly freed, and the white-owned plantation system fully disintegrated in the decades following emancipation.
This chapter considers initial archaeological work at one of these free black
"smallholder" farms, highlighting the creative negotiation of the women
and men who held their own land despite living in an oppressive empire.

As discussed in the introduction to this volume, while much attention
has been rightly focused on the large sugar estate as the dominant form of
economic entity in the historic Caribbean, other less-common sites that
were nonetheless a major part of the Caribbean experience have not received enough attention. The entire postemancipation period may be such
a context in need of further study (Kelly et al. 2011). While this chapter
seeks to contribute to the discussion of these sites that have so far largely
fallen through the cracks of archaeological attention, only initial excavation
of this site has been conducted to date, and the conclusions discussed here

must be seen as preliminary. I view these interpretations as hypotheses that may be evaluated by full-scale study and comparisons to other sites.

* * *

On private property on a small island called Great Camanoe, gardeners clearing a patch of woods in the summer of 2013 discovered the foundations of a small building. Artifacts and construction, discussed below, suggested a mid-nineteenth-century occupation date, by which time virtually all the white population of the BVI had abandoned it; by 1856 there were only 201 whites compared to 5,892 African-descended people, with whites making up just 3.4 percent of the population (Dookhan 1975:129, 141). This is a substantial decrease from 1823, when they composed 6.3 percent (House of Commons Parliamentary Papers, Papers Relating to Captured Negroes, Slave Trade, 1826 (81) XXVII.110), or a century earlier when there were 760 whites from a total population of 2,190, or 34.7 percent (Burns 1965:461). The remaining whites were mainly government officials based in Road Town, the territory's capital and only substantial settlement, and a few large landholders. The "Out Islands" like Great Camanoe were not the sites of large estates since they were less suited for agriculture, especially sugar, and generally poorer than the main island of Tortola or larger Caribbean islands (Chenoweth 2011:293). Despite the fact that there are no currently accessible land records to clarify ownership, then, it can be suggested that this site was most likely home to a family of free people of African descent, the eldest of whom probably had lived in slavery while perhaps the younger hoped to build a future in the postemancipation colonial system.

The British Virgin Islands and the Economic Context of Smallholding

The BVI are a group of about 40 small islands centered on today's regional population center of Tortola. The earliest British surveys of Tortola found it "Very Mountainous, not capable of making many Sugarworks" in 1716 (National Archives, London, CO 152/11#6 encl. (v)). Another early report, in 1711, states that of the whole of the BVI "only Spanishtown [today called Virgin Gorda] has a good harbor and . . . the soil of that island is good, but most of the rest are little better than Rocks" (National Archives, London, CO 314/1#1). Likely due to this poor agricultural potential, the BVI were settled later in the colonial process than many other Caribbean islands, with white settlers not arriving in force until the 1720s. These first

European occupants were poor and arrived informally rather than as part of a planned settlement.

A plantation system did develop in the BVI, based first on cotton, which was profitable after 1770 (Dookhan 1975:46), particularly when the American Revolution cut Britain off from its mainland cotton-producing colonies. At other times, such as in the 1820s, the price of cotton was so low that it was not worth planting. Sugar passed cotton as the major BVI export in terms of value by 1759 (Dookhan 1975:49), and it briefly was quite profitable toward the end of the eighteenth and beginning of the nineteenth centuries. However, overall Tortola was ill-suited to sugar growing (Martin 1834:381), at least compared to the major sugar islands such as Jamaica and Barbados, and it was never home to such large estates and wealthy elite planters. The Out Islands and large parts of Tortola continued to be used primarily for cotton as they were unsuited to sugar growing.

A combination of factors brought even the relative economic stability of the late eighteenth century to a close in the early nineteenth century. These included international peace after the Napoleonic Wars, which decreased illicit smuggling—always a source of wealth in the BVI—and a switch in consumer preference to green-seed cotton from the American South instead of the sea-island variety grown in the Caribbean. The economy was further upset by the collapse of sugar prices due to economic depression in Britain and increased sugar production by other European countries (Dookhan 1975:46, 61). Perhaps the greatest blow to the economy of the BVI in the early nineteenth century was the hurricane of September 1819, which killed almost a hundred people and destroyed buildings and goods reported to have values from £150,000 (Martin 1834:509) to over £300,000 (Dookhan 1975:64). It was reported that this hurricane "laid low every building in the islands" and encouraged a great number of planters to take the enslaved people they held and relocate to Trinidad (Watkins 1924:137). One visitor, Trelawney Wentworth, arrived on Tortola the year after the hurricane and reported that "every set of [sugar] works in the island had been more or less injured, and many were totally laid waste; every estate too, was more or less mortgaged, and many without resources to rebuild the works or continue cultivation" (Wentworth 1835:170).

As a result of this combination of factors, many planters were unable to pay their taxes, and some also accumulated large amounts of debt trying to repair the damage done by the storm. The recent economic upheaval had left these planters with damaged credit, making repairs even more difficult, and many simply abandoned their plantations and emigrated (Dookhan

1975:65). By the last few years of slavery, the economic situation in the BVI was such that "not above two or three" British ships called each year (Martin 1834:508). The last BVI sugar was exported directly to Britain in 1848, and by 1859 virtually all trade was with nearby Danish St. Thomas, since the smaller profit margins of the products of the BVI made this the only effective market (Dookhan 1975:139). Exports also came almost exclusively through St. Thomas, even those of British manufacture. Production of sugar and cotton nearly ceased in the BVI and most of the land was turned over to cattle and provisioning crops over the course of the nineteenth century (Dookhan 1975:138–139).

Ultimately many factors, from changes in world trade patterns to the preexisting environment and geology of the BVI, to specific events like the 1819 hurricane, brought an end to the plantation system of the BVI. Those who remained were largely the African-descended population, legally freed after 1838 but with little support from the colonial government, which cared primarily for the colonies that still produced tax revenues using paid (and controlled) labor. Although the weather and the global economic situation were beyond the control of the black British Virgin Islanders who lived through this slow collapse, their decisions in the aftermath of the plantation system produced a unique history that has remained largely unexplored, particularly archaeologically.

Historian Michael O'Neal argues that the economic marginality of the BVI accorded powers to their laborers that those of African descent were sometimes able to assert even before enslavement ended. He cites a case of rebellion on the Isaac Pickering estate in 1823, in the midst of this economic decline, in which the enslaved Africans recognized "the degree of bargaining power which their labour represented within the context of the social relations of production of a declining plantation economy. Thus . . . by means of a work stoppage, the Pickering slaves were able to force the removal of a disliked overseer" (O'Neal 2012:48). While not unheard of in other contexts during slavery, such exercises of power by the legally enslaved may have had more lasting effects in the BVI, considering the unstable economy.

After emancipation, the economic difficulties of the colony and the inability of plantation owners to pay their taxes provided an opportunity for the latent power of the laboring majority of the BVI to bear fruit. In 1864 the colonial government eased the land transfer tax that had been a major roadblock to small purchases of land and in 1865 sold off eight estates totaling 315 hectares (780 acres) or fully 5 percent of the total land of Tortola, in parcels to anyone—black or white—who could pay. O'Neal concludes, "With the sale of these properties at an average price of £1.53 per acre falling well within the purchasing power of many of the former slaves [Dookhan 1975:135], this event constituted both the symbolic and effective demise of the plantation economy in the British Virgin Islands. And thus was born a society of free black smallholders" (O'Neal 2012:55). The term "smallholder" is discussed in some detail by O'Neal as representing those who owned their own land and produced a mix of cash and subsistence crops but who pursued other opportunities including charcoaling, fishing, and livestock husbandry (O'Neal 2012:65–70). In this way the European-imposed plantation model fully gave way to a very different system, with many small landholders making ends meet creatively. By the end of the 1860s, 1 in every 10 British Virgin Islanders was a "freeholder" and 1 in 6 owned enough property (land or cattle) to be taxed (Harrigan and Varlack 1975:70, 1991). By 1865 a majority of the land of the BVI was legally held by blacks, and by the end of the century it was virtually all held by small landowners in lots of less than 100 acres, with only 32 resident whites in the whole colony (Dookhan 1975:129, 136). Similar smallholdings existed on marginal lands and the white-owned plantation system persisted on the best lands nearby in places like Jamaica; in the BVI, the smallholders represented virtually the entire economy.

It is a fundamental principle of historical archaeology that written records cannot encapsulate all there is to know about a past time and place. Governmental records in particular are usually created with an economic focus, especially in the extractive colonial economy of the eighteenth- and nineteenth-century Caribbean. Mainstream histories of the BVI such as those cited here (Dookhan 1975; Harrigan and Varlack 1975) have until recently focused on economics, in part because this was the subject best recorded in written documents. As a result, the history of the BVI may sometimes be written so as to appear wholly a function of colonial forces: the decisions made in London to tax, import, purchase, and so on. Such histories have little to say of the enslaved and freed Africans and their agency, but, as O'Neal has shown, this was a force to be reckoned with even before the establishment of legal freedom. Moreover, documents for the postemancipation period in the Caribbean can, perhaps surprisingly, be less abundant and informative than for earlier times. Laurie Wilkie and Paul Farnsworth (2011:66–67) discovered this for the Bahamas, and it is similarly true for the BVI. Archaeological work has the potential to help in narrowing these gaps.

Archaeology and the Rowe Site

Colonial systems are built in part on record keeping, but the records kept are those that benefit the system itself. Those for the BVI are concentrated between about 1760 and 1840, with a virtual silence after this date until after World War II. The economic marginality of this colony prevented the colonial system from profiting from it, so those in London took little note of this area. Archaeology has a great potential to inform us about the lives of people in this period when we have so few other sources. As noted earlier, the project discussed here is quite preliminary, consisting of only limited work at one site dating to the postemancipation period. Rather than arguing for broad conclusions based on these limited data, it is meant to raise questions and suggest the untapped potential of studying this period that was so influential to later BVI culture and of which so little is known from the documentary record.

A brief field season in 2013 identified a set of foundation walls, known as "Structure B" or the "Rowe Site," after the current landowners. The site rests about 22 m above the sea on a gentle rise, the slopes of which extend down to the coast about 125 m away. This placement results in very shallow archaeological deposits but would have provided both a clear view of the neighboring islands and good breezes while the taller center of the island would have sheltered the site from most storms. A short walk would have allowed residents access to both the best growing areas for either provisions or cash crops at the higher elevations and the resources of the sea.

The structure itself consists of a single mortared-stone rectangular wall measuring 6.8 m × 5.0 m on the outside, enclosing an area of 18.7 m^2 (Figure 10.1). This interior would probably have been divided in half, although there is no surviving indication of this in the walls or ground. Different sides of the enclosure vary from 60 cm to 80 cm in width, although measurements are difficult in some areas due to collapse, so the walls may have all been about 60 cm in diameter originally. The foundation survives to a height of up to 1 m in places, and surviving portions are finished at this level, showing that this was the original height. Above this, the walls of the structure were probably wood-framed with post-in-ground construction, there being no evidence for postholes visible in the walls; this is a technique common in the BVI, especially in the eighteenth century. Alternately, the walls may have sat on "sleeper" beams placed on the top of the stone foundation, a technique more common in the nineteenth century. On

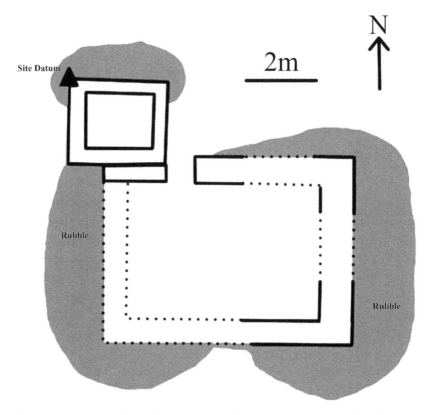

Figure 10.1. Map of the Rowe Site foundations, Great Camanoe Island, British Virgin Islands. (Image by John M. Chenoweth)

comparable BVI sites, however, this construction is usually accompanied by layers of mortar that secured the sleepers to the foundation and created a slope, directing rainwater away from the wood. No traces of such mortar sleeper trenches are visible, and the walls appear to have been finished smooth and level on the tops where these survive. No pieces of mortar impressed with wattle shapes were encountered, suggesting wattle-and-daub (mud as opposed to mortar over wooden wattles) or clapboard walls. There is a well-preserved doorway in the north wall whose low threshold suggests that the structure most likely had a dirt floor.

On the northwest corner stands a better-preserved enclosure measuring 2.2 m × 2.7 m on the outside, with an internal area of just under 3 m^2 abutting the main foundation. This structure was clearly added at a later date, adjoining the main building, and is interpreted as a cistern, likely storing water collected from the structure's roof, as it has slightly rounded interior corners and no doorway. Unfortunately, the unstable nature of this wall prevented any excavation inside the structure, and plant growth had destroyed any mortar flooring or sign of waterproofing.

A cistern would have been a vital part of this home. P.H.A. Martin-Kaye's (1954:69) modern survey of the BVI's water supplies expresses dim prospects for well water on the Out Islands such as this. Fresh water was always a problem in the BVI in general, as there are no rivers or steady streams and rainfall is erratic. The BVI's rainfall can be as little as 76 cm in a year and is less overall at lower elevations, including on the cays such as Great Camanoe (Martin-Kaye 1954).

The two phases of construction in the walls of the Rowe Site—the main foundation and cistern—are built of somewhat different materials. The first phase is composed primarily of rough-faced local stone mortared together in a style common to structures of the BVI since the middle of the eighteenth century. The cistern is made in a different style, with substantially more mortar between the stones and a wider variety of materials: rough-faced (usually single-faced) stone blocks, cut coral blocks, and even flat mortar pieces reused from an earlier building (Figure 10.2). Both coral

Figure 10.2. Repurposed mortar block in the foundations of the cistern, Rowe Site. (Photograph by John M. Chenoweth)

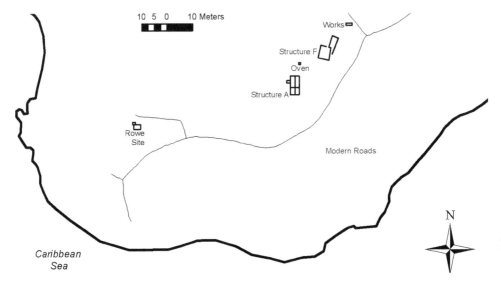

Figure 10.3. Map of the ruins near the Rowe Site, Great Camanoe Island, British Virgin Islands. (Image by John M. Chenoweth)

and brick have associations with higher-status building in the BVI. For instance, huge amounts of cut coral were used in a late phase of a very large plantation house on Norman Island, which I surveyed in 2014. Brick arrived as ballast and was not produced in the BVI, where it was in demand for building and hearths. Yet coral could be acquired from the local reefs at any time, and single bricks could be reused or sold. In contrast, hardened mortar blocks must have been taken from earlier buildings that had been abandoned and could be disassembled without residents objecting.

The probable source of at least some of these materials is a complex of earlier buildings that begins about 170 m east of the Rowe Site, at an altitude 30 m higher, 50 m above the nearby sea (Figure 10.3). These have been identified as a multiphase plantation house (structure A), and oven, a small sugar train (the part of the works where sugar is boiled down), and a large associated building (structure F) that may have served as the owners' residence earlier in the site's history before being converted to industrial or storage use. Artifacts consistent with a mid-eighteenth to mid-nineteenth century occupation were recovered from structures A and F, including tin-enameled wares, lead-glazed slipwares, creamwares, and pearlwares. This places these structures earlier than the Rowe Site (the chronology of which is discussed in more detail below). The journey between structures A and F and the Rowe Site would be about 250 m by the modern road, which probably follows the line of an earlier track.

Several pieces of glass were visible in the mortar of the Rowe Site cistern, including one clear glass bottle base that was loose and was removed for analysis. This piece appears to be dip-molded, exhibiting vertical ribbed decoration on the sides and an eight-pointed star or starburst motif decoration on the kickup, a slight narrowing toward the base, straight sides, and no mold seams. Unfortunately, dip molding is not a useful chronological indicator, but it is clear that this material was at hand during the construction of the cistern, suggesting a period of occupation between the construction of the Rowe Site's main foundations and the cistern addition.

The scale and dating of the earlier structures A and F suggest that they were most likely the homes of white plantation owners. Although analysis of the artifacts recovered from this complex has not yet been completed, it appears to have been abandoned by the middle of the nineteenth century. The different construction materials in the different parts of the walls of the Rowe Site suggest that the second phase—the cistern—may have been built when it was more practical to take these more-difficult-to-acquire but easier-to-use pieces from this earlier structural complex. In other words, the first phase of structure B was probably built before the plantation house up the hill was abandoned and the cistern after. The occupation of the Rowe Site likely continued after the former owners of the plantation left the island, and the Rowe Site occupants thereafter became the legal owners of the land. The abandoned buildings up the hill then became quarries for those who remained.

Archaeological Excavation

A test unit placed in the interior of the Rowe Site near the southwest corner was excavated to a depth of 24 cm below the surface before encountering bedrock. No ceramics or pipe stems were found to provide dates, but several finds add to our knowledge of the structure's occupants. Two halves of a copper-alloy hook from a hook-and-eye clothing fastener were found in the lowest excavated level. These fasteners were quite simple, generally invisible in use, and were found on both men's and women's clothing (White 2005:74–75). This example is slightly flattened, suggesting a post-1770s date.

Another clothing-related item is a backing to an imported, two-piece button, most similar to South's (1964) type 24: a back with a single hole and with small grooves radiating out on one side to keep the free ends of a wire shank from spinning, but of copper alloy rather than iron. These features suggest an early- or mid-nineteenth-century date (the context for South's similar find dated to 1837–1865). The diameter of approximately 11 mm, with the finished button slightly larger, suggests a medium-sized button, often used on sleeves (White 2005:57). Buttons were decorative as well as functional and varied tremendously in cost (White 2005:57), but this was not of the most basic and functional bone or shell, which could have been manufactured locally.

Other finds include a copper-alloy, square-sided, hand-wrought nail, a nondiagnostic can fragment, and several fragments of wrought iron nails. Food canning became widespread starting in the early nineteenth century (Busch 1981). None of the nails show any signs of being cut nails of any type (although many are too corroded to discern manufacturing technique clearly); this is surprising, given the other dating evidence for the site that suggests a mid-nineteenth-century occupation and the late-eighteenth-century date for the introduction of cut nails (Wells 1998). This absence may speak to the isolation of the BVI from commercial trading routes, suggesting that older nails were reused and newer nails were not always available. This evidence is consistent with reports of difficulty acquiring manufactured goods, particularly iron nails, in the more rural parts of the Lesser Antilles in much more recent times, as late as the 1970s (Pyle 1981:86).

*   *   *

Two highly fragmented pieces of unidentifiable mammal bone suggest that nothing was wasted in food preparation, as does the presence of the one identifiable shell: a single, complete *Americardia media* or Atlantic strawberry cockle. This species is common and easy to acquire, living in sandy shallows (Rehder 1981:746), but was not commonly eaten (Humfrey 1975:244). This may suggest some food pressure, with the inhabitants of the site turning to less-preferred species for food. The lack of any examples of *Cittarium pica*, the West Indian top shell, was a surprising result, despite the limited nature of the excavations. Work on a site of the previous century on nearby Little Jost van Dyke produced *C. pica* fragments at almost 100 per m² and minimum number of individuals of 11 per m² (Chenoweth 2011). This species, locally called "whelk," was an important historic and prehistoric food resource (Abbott and Morris 1995:137) and probably remains the most common shoreline gastropod in the West Indies, but their populations have suffered in recent decades (Toller and Gordon 2005:9–11), suggesting a long-term decline that may have made this resource unavailable postemancipation.

While the sample is of course limited, the bone and shell finds may suggest some food stress. Enslaved people in the BVI were usually responsible for their own food and were accorded land and some time each week to grow and gather what they could (see Chapters 4 and 5 in this volume for analyses of Jamaican provisioning areas). Thomas Woolrich, a merchant living in the BVI for several decades, suggests that on his first arrival in 1753, the enslaved people had sufficient land for this purpose (House of Commons 1790:268). However, later in his stay, by the 1770s, the enslaved population was much larger as planters attempted to increase profits by increasing their workforce, mimicking the intensification of plantations on better-suited islands such as Jamaica and Barbados. Population records show the sharp increase toward the end of the eighteenth century as planters tried to increase production, pushing themselves deeper into debt and pushing those they held closer to starvation. In 1756, a few years after Woolrich's arrival, the population of the colony is given as 7,289, of whom 6,121 were enslaved (National Archives, London, CO 152/28#BC83). This was an increase from a population of 2,190 a generation earlier in 1724, and just 1,205 in 1720 (Dookhan 1975:24). By the end of Woolrich's stay in Tortola, in 1774, the population was over 10,000, with all of the increase within the enslaved population, who now had increased 50 percent over the 1756 figure to about 9,000 (Burns 1965:510).

As more land was put under cultivation for cash crops and more enslaved people relied on the smaller provisioning grounds that were left, planters were forced to rely on imported, purchased foods. Although not without hardship to the enslaved people, this was sufficient when plantations were profitable, but these supplies were surely the first expenses to be cut as the plantation system failed in the BVI during the first half of the nineteenth century. Postemancipation, this resource would have been cut altogether. This may have caused a greater reliance on local resources, possibly including overexploitation of *C. pica* and use of less-preferred shellfish. The food-related remains here are too scant to be clear, but they raise the issue of food stress, evidence for which may be sought on related sites.

Surface Artifacts

Although not encountered in excavation, substantial numbers of ceramic and glass artifacts were present on the Rowe Site as surface finds, primarily collected shortly before the project by workers clearing the area for a garden planting. The ceramics are the clearest chronological indicators present on the site and are all consistent with a mid-nineteenth century date: whitewares with thick-line ("peasant style") floral designs (Majewski and O'Brien 1987:158) and light blue transfer prints predominated. No creamwares or pearlwares were encountered, although this was a judgmental sample. One ceramic printed with the mark of the manufacturer, Copeland and Garrett, dates its production to 1833–1847 (Godden 1964:173). These sherds confirm the occupation dates discussed above, with substantial components that are postemancipation.

Both clear and black-glass bottle fragments were common, and at least two glass pieces from the Rowe Site show signs of intentional modification. A bottle base exhibits conchoidal fracturing with a clear bulb of percussion resulting from an impact on the underside of the base. This resulted in one flake taken from the edge (probably a waste flake, since it was also recovered and refit) and a line of thinner, smaller flakes taken across the middle of the inside of the kickup. These latter may have been fit into a composite blade. Conte and colleagues (2008) warn us to be conservative in assessments of worked glass, relying on both marks of working and of use to identify such pieces. The examples here do not show obvious signs of use but may best be seen as waste products from the production of other probably expedient flakes that were used as tools and were not recovered.

Worked glass has received substantial attention, particularly in Native American (Lightfoot et al. 1998:214; Silliman 2010; Martindale and Jurakic 2006), Native Hawaiian (Flexner and Morgan 2013), and Aboriginal Australian (Harrison 2000, 2003) contexts, as well as on several sites associated with African-descended peoples (Klingelhofer 1987; Ryzewski and Cherry 2015:373; Ryzewski and Cherry, this volume). Wilkie reviewed the literature on the subject some two decades ago and did not find any examples of glass-working in clearly Euroamerican contexts (Wilkie 1996:47). At the same time, she suggested that worked glass was used for a variety of cutting and scraping tasks but was mainly replaced by the early twentieth century as razors and other manufactured tools became cheaper and more available.

A more recent review by Todd Ahlman and colleagues (2014) also notes several interpretations of glass tools in African Caribbean contexts being used for woodworking. They suggest that planters did not always supply their enslaved laborers with metal tools if the work they were required to perform did not require them, leading the enslaved people to look to expedient glass tools for many tasks, particularly household ones (Ahlman et al. 2014:17–18). The chronology of the Rowe Site discussed earlier suggests a postemancipation primary occupation, and the changes to the structure noted above have even suggested that much occupation took place after the plantation house itself was abandoned. Therefore, direct control of supervisory whites was not likely the reason for the use of glass tools on this site.

To contextualize these materials, it must be remembered that the BVI were in many respects similar to the Bahamas where Wilkie worked, in that neither was part of the Caribbean core of sugar-producing plantation colonies. Materials and tools easily acquired even by the enslaved in Jamaica or Barbados could be scarce and therefore more costly in these more marginal locations. In the 1730s there was "no immediate intercourse" between Britain and the BVI (Commissioners for Trade and Plantations 1734/5:10), and a similar statement is made of the 1760s, with only two or three ships a year from London and some minimal trade with the newly independent American states by the 1770s (House of Commons 1790:279). As noted earlier, by the 1830s still "not above two or three" British ships called on the BVI in a year (Martin 1834: 508), and Douglas Pyle (1981) suggested difficulty getting some materials into the 1970s. Even today most imports to the BVI come through St. Thomas, with residents taking the ferry to shop there regularly.

While improvised glass tools certainly had a practical purpose, they have also been seen as socially meaningful. In the context of the BVI, they may have taken on meanings as products that were not directly related to the systems of colonial trade, which were limited and, when accessible, always favored white merchants and manufacturers. Instead, "homemade" pieces were of local tradition and origin.

Stone-tool traditions have long been seen by prehistorians as markers of cultural identity, and this has been applied to historic assemblages made in glass with great effect (Shackley 2001). In a Jamaican plantation context, Armstrong has read the modification of glass found in the burial of an enslaved person as a way of giving new symbolic meaning to the object, and has also noted fragments being used to shape wood both archaeologically and in recent times (Armstrong 1998:390–391). Improvising tools from glass has also been seen as a mode of resistance through keeping traditions alive for native youths held at an Indian School (Lindauer 1997:49–50). No connection to an ancient African tradition of stone-tool making need be implied here, however, for these tools to hold value for British Virgin Islanders.

In all these cases, knapped-glass tools could have been quite practical, costing less and being more accessible than purchased metal ones, but equally such tools allowed for a measure of independence, an important social function. Manufactured goods required dependence on outsiders and a cash economy, where many groups including BVI postemancipation smallholders were always at a disadvantage. While engagement with cash economies was often necessary for some aspects of daily life (indeed, the glass itself was acquired as a result of trade), the self-sufficiency provided by making one's own tools allowed a measure of distance from the economic and social systems of whites. In other words, such tools may not simply represent the inability to acquire metal equivalents but suggest that disadvantaged people were making conscious, active choices about when to purchase and when to innovate, rather than always being at the mercy of the merchant or shopkeeper.

Discussion

The story of slavery in the Caribbean is sometimes written as if its effects did not extend past 1838, but the stories of those who were enmeshed in this system continue for many years after. This site represents a modest house dating to the middle decades of the nineteenth century, after slavery had ended—a period about which surprisingly little is known in the BVI as it is well before the memories of any living people but during a period of little colonial interest and therefore few documentary records.

Archaeology has shown two separate phases of construction that probably date to before and after the plantation house up the hill had been abandoned, and has suggested that food resources were not always plentiful. Nonetheless, the addition of a cistern on this site, probably after about 1850 (based on the expectation that the plantation house had been abandoned before the cistern's construction and the known population trends for the BVI), represents a substantial investment in this place. At this time, not only the white but also the black population of the BVI was emigrating in search of opportunities elsewhere: 1854 the population was down to under 6,000 from its highs near 10,000 (Dookhan 1975:176), and by 1891 it was only 4,600 (O'Neal 2012:175).

The location of the house itself was probably carefully chosen. Under the plantation system, enslaved laborers were often limited as to where they were allowed to build their homes, but these limits would not have applied after emancipation and the departure of the former owners. There are other concerns discussed for the location of plantation houses that would have applied to the siting of freeholder houses as well, such as ventilation and intervisibility between neighbors (Chenoweth 2014; Clement 1997). For these concerns, the best site for a house in the area was probably that occupied by the slavery-era plantation complex, structures A and F: that site was at a higher elevation, providing more view, more breezes, and cooler temperatures, yet was still sheltered from storms by the heights of the island. Rather than taking this property that was abandoned before the Rowe Site and was not reoccupied, however, the freeholders of the Rowe Site chose to continue in their own space, perhaps on a site that had been theirs de facto even during the last years of slavery. In one reading, this choice may be surprising. Relocation to the former planters' structure would have provided more space, more substantial walls, and access to a preexisting water catchment system, which was built into structure F's southwest corner. This feature would have alleviated the need to build the similar cistern attached to the Rowe Site house, and yet since this cistern contained elements probably scavenged from the complex uphill, its construction most likely postdates the abandonment of structures A and F.

The location of the Rowe Site was certainly motivated in part by practical considerations. If they were anything like the average smallholder described by O'Neal (2012), the residents here survived and prospered based on a mix of cash and subsistence cropping (which worked best at higher elevations), the harvesting of sea resources, and making use of other opportunities requiring access to the sea, such as charcoaling and foraging on nearby cays. Placement between the higher elevations of the plantation structures and the sea resources below made both accessible. If taking the literal place of their former enslavers in structures A and F had been a goal, as economic histories sometimes assume, these concerns could have been managed. For the smallholders of the Rowe Site, however, the large structures that had been at the center of the system of slavery were not seen as improvements over what they had created for themselves in the decades after slavery ended. Although it would have been possible for them to occupy these larger and more substantial structures, they did not choose to do so, preferring their smaller-scale structure. Nonetheless, they did not ignore the abandoned plantation complex, returning to literally (re-)appropriate the building, the product primarily of their own or their enslaved predecessors' labor, and with it perhaps a measure of symbolic control over past and present oppressions.

Archaeology also demonstrates that the inhabitants of the Rowe Site had the ability to acquire trade goods throughout the occupation, and that these were not always of the cheapest and most basic types. Whitewares with hand painting and transfer prints became less expensive than they had been, but they were still more expensive and formal than yellowwares, "cream colored" wares, or factory slipwares found elsewhere on the island.

Other finds echo this balance between practical limitations and the acquisition of meaningful goods. Imported composite buttons are not necessary, and indeed the hooks-and-eyes recovered show that the occupants had other, less costly means of fastening clothing as well, but buttons were a means of adornment. At the same time, they may have chosen to make some of their own tools from bottle glass rather than exclusively relying on imported ones.

It may be somewhat contradictory to suggest that worked glass was employed in part to limit involvement in trading that placed BVI smallholders at a disadvantage while at the same time they clearly purchased middle-quality ceramics and buttons. It was argued above that, compared to much of the rest of the Caribbean, traded materials were more difficult to acquire in the BVI, but it was also suggested that, in part because of this difficulty, they took on a particular value in terms of social negotiation. Engagement with this system primarily benefited those at the top, perhaps more than a particular tool or supply might be a benefit to some customers. Although constrained by a colonial system still focused on extraction and disinterested when profits were small, the residents of the Rowe Site were making these choices actively, engaging with or avoiding these markets on their own terms. Evidence suggests that they selectively engaged in the market economy to acquire items of particular importance at some times, and were creatively resourceful in avoiding it at others.

Although small players in the colonial game, these actors were neither powerless nor unaware. Minimizing their acquisition of traded goods benefited them and hurt the system. Like the enslaved people held on Isaac Pickering's estate who protested in 1823 (O'Neal 2012:48), the free people of a generation later had power that they exercised as consumers (or nonconsumers).

Conclusion

The work on this site is preliminary, so it would be premature to draw broad conclusions. Rather, the discussions here provide us with both a set of questions to be considered and a preliminary picture of some possible motivations and ideas at work on small postemancipation farms. Is there a broader pattern in the purchase of manufactured goods similar to that seen here? Do knapped-glass tools and other "improvised" materials appear more readily in postemancipation contexts? Are plantation houses on other sites occupied by freed people after abandonment? How do these negotiations in more marginal colonies compare to those elsewhere?

While these questions await further research, we can nonetheless suggest some elements of worldview at work on this site. In her recent book *Black Feminist Archaeology*, Whitney Battle-Baptist combines the focus on yard spaces in African American homes with bell hooks' idea of the "home-place" to introduce the concept of "homespace" as a model for viewing the domestic spaces of captive Africans. Battle-Baptist (2011:95) writes of this homespace that "it was a place to regroup, to learn strategies of survival, find strength, and create thoughts of resistance." While the situation for postslavery peoples was different, especially for those who were legally recognized as landowners, this concept is nonetheless useful in considering the archaeology of the Rowe Site.

For both hooks and Battle-Baptist, African American and African Caribbean homes were places of humanization as well as resistance, the comfort of family as well as practical considerations of food and shelter. More than just cramped islands in a sea of oppression, these homes were part of broader landscapes of meaning, shaped particularly by women and at the heart of identity formation: "Without the social space to sit down and communicate, social reproduction of the African American identity would have been nearly impossible" (Battle-Baptiste 2011:102). Many British Virgin Islanders were forced to leave their homespaces in search of work in the decades after enslavement—a diaspora within a diaspora. Those who remained behind and survived in the difficult social and environmental conditions of the nineteenth century were aware of the social and economic advantages of having such a space.

The material goods found on this site and its size and setting could all be used to describe this site as poor, but this makes assumptions about the goals of the site's inhabitants. In particular, while imported materials were purchased, presumably this was done on the inhabitants' own terms, and although the occupation of the larger plantation house may have been possible, the homespace down the hill was preferred. These occupants did not want to walk in the footsteps of those who had "owned" them, nor did they think bigger houses and newer purchased goods were always better. Archaeology has shown us people aware of their situation, making choices:

acquiring manufactured goods or doing without them selectively, choosing the placement of their home quite consciously and not at all in emulation of their former enslavers, investing further in their home when whites had written off the colony.

One day a woman or man living at the Rowe Site decided to improve the family homespace by ensuring a supply of fresh water through the construction of a cistern. Perhaps it was a communal decision. Unshaped rocks were at hand, but a better and perhaps a more aesthetic structure could be achieved with coral, bricks, and squared blocks of mortar from up the hill. There sat a ruin that was not meaningless to them, but it did not represent a goal. It was a resource for goals of their own, perhaps including a secure homespace.

Acknowledgments

My thanks go to Marillyn Suzuki for making this season of archaeological work possible and to the Rowe family for permission to examine this particular site. Funding for this research was provided by Stanford University's Thinking Matters program, and the work was conducted with the assistance of Alex Baer, Elliot Blair, Rachel Cajigas, and Anna Harkey. I would like to thank the anonymous reviewers, James A. Delle, Lynsey A. Bates, and the participants of the SHA 2014 session where a version of this paper was first presented for their comments throughout the development of this chapter and this volume.

References Cited

Abbott, R. Tucker, and Percy A. Morris
1995   *A Field Guide to Shells: Atlantic and Gulf Coasts and the West Indies, Fourth Edition*. Houghton Mifflin, New York.
Ahlman, Todd M., Bobby R. Braly, and Gerald F. Schroedl
2014   Stone Artifacts and Glass Tools from Enslaved African Contexts on St. Kitts' Southeast Peninsula. *Journal of African Diaspora Archaeology and Heritage* 3(1):1–25.
Armstrong, Douglas V.
1998   Cultural Transformation within Enslaved Laborer Communities in the Caribbean. In *Studies in Culture Contact: Interaction, Culture Change, and Archaeology*, edited by James G. Cusick, pp. 378–401. Southern Illinois University, Carbondale.
Battle-Baptiste, Whitney
2011   *Black Feminist Archaeology*. Left Coast Press, Walnut Creek, California.

Burns, Alan
1965   *History of the British West Indies.* Allen and Unwin, London.
Busch, Jane
1981   An Introduction to the Tin Can. *Historical Archaeology* 15(1):95–104.
Chenoweth, John M.
2011   *Religion, Archaeology, and Social Relations: A Study of the Practice of Quakerism and Caribbean Slavery in the Eighteenth-Century British Virgin Islands.* Unpublished Ph.D. dissertation, Department of Anthropology, University of California, Berkeley.
2014   Practicing and Preaching: Creating a Religion of Peace on a Slave Plantation. *American Anthropologist* 116(1):94–109.
Clement, Christopher Ohm
1997   Settlement Patterning on the British Caribbean Island of Tobago. *Historical Archaeology* 31(2):93–106.
Commissioners for Trade and Plantations
1734/5   *Representation from the Commissioners for Trade and Plantations Relating to the State of the British Islands in America, with Regards to their Strength, Trade, and Fortifications, and to What May Be Further Necessary for the Encouragement and Security of Those Islands.* J. Baskett, London.
Conte, Ignacio Clemente, and Facundo Gómez Romero
2008   Microwear Analysis of Retouched Glass Fragments from Fortlet Miñana, Azul, Argentina, 1860–1863. *International Journal of Historical Archaeology* 12(3):248–262.
Dookhan, Isaac
1975   *A History of the British Virgin Islands, 1672 to 1970.* Caribbean Universities Press in association with Bowker, Epping, United Kingdom.
Flexner, James L., and Colleen Morgan
2013   The Industrious Exiles: An Analysis of Flaked Glass Tools from the Leprosarium at Kalawao, Moloka'i. In *The Archaeology of Hybrid Material Culture,* edited by Jeb J. Card, pp. 295–317. Southern Illinois University Press, Carbondale.
Godden, Geoffrey A.
1964   *Encyclopaedia of British Pottery and Porcelain Marks.* Crown, New York.
Harrigan, Norwell, and Pearl Varlack
1975   *The Virgin Islands Story.* Caribbean Universities Press, Kingston, Jamaica.
1991   The Emergence of a Black Small-Holders Society in the British Virgin Islands. In *Caribbean Perspectives: The Social Structure of a Region,* edited by Joseph Lisowski, pp. 18–29. Transaction Publishers, New Brunswick, New Jersey.
Harrison, Rodney
2000   "Nowadays with Glass": Regional Variation in Aboriginal Bottle Glass Artefacts from Western Australia. *Archaeology in Oceania* 35(1):34–47.
2003   "The Magical Virtue of These Sharp Things": Colonialism, Mimesis and Knapped Bottle Glass Artefacts in Australia. *Journal of Material Culture* 8(3):311–336.
House of Commons
1790   *Minutes of Evidence Taken before a Committee of the House of Commons . . . to Consider Further of the Circumstances of the Slave Trade.* House of Commons, Parliament of Great Britain, London.

Humfrey, Michael
1975   *Sea Shells of the West Indies: A Guide to Marine Molluscs of the Caribbean*. Ta-
        plinger Publishing, New York.
Kelly, Kenneth G., Mark W. Hauser, and Douglas V. Armstrong
2011   Identity and Opportunity in Post-Slavery Jamaica. In *Out of Many, One People:
        The Historical Archaeology of Colonial Jamaica*, edited by James A. Delle, Mark
        W. Hauser, and Douglas V. Armstrong, pp. 243–257. University of Alabama
        Press, Tuscaloosa.
Klingelhofer, Eric
1987   Aspects of Early Afro-American Material Culture: Artifacts from the Slave
        Quarters at Garrison Plantation. *Historical Archaeology* 21(2):112–119.
Lightfoot, Kent G., Antoinette Martinez, and Ann M. Schiff
1998   Daily Practice and Material Culture in Pluralistic Social Settings: An Archae-
        ological Study of Culture Change and Persistence from Fort Ross, California.
        American Antiquity 63(2):199–222.
Lindauer, Owen
1997   *Not for School, but for Life: Lessons from the Historical Archaeology of the Phoenix
        Indian School* (Office of Cultural Resource Management Report 95). Department
        of Anthropology, Arizona State University, Tempe.
Majewski, Teresita, and Michael J. O'Brien
1987   The Use and Misuse of Nineteenth-Century English and American Ceramics in
        Archaeological Analysis. *Advances in Archaeological Method and Theory* 11:97–
        209.
Martin, Robert Montgomery
1834   *A History of the British Colonies*, Volume 2. Cochrane and McCrone, London.
Martin-Kaye, P.H.A.
1954   *Water Supplies of the British Virgin Islands*. B. G. Lithographic Co., Georgetown,
        Demerara, British West Indies.
Martindale, Andrew and Irena Jurakic
2006   Identifying Expedient Glass Tools from a Post-Contact Tsimshian Village Using
        Low Power (10–100×) Magnification. *Journal of Archaeological Science* 33(3):414–
        427.
O'Neal, Michael E.
2012   *Slavery, Smallholding, and Tourism: Social Transformations in the British Virgin
        Islands*. Quid Pro Books, New Orleans.
Pyle, Douglas C.
1981   *Clean Sweet Wind: Sailing Craft of the Lesser Antilles*. Easy Reach Press, Preston,
        Maryland.
Rehder, Harald A.
1981   *The Audubon Society Field Guide to North American Seashells*. Knopf, New York.
Ryzewski, Krysta, and John F. Cherry
2015   Struggles of a Sugar Society: Surveying Plantation-Era Montserrat, 1650–1850.
        International Journal of Historical Archaeology 19(2):356–383.
Shackley, M. Steven
2001   The Stone Tool Technology of Ishi and the Yana of North Central California: In-

ferences for Hunter Gatherer Cultural Identity in Historic California. *American Anthropologist* 102(4):693–713.

Silliman, Stephen

2010   Indigenous Traces in Colonial Spaces: Archaeologies of Ambiguity, Origin, and Practice. *Journal of Social Archaeology* 10(1):28–58.

South, Stanley

1964   Analysis of the Buttons from Brunswick Town and Fort Fisher. *Florida Anthropologist* 17(2):113–133.

Toller, Wes, and Shenell Gordon

2005   *A Population Survey of West Indian Topshell or Whelk (Cittarium pica) in the U.S. Virgin Islands*. Bureau of Fisheries, Department of Planning and Natural Resources, U.S. Virgin Islands.

Watkins, Frederick Henry

1924   *Handbook of the Leeward Islands*. West India Committee, London.

Wells, Tom

1998   Nail Chronology: The Use of Technologically Derived Features. *Historical Archaeology* 32(2):78–99.

Wentworth, Trelawney

1835   *The West India Sketch Book*. Whittaker & Co., London.

White, Carolyn L.

2005   *American Artifacts of Personal Adornment, 1680–1820*. Alta Mira, Oxford.

Wilkie, Laurie A.

1996   Glass-Knapping at a Louisiana Plantation: African-American Tools? *Historical Archaeology* 30(4):37–49.

Wilkie, Laurie A., and Paul Farnsworth

2011   Living Not So Quietly, Not So on the Edge of Things. In *The Materiality of Freedom: Archaeologies of Postemancipation Life*, edited by Jodi A. Barnes, pp. 58–68. University of South Carolina Press, Columbia.

11

Postemancipation Shifts

Land, Labor, and Freedom on the Bois Cotlette Estate,
Dominica, after 1838

KHADENE K. HARRIS

In 1838, following a four-year transition in labor known as the "apprentice-ship," the enslaved population of Britain's West Indian colonies was fully emancipated. A watershed moment in Caribbean history, emancipation ushered in a critical period of cultural, social, and economic change in Caribbean society. The significance of "full freedom" lay not only in Afro-Caribbean peoples' freedom from enslavement but in the freedom to explore opportunities once denied to those who previously had no choice but to labor on estates and in other colonial enterprises. With freedom came new and challenging opportunities for Afro-Caribbean people to redefine their relationship with the land and each other—a process that ultimately reshaped the physical landscape and both individual and collective identities. For this reason, the immediate postemancipation period was extraordinarily significant in shaping the social and material realities of the British Caribbean territories, including the island colony of Dominica.

This chapter examines changes that occurred on a Dominican plantation after 1838 using spatial and archaeological data in order to cast new light on the distinctive character of postemancipation life. I attempt to understand social and cultural shifts by examining changes in the use of space and the built environment in the immediate postemancipation years. Specifically, I focus on laborer houses that were built on the Bois Cotlette Estate in Dominica after slavery to explore what their location and layout reveals about a community in flux.

The process of emancipation was not seamless for Afro-Caribbean peoples. It was fraught with political upheaval, economic competition, and gross levels of social inequality. Archaeologists and historians alike have agreed that formal emancipation in 1838 did not result in immediate equality for the newly free populace, nor did it affect a sudden transformation in social and power relations. Nevertheless, for the newly free, emancipation altered the old order of things and opened up new opportunities to pursue land ownership and political enfranchisement—important markers of freedom. The postemancipation period, whose complexities we are only now beginning to understand, defies the methodological and conceptual confines of a single disciplinary approach. These years complicate traditional narratives—and our archaeological perceptions—of "free" and "unfree." This chapter, in keeping with the larger theme of this volume, is an attempt at unpacking these tensions through archaeological analysis.

The Postemancipation Caribbean

In exploring the postemancipation period in the British Caribbean, a greater understanding of the political, social, and economic climate of the early nineteenth century provides much-needed context for the social lives of newly freed people. Before the passage of the Slavery Abolition Act, metropolitan interest in the use of enslaved labor as a mode of production waned in the face of a burgeoning capitalist market. Further, slave uprisings—particularly in the early 1800s—cast the region as unstable and discouraged investment (Blackburn 1988; Craton 1997; Delle 2014; Green 1976; Holt 1992; Williams 1994). With the abolition of slavery, the region experienced further turmoil given that the sugar industry was nearing certain decline and there was a growing recognition that social hierarchies were being reshaped. This kind of regional turmoil would ensure that emancipation took on an uneven quality within the British Caribbean.

The plantation economy structured the lives of many who lived and labored throughout the Caribbean, even after emancipation. Elsa Goveia's (1980) study of the eighteenth century reveals the ways in which laws were constructed to maintain a society dedicated to the profitable production of cash crops. So grave was the concern for land and labor in the postemancipation period that Parliament worked to minimize the social impact of emancipation by instituting apprenticeship, which allowed for the continued subjugation of the laboring class for a further five years. Howard Johnson (1991:72) points out that "in some sugar colonies, the planter class attempted, through a variety of legal compulsions, to recreate the social relations of production that had previously existed on the plantations." Bills enacted after the end of slavery sought to actively discourage formerly enslaved people from engaging in any work beyond plantation labor or any other economic activity that would deplete the labor supply available to estates.

Colonial authorities were primarily concerned with the land from which profits were derived and the labor that produced them. They protected their interests by attempting to maintain the plantation system and its profitability after slavery. During slavery, opportunities for Afro-Caribbean laborers to operate outside of this framework were few. Enslaved laborers had access to provision grounds—typically marginal, unproductive land on which they would grow crops in place of or to supplement rations from owners (see also Bates, this volume; Delle, this volume). The internal organization of the provision grounds was left largely to the enslaved people themselves. The planters would, in some cases, subdivide the plots and allocate them to particular individuals, but beyond this they took very little interest apart from making occasional inspections (Higman 1998; Sheridan 1976). The provision-ground system was also an opportunity for independent economic activities by enslaved men and women because in many cases they were allowed to keep and sell any excess produce. This practice soon proved to be one of the most important sources of empowerment for the newly freed population (Delle 2014; Mintz and Hall 1960).

It should come as no surprise, then, that in the postemancipation years land and the economic opportunities associated with land ownership were paramount in Afro-Caribbean peoples' decisions about where to go and what to do. Michel-Rolph Trouillot (1988: 69) writes, "These grounds are at the core of the social genesis of many Caribbean nations; and for many of these peasants, the social and cultural significance vested in these lands under slavery has not lost its significance." Emancipation was in many the catalyst for the rise of a dynamic peasantry throughout the Caribbean (see also Chenoweth, this volume). Large groups of small farmers throughout the Caribbean were ultimately responsible for the emergence and growth of a semiautonomous mode of production that was integral to the social and economic lives of the newly free.

*　*　*

With Caribbean sugar's poor performance on the world market in the middle of the nineteenth century and the new demands for acceptable wages from the newly freed, the planter class viewed emancipation as a labor "problem" (Holt 1992). The laboring and planter classes employed different strategies to contend with the realities of land and labor within and between colonies. The measures employed by different plantations were by no means uniform. In the larger colonies with surplus land like Jamaica and British Guiana, many formerly enslaved people removed themselves from the estates and established communities elsewhere. The planters responded to this action by importing labor from India, China, and Africa under contracts of indenture.

Those who left plantations would either purchase property or squat on Crown land. The purchasing of Crown land for the establishment of free villages and small farms was a possibility for some freed peoples, but they faced planter opposition. Planter-dominated legislatures refused to initiate surveys of Crown land, a required first step to smallholder settlements. In many cases, the planters either refused to sell surplus or marginal land or they charged exorbitant prices for small portions. They also levied land taxes that discriminated against the owners of smallholdings (Marshall 1968).

Those who continued to work on estates did so as wage laborers or tenants. Working as wage laborers was a more flexible option. Laborers would often work on estates part time whenever there was work. Wages, however, were often kept deliberately low by planters. Tenancy, or métayage, was a riskier option. Under this agreement, also called sharecropping, laborers would share either their crops or their earnings from the sale of their crops as payment for living and working on estates.

Tenancy

By 1842 métayage was common practice on many estates, with the efforts of métayers accounting for 20 percent of Dominica's sugar crop (Chace 1989; Marshall 1996). The popularity of métayage in Dominica reflected postemancipation desires on the part of freed people for greater autonomy and social liberty and a direct response to planter efforts meant to coerce the newly free to work under familiar terms. Between 1838 and the turn of the twentieth century, there were four large-scale incidents of violent protests in Dominica by the laboring class; several scholars have argued that this political unrest among the laboring class arose from tensions emerging from conflict over rent, wages, and access to arable land (e.g., Honychurch 1995; Lenik 2014; Trouillot 1988).

Our opportunities to understand the social lives of freed people can be expanded by looking closely at patterns of movement across the physical landscape and how land and labor concerns were reflected in these movements. Changes in land tenure practices and labor relations on plantations are very often reflected in the way space is organized and used. The way people organize living spaces defines and is defined by all aspects of their lives—social, political, economic, and ritual (Robin and Rothschild 2002:161). Where people decide to build their homes and plant crops has been shaped and molded from historical and natural elements, which is itself a political process (Lefebvre 1991).

Douglas Armstrong's (1990) archaeological study of the Drax Hall plantation in Jamaica during the both pre- and postemancipation periods reveals that, immediately following emancipation, many formerly enslaved people moved from the nucleated slave village to freehold parcels in a new community called The Priory. The slavery-era houses on some estates continued to be occupied by tenant farmers in the postemancipation era up until the mid-twentieth century, when they were eventually knocked down. The proximity of free communities like The Priory to estates like Drax Hall was deliberate. In the decades after emancipation, the newly free were acutely aware of the opportunities that existed beyond the estate, but their attempts at carving out new lives did not mean wholesale dismissal of estate work (Bolland 1981; Campbell 2002; Trouillot 1984). What this suggests is that decisions that the newly free made reflected their expectations for social legitimization, greater possibilities to accumulate economic resources, and open access to social and political institutions (Shepherd and Beckles 1996).

Laurie Wilkie and Paul Farnsworth's study (2011:60) of the postemancipation settlement on the Clifton Plantation in the Bahamas reveals similar shifts. Their archaeological research showed that the postemancipation period was fragmented, with particular buildings and spaces of the landscape used, abandoned, and used again at different times. According to Wilkie and Farnsworth (2011:61, 64), at least three of the eight cabins still standing in the main African village were refurbished in the postemancipation period, though not necessarily concurrently. Crumbling walls were repaired, new layers of mortar and paint applied, and in one instance a tin roof added. Their excavation of the area around a house yielded material culture that demonstrated both evidence of self-sufficiency and connectedness to the global economy.

Archaeological research into the "afterlives"—to borrow from Wilkie and Farnsworth (citing Hicks 2007)—of plantations can reveal the creative and resourceful ways that newly freed men and women formed communities, extended kinship networks, and demanded political transformation.

Understanding the everyday life of free peoples who continued to live on estates after emancipation is an attempt at uncovering the ways in which material culture is recontextualized as products of a newly altered world.

Postemancipation Dominica

Dominica, located in the Eastern Caribbean (see Figure 1.2), has a rich history inextricably tied to its physical environment. Flat fertile landscapes ideal for large-scale sugar cultivation are scarce (Lenik 2014). The island is mountainous and densely forested in the interior—a difficult landscape when compared to such islands as Barbados and Cuba.

The Bois Cotlette Estate in the Soufrière enclave is one of the oldest estates on the island, dating from the mid-eighteenth century. The property was originally owned by French leaseholders who agreed to become British subjects in order to remain on the island after it was ceded to the British in 1763 (Candlin 2012). Bois Cotlette began as a provisioning estate for larger sugar plantations in Martinique. Subsequently, coffee and sugar would be cultivated alternately, depending upon market conditions, until the late nineteenth century, when the estate began focusing on lime and cocoa.

In the years following full emancipation in 1838, Dominica's colonial policies maintained limits on laborers' access to land, even where it was plentiful (Honychurch 2001). As was the case in most of the British Caribbean, crown land in Dominica was priced high enough to keep many landless, but not too high to discourage the most "industrious" workers from saving their wages in the hope of purchase (Honychurch 2001:6). Despite the difficulties of purchasing land, the newly freed laboring class was able to dictate the terms under which labor battles would be fought. This was no less true on the Bois Cotlette Estate, where interesting patterns emerge in the postemancipation period.

One result of the Slavery Abolition Act of 1833 was the widespread appointment of stipendiary magistrates recruited in Britain to oversee and adjudicate the system of apprenticeship that followed initial emancipation in 1834. They were to hear the grievances of the apprentices against planters and facilitate issues surrounding manumission. William Lynch was one such magistrate who monitored the southern parishes of Dominica where Bois Cotlette is located. Lynch's records provide a list of estates and the main crops they produced along with the number of apprentices on each estate on the last day of apprenticeship, July 31, 1838 (Trouillot 1984: 77–79, see also Trouillot 1988 for greater detail). His records also reveal the average number of laborers at work in the first month of full freedom, August 1838, and the average number of laborers at work in the two subsequent months.

Lynch's records suggest four important trends that have interesting implications for Bois Cotlette's postemancipation period. First, there was a sharp decline in the labor force immediately after emancipation in the months of August and September. Second, there was a rise in the labor force after September, suggesting that the newly free in some cases returned to plantation labor after they had explored alternatives. Third, the smaller the estate, the better was its chance to successfully retain its labor force. And fourth, estates that allowed sharecropping were more successful in retaining labor while those that experienced the worst labor shortages primarily used wage labor. From this trend we understand that newly freed Dominicans were more attracted to estates that allowed them to have their own plots of land, in some ways ensuring some level of autonomy. As Trouillot (1984:79) notes, the final decision of the estate on which to work was certainly not made only in terms of the characteristics of the estate and the behavior of its owner but also on the basis of all the alternatives available in a particular area. In this way, formerly enslaved people are shown to be active subjects and self-interested, rational beings.

This becomes especially clear when one focuses on the Bois Cotlette Estate as represented in Lynch's records. Lynch's report showed that on Bois Cotlette the size of the labor force dramatically dropped immediately after full emancipation, from 31 in July to 4 in November—a decrease of 87.09 percent. A cursory examination of Lynch's report would suggest that the estate was left with only 4 laborers after 1838. The story that these numbers tell, while important, is incomplete and requires a more layered analysis of these trends. The goal is not to prove or disprove Lynch's numbers but to highlight the unevenness that is characteristic of the postemancipation period. As I have suggested, this was a time of improvisation and rapid change in individuals' circumstances. The process of establishing new lives after enslavement was not a linear one. Decisions were made and unmade and the desire for autonomy and personal freedom meant that spaces in which human activity occurred experienced frequent changes.

A Postemancipation Archaeology

The first steps to understanding the complexity of the postemancipation period is to determine where laborers lived on Bois Cotlette in the years immediately following emancipation and what insight the location and layout of these postemancipation houses can offer. Archaeological evidence suggests that Lynch's estimates are misleading. Lynch's figures perhaps did not account for the possibility that free laborers moved out of the enslaved village and established a new village on or near the estate, and thus may have escaped Lynch's notice or, employing similar house yard design but under different systems of land tenure and labor relations, were not considered to be attached to the estate. My primary data for this idea is the analysis of the house yard.

The Caribbean house and house yard has been linked through ethnographic and ethnohistorical information to community and the ways in which a person might fashion their own identity. Developed through observations of Puerto Rican and Jamaican peasantries in the mid-twentieth century, Sidney Mintz (1974, 1983) argues that the house yard was the center of the household and by implication dissolved the distinction between inside and outside for economic and social activity. It was a foundational space in which identity was created and transformed. Daily life, including cooking, cleaning, playing, and food processing took place in a yard. The house that stood in the yard was a place where people stored things and slept. Assumptions could also be made about the relative status of the owner by examining the kinds of material used to construct a house. The Caribbean yard, then, is a useful device for observing how the newly free negotiated uneven terrains—literally and figuratively.

Archaeological investigations of postemancipation house yards at Bois Cotlette began in July 2012 with a pedestrian survey of the entire estate. Based on historical maps, agricultural fields were identified by field walls and terraces. Field walls were meant to separate various crops at differing stages of production and terraces were meant to prevent erosion and facilitate better human access to the steeply sloping terrain. Within three separate fields, we came across stone features that indicated the presence of a domestic dwelling and a leveled platform that likely required a considerable amount of labor to construct. The possibility that this was only a small garden was ruled out by the discovery of a stone floor that was a part of a structure at least 8 m × 4 m in size. The pedestrian survey also identified three house areas (hereafter HA-1, HA-2, and HA-3) with stone walls, terraces, and stone floors, many in a state of decay.

Bois Cotlette has been the site of ongoing archaeological investigations exploring the community histories and material record of slavery in the Dominican enclaves of Soufrière and Portsmouth (see Hauser 2014). Based on the survey and mapping data, we were able to draw parallels between

Figure 11.1. Artifacts from the HA-1 test unit, Bois Cotlette Estate, Dominica. (Photograph by Khadene K. Harris)

slavery-period housing and the features encountered in the 2012 survey. House structures in the enslaved village are identified by an alignment of locally sourced stones. To determine if the stone alignments discovered in 2012 were indeed foundations of postemancipation house structures similar to those discovered in the village, we mapped and recorded all observed features using the same methodology. Additionally, two 1 m × 1 m test units placed in HA-1 yielded European ceramics, glass, and nail fragments (Figure 11.1). The combination of stone alignments and the recovery of artifacts associated with domestic spaces confirmed that there was a structure erected within the boundaries of the field walls sometime after slavery ended when Bois Cotlette's laborers were demanding and witnessing changes in labor conditions and land tenure.

More thorough test excavations were conducted in 2013 to determine the layout and boundaries of what appeared to be another house yard located 6 m away from HA-1, which was named HA-2. Six 1 m × 1 m units were excavated, which yielded very few artifacts but interesting spatial data. A stone floor measuring 3 m × 3 m with several circular depressions (Figure 11.2) was uncovered. No artifacts were found inside the depressions. One meter to the east of the circular depressions, a house floor was also uncovered measuring approximately 6 m × 4 m. No floor with similar circular depressions has been found in the pre-emancipation enslaved village. Its presence in this postemancipation context suggests a shift in the way the house yard was organized and likely used by its occupants. This suggests that under sharecropping agreements, domestic spaces were also workspaces and the layout of the house yard would reflect both personal activities like cooking and cleaning and activities associated with agricultural production.

Preliminary analyses of ceramic finds prove interesting as well. Of the 124 artifacts recovered from the 6 units excavated, only 23 were imported ceramics. Among these, 14 were identified as Huveaune, a French-made

Figure 11.2. Circular depressions in the stone floor of HA-2, Bois Cotlette Estate, Dominica. (Photograph by Khadene K. Harris)

earthenware found throughout Martinique and Guadeloupe. Difficult to date, Huveaune ceramics are all slip decorated and their background is typically red or yellow. Bowls, basins, and chamber pots were the most commonly exported forms (Avery 2007:133). These types of ceramics were multifunctional, used for cooking as well as for other domestic chores such as cleaning the house or doing the laundry (Arcangeli 2014:14), and came in various shapes and sizes. The remaining 9 ceramics uncovered were English made refined earthenwares: 2 annular ware mocha (1795–1895), 6 plain undecorated whiteware (1830–present) and 1 locally made earthenware.

The low numbers of ceramics recovered from test excavations speaks volumes, especially when compared to the number of materials recovered from ongoing excavations in the enslaved village. Remarking on the intense and diverse assemblage recovered from the study of the enslaved village, Hauser (2014:61) notes, "for the enslaved who lived at Bois Cotlette, they were able to materialize a surplus in what they purchased." What does this mean, then, for postemancipation exchange networks if there is a perceptible shift in the kinds of material culture that the newly free are now able to access?

Conclusion

Several conclusions can be drawn concerning postemancipation shifts on the Bois Cotlette Estate. First, laborer engagement with the plantation economy was a dynamic one that was constantly adjusting to changing conditions. The presence of stone floors and ceramic finds in an area that was once fully cultivated by estate crops point to such a shift. The changes in the way space was used gives and is given meaning through the larger political and economic context in which Bois Cotlette's residents move. If we consider as well that Lynch's records suggest that Bois Cotlette attempted to move away from wage labor into sharecropping and tenancy, we can argue that house yards built within cultivation fields reflect such a shift. In the pre-emancipation period, enslaved villages were quite often nucleated, indicating that work on plantations was a communal enterprise. In contrast, under sharecropping or tenancy arrangements, work was a more individualized endeavor, organized primarily around the household, which could explain why postemancipation house yards are located within enclosed field boundaries. The presence of laborer house areas within enclosed field walls indicates a move away from wage remunerations and the adoption of a sharecropping system—a move on Bois Cotlette that was perhaps influenced by the success of other plantations that incorporated such an approach.

Second, while overall the occupants of the postemancipation sites HA-1, HA-2, and HA-3 employed similar architectural strategies to those living at the slavery-period village, new labor demands resulted in observable shifts in the way space was organized, as evidenced by the presence of stone floors. The location of cleared house areas with greater space and a curious stone floor with circular depressions offer insight into how we may track these changes. We can also argue that freedom did not necessarily provide laborers with greater opportunities to accumulate wealth in the form of portable goods. Laborers, métayers in particular, were more prone to the risks associated with agricultural production such as hurricanes, floods, or drought. The efforts of the newly free on Bois Cotlette reveal a pattern of interaction with the physical landscape that is active, self-interested, and changeable—a reflection, no doubt, of the postemancipation era.

As Barnes (2011) maintains, the years after freedom are not a sequel to slavery. The changes that occur during this period display both continuities and breaks in the material record. The patterns that we uncover tell a story of rapid change and provide clues as to how individuals adjusted to such realities. Research on the postemancipation village at Bois Cotlette and similar sites in the Americas are great opportunities to examine the emergence of postemancipation identities and the "rooting and uprooting" (Besson 1995) that took place in its formative years, and perhaps to better understand the layers of complexity that defined the ever-changing relationship between the colonial state and those who lived within its confines.

References Cited

Arcangeli, Myriam
2014   Un canari dans la cuisine: What Ceramic Cookware Shows About Enslaved Cooks in Colonial Guadeloupe. Paper presented at The Society for Historical Archaeology, Quebec City, Quebec, January 12–14.
Armstrong, Douglas
1990   *The Old Village and the Great House*. University of Illinois Press, Urbana.
Avery, G. E. (editor)
2007   French Colonial Pottery: An International Conference, Northwestern State University Press, Natchitoches, Louisiana.
Barnes, Jodi A. (editor)
2011   *The Materialities of Freedom: Archaeologies of Postemancipation Life*. University of South Carolina Press, Columbia.

Besson, Jean
1995   Land, Kinship and Community in the Post-Emancipation Caribbean: A Region-
        al Review of the Leewards. In *Small Islands, Large Questions: Society, Culture and
        Resistance in the Post-Emancipation Caribbean,* edited by Karen Fog Olwig, pp.
        73–99. Routledge, New York.

Blackburn, Robin
1988   *The Overthrow of Colonial Slavery.* Verso, London.

Bolland, Nigel
1981   Systems of Domination after Slavery: The Control of Land and Labor in the Brit-
        ish West Indies after 1838. *Comparative Studies in Society and History* 23(4):591–
        619.

Campbell, Carl
2002   The Early Post-Emancipation Jamaica: The Historiography of Plantation Cul-
        ture. In *Jamaica in Slavery and Freedom: History, Heritage and Culture,* edited by
        Kathleen E. A. Monteith and Glen L. Richards, pp. 52–69. University of the West
        Indies Press, Mona, Jamaica.

Candlin, Kit
2012   *The Last Caribbean Frontier, 1795–1815.* Palgrave Macmillan, New York.

Chace, R. E.
1989   Protest in Post-Emancipation Dominica—The Guerre Negre of 1844. *Journal of
        Caribbean History* 23(2):118–141.

Craton, Michael
1997   *Empire, Enslavement, and Freedom in the Caribbean.* Ian Randle, Kingston.

Delle, James A.
2014   *The Colonial Caribbean: Landscapes of Power in Jamaica's Plantation System.*
        Cambridge University Press, Cambridge.

Goveia, Elsa V.
1980   *Slave Society in the British Leeward Islands at the End of the Eighteenth Century.*
        Greenwood Press, Westport, Connecticut.

Green, William A.
1976   *British Slave Emancipation: The Great Sugar Colonies and the Great Experiment
        1830–1865.* Oxford University Press, Oxford.

Hauser, Mark W.
2014   Land, Labor and Things: Surplus in a West Indian Colony (1763–1897). *Economic
        Anthropology* 1:49–65.

Hicks, Dan
2007   *The Garden of the World: An Historical Archaeology of Sugar Landscapes in the
        Eastern Caribbean.* British Archaeological Report International Series 1632,
        Studies in Contemporary and Historical Archaeology 3. Archaeopress, Oxford.

Higman, Barry W.
1998   *Montpelier, Jamaica: a Plantation Community in Slavery and Freedom, 1739–1912.*
        University of West Indies Press, Mona, Jamaica.

Holt, Thomas
1992   *The Problem of Freedom: Race, Labor, and Politics in Jamaica and Britain, 1832–1938*. Johns Hopkins University Press, Baltimore.
Honychurch, Lennox
1995   *The Dominica Story: A History of the Island*. Macmillan, Oxford.
2001   Slave Valleys, Peasant Ridges: Topography, Colour and Land Settlement on Dominica. Paper presented to the University of the West Indies, Cave Hill. Macmillan, Oxford.
Johnson, Howard
1991   *The Bahamas in Slavery and In Freedom*. Ian Randle Publishers, Kingston, Jamaica.
Lefebvre, Henri
1991   *The Production of Space*. Blackwell, Oxford.
Lenik, Stephan
2014   Plantation Labourer Rebellions, Material Culture and Events: Historical Archaeology at Geneva Estate, Grand Bay, Commonwealth of Dominica. *Slavery and Abolition* 35(3):508–526.
Marshall, Woodville
1968   Agricultural Development and Planning in the West Indies *Social and Economic Studies* 17(3):252–263.
1996   Métayage in the Sugar Industry of the British Windward Islands, 1838–1865. In *Caribbean Freedom: Economy and Society from Emancipation to Present*, edited by Verene Shepherd and Hilary Beckles, pp. 64–79. Ian Randle, Kingston, Jamaica.
Mintz, Sidney W.
1974   *Caribbean Transformations*. Aldine, Chicago.
1983   Reflections on Caribbean Peasantries. *New West Indian Guide/Nieuve West-Indishce Gids* 57(1/2):1–17.
Mintz, Sidney W., and Douglas Hall
1960   *The Origins of the Jamaican Internal Marketing System*. Yale University Publications in Anthropology, New Haven, Connecticut.
Robin, Cynthia, and Nan A. Rothschild
2002   Archaeological Ethnographies Social Dynamics of Outdoor Space. *Journal of Social Archaeology* 2(2):159–172.
Shepherd, Verene, and Hilary Beckles (Editors)
1996   *Caribbean Freedom: Economy and Society from Emancipation to present*. Ian Randle, Kingston, Jamaica.
Sheridan, Richard B.
1976   "Sweet Malefactor": The Social Costs of Slavery and Sugar in Jamaica and Cuba, 1807–54. *Economic History Review* 29(2):236–257.
Trouillot, Michel-Rolph
1984   Labour and Emancipation in Dominica: A Contribution to the Debate. *Caribbean Quarterly* 30(3/4):73–84.

1988   *Peasants and Capital: Dominica in the World Economy*. John Hopkins University Press, Baltimore.

Wilkie, Laurie A., and Paul Farnsworth

2011   Living Not So Quietly, Not So on the Edge of Things: A Twentieth Century Bahamian Household. In *The Materiality of Freedom: Archaeologies of Postemancipation Life*, edited by Jodi A. Barnes, pp. 58–68. University of South Carolina Press, Columbia.

Williams, Eric

1994   *Capitalism and Slavery*. University of North Carolina Press, Chapel Hill.

12

Military Material Life in the British Caribbean

Historical Archaeology of Fort Rocky, Kingston Harbor, Jamaica (ca. 1880–1945)

STEPHAN T. LENIK AND ZACHARY J. M. BEIER

With the outbreak of World War I, the Caribbean peoples who served as soldiers and in auxiliary roles in the armed services hoped that their patriotism and sacrifice would aid in "demonstrating [the] worth . . . of coloured people" (Metzgen and Graham 2007:89). Joining similar efforts from throughout the empire, Britain's Caribbean colonies raised material goods and money to support the war effort in an initial surge of "patriotic fervour" (Metzgen and Graham 2007:87; see also Cundall 1925; Smith 2014). The thousands of Caribbean volunteers who went overseas as part of the British West Indies Regiment (BWIR), however, experienced structural racism as they were compelled to do manual labor and rarely saw combat. The BWIR troops commanded by white British officers had no prospects for promotion (Joseph 1971), and there were concerns that black soldiers should be excluded from contact with the white population in Britain (Smith 2014:108–110). Among the consequences of such treatment was a mutiny by BWIR soldiers in Taranto, Italy, that exploded in 1918.

For colonized peoples from the Caribbean and elsewhere, World War I represented "a major impetus for the rise of nationalism and discontent throughout the British empire" (Smith 2004:4), and coming home to the islands at war's end cemented a sense of disenchantment among veterans (Dyde 1997; Joseph 1971; Metzgen and Graham 2007:93–100; Smith 2004). George Blackman (1897–2003), a Barbadian recruit who briefly served at the base in Taranto, recounts the manual labor that occupied most of his time and the difficult return home: "I said, 'The English are no good.' I went to Jamaica and I meet up some soldiers and I asked them, 'Here boy, what the government give you?' They said, 'The government give us nothing.'

I said, 'We just the same'" (Rogers 2002). Marcus Garvey, whose Universal Negro Improvement Association had approved a resolution affirming loyalty to king and empire in 1914 (Smith 2014:102), references the unfulfilling wartime experience for Jamaicans that "helped a great deal in arousing the consciousness of the colored people to the reasonableness of our program, especially after the British at home had rejected a large number of West Indian colored men who wanted to be officers in the British army" (Garvey 2004:4).

While many Caribbean men shared this overseas experience, many other troops manned a series of garrisons, batteries, and signal posts that spanned Britain's Caribbean colonies. Men of African descent had long served the colonial military. In 1795, in reaction to the extremely high mortality rates white European soldiers had suffered in the islands during the initial centuries of colonization, Britain formed a corps of West India Regiments (WIR)—not to be confused with the British West Indies Regiment (BWIR) mentioned above—composed of enslaved African soldiers (Buckley 1979, 1998; Handler 1984; Voelz 1993). Consisting of as many as twelve different regiments at their peak, after 1817 the WIR were gradually reduced and reorganized. Most British Caribbean fortifications were abandoned in 1854, and remaining WIR units were dispersed across a few installations while periodically serving in Britain's West African colonies. Linked to the Cardwell Reforms of 1868 to 1874, which sought to modernize the British military, Britain began to supplement its armed forces with volunteer militias composed of recruits from the colonies (Black 2006:85–86; Maurice-Jones 2009:160–161), known as Local Forces. For African Jamaican militia on the "home front," their acts of volunteering suggest a desire for advancement in social standing and at least some measure of loyalty to the empire, a regime that had enslaved their ancestors and continued to oppress the populace. These volunteers served even as patriotic sentiments soured after World War I and Jamaica experienced a rise of political consciousness with labor unionization, Garveyism, Rastafarianism, decolonization, and other social and political movements (Beckles and Shepherd 1996; Campbell 1985; Lumsden 1999). Colonial troops at Caribbean military installations submitted themselves to a regime that strove to instill strict military discipline, demanding long hours of drill, target practice, and physical exertion. The continued existence of WIR units and their successors raises a series of questions: Is there evidence that the "arousing of consciousness" referenced by Garvey materialized among colonial troops on the home front in Jamaica? Within disciplined military space, was there room for discontent or outright opposition among the Local Forces? And how might such opposition be manifested in the material realm?

To explore these questions, this chapter examines a case study of Rocky Point Battery, also known as Fort Rocky, in Jamaica. Located on the Palisadoes Peninsula near Port Royal, construction at Rocky Point began in 1882, and possibly earlier. It was one of four batteries built or modified in the late nineteenth century to defend Kingston Harbor, as improvements in land-based and naval artillery required reinvestment in defense (Buisseret 2008:29–32). Monitoring the harbor during both World Wars and in peacetime as well, Fort Rocky was abandoned after World War II. In the late nineteenth century, with labor patterns reoriented after emancipation, full-time garrisoned armed forces in the colonies were replaced by militias. In Jamaica, the 1879 Militia Act led to the creation in 1891 of Militia Infantry and Militia Artillery as "native companies" to be stationed at outposts like Fort Rocky (Barker 1980:201; Cundall 1922:57). Militia units stationed at Rocky Point were native companies of Royal Garrison Artillery and Royal Garrison Engineers, including the St. Andrew's Rifle Corps of Militia Infantry, Kingston Infantry Volunteers, and Jamaica Infantry Volunteers (National Archives, London, WO 33/345, p. 128–129; Cundall 1922:57).

We argue that a productive route toward answering the questions we state above draws from the work of postcolonial theorists who have identified and critiqued colonial discourses, especially the distinction of colonizer versus colonized "other" enforced by the colonial system (Bhabha 1994; Fanon 1967, 1968; Said 1978). Military service influenced the thinking of some of these writers, particularly Frantz Fanon, a colonial soldier who fought for France in World War II and later aided Algeria's liberation movement (Fanon 1967, 1968). Such work has been deployed by anthropological archaeologists in thinking about postcolonialism and hybridity (e.g., Card 2013; González-Ruibal 2010, 2011; Liebmann and Rizvi 2008; Lydon and Rizvi 2010; Naum 2010; Silliman 2015; Singleton 2010; van Pelt 2013). These works have framed our interpretation of archaeological data from Rocky Point and lead us to question the colonizing effect of assumed categories, especially the hierarchical "colonizer" versus "colonized" distinction that appears in some analyses of British military sites (e.g., Farry 2005).

Military installations enacted a strict chain of command that manifested in patterned ways via spatial layouts related to military strategies, disciplinary modes reinforcing status differences or race relations, and specific objects or principles enforcing material uniformity, particularly in dress (Tynan 2013) and weaponry. Our study of the militia at Rocky Point, which

operated within the rigidly divided space and routine of drill, target practice, and monitoring ocean traffic, finds routes for analysis that allow for
hybridity or in-betweenness and colonial mimicry and subversion. Even
as military rules required standardized institutional objects that sought to
prevent hybrid forms, hybridized practices may appear in everyday material culture.

To explore these ideas, we draw from historical records and the artifact
assemblage recovered from Rocky Point Battery. Analysis of four artifact
types reveals how evidence of "in-betweenness" may appear at military installations where institutional specifications dictated spatial organization,
uniforms, rules for the mess hall, and other activities subject to inspection.
We evade analytical frameworks derived from a colonizer/colonized dual-
ity in which one either internalizes or resists empire or adopts imported
manufactured goods as opposed to local products. To this end, we suggest a
distinction in this context of buttons and tableware ceramics as institutional
material culture, part of the British military's provisioning that required
uniformity, versus smoking pipes and glass bottles, understood as personal
material culture brought to the fort by the soldiers, reflecting avenues for
negotiating in-betweenness. At this isolated outpost guarding Kingston
Harbor, we find that multiple desires could be expressed or manifested in
certain types of material culture. This evidence suggests that, among people
who declared allegiance to Britain, the display of individual style may not
have operated as inflexibly as the military establishment intended.

Colonial Institutions, Spaces in Between, and Material Culture after Emancipation

Social and racial hierarchies in the colonial Caribbean were shaped by institutions, including plantations, missions, and forts, that dictated certain
roles, social relations, and market access. Before emancipation, these regimes governed power relationships that changed as conditions required
varied forms of reinforcement or "amelioration." Power relations within
these institutions were administered by manipulation of the landscape, or
by institutional material culture as specific objects or principles ensured
uniformity of material life. Of course, not all Caribbean peoples willingly
submitted to colonial regimes; through market systems, provision grounds,
mortuary practices, *marronage*, and other avenues of social action, many
exploited spatial and temporal liminalities between and among the matrices

of plantations, missions, and forts (for example, see Smith and Bassett, this volume; Bates, this volume).

Many of these alternative formations persisted in Britain's Caribbean colonies after emancipation, even as "spaces between" experienced a series of shifts. While agroindustrial production continued, many African Caribbean peoples exited the plantation setting while maintaining provision grounds and market systems. In Jamaica, churches purchased land to found "free villages" for peasant populations (Mintz 1958), and some, particularly in less prosperous colonies, were able to acquire their own lands (see Seiter, this volume; Chenoweth, this volume). The military was not immune to postemancipation change, as most Caribbean fortifications were abandoned by the British in 1854 and the West India Regiment units were distributed among the few remaining installations. As the WIR units were reduced, the locally raised militias that replaced the regiments retained many ordering regimes such as spatial segregation, uniform and drill requirements, and institutional provisioning.

Military Material Culture and Space in the Pre- and Postemancipation Caribbean

Historical archaeologists have been concerned with the investigation of fortifications for decades (Campbell 1967; Orser 2002:227–229). In the Caribbean, an early focus of historians and historical archaeologists alike was in documenting and preserving monumental colonial settlements to underscore the legacies of various imperial powers (Armstrong and Hauser 2009) while studies investigating the nature of military communities were largely absent (Buckley 1998; Leech 2010; Watters 2001). Like traditional studies of North American fortifications, early military sites research in the Caribbean focused on the institutional qualities of these settings in studies of architecture, weaponry, and buttons. This research benefited from the conversion of forts into "open air" museums or national parks that commodify heritage and encourage cultural tourism, a path used to attain UNESCO World Heritage status (Halloran 2009). Archaeology at forts that date from the early colonization phase in the Greater Antilles (Deagan 2010; Smith and Reyes 2013) and Bermuda (Harris 2010) traced the rise of institutionalized settlement plans, the interaction of social groups, and associated behavior patterns.

Recent work has also explored the diversity of military communities. Deagan's (1978, 1995, 2010) studies in early Spanish Florida and Hispañiola consider the critical role of early towns and military installations as loci of European-indigene-African cultural and social transformation. At Brimstone Hill Fortress, St. Kitts, excavations directed by Gerald Schroedl track expressions of cultural identities and individuality, despite oppression and subordination, in ceramic production, exchange, and personalized markings (Ahlman et al. 2008, 2009; Schroedl and Ahlman 2002). Research by Zachary Beier (2011, 2014) at the Cabrits Garrison, Dominica, reveals how enslaved laborers and WIR soldiers accessed exchange networks to acquire locally and regionally made coarse earthenwares and a variety of pots imported from Europe. This is also taken as evidence of creole cooking strategies and diverse eating practices. To broaden perceptions of the sociocultural composition of forts, archaeology at Shirley Heights, Antigua (Cripps 2003), and Fort Charles, Nevis (González-Tennant 2014), reveals lives of women, children, and enslaved African laborers or WIR soldiers silenced in primary documents or popular histories.

Although some late-nineteenth- and twentieth-century military contexts became national symbols after decolonization, the mixture of European, Creole, and African Caribbean personnel at military sites from this period of global hostilities has rarely been studied (Watters 2011). In contrast to forts from earlier periods, military sites dating from emancipation to the World Wars are seldom developed for heritage tourism and are peripheral to UNESCO World Heritage initiatives. Beyond identifying continuity in institutional architecture, technology, and routines, the material and spatial patterns and shifting notions of affiliation and citizenry at these sites reveal experiences of local forces on the home front (Needham 2011; Watters 2011).

Postcolonial Approaches

The overseas experience of colonial troops and the regional identities forged among units like the BWIR in World War I raised awareness among common soldiers of structural inequalities of the military experience that were symptomatic of larger exploitative relationships enforced by colonial order. Although Fanon's writings relate to the French Empire, his experiences describe colonial discourses that also existed in the British Empire. Born in the French colony of Martinique, Fanon fought for France in World War II and, following his education in metropolitan France, served as a psychiatrist in Algeria, where he joined the liberation movement. His works, especially *Black Skin, White Masks* (first published in 1963) and *The Wretched of the Earth* (first published in 1952) are influential postcolonial texts. In the former, Fanon presents a devastating critique of black/white hierarchies manifesting in realms such as language or appropriate choice of spouse that were internalized by and used to oppress the colonized. By breaking down the black/white dichotomy to foster an international post-colonial consciousness, Fanon pried open the door for further critiques, including Edward Said's *Orientalism* (1978), which analyzes discourses by which Europeans constructed the exotic "other."

Homi Bhabha (1994) goes further toward escaping the colonizer/colonized dichotomy by exposing liminal, interstitial categories constituting "hybrid" forms, what he refers to as "third space": "a realm of inventions and convention, initiated and maintained by day-to-day situations and encounters" (Naum 2010:106). Thus, "homogenous national cultures" are effectively imagined entities because their purity is illusory (Bhabha 1994: 7–8). As such, the past is also an "in-between" space (Bhabha 1994:9) characterized by the liminal or interstitial (Lydon and Rizvi 2010:21).

At a military installation like Rocky Point Battery where disciplinary modes were enforced, there is evidence that individuals could work around or within such colonial discourse. Likewise, Stephan Palmié's (2013:465) discussion of "classificatory regimes" that produce hybrids and hybridity finds that "the more one strives for classificatory purity, the more 'hybrids' will begin to multiply"; thus, the colonizer/colonized distinction, which requires a conceived purity of forms, affects the development of hybrids. Yet, instead of focusing on the production or origins of objects, Stephen Silliman (2015:10–11) suggests approaching hybridity as a quality or state such that analysis may benefit from more emphasis on use or practice.

To return to the military setting, Fanon (1962:16) writes, "The colonized subject is a persecuted man who is forever dreaming of becoming the persecutor. The symbols of society such as the police force, bugle calls in the barracks, military parades, and the flag flying aloft, serve not only as inhibitors but also as stimulants. They do not signify: 'Stay where you are.' But rather 'Get ready to do the right thing.'" To borrow from Fanon, we may ask if the militia at Rocky Point "did the right thing" when stimulated by these material and symbolic reminders. Can we detect, in material or written records of their activities, forms of subversion or hybrid practices?

Postemancipation Military Material Culture

Military architecture and material culture stressed homogeneity in clothing, tablewares, diet, and structures. The prevalence of mass-produced goods might further restrict the ways in which material things could be deployed to reflect individuality or in-betweenness. We believe it is a false simplification to interpret material culture according to a colonizer versus colonized dichotomy, in which certain objects or spaces reflect internalization of or dependence upon Britain (possibly reflected as homogeneity or an absence of noninstitutional objects) and others are seen as assertions of local affiliation or individual identity.

To avoid this fallacy, we isolated two broad artifact categories in the Rocky Point assemblage: (1) buttons and ceramics as institutional material culture and (2) smoking pipes and glass bottles as personal objects. We do not aim to present an exhaustive list or typology of the artifact collection, but the definition of these two categories helps interpret the data. The first, following the lead of Lynne Sussman (1978) for British military settings, can be considered "institutional material culture." While this term appears periodically (e.g., Beisaw and Gibb 2009), attempts to define this idea are limited. By institutional material culture, we mean objects made or acquired as part of the system of British military provisioning and subsequently distributed to users. Institutional material culture also includes standardized objects that individuals or groups were expected to acquire for themselves but that had to conform to uniform appearances or patterns according to the institution's demands. Institutional material culture can also include buildings designed, constructed, and maintained in standardized ways. Here we consider uniform buttons and tableware ceramics as institutional material culture. These objects would appear to lend themselves to a colonizer/colonized distinction in the context of African Jamaican militia, but this institutional material culture may also be interpreted as evidence of in-betweenness based on context(s) of use.

The second category is personal material culture, understood within institutional settings. An individual or group acquires these objects for personal uses that are not provided for directly by the institution. The use or possession of personal material culture may be forbidden or discouraged but not necessarily "illegal." Mass-produced or locally manufactured objects could both fall into this category if acquired via purchase in a market or through household production, smuggling, or a variety of other ways. At Fort Rocky, we consider clay smoking pipes and glass bottles related to personal hygiene, appearance, or medicinal use as personal material culture. Again, these are material realms enabling alternative, subversive, or hybrid practices.

Rocky Point Battery: Chronology and Archaeology

Britain entered its final phase of investment in Jamaica's defenses in the 1880s as the development of more powerful weaponry necessitated revision of coastal defenses in Kingston, which had become Jamaica's capital in 1872. Investment was needed to upgrade and reposition batteries and to install new guns, with the heaviest pieces being 9.2-inch guns that fired 380-pound shells to a distance of 16 km (Buisseret 2008:30). To protect the harbor and its entry point off Port Royal, four batteries were erected or modified starting in the 1880s: Rocky Point east of Port Royal, Victoria Battery in Port Royal, and Fort Clarence Battery and Apostles Battery on the west side of the channel (Barker 1980:202–204; Buisseret 2008:29–32). A two-mile-long railway joined Port Royal to Rocky Point from 1887 until the middle of World War I (Needham 2007; Panning 1998).

Rocky Point Battery was built in at least three stages. Construction of the five gun emplacements, fortifications, and barracks began as early as 1882 (Government of Jamaica 1882/83). In March 1889, Inspector General of Artillery W. H. Goodenough conducted an inspection of Kingston Harbor's defenses and reported that Rocky Point Battery has its "old armament of three 7-inch guns, and two 64-prs [pounders]," although plans were for it "to have one 9.2 inch, two 6-inch B.L. [breech loaders], and two 64-prs" (Goodenough, Report of Inspection in the West Indies by the Inspector General of Artillery, No 2, 1890. National Archives, London, WO 106/6329:4). By completion of the first phase on November 18, 1892, the battery consisted of walls and gun emplacements on the south side, a barrack room, kitchen, artillery store rooms, and machine gun emplacements (Jamaica Defenses Port Royal. Record Plan of Rocky Point Battery, 1896, National Archives, London, WO 78/4905), along with the railway connecting Rocky Point to Port Royal. A second construction phase from October 1908 to October 1911 added a number of features recorded on a 1912 "General Plan" (Jamaica–Rocky Point Record Plan, 1912, National Archives, London, WO 78/4905): an engine room and oil store on the east wall, electric light emplacements facing south, a three-story Battery Commander post, shelter, an ablution, a new cookhouse, two latrines, and a Royal Artillery workshop. There is no specific documentation of this, but damage suffered during an earthquake that struck Kingston on January 14, 1907, may have required this new construction.

A final stage of construction for Rocky Point, probably from the interwar period or World War II, when the site's name changed to "Fort Rocky," consisted of further additions and modifications. After removal of the railway, a new barracks was added in the fort's center along with a cookhouse, officer quarters, outbuilding, chapel, and rooms on the south wall.

Units assigned to Rocky Point may be identified from various sources, but a detailed log of all personnel has not been located. As mentioned earlier, militia units were raised in 1891 in accordance with the 1879 law. One of these units stationed at Rocky Point was the St. Andrew Rifle Corps, which was disbanded in January 1914 only to be re-embodied as the Kingston Infantry Volunteers during World War I (Cundall 1922:57), a unit later known as the Jamaica Infantry Volunteers. A 1905 report lists 32 Europeans and 50 men of a "Native Company" of Royal Garrison Artillery at Rocky Point (Military Report and General Information Concerning the Colony of Jamaica and Its Dependencies, 1905, National Archives, London, WO 33/345:128–129). The same strength is repeated in a 1912 report recording a "usual occupation" of Royal Garrison Artillery and Engineers (Military Report on Jamaica, Vol. 1, General Staff, 1912, National Library of Jamaica, Kingston:124–125). In an unpublished manuscript titled "The Jamaica Local Forces," Bruce Barker writes that during World War II there were engineers, militia artillery, and infantry at Fort Rocky, at a strength of 5 officers and 95 other ranks (see also Jamaica Militia Artillery War Diary August 1939–December 1941, National Archives, London, WO 176/26).

Archaeological fieldwork at Fort Rocky satisfied three goals. First, two archaeology field schools offered educational opportunities for students from the University of the West Indies, Mona, and several American universities as well as staff from the Jamaica National Heritage Trust and Jamaican Military Museum. Second, following a previous assessment (Heritage Preservation and Planning Unit 2011), excavations recorded aboveground and subsurface resources to guide the Jamaica National Heritage Trust's management of the site (Lenik 2015). Third, the assemblage would reveal details of daily life and provide dates for deposits and structures in order to associate them with military units. A composite map was built using ESRI ArcGIS 10.1 software with aerial photographs, historic maps, and spatial data collected during a total station survey (Figure 12.1). A systematic shovel test pit (STP) survey at a 10 m interval tested interior and limited exterior areas to record stratigraphy and horizontal artifact distributions and to locate subsurface deposits. A total of 31 1 m × 1 m excavation units were placed, some in a midden found during the STP survey and the rest adjacent to selected structures and walls. The goal of the latter units was to establish construction methods and occupation dates and to associate

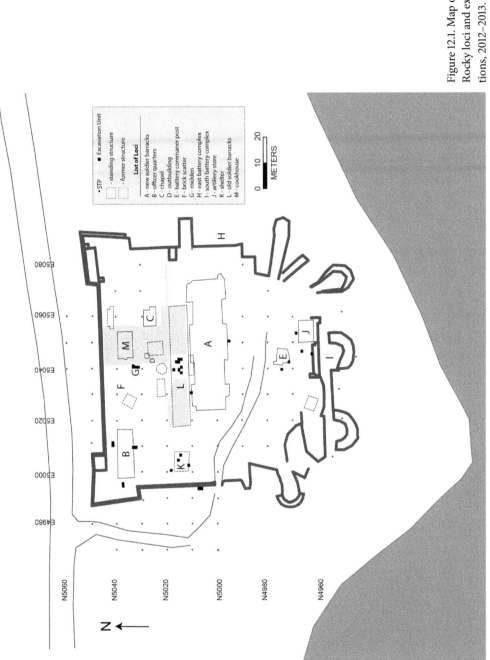

Figure 12.1. Map of Fort Rocky loci and excavations, 2012–2013.

artifacts with specific structures for purposes of comparison. All soil was screened through quarter-inch mesh, and excavation followed natural levels, divided into 10 cm arbitrary layers when necessary. During the two field seasons, 13,194 artifacts were collected. Objects from the surface and the topsoil stratum are excluded from analysis unless otherwise noted.

Our analysis indicates that material realms allowed in-betweenness or hybridity of practices among militiamen at Rocky Point. While there may be objects that could be deployed to signify individuality, affiliation, or resistance, we seek to avoid interpreting data according to dichotomies such as imperial/colonial or European/African, even though institutional material culture stressed homogeneity in diet, dress, and structures (Sussman 1978). Thus, there are dual implications of institutional material culture. The apparent degree of unity in regard to tableware and buttons is interspersed with alternative uses of materials via stylized ceramics and informal versus formal use of buttons. As personal material culture, troops brought smoking pipes and glass bottles to Rocky Point via Port Royal, as the battery was not accessible from the east, where Norman Manley International Airport is now located.

Institutional Material Culture: Uniform Buttons and Tablewares

We identify uniform buttons and tableware ceramics as two object classes that reflect institutional qualities of military culture. Regimented daily schedules and standardized material use in the military under closely monitored living conditions restricted individual expression. Individuals in such settings were encouraged to rally around common activities, theoretically resulting in an ordered schematic composed of socially separated groups with relatively standardized material assemblages. Practices of eating and dress were principle foci of concern for military administration.

Buttons

Uniform buttons as institutional material culture are traditionally interpreted as evidence of varying social functions and the British military's hierarchical structure. When identifiable markings are present, buttons indicate class or rank (e.g., Emilio 1911; Wilkinson-Latham 2008), and, for archaeologists, buttons can associate a military unit with a particular encampment or location in a battlefield. In analyzing manufacture type, context, and decoration of the 82 buttons recovered from all contexts at Fort Rocky, we seek to avoid a colonizer/colonized distinction and do not assume that wearing a Royal Artillery button reflects intentional identification with the empire or that wearing buttons with insignia specific to Jamaica necessarily signals expression of colonial or nationalist sentiments. Certainly, British military uniforms could "embody racial and ethnic differences" by marking colonial types (Tynan 2013:130), and, following Tynan, we agree that buttons established boundaries and enforced status hierarchies within institutional material culture in the military. We continue this line of argument by showing how buttons allowed complex, overlapping meanings in fluid contexts of use depending on who wore a particular button, where, and when. Manufacture types in the assemblage include cast, stamped, carved or drilled, and molded buttons as well as snap fasteners (Table 12.1). Three broad types related the formality of dress can be defined by comparison to buttons in the collection of the Jamaican Military Museum at Up Park Camp in Kingston and input from members of the Jamaica Defence Force who serve as museum staff. Ceremonial "dress" occasions require uniforms with cast buttons like the examples in Figure 12.2, whereas "drill" or everyday activities would use stamped buttons. Carved and molded buttons are of insufficient quality for military usage and represent a third, nonmilitary category. Usage of snap fasteners is difficult to associate with a particular degree of formality.

As shown in Table 12.1, stamped "drill" buttons were recovered from seven loci inside the fort, and the probable nonmilitary carved and molded buttons are sparse and not directly associated with living quarters. The high frequency of formal "dress" cast buttons in the midden (Locus G in Figure 12.1) is difficult to explain. Activities requiring dress uniform may have occurred elsewhere, but cast buttons from the midden, which predates the 1908–1912 construction phase, suggest that dress activities requiring cast buttons took place more often in the earlier period. The low frequency of cast buttons (n = 4) in other contexts suggests a shift away from use of dress uniforms in the period when Rocky Point was manned solely by militia.

Decorative elements on cast buttons and maker's marks on stamped buttons, shown in the upper two rows of Figure 12.2, record place of manufacture and identify particular units of the armed forces. British military insignia are present on four cast buttons that bear the Royal Coat of Arms and on four Royal Artillery buttons with a cannon and crown. Manufacturing dates in the late nineteenth century are given by maker's marks: "W. Twigg & Co. Ltd. Birmingham" (manufactured 1856–1857; 1899 [Nayler 1993:69]); "B-Ham Buttons Limited" and "Smith & Wright Limited Birmingham" (manufactured 1882–1899 [Nayler 1993:64]).

Table 12.1. Fort Rocky button manufacture types by locus

Manufacturing Type	Locus									
	New Barracks	Officer Quarters	BC Post	Midden	Artillery Store	Shelter	Old Barracks	Exterior Wall	Other	Sum
Carved	0	0	0	0	0	3	0	0	0	3
Carved-drilled	0	0	0	0	0	0	2	0	0	2
Cast	0	1	0	29	0	0	2	1	1	34
Cut-carved	1	2	0	0	0	0	0	0	2	5
Molded	0	0	1	0	0	0	1	0	0	2
Snap	0	0	0	0	0	1	0	0	5	6
Stamped	1	4	1	14	1	2	5	0	0	28
Unidentified	0	0	0	0	0	0	1	0	0	1
Sum	2	7	2	43	1	6	11	1	8	81

Figure 12.2. *Top*: Military buttons bearing Royal Coat of Arms and Royal Artillery insignia. *Bottom*: Crocodile and "JC" buttons.

Jamaican insignia are seen on two buttons on the bottom row of Figure 12.2. The first, shown on the left, is a stamped button with an American crocodile (known in Jamaica as an alligator), a symbol associated with militia badges of colonial Jamaica including a buckle recovered from Drax Hall (Armstrong 1990:179), and an 1810 Jamaican militia gorget (Gorget of the Jamaica Militia, 1810, NAM Accession Number 1984-06-163-1, National Army Museum, London). Jamaica's Arms features an alligator as its crest and the Jamaica Defence Force also uses this symbol. The second, a snap with the letters "JC," likely represents the "Jamaica Company" of Royal Artillery. A bar across the "JC" has the letters "JUSTIN," but the full word is indecipherable. Founded in the 1780s, this unit is listed as "Black Troops" for Jamaica in an 1893 report (Army Medical Department 1895:61). Rather than interpreting these as assertions of affiliation or intentional acts of identification, these buttons may be understood as part of a complex system of military insignia active in the daily life of troops, as they parallel the variety of dress, drill, and everyday-use buttons.

Ceramics

Tableware ceramics recovered from British military sites are typically interpreted as evidence of provisioning, either given to troops or purchased by soldiers or officers in conformance with a uniform style or specific insignia (Demers 2009; Sussman 1978). Segregation of food production and consumption at nineteenth-century military sites is manifested in discrete preparation and consumption areas in locales such as mess halls, although archaeological and historical evidence at eighteenth-century military sites show that food consumption was decentralized (Buckley 1998:349). A mess does not appear in documentation of Rocky Point Battery, as the only identified buildings relating to food preparation or consumption are three cookhouses. One of these appears on an 1896 map (Jamaica Defenses Port Royal, Record Plan of Rocky Point Battery, 1896, National Archives, London, WO 78/4905) in the southern half of the battery, and a second is located in the northern part on the 1912 map (Jamaica-Rocky Point Record Plan, 1912, National Archives, London, WO 78/4905). A third cookhouse recorded during fieldwork is a structure with a collapsed brick chimney (see Figure 12.1).

The Rocky Point tableware ceramic assemblage consists of 309 sherds (3,909.0 g), excluding those recovered from topsoil layers. Institutional ceramics are represented by plain white granite/ironstone wares that compose 58.2 percent of the collection by count (62.8 percent weight). Patterns consistent with those found at British military sites from earlier periods (Demers 2009; Sussman 1978) are not observed. A variety of decoration types are present, including transfer-printed (n = 24), hand-painted (n = 11), sponge-decorated (n = 8), annular (n = 3), and flow blue (n = 2) wares. We argue that decorated and undecorated tablewares that are *not* white granite wares represent vessels brought in by troops for their own use. Assuming a strong relationship between the locations of deposition and use, spatial segregation of institutional versus noninstitutional ceramics can be taken to suggest where institutional ceramics were and were not being used.

Because sample sizes consist of fewer than 10 sherds, the new barracks, Battery Commander post, and artillery store are omitted from consideration in Table 12.2, which calculates percentages of institutional white granite wares versus noninstitutional wares by count and by weight in

Table 12.2. Fort Rocky percentage of decorated versus undecorated tablewares by locus

Locus	Description	Total Count	Total Weight (g)	Inst. Ct %	Non-Inst. Ct %	Inst. Wt %	Non-Inst. Wt %
B	Officer Quarters	10	20.7	50.0	50.0	24.6	75.4
G	Midden	143	1723.5	67.1	32.9	88.1	11.9
K	Shelter	40	250.0	15.0	85.0	3.8	96.2
L	Old Barracks	21	103.9	47.6	52.4	59.2	40.8
W	Exterior Wall	25	604.1	52.0	48.0	16.1	83.9

grams (g) for each locus. This evidence shows that institutional tablewares appear most frequently in the midden, which dates from before the second construction phase. Low percentages of noninstitutional ceramics, when measured by weight, appear most clearly in the shelter inside the main entrance and along the exterior wall, where excavation units uncovered a buried artifact deposit atop a widened concrete base of the wall extending from 20 to 50 cm below the surface.

It is likely that materials were deposited over the wall or thrown out before entering the fort. These findings indicate that areas near the main gate were liminal or communal spaces, where rules regarding uniformity could be bent or broken, which was less likely in soldiers' living quarters where more plain institutional wares are found. While precise meanings and intentions of use for these ceramics are not straightforward, we interpret this evidence to mean that interior and exterior areas near the west wall entrance, which offers a view of the harbor and traffic to and from Port Royal, allowed opportunities outside of formal arenas of habitation or food preparation for troops to use more noninstitutional wares while adhering to institutional practices inside the fort.

Personal Material Culture: Tobacco Pipes and Bottle Glass

Archaeological evidence suggests that several types of personal material culture were used by the men stationed at Rocky Point. Clay smoking pipes and glass bottles related to hygiene, health, and personal appearance reflect material realms that permit subversion and in-betweenness.

Smoking Pipes

The 67 white clay smoking pipe fragments in the assemblage reveal that people smoked at Rocky Point, but it is the continued use of white clay pipes that is somewhat surprising, considering the invention of the cigarette rolling machine in the United States in 1880 and a cigar-making tradition in Jamaica maintained by Cuban migrants. Because of the battery's narrow occupation date, these pieces offer little temporal information. In 64ths of an inch, the mean bore diameter of measurable stems is 4.47, and the standard formula dating methods greatly underestimate the date, which is understandable as methods devised by J. C. Harrington, Lewis Binford, and others were designed for much earlier time periods. It is rather the decorative markings on these pipes and their contexts that suggest the role of smoking. As others have noted, how one smoked and the resultant markings on a pipe can be read as intentional acts of resistance or subversion (Brighton 2009:148–152; Hartnett 2004), and we adopt a similar position here.

The percentage of decorated pipes from Rocky Point can be compared to three earlier British Caribbean military installations: Cabrits Garrison, Dominica (1763–1854 [Beier 2014]); Brimstone Hill, St. Kitts (1690–1854, [Hill and Schroedl 2003:21]); and Shirley Heights, Antigua (1781–1854 [Cripps 2003]). At 25.4 percent, the ratio of decorated to undecorated fragments at Rocky Point is considerably higher than those from pre-1854 contexts (Cabrits Garrison contexts related to enslaved people = 10.6 percent, soldier = 4.5 percent; Brimstone Hill = 2.1 percent; Shirley Heights = 11.3 percent). These findings suggest that smoking pipes as personal material culture continued to be used during the earlier period of Fort Rocky's occupation, and, compared to pre-emancipation sites, the significance of decorations and other markings may have increased.

Markings offer some clues into the usage of pipes. A "McDougall Glasgow" stamp on six fragments reflects a manufacturer in Scotland that operated from the mid-nineteenth century to the early-twentieth century (Sudbury 2007). Three bowls suggest some form of affiliation with particular owners. A complete knobbed bowl has the letters "EW" scratched into it, and, while the precise meaning cannot be determined, the marks may represent a form of personalized marking resembling letters and X's scratched into ceramic plates at Brimstone Hill (Schroedl and Ahlman 2002). A bowl fragment from the exterior wall near the gate has an embossed image of a steam locomotive and a boat. Such a pipe may have been selected to identify with this coastal battery, which also had a railroad and monitored ocean traffic. Third, a bowl with animal horns above the letters "RAOB" stands for "Royal Antediluvian Order of Buffaloes," a worldwide philanthropic society associated with British working-class men, who may have visited the battery as engineers or army regulars. Ritually broken during initiation ceremonies, RAOB pipes marked membership in a group that spanned the British Empire (Resources for Learning in Scotland 2014). This pipe reveals an interwoven field of identity associated with working-class Europeans within the material life of Rocky Point.

The spatial distribution of pipes shows that over 77 percent of the fragments were recovered from the midden (n = 34) and the old soldiers' barracks (n = 18). Small numbers of pipes were collected near the exterior wall (n = 7), shelter (n = 2), Battery Commander post (n = 1), and new barracks (n = 1), and dispersed across the site in the STP survey (n = 4). No fragments were found at the officer's quarters, which may suggest use of paper cigarettes or cigars. The contexts of these finds suggest status differences could be expressed through smoking pipes used by militia.

Bottle Glass

A second type of personal material culture offering prospects for interpreting hybridizing practices is glass, the most frequently occurring artifact type at the site, including an array of bottles, stemwares, light fixtures, and architectural glass attributable to the rise of mass production of these items during this period. The surface and topsoil stratum yield the most fragments, at 61.7 percent of the total count of glass artifacts, mainly soft drink, liquor bottles, and the ubiquitous Red Stripe bottle, indicating post-abandonment activity that is excluded from this analysis. Bottles related to hygiene or appearance and pharmaceuticals total 68 fragments (545.6 g), which are 1.8 percent (3.2 percent by weight) of nonarchitectural glass from all contexts.

Among the bottle fragments related to hygiene, personal appearance, and pharmaceuticals (again excluding topsoil strata), most are located in the midden (n = 50; 227.6 g), with small quantities from the officer's quarters (n = 2; 26.6 g), Battery Commander post (n = 1; 0.4 g), shelter (n = 1; 5.8 g), and STP contexts (n = 3; 33.7 g). Fragments were not found associated with either barracks. Several bottles with identifiable markings indicate uses by the militia, and, although reuse of bottles is possible, the toxicity of the contents makes secondary use unlikely.

First, troops contended with body odor and sweat in the hot, sunny conditions, shown by a cylindrical milk-glass jar recovered from a STP topsoil layer with remains of a decal label for deodorant antiperspirant and a fragment of a cylindrical bottle with the embossed letters "LANMAN / STS / ORK" from the midden. This bottle appears to be "Florida Water," a perfumed spirit used as toilet water or fragrance made by Murray and

Figure 12.3. Glass bottles related to hair care. *Left*: Vaseline jar, Chesebrough Manufacturing Co.; *center*: "Barry's Tricopherous for the Skin and Hair"; *right*: possible hair straightener bottle.

Lanman in New York (Sullivan 1994). Second, a number of pharmaceutical sherds show that soldiers used patent medicines common at many sites from this period. From the midden was recovered a complete bottle of "Dr. Morse's Indian Root Pills," which promised to remedy a wide variety of illnesses and was manufactured by W. H. Comstock after 1855 (Shaw 1972). These finds show that troops accessed patent medicines while remedies based on medicinal plants and herbs were also available but are unlikely to be identified archaeologically. Third, three glass fragments (Figure 12.3) are associated with hair treatments. From the midden is a Vaseline jar with a tooled lip made by "Chesebrough Manufacturing Co." of Perth Amboy, New Jersey. Patented in the United States in 1872, Vaseline has many applications, including use as pomade for styling hair (Whitten 2014). Recovered from the exterior wall is a bottle of "Barry's Tricopherous for the Skin and Hair," a mixture featuring 97 percent alcohol used to stimulate hair growth or prevent loss (Sherrow 2006:175). Finally, a fragment from the shelter is embossed with the letters "-AIR" above "AIT-NER" and appears to be a hair straightener (spelled "strait-ner"), which often consisted of lye to relax hair before straightening, usually with a heavy metal comb.

These data show that troops acquired mass-produced goods to address health issues with patent medicines, to contend with hot conditions using toilet water and antiperspirants, and to treat their hair. Within the military regime at Rocky Point, the militiamen were concerned with personal appearance and body odor in ways that could operate alongside but independent of military discipline. Beneath a uniform cap, one's hair style could match latest fashions, or a soldier could choose to express individuality and evade uniformity by wearing scents. While the specific intentions behind use of these products may not be recoverable, these fragments reflect the presence of multiple ways of manipulating appearance despite the military's uniform requirements.

Conclusion

Archaeological findings from Fort Rocky reveal the lived experience of African Jamaican volunteers, which is either lacking in documents from the period or generalized as propaganda or cautionary measures. In this way, this investigation has sought evidence derived directly from the people being studied rather than traditional top-down or Eurocentric approaches to understanding the twentieth-century World Wars. Institutional and personal forms of material culture demonstrate to varying degrees how social boundaries underpinning British imperialism and military hierarchy could be tested or exceeded in everyday practice, revealing the brittleness of the colonial structure as well as the potential for research probing the in-betweenness that would otherwise be obscured by the idealized colonizer/colonized dichotomy. In particular, this analysis reveals that for institutional material culture, colonial desires were not being manifested in plain white granite tablewares. Rather, evidence indicates that bringing in one's own ceramics and using them in areas in between sites of imperial power, such as the west wall entrance, one could get around the rules. For buttons, there are hierarchies of use along multiple scales, as contexts dictated buttons associated with dress versus drill uniforms and incorporated insignia associated with Jamaica or the British Empire. Buttons express a variety of affiliations and would assume different meanings depending on where, when, how, or on whom they worn.

Smoking pipes and glass bottles containing substances related to hygiene and personal appearance indicate fluidity within restrictions at this outpost. Possession and use of decorated clay pipes at postemancipation military sites, contemporaneous with the rise of paper cigarettes and use of cigars, indicate that smoking was a way troops could represent themselves in relation to others. The lack of pipes from the officer's quarters suggests they may have smoked cigarettes or cigars while clay pipes could have been used by Jamaican militia. Thus, there were inflexible identities in certain contexts, but other realms of identification escaped the colonized/colonizer hierarchy that the military regime tried to enforce. The initials scratched on a pipe but not on any ceramics may perhaps indicate more personal connection to this class of material. However, decorated tablewares were also brought to Rocky Point and used alongside plain institutional wares. In a glass assemblage that shows how militia accessed mass-produced goods, pharmaceuticals and substances related to hair or body odor could be used to look and feel a certain way. These types of glass tend to be used and discarded in communal areas near the entrance to the battery.

The archaeology at Rocky Point suggests that there were venues for contested and complex identities and practices within hierarchies manifested in uniforms, daily life, labor, and social relations in Caribbean military spaces. Reflexive approaches of postcolonial writers and theorists help sidestep colonial categories imposed upon African Jamaican militia, who appear in written records according to such categorizations and were subject to sociospatial relations structured by colonial powers. There is no evidence of overt rebellion by militiamen at the Kingston Harbor batteries, and we cannot confirm whether the individual material negotiations detected here were intentionally subversive acts, but it is evident that material culture offered opportunities for blurring boundaries through the pipes used to smoke, when and where buttons were worn, the plates and bowls used to eat, and glass associated with personal care. The degree to which this evidence is connected to contemporaneous emergence of political consciousness in Jamaica (Lumsden 1999) is debatable, but what this analysis of Fort Rocky does—similar to Alfredo González-Ruibal's (2010) deconstruction of "good fascism" at twentieth-century Italian outposts in Ethiopia—is to help reevaluate the myth of the "loyal colony" by bringing attention to the places in between imperial ordering and segregation. Although memory of the World Wars has faded, the abandoned Fort Rocky is a reminder that, even though Jamaicans were once colonized peoples, this same system offered the means to subvert and escape colonial domination that lasted for more than three centuries.

Acknowledgments

A Special Initiative Grant and Study and Travel Grant from the University of the West Indies, Mona, supported archive research and laboratory analysis. We thank the Jamaica National Heritage Trust for support during all phases of the project, and students from UWI, Mona, St. Mary's College of Maryland, and Appalachian State University who participated. Maj. Michael Anglin and Capt. Staci-Marie Dehaney from the Jamaican Military Museum generously provided their support. We also thank David

Buisseret, Liza Gijanto, Merrick Needham, James Robertson, and Christopher Waters for their assistance.

References Cited

Ahlman, Todd M., Gerald F. Schroedl, and Ashley H. McKeown
2009   The Afro-Caribbean Ware from the Brimstone Hill Fortress, St. Kitts, West Indies: A Study in Ceramic Production. *Historical Archaeology* 43(4):22–41.
Ahlman, Todd M., Gerald F. Schroedl, Ashley H. McKeown, Robert J. Speakman, and Michael D. Glascock
2008   Ceramic Production and Exchange among Enslaved Africans on St. Kitts, West Indies. *Journal of Caribbean Archaeology* 2:109–122.
Armstrong, Douglas V.
1990   *The Old Village and the Great House: An Archaeological and Historical Examination of Drax Hall Plantation, St. Ann's Bay, Jamaica.* University of Illinois Press, Urbana.
Armstrong, Douglas V., and Mark W. Hauser
2009   A Sea of Diversity: Historical Archaeology in the Caribbean. In *International Handbook of Historical Archaeology*, edited by David Gaimster and Teresita Majewski, pp. 583–612. Springer, New York.
Army Medical Department
1895   *Army Medical Department Report for the Year 1893, with Appendix.* Volume XXXV. Harrison and Sons, London.
Barker, Bruce
1980   A Few Notes on Coastal Artillery in Jamaica. *Jamaican Historical Society Bulletin* 7(15):199–204.
Beckles, Hilary, and Verene Shepherd (editors)
1996   *Caribbean Freedom: Economy and Society from Emancipation to the Present.* Markus Wiener, Princeton, New Jersey.
Beier, Zachary J. M.
2011   Initial Feasibility and Reconnaissance at the Cabrits Garrison, Dominica. In *Proceedings of the XXIII Congress of The International Association for Caribbean Archaeology*, June 29–July 3, 2009, Antigua, edited by Samantha A. Rebovich. Dockyard Museum, English Harbour, Antigua.
2014   The Cabrits Garrison. In *The Encyclopedia of Caribbean Archaeology*, edited by Basil Reid and R. Grant Gilmore III, pp. 83–84. University Press of Florida, Gainesville.
Beisaw, April M., and James G. Gibb
2009   *The Archaeology of Institutional Life.* University of Alabama Press, Tuscaloosa.
Bhabha, Homi K.
1994   *The Location of Culture.* Routledge, New York.
Black, Jeremy
2006   *A Military History of Britain: From 1775 to the Present.* Praeger Security International, Westport, Connecticut.

Brighton, Stephen A.
2009   *Historical Archaeology of the Irish Diaspora: A Transnational Approach*. University of Tennessee Press, Knoxville.

Buckley, Roger N.
1979   *Slaves in Red Coats: The British West India Regiments, 1795–1815*. Yale University Press, New Haven, Connecticut.
1998   *The British Army in the West Indies: Society and the Military in the Revolutionary Age*. University Press of Florida, Gainesville.

Buisseret, David
2008   *The Fortifications of Jamaica*. The Elsa Goveia Memorial Lecture. Department of History and Archaeology, University of the West Indies, Kingston, Jamaica.

Campbell, Horace
1985   *Rasta and Resistance: From Marcus Garvey to Walter Rodney*. Hansib, St. John's, Antigua, West Indies.

Campbell, J. Duncan
1967   Military Sites. *Historical Archaeology* 1:38–40.

Card, Jeb J. (editor)
2013   *The Archaeology of Hybrid Material Culture*. Occasional Paper No. 39, Center for Archaeological Investigations, Southern Illinois University, Carbondale.

Cundall, Frank
1922   *Jamaica in 1922: A Handbook of Information for Intending Settlers and Visitors with some Account of the Colony's History*. Institute of Jamaica, Kingston, Jamaica.
1925   *Jamaica's Part in the Great War, 1914–1918*. Institute of Jamaica, Kingston, Jamaica.

Cripps, Beau F.
2003   The Garbage of Gentlemen: Investigations of a Military Refuse Midden from the Shirley Heights Officers' Quarters (PAH 127) Antigua, West Indies. Unpublished Master's thesis, Faculty of Arts and Science, Trent University, Peterborough, Ontario.

Deagan, Kathleen
1978   The Material Assemblage of 16th Century Spanish Florida. *Historical Archaeology* 12:25–50.
1995   *Puerto Real: The Archaeology of a Sixteenth-Century Spanish Town in Hispaniola*. University Press of Florida, Gainesville.
2010   Strategies of Adjustment: Spanish Defense of the Circum-Caribbean Colonies, 1493–1600. In *First Forts: Essays on the Archaeology of Proto-colonial Fortifications*, edited by Eric Klingelhofer, pp. 17–39. Brill, Boston.

Demers, Paul
2009   "Crestspeak": British Military Crested Ceramics, Military Socialization, and Collective Memory. *International Journal of Historical Archaeology* 13(3):366–384.

Dyde, Brian
1997   *The Empty Sleeve: Story of the West India Regiments of the British Army*. Hansib, St. John's, Antigua, West Indies.

Emilio, Luis Fenollosa
1911   *The Emilio Collection of Military Buttons: American, British, French and Spanish, with Some Other Countries, and Non-Military in the Museum of the Essex Institute, Salem, Mass.* The Essex Collection, Salem, Massachusetts.

Fanon, Frantz
1967   *Black Skin, White Masks.* Reprinted. Grove Press, New York. Originally published 1952, Editions Du Seuil, Paris.
1968   *The Wretched of the Earth.* Reprinted. Grove Press, New York. Originally published 1963, Francois Maspero editeur, Paris.

Farry, Andrew
2005   Regulars and "Irregulars": British and Provincial Variability among Eighteenth-Century Military Frontiers. *Historical Archaeology* 39(2):16–32.

Garvey, Marcus
2004   The Negro's Greatest Enemy. In *Selected Writings and Speeches of Marcus Garvey,* edited by Bob Blaisdell, pp. 1–9. Dover Publications, Mineola, New York.

González-Ruibal, Alfredo
2010   Fascist Colonialism: The Archaeology of Italian Outposts in Western Ethiopia (1936–41). *International Journal of Historical Archaeology* 14:547–574.
2011   A Social Archaeology of Colonial War in Ethiopia. *World Archaeology* 43(1): 40–65.

González-Tennant, Edward
2014   The "Color" of Heritage: Decolonizing Collaborative Archaeology in the Caribbean. *Journal of African Diaspora Archaeology and Heritage* 3(1):26–50.

Government of Jamaica
1882–1883 *Blue Book for the Island of Jamaica, 1882/83.* Government Printing Office, Kingston.

Halloran, Vivian Nun
2009   Exhibiting Slavery: The Caribbean Postmodern Novel as Museum. University of Virginia Press, Charlottesville.

Handler, Jerome S.
1984   Freedmen and Slaves in the Barbados Militia. *Journal of Caribbean History* 19:1–25.

Harris, Edward Cecil
2010   Bermuda's First Forts, 1612–1622. In *First Forts: Essays on the Archaeology of Proto-colonial Fortifications,* edited by Eric Klingelhofer, pp. 105–125. Brill, Boston.

Hartnett, Alexandra
2004   The Politics of the Pipe: Clay Pipes and Tobacco Consumption in Galway, Ireland. *International Journal of Historical Archaeology* 8(2):133–147.

Heritage Preservation and Planning Unit, Archaeology Division
2011   *Development Proposal for Fort Rocky, Port Royal.* Report on file at the Jamaica National Heritage Trust, Kingston, Jamaica.

Hill, Amy D., and Gerald F. Schroedl
2003   *Clay Tobacco Pipes from the Brimstone Hill Fortress, St. Kitts, West Indies.* Brimstone Hill Archaeological Report No.23. Report on file at The Brimstone Hill Fortress National Park Society, St. Kitts.

Joseph, C. L.

1971   The British West Indian Regiment 1914–1918. *Journal of Caribbean History* 2:94–124.

Leech, Roger H.

2010   "Within musquett shott of Black Rock": Johnson's Fort and the Early Defenses of Nevis, West Indies. In *First Forts: Essays on the Archaeology of Proto-colonial Fortifications*, edited by Eric Klingelhofer, pp. 127–138. Brill, Boston.

Lenik, Stephan T.

2015   *Report of Archaeological Investigations of Fort Rocky (Rocky Point Battery) 2012–2013*. Report on file at the Jamaica National Heritage Trust, Kingston, Jamaica.

Liebmann, Matthew, and Uzma Z. Rizvi (editor)

2008   *Archaeology and the Postcolonial Critique*. Altamira Press, Lanham, Maryland.

Lumsden, Joy

1999   A Forgotten Generation: Black Politicians in Jamaica, 1884–1914. In *Before and After 1865: Education, Politics and Regionalism in the Caribbean*, edited by Brian Moore and Swithin Wilmot, pp. 112–122. Ian Randle, Kingston, Jamaica.

Lydon, Jane, and Uzma Z. Rizvi

2010   Introduction: Postcolonialism and Archaeology. In *Handbook of Postcolonial Archaeology*, edited by Jane Lydon and Uzma Z. Rizvi, pp. 17–33. Left Coast Press, Walnut Creek, California.

Maurice-Jones, K. W.

2009   *The History of Coast Artillery in the British Army*. Naval and Military Press, Uckfield, United Kingdom.

Metzgen, Humphrey and John Graham

2007   *Caribbean Wars Untold: A Salute to the British West Indies*. University of the West Indies Press, Kingston, Jamaica.

Mintz, Sidney W.

1958   Historical Sociology of the Jamaican Church-Founded Free Village System. *New West Indian Guide* 38(1):46–70.

Naum, Magdalena

2010   Re-Emerging Frontiers: Postcolonial Theory and Historical Archaeology of the Borderlands. *Journal of Archaeological Method and Theory* 17:101–131.

Nayler, Peter

1993   *Military Button Manufacturers from the London Directories, 1800–1899*. Minister of the Department of Canadian Heritage, Parks Canada, Ottawa.

Needham, Merrick

2007   Jamaican Military Railway. *The Gleaner*, September 14. Kingston, Jamaica

2011   "They Possess . . . Many Excellent Qualities as Soldiers": The West India Regiments. *Jamaica Journal* 33(3):8–9.

Orser, Charles E., Jr. (editor)

2002   *Encyclopedia of Historical Archaeology*. Routledge, New York.

Palmié, Stephan

2013   Mixed Blessings and Sorrowful Mysteries: Second Thoughts about "Hybridity." *Current Anthropology* 54(4):463–482.

Panning, Stephen F.
1998   Evidence of a Light Railway at Port Royal—Circa 1900. *Jamaican Historical Society Bulletin* 11(1):19–21.
Resources for Learning in Scotland
2014   Pathfinder Pack on The Royal Antediluvian Order of Buffaloes. Electronic Document, http://rls.org.uk/database/record.php?usi=000-000-001-348-L.
Rogers, Simon
2002   "There Were No Parades for Us," *Guardian*, November 6.
Said, Edward W.
1978   *Orientalism*. Vintage Books, New York.
Schroedl, Gerald F., and Todd M. Ahlman
2002   The Maintenance of Cultural and Personal Identities of Enslaved Africans and British Soldiers at the Brimstone Hill Fortress, St. Kitts, West Indies. *Historical Archaeology* 36(4):38–49.
Shaw, Robert B.
1972   *History of the Comstock Patent Medicine Business and Dr. Morse's Indian Root Pills*. Smithsonian Institution Press, Washington, D.C.
Sherrow, Victoria
2006   *Encyclopedia of Hair: A Cultural History*. Greenwood, New York.
Silliman, Stephen W.
2015   A Requiem for Hybridity? The Problem with Frankensteins, Purées, and Mules. *Journal of Social Archaeology* 15:1–22.
Singleton, Theresa A.
2010   Liberation, and Emancipation: Constructing a Postcolonial Archaeology of the African Diaspora. In *Handbook of Postcolonial Archaeology*, edited by Jane Lydon and Uzma Z. Rizvi, pp. 185–198. Left Coast Press, Walnut Creek, California.
Smith, Hale Gilliam, and Ricardo Torres Reyes
2013   *Archaeological Excavations at El Morro, San Juan, Puerto Rico: With Historical Background Sections*. Literary Licensing, Whitefish, Montana.
Smith, Richard
2004   *Jamaican Volunteers in the First World War: Race, Masculinity and the Development of a National Consciousness*. Manchester University Press, Manchester.
2014   Propaganda, Imperial Subjecthood and National Identity in Jamaica during the First World War. In *World War I and Propaganda*, edited by Troy R. E. Paddock, pp. 89–112. Brill Academic, Boston, Massachusetts.
Sudbury, J. Byron
2007   *Historic Clay Tobacco Pipe Studies*, Vol. 1. Phytolith Press, Ponca City, Oklahoma.
Sullivan, Catherine
1994   Searching for Nineteenth-Century Florida Water Bottles. *Historical Archaeology* 28(1):78–98.
Sussman, Lynne
1978   British Military Tableware, 1760–1830. *Historical Archaeology* 12:93–104.
Tynan, Jane
2013   *British Army Uniform and the First World War: Men in Khaki*. Palgrave Macmillan, New York.

van Pelt, W. Paul (editor)

2013   Archaeology and Cultural Mixture. *Archaeological Review from Cambridge* 28(1):1–363.

Voelz, Peter M.

1993   *Slave and Soldier: The Military Impact of Blacks in the Colonial Americas*. Garland, New York.

Watters, David R.

2001   Historical Archaeology in the British Caribbean. In *Island Lives: Historical Archaeologies of the Caribbean*, edited by Paul Farnsworth, pp. 82–99. University of Alabama Press, Tuscaloosa.

2011   Is the Archaeology of World War II Now a Valid Field of Study? Paper presented at the XXIV International Congress for Caribbean Archaeology, Martinique, July 25–30, 2011.

Whitten, David

2014   Chesebrough Manuf'g Co / Vaseline Jars. Electronic document, http://www. glassbottlemarks.com/chesebrough-manufg-co-vaseline-jars/. Accessed October 1, 2014.

Wilkinson-Latham, Robert

2008   *Discovering British Military Badges and Buttons*, 3rd ed. Shire, Oxford.

13

Double Consciousness and an African American Enclave

Being Black and American on Hispañiola

KRISTEN R. FELLOWS

> It is a peculiar sensation, this double-consciousness, this sense of always looking at one's self through the eyes of others, of measuring one's soul by the tape of a world that looks on in amused contempt and pity. One ever feels his two-ness,—an American, a Negro; two souls, two thoughts, two unreconciled strivings; two warring ideals in one dark body, whose dogged strength alone keeps it from being torn asunder.
>
> W.E.B. Du Bois, *The Souls of Black Folk*

> Away back in the days of bondage they thought to see in one divine event the end of all doubt and disappointment; few men ever worshipped Freedom with half such unquestioning faith as did the American Negro for two centuries. To him, so far as he thought and dreamed, slavery was indeed the sum of all villainies, the cause of all sorrow, the root of all prejudice; Emancipation was the key to a promised land of sweeter beauty than ever stretched before the eyes of wearied Israelites.
>
> W.E.B. Du Bois, *The Souls of Black Folk*

In *The Souls of Black Folk*, W.E.B. Du Bois introduced readers to the tensions inherent within an African American identity; he labeled this a "double consciousness," which is a concept that speaks to scholars of race and racism to this day. In the beginning of *Souls*, Du Bois points out that for African and African-descended people in the United States, "Freedom" was the cure to their plight; for two hundred years, "Emancipation" was the end goal. For blacks in the United States, Freedom was not just legal freedom; it would bring recognition, citizenship, and a reconciliation of the "two-ness" that characterized being black in America. Du Bois capitalizes "Freedom" and "Emancipation" in order to emphasize the idealism behind these concepts for both slaves and freedmen; these terms embodied more than just manumission. Although Du Bois' work focused on postbellum African Americans, his research was often historical in nature. In *Souls* he tells us, "The history of the American Negro is the history of this strife,—this long-ing to attain self-conscious manhood, to merge his double self into a better and truer self" (Du Bois 2003 [1903]:9; see also Zamir 2014). In the sec-ond quote that opens this chapter, we also see him referencing the days of slavery. Thus, Du Bois' double consciousness serves as a useful framework for the exploration of changing conceptions of identity within a free-black community, a community that predated the American Civil War and that consisted of freedmen living in a slaveholding society. In the 1820s, free blacks emigrated from the United States to settle in the free-black republic of Haiti. In this chapter, one group of emigrants and their descendants will serve as a case study through which to explore the processes of community formation and maintenance and the impact multiple racialized nationali-ties had on the development of a diasporic identity.

Following the Haitian Revolution (1791–1804), the newly formed free-black nation unified the Spanish and formerly French sides of the island of Hispaniola for a period of twenty-two years (1822–1844) (Moya Pons 1998). In 1824 Haitian president Jean-Pierre Boyer sent an agent to the United States to begin recruiting potential immigrants from the free-black com-munities of the major northern cities. The purpose behind this endeavor was to help bolster population numbers with skilled agriculturalists while also making a bid to gain political recognition from the United States. By the end of 1825 approximately 6,000 freedmen had been recruited to im-migrate to and settle on the island (Davis 2007; Hoetink 1962; Smith 1986, 1987; Weeks and Ramírez Zabala 2005; Winch 1988, 1989). Inspired by President Boyer's promises of citizenship and notions of black nationalism, around 200 emigrants settled in the town of Santa Bárbara de Samaná, on the Samaná Peninsula, in what is now the Dominican Republic (see Figure 1.2). Both the town and the peninsula are commonly referred to simply as Samaná. The remote location of this settlement allowed the Americans to remain relatively geopolitically isolated for well over 100 years. This African American community has been characterized by the use of English as their first and primary language, their devotion to Methodism (in a country of devout Catholics), their unique American surnames and culture, and their family stories of the United States, slavery, and early life on the island. Al-though this group was once rather insulated, in the twentieth century it became more integrated into the larger Dominican society. Today younger generations primarily speak Spanish, there has been a rise in the number of conversions to Catholicism, and the descendants are no longer a cohesive community (Davis 2007; Hoetink 1962; Ramírez Zabala 2005; Smith 1987; Weeks and Ramírez Zabala 2005).

It is important to contextualize the North American black community prior to their emigration from the United States. Although African Americans left for Haiti from multiple northern cities in the United States, the group settling in Samaná originated primarily from Philadelphia; accordingly, this chapter will also consider the free-black community of that city. While material culture is the traditional focus of archaeological research, anthropological analysis of the documentary record has contributed vastly to historical archaeological studies. Thus, ethnohistorical and archival sources will help to shed light on the Americans in Samaná after settlement. The most significant of these documents is the Report of the 1871 U.S. Commission of Inquiry on Santo Domingo, which sought to determine what the Dominican population and the American settlers thought about a possible annexation by the United States. Serving as a subsecretary for this commission, Frederick Douglass interviewed a number of the Americans in both Santo Domingo and Samaná and published their responses in the back of the report, thus providing a glimpse of the community just shy of 50 years after settlement (Government Printing Office [GPO] 1871). The documentary record allows for an exploration of how the development of multiple racialized national projects affected a diasporic identity within this African American community while living in the United States, then as they settled in Haiti, and finally as they lived after their land became part of the Dominican Republic. The free blacks leaving the United States rejected, in a sense, their African American identity for citizenship in a black republic. Yet, after arriving in what was then Haiti, the enclave in Samaná worked hard to reestablish this identity in order to distance themselves from local Dominicans and Haitians. By 1871 we will see this community fully identifying as African American; interestingly, at this point in time they seem to have achieved a degree of relief from the tensions inherent in their double consciousness.

Philadelphia's Free-Black Community in the Late-Eighteenth and Early-Nineteenth Centuries

During the late eighteenth century, segments of Philadelphia's black community, the largest free-black community in the United States at that time,

worked hard not only to establish fruitful careers but also to cultivate respect within the larger population and a sense of identity independent
from their plantation past. While still retaining many practices originating
in Africa, Anglo cultural ways were also adopted. Northern blacks were
beginning to identify as both American *and* as black. Gary Nash (1988)
studied naming practices within the community in Philadelphia to demonstrate the development of this unique African American identity, or rather,
W.E.B. Du Bois' "double consciousness." As former slaves changed their
names and black institutions were founded and grew within the city, the
names taken on by individuals as well as those given to social, religious, and
aid societies conveyed the tension between creating an identity that would
be seen as respectable within the larger American society while maintaining a connection to a past identity from which they had been physically
and forcibly removed. According to Nash (1988), newly freed people in
Philadelphia often chose new Anglo first names, abandoning the ridicu-
lous, mocking, classical names they had been given by their masters (e.g.
"Hercules"). Additionally, they decided on surnames that would distance
themselves from their former owners. A very different practice was seen in
the U.S. South, where many former slaves retained the surname (and thus
patronage) of their former masters (Nash 1988).

Black institutions were created during this time based on the structure
and mission of white benevolent societies. For instance, the Free African
Society was established in 1787. Nash (1988) points out that it was not the
"Free Black/Negro/Colored Society," but the "Free African Society." While
this institution was based on white models, it took on a name that spoke
to a shared African past and did not draw on the racialized language of the
plantation. Also significant in the use of "African" by various black institutions was the newly formed concept of a Pan-African identity. Despite
the fact that multiple generations of enslaved people had been born in the
United States by the late eighteenth century, there were still those who came
from diverse places and ethnic groups in Africa; it was not a given that
those newly freed or free blacks not born into slavery would have readily
identified as a single, cohesive group prior to this time (Berlin 1998; Nash
1988). A particularly relevant example of these institutional, Pan-African
naming practices is seen in the formation of the African Methodist Episco-
pal (AME) Church. This institution's Pan-African leanings can also be seen
in its support for the Haitian emigration scheme. The various black institutions created during the end of the eighteenth century and beginning of the

nineteenth century also indicated the need for a communalism within this minority population (Berlin 1998; Dixon 2000; Nash 1988; Newman 2008).

The Pan-Africanism of the aid societies and black churches demonstrated the rising sense of an African American identity within Philadelphia. As Du Bois explains, identity is not something that is entirely self-ascribed. He shows that for blacks in the United States, self-image is largely viewed through the eyes of the dominant white majority. In Du Bois' (2003 [1903]:9) words, blacks were "measuring [their] soul[s] by the tape of a world that looks on in amused contempt and pity." Labor hierarchies within the city were increasingly aligning with racial hierarchies, especially as the industrial sector expanded, and U.S. nationalism was increasingly (if not already fully) being characterized as white. While the African American community in Philadelphia was legally free, slavery and the lack of freedom led to their sense of two-ness.

Beginning in the first decade of the nineteenth century, a rise in racial tensions within Philadelphia made life more difficult and personal safety harder to guarantee for the city's substantial African American community. A number of factors contributed to the increase in racial hostility, including the Haitian Revolution (1791–1804), changing demographics within the city, rising class disparities, and changes in legislation. News of the violent Haitian Revolution quickly reached the port city of Philadelphia and inspired an increased fear of racial violence (Berlin 1998; Nash 1988). Simultaneously, new waves of Southern freed people were migrating to the city. These freedmen and women often arrived in poor health and with few skills applicable to their new urban environment. While newly arrived German and Irish immigrants were given jobs in the factories that were popping up throughout the city, the African Americans were left with lower-wage day labor (Nash 1988; Richardson 1982). In addition to the continued existence of a racialized class system in Philadelphia, numerous pieces of legislation were being proposed that would limit the already small number of rights and freedoms enjoyed by African Americans. Furthermore, a combination of old and new laws caused free blacks in Philadelphia to be fearful of the prospect of being delivered into slavery (Nash 1988).

Many readers will be familiar with the recent film *12 Years a Slave* (McQueen 2013; see also the narrative that inspired the film, Northup 2012 [1853]), which depicted the kidnapping and enslavement of Solomon Northup. This movie offers a powerful look at the violence that could be enacted on a free person living in the northern United States, a reality that must have led to a pervasive underlying fear that individuals lived with on a daily basis. Unfortunately, by 1841, the year of Northup's kidnapping, free blacks had been living in fear of this heinous crime for decades. The Fugitive Slave Act of 1793 did not require a warrant to claim a fugitive slave and return her or him to bondage; however, punishment for kidnapping free blacks, many of whom had never been enslaved, was rarely more than a slap on the wrist. Following the end of the slave trade in 1808, the number of kidnappings rose dramatically (Nash 1988). A very telling case can be seen in the attempted kidnapping of the Reverend Richard Allen in 1806. Founder of the AME Church and supporter of the Haitian emigration scheme, Reverend Allen was a widely known and respected leader of the free-black community and was also firmly established in the middle class. Allen's status as a well-known public figure enabled him to turn the tables on his kidnapper, but the criminal spent a mere three months in jail for failure to pay a fine and was eventually released to return home and, one would presume, resume his nefarious activities (Nash 1988).

Other forms of racialized violence were also increasing throughout the city. In 1825 the Mother Bethel AME Church was the target of one such act when white youths slipped pepper and salt into a wood-burning stove during a service. Thinking a fire had started, the congregation stampeded to evacuate the building, trampling two people to death in the process (Nash 1988). The fear, hostility, and the degradation of race relations in Philadelphia contextualizes the black community and the hardships they were increasingly facing in the early nineteenth century. It seems obvious that the progressively hostile situation in Philadelphia, and more generally the northern United States, would inspire the desire to emigrate within the free-black community.

Emigration Schemes and Settlement in Samaná

The Haitian emigration of 1824 was not the first colonization scheme proposed to northern freed people in the United States (Dixon 2000; Miller 1975; Winch 1989). The American Colonization Society (ACS) led the effort to establish a black American colony on the West Coast of Africa that came to be known as Liberia. For Southern slave-owning members of the ACS, this was an opportunity to put a great distance between those they continued to enslave and potentially rabble-rousing (or rebel-rousing) free blacks. Yet the free-black community quickly saw through the racist desire of some members of the ACS to get rid of the so-called negro problem within the

United States, and the Liberian movement never attracted large numbers of emigrants (Dixon 2000; Hidalgo 2001). It is worth noting that the sentiment that African-descended peoples were a "problem" was still present as Du Bois was writing *Souls*. In fact, he says, "To the real question, How does it feel to be a problem? I answer seldom a word" (Du Bois 2003 [1903]:8).

In 1824 Haitian president Boyer offered the free-black community an alternative to the Liberian emigration scheme when he sent an agent of the Haitian government to the United States to recruit free blacks for migration to Haiti (García 1894; Winch 1989). Potential emigrants were offered passage to the island, 36 acres of land for every 12 emigrants, 4 months' worth of supplies upon arrival, and return passage to the United States should the arrangement not be considered favorable. In order to fund the project, the Haitian agent was sent with a cargo of coffee that was to be sold once he arrived in the United States (Davis 2007; Hoetink 1962; Smith 1986, 1987; Weeks and Ramírez Zabala 2005; Winch 1988, 1989). Despite initial reservations, the black community began to warm to this migration plan. Black leaders such as Richard Allen of the AME Church began to aid in recruitment efforts and free blacks of good repute were the most sought-after volunteers (Nash 1988; Winch 1988, 1989).

Between 1824 and 1825 approximately 6,000 individuals left the United States from Philadelphia, New York City, Baltimore, and Boston and made their way down to the island Republic of Haiti. Some accounts place the number as high as 13,000, although the official number authorized by the Haitian government was 6,000 (Hoetink 1962). They settled in a variety of places around the island: Cap-Haïtien (approximately 1,000 immigrants), Les Cayes (500), Gonaives (500), Jacmel (600), Port-au-Prince (1,000), Puerto Plata (1,000), Samaná (200), and Santo Domingo (1,200) (see Figure 13.1) (Weeks and Ramírez Zabala 2005). Unfortunately, as many as one-third of the émigrés died en route or shortly after arrival; the harsh conditions at sea and tropical diseases took their toll. Furthermore, it is estimated that 2,000 members of the original 6,000 returned to the United States (García 1894; GPO 1871; Winch 1988, 1989). Despite these melancholic numbers, 200 people settled in Santa Bárbara de Samaná, where their descendants have remained for 190 years.

The emigration scheme lasted only a short while, ending in 1825. Accusations of deceit were made against ship captains, who were said to be cheating the Haitian government out of unused fares both going to the island and returning to the United States (Winch 1989). It is also likely that the high mortality and return rates did not encourage future migration.

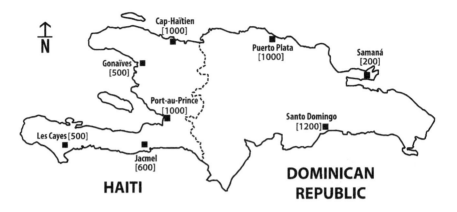

Figure 13.1. Map of Haiti with locations of settlement and numbers of projected settlers (Weeks and Ramírez Zabala 2005).

Despite the brief duration of this migration effort, more free blacks left for Haiti than for the Liberian colony. It was also not the last time that Haiti was looked to as a refuge—or dumping ground, depending on one's perspective—for African Americans (see, e.g., Dixon 2000).

Of course, the American emigrants' story did not end when they left the United States. President Boyer intended for the bulk of the immigrants to form rural agricultural communities, although this arrangement did not suit the majority of the U.S. blacks who had been nonagriculturalist city-dwellers. Many who stayed on the island ignored Boyer's directives and ended up living in the larger cities, including Port-au-Prince, Santo Domingo, and Puerto Plata (see Figure 13.1). Historical sources, such as letters from the immigrants published in the *Genius of Universal Emancipation*, travelers' accounts, and the U.S. commission report of 1871 described earlier show that within a generation the immigrant communities in the various cities were assimilating into the surrounding dominant societies (Torres-Saillant 2010; Weeks and Ramírez Zabala 2005; Winch 1988). Nevertheless, the descendants of the 200 people who settled in Samaná retained a sense of being a separate community for over 150 years.

The Samaná Peninsula was relatively geopolitically isolated for much of the American enclave's history. However, the lives of the immigrants and their Dominican and Haitian neighbors were greatly affected by the events that unfolded during a particularly tumultuous period following their settlement on the island. The Americans arrived in 1824 to what was then Haiti. The Haitian government maintained control over the entire

island until February 27, 1844, when the Dominicans declared independence (Moya Pons 1998; Torres-Saillant 2010). That the Dominicans declared independence from the Haitians and not a European colonial force
is particularly noteworthy (Torres-Saillant 2010). Following independence,
the country was run by caudillos and "strong men," which produced a tremendous amount of instability, especially for populations in outlying areas
(Moya Pons 1998). In 1861, with the support of the elites who controlled
the government in Santo Domingo, Spain annexed its former colony. This
annexation, however, did not last long, and the ensuing War of Restoration ended in the summer of 1865 (Crassweller 1966; Krohn-Hansen 2009;
Moya Pons 1998; Torres-Saillant 2010). According to Silvio Torres-Saillant
(2010), Dominicans celebrate the War of Restoration with as much convic-
tion as they do their independence from Haiti. In 1871 the U.S. government
showed an explicit interest in annexing the Dominican Republic and, more
specifically, the Samaná Peninsula for use as a naval station (GPO 1871).
This was not the first time the United States considered annexing the Dominican Republic, as an annexation proposal had been considered 20 years
previously. While the planned annexation failed, the United States did send
in the Marines in 1916, and they occupied the Dominican Republic until
1924 (Krohn-Hansen 2009; Moya Pons 1998). However, the most significant forces the Americans in Samaná had to contend with were the governments of Rafael Trujillo and Joaquín Balaguer in the twentieth century
(Fellows 2013).

Isolation and Boundary Making in Samaná

After settling in Samaná, the American immigrants remained relatively isolated, in large part due to the physical boundaries created by the estuary-
like area leading into the peninsula and the mountains running its length,
which made overland journeys difficult. Both the geographical situation
of Samaná and the relatively low population density within the peninsula
played a large role in the long-term integrity of the local immigrant community. Geologically, the Samaná Peninsula seems to have once been an
island although the area connecting the land masses became known as the
Gran Estero, which is still a relatively marshy place (GPO 1871; Hoetink
1962; Schomburgk 1853). Travel accounts from the mid- to late nineteenth
century also commented on the rough and mountainous terrain encountered on the peninsula (e.g., Hazard 1873; Stuart 1878). It seems that the
lack of maintained roads meant that it was often easier to access Samaná by

Figure 13.2. A view of Santa Bárbara de Samaná from the Bay of Samaná. (Image from Hazard 1873)

boat. While being interviewed by Frederick Douglass for the 1871 commission report, Rev. Jacob James gives us a sense of what the physical isolation meant for the economy of the town: "If we only had roads, which could be built without very great expense, leading up into the country, everything would be more valuable there. Things can only be disposed of at the water side to vessels. Every family now produces more vegetables and fruits than they want, leaving them to rot and waste" (qtd. in GPO 1871:230).

Within Samaná, both social and physical boundaries were established that enabled the American enclave to remain a distinct minority group in the town for over 150 years. As mentioned earlier, physical isolation of the peninsula meant that the general population of Samaná remained relatively isolated, which, in part, kept the overall number of residents on the peninsula rather small. When Harry Hoetink (1962) was doing research in Samaná in the 1960s, he approximated the town's population to be between 3,000 and 4,000 people. The American immigrants may have been a minority within a local population historically made up of Dominicans and Haitians, but, especially until the mid-twentieth century, they were never a negligible group. This in turn allowed the American enclave to retain a prominent place within Samanesa society, despite their minority status (Fellows 2013). Their standing within Samaná stands in stark contrast to the Americans who had settled in the larger cities (e.g., Santo Domingo and Puerto Plata). For instance, an aboveground study of the cemetery in Samaná, undertaken as part of this project, points to the more prominent status of the American enclave earlier in the town's history, although the data is not definitive and dates to the early twentieth century.

The documentary records have shown that the American immigrants and their descendants also worked to socially and physically separate themselves from local Dominicans and Haitians within the town. In 1871 Reverend James explained, "We try to keep our people together here as Americans, so that they shall not fall away into the ways of the natives and almost become natives, as they have done too much at Puerto Plata, where they are all mixed up. Our people are honest working people" (GPO 1871:229–230). This quote illustrates the perceived social distance between the "natives" of Samaná and the American immigrants. As minister of the Methodist congregation, James was a leader within the immigrant community. It seems safe to assume that the majority of the Americans shared his sentiments of the "natives." Standing in opposition to these other locals, the Americans defined themselves through an adherence to a Protestant work ethic, prioritizing education, maintaining their living spaces in an orderly fashion, and being a God-fearing people (GPO 1871; Fellows 2013). Interestingly, a number of historical sources presented the Americans in a similar manner and in opposition to the rest of Samanesa society; the "natives" were viewed by outsiders as more indolent and ill-informed (e.g., Cazneau 1878; Hazard 1873; Schomburgk 1853; Stuart 1878).

Analyses of baptism and marriage records from the Wesleyan Methodist Church have shown that as late as the early twentieth century, the Americans were clustering in specific neighborhoods in Samaná where everyone spoke English, practiced Protestantism, and shared cultural practices and foodways brought with them from the United States. Four primary areas dominated the listed residence for Americans marrying and baptizing children in Samaná; they included the districts of Clara, Honduras, Northwest, and the town of Samaná proper. By creating living spaces dominated by members of their own community and that extended beyond the confines of the home, the American immigrants were ensuring that their children would grow up with a well-defined communal identity. All of their closest neighbors would have been English-speaking Protestants who helped to reinforce the cultural practices brought over from the United States.

Living spaces in tropical areas, such as the Dominican Republic and even the U.S. South, extended beyond the immediate confines of the walls of the house. Yard space provided areas for cooking, congregating, and performing a variety of activities that required well-lit and cooler spaces. There is a long tradition of the use of yard spaces in Africa and the African

Diaspora. Archaeologists have discussed the importance of yards in both North America and the Caribbean, and yards are still important to living populations throughout the Caribbean. (For some archaeological examples, see Armstrong and Kelly 2000, Heath and Bennett 2000; also Blouet, this volume; and Harris, this volume.) Interaction with primarily American neighbors in yards would have been inevitable (Fellows 2013). Oral histories support the suggestion that members of the community were living in areas that were dominated by immigrants to the exclusion of other locals (Fellows 2013; Poplack and Sankoff 1987). This is not to say that there was no interaction between the various groups within the area; however, data from the documentary and oral historical records show that the American immigrants were living in clusters that most likely increased their daily interaction in yard spaces.

The American community also established two Methodist churches in the town: the first was the Wesleyan Methodist Church, run by British missionaries, and the second was the AME Church, which was the home institution of many of the original emigrants. The community's focus on these two English-language Methodist churches worked to further distance the Americans from the Spanish-speaking and Haitian Creole–speaking Catholic inhabitants in the town. The Methodist churches also established English-language schools, which provided further institutional support for the community's relatively distinctive religion and the transmission of a standardized English to the younger generations.

The two Protestant churches offered physical spaces outside of the home and neighborhoods where the Americans would congregate, often to the exclusion of the rest of Samanesa society. The original Wesleyan church, now referred to as "La Chorcha," is still standing and continues to serve congregants with surnames like Jones, Johnson, and Green. La Chorcha is even included in guide books of the area, which speak of the history of this church and the original American congregation (Fellows 2013). The presence and continuation of English and Methodism functioned as boundary-creating characteristics of this enclave and were crucial components to the survival of this minority community (Davis 1980; Fellows 2013; Hoetink 1962; Smith 1986, 1987). Taken all together, this evidence demonstrates the significance of the spatial, sociocultural, religious, and linguistic boundaries to the maintenance of the communal identity of the African Americans in Samaná.

The Double Consciousness Persists: "But now the United States is a country of freedom."

The Report of the 1871 U.S. Commission of Inquiry to Santo Domingo was produced in order to assess the feasibility of annexing the Samaná Peninsula for the purposes of a naval coaling station (GPO 1871). This important document has allowed for insight into the perceptions of social boundaries within Samaná, but it also enables a better understanding of how the Americans felt regarding the Spanish and proposed American annexations and of their sentiments on the American Civil War and the end of slavery in the United States.

Visitors from the 1871 U.S. Commission asked their informants about the 1861 Spanish annexation as well as the proposed U.S. annexation, and the responses given in both Santo Domingo and in Samaná expose local understandings of race and speak to the weak sense of Dominican nationality within the general population. For most people, the primary concern was day-to-day safety and long-term stability, regardless of the national package in which it came.

Prior to Spanish annexation in 1861, political volatility and associated military and paramilitary actions were nothing new to the Spanish side of Hispañiola. The general sentiment throughout the Dominican Republic was that annexation by the United States would bring constancy to the government and thus to daily life. Gen. Theophilus James, an African American in Samaná, explained, "[Dominicans] desire annexation to the United States for the sake of peace and tranquility; that each man may enjoy what he earns by his labor" (qtd. in GPO 1871:228). Similar notions were expressed by informants in Santo Domingo. Theodore Hall, who lived in the capital, told the commission, "When there are troubles the men are always called off to war. First, it was with Hayti [the 1844 War of Independence]. . . . The next time the men would get to work and make a little money, and then they would be called away again" (qtd. in GPO 1871:253). The threat of loss of life, personal property, and wealth seem to have been real enough for the majority of Dominicans to be in favor of annexation to the United States, and there was not a strong sense of a Dominican nationality that would have prevented the population's willingness to adopt a new nation-state through annexation. However, while those living in Santo Domingo seemed to worry about conscription and the disruption this would bring to their earning ability, those in Samaná may have felt the political instability in a more material way.

Figure 13.3. This sketch from the Wesleyan Missionary Notices (1858) depicts the mission's chapel and related buildings in Samaná. Reverend James referenced the destruction of these structures in the 1871 Government Printing Office report.

In a published report from 1858, the Assistant Missionary in Samaná, Peter Van der Horst (an American immigrant), described a revolt by a segment of the Dominican population known as the Cibaeños. They had laid siege to the town of Samaná and were attempting to capture the government men stationed at Fort Buenaventura as they left the fort on provision procuring missions. The siege impacted more people than just the soldiers stationed in Samaná; multiple families fled their homes in the surrounding countryside and took refuge in the town (Wesleyan Missionary Notices 1858). In 1871 Reverend James described the effects of the instability on the morale in the town, "The revolutions and wars have got us down so that we cannot do as we would have done. We once had a church here, and a school-house and a mission house . . . but all was destroyed and burned up in the wars. . . . Now we are hoping for better things from [U.S.] annexation" (qtd. in GPO 1871:230). The places and spaces—the neighborhoods and churches—that helped the Americans maintain their communal identity apart from the rest of Samanesa society were threatened by the political unrest.

Some of the interviewees from 1871 felt that if the United States was not going to annex the Dominican Republic, the nation would benefit from annexation to a different, yet still powerful nation, as long as that nation was not Spain (e.g., Gen. Theophilus James, in GPO 1871:228). In fact, Spain was never an option for the majority of Dominicans prior to—and especially following—the 1861–1865 annexation since the black and mixed-race Dominican majority feared a return to slavery (Torres-Saillant 2010). However, the 1871 report demonstrates that the racial dimensions of this conflict may have made more of a lasting impression on some populations within the Dominican Republic than others. One informant in Samaná pointed out that the Spanish had "mistreated the poor colored people" (Joseph Hamilton, qtd. in GPO 1871:222). George Judd, a white American school teacher living among the African American enclave, explained that the Spanish "came with guns and bayonets, and treated the people almost as slaves. . . . Besides, this people knew, for they are intelligent, that the Spaniards were slaveholders in Cuba on one side and Porto Rico on the other. The Spaniards sometimes would say that they would make them all slaves . . . but now they know the Americans have abolished slavery and there is no fear of them" (qtd. in GPO 1871:227). Mr. Judd was not the only person to point out that the Americans were no longer slaveholders. Reverend James explained that there had been talk of annexation by the United States 20 years prior to 1871 but that people were less supportive of the move then, as the United States was still a slaveholding nation. He goes on to say, "But now the United States is a country of freedom. We all know that, and all want to join the United States" (qtd. in GPO 1871:230). Reverend James also informed the commission that during the American Civil War his community had kept abreast of the news of what he refers to as the "rebellion" through newspapers. This speaks to Du Bois' argument that Emancipation/Freedom was the end goal for blacks, free and enslaved, in the antebellum United States.

Despite the fact that the United States was a slaveholding nation for almost four decades after the immigrants settled in Samaná, they seem to have maintained a sense of loyalty and patriotism for the United States. Reverend James explained, "Although we have been here so long, we have preserved our feelings as Americans" (qtd. in GPO 1871:230). Mr. Judd, the white American previously quoted, offered external verification of Reverend James' sentiments when he said, "This American colony about here have preserved their nationality with great persistency for the forty years they have been here, in spite of revolutions" (qtd. in GPO 1871:228). Mr. Judd's statement is particularly telling in that he not only reiterates the African American's self-ascribed American identity, he also begins the sentence by confirming a perceived association between the community and the United States. That the immigrants and their descendants continued to identify with the United States may have been influenced by the fact that it represented a more stable life, but their patriotic sentimentality was strengthened after the American Civil War ended slavery.

Tellingly, the only informants in the 1871 report who spoke of the racial prejudice practiced by the Spanish and the freedom now enjoyed by all Americans were located in Samaná. We also see multiple members of the American community in Samaná refer to themselves as "full black" in the report (GPO 1871:229). Reverend James explained, "We [the Americans] are all colored people" (qtd. in GPO 1871:229). Furthermore, one of the white outsiders who had lived in the town for a couple of years, said, "There is a greater proportion of blacks in Samana than in any other part of Dominica" (qtd. in GPO 1871:227). This last sentiment persists among Dominicans to this day (Fellows 2013). Some of the original immigrants were still living 48 years after the 1824 migration, and the second and third generations were growing up hearing stories of the United States from their self-identified black parents and grandparents.

The Spanish Annexation of the 1860s reinforced the community's disdain for and anxiety over the institution of slavery. Remnants of the fear of racial persecution and even enslavement that led the American emigrants to flee the United States seem to be present in the community as of 1871. With the Spanish annexation having ended only six years prior, the fear of enslavement and racial persecution would have been even more present for the African Americans. It is this fear that served to underpin the continuation of the African American's double consciousness.

Conclusions

Rising racial tensions, racialized violence, newly racialized labor hierarchies, and the persistent presence of slavery that characterized the early-nineteenth-century United States meant that it was becoming increasingly difficult to reconcile African descent with an American national identity. Moreover, as naming practices in the North have shown, the blackness of the free community was coming to be defined in a broader, Pan-African manner. It could be argued that the rising sense of Pan-Africanism that played a role in the naming of the AME Church also led to a sense of shared history with the former slaves. This Pan-African sense of blackness experienced by the African American community allowed for an interest in, and feeling of solidarity with, the former slaves of the new black Republic of

Haiti. In fact, the free-black community in Philadelphia looked upon the success of the Haitian Revolution with pride.

President Boyer's Haitian emigration plan, which was initiated and run by black men, stood in stark contrast to the American Colonization Society's Liberian scheme. Haiti offered the promise of a black nationalism stemming from the only truly successful slave revolt, which spoke to a Pan-African sensibility. Seeing themselves through an incipient American nationality that was increasingly being characterized by whiteness, the free-black community in Philadelphia was beginning to identify as both black and American; they were developing a "double consciousness," an identity with an inherent two-ness, as Du Bois (2003 [1903]) would say. Emigrating to a black republic was, perhaps, a way to escape the strife that came with being African American.

Relocating to a foreign country and adapting to new cultures and languages were extreme acts of communal resistance to the growing racism and continued practice of slavery in the United States. The emigrants' physical and legal separation from the United States would also mean a realignment of how national and racial identities would intersect. These individuals knew (or at least hoped) that the decision to emigrate and cross national borders would bring new social realities and would allow them to discard the dual nature of their identity. And yet analysis of the documentary records associated with the American community in Samaná has revealed that, despite their physical relocation to a new nation and their attempted rejection of their double consciousness, this community would come to use their African American identity as a means to distance itself from local Dominicans and Haitians. For African Americans in Samaná, being "American" indexed the religious, linguistic, and cultural differences separating the settlers from the "natives," and they worked hard to maintain these social and physical boundaries. By maintaining an American identity, however, African Americans in Samaná were also retaining their double consciousness; they remained both black and American.

Identifying as African American became much more comfortable following what one prominent settler referred to as the American "rebellion," more commonly known as the Civil War. While it may have been unintentional, the choice to describe the Civil War as a "rebellion" links the United States with Haiti and the Haitian Revolution; both wars ended slavery in their given territories, and this, it seems, was the primary purpose of each conflict for the Americans in Samaná. The American Civil War seems to have helped this community reconcile their blackness with their

Americanness. Interestingly, this African American community in Samaná was far removed from the effects of Reconstruction in the United States, which perhaps made the integration of the different parts of their identity easier. Such physical distance may have enabled a more romantic view of the post-slavery United States.

In the second of the two quotes that opened this chapter, Du Bois talked of the centuries-long desire for Freedom among slaves and free blacks alike. In *The Souls of Black Folk*, he purposefully capitalizes "Freedom" and "Emancipation" to emphasize that, in the days of slavery, these were not merely ideas but ideals to which black communities, both free and enslaved, aspired. Du Bois (2003 [1903]:11), however, goes on to say, "The Nation has not yet found peace from its sins; the freedman has not yet found in freedom his promised land. Whatever of good may have come in these years of change, the shadow of a deep disappointment rests upon the Negro people,—a disappointment all the more bitter because the unattained ideal was unbounded save by the simple ignorance of a lowly people." Note that in this quote, when referencing historical events, Du Bois does not capitalize "freedom"; the emancipation that came for slaves in the United States in 1863 did not bring the Freedom that all blacks had hoped it would. Du Bois later explains the trajectory of the ideals of African Americans—the various ideals being what would help to bring freedmen into the nation and allow them to no longer be "a problem." After realizing that freedom would not bring a life free from prejudice, of full citizenship and respect, the ideal became the right to vote. After gaining the ballot failed to be the answer, the ideal shifted to one of education as a means through which black men could rise within the United States.[1] By the end of his discussion, Du Bois (2003 [1903]:15) tells us that in reality, "the bright ideals of the past,—physical freedom, political power, the training of brains and the training of hands . . ." are all necessary and part and parcel of each other. Yet, when Du Bois was writing, they had not been fully realized.

For the African American enclave in Samaná, we see Du Bois' description of the driving ideals at play. For the emigrants leaving the United States, Haiti offered Freedom in the unbounded idealistic sense for which the freedmen and slaves strove. Full citizenship, land, and freedom from prejudice came in the package of a black Republic. In a sense, the emigrants had an advantage over those still enslaved for they recognized that legal freedom did not actually bring Freedom in the United States. It was, in fact, the increasing reality of racial persecution and violence enacted against the already *free*-black community that led to the Haitian emigration. Yet by the 1870s we see the settlers and their descendants emphasizing physical and legal freedom as Freedom. The tensions inherent within an African American identity were made manifest in the settlers' migration to Haiti and then their continued loyalty to the United States.

After the American Civil War, the tensions in the enclave's double consciousness had eased, at least to an extent, because the United States was no longer a slaveholding nation-state. Any doubt they had regarding U.S. annexation in the 1850s was gone, while they remained adamantly opposed to Spanish rule due to the slaveholding status of that nation. "But now the United States is a country of freedom" (GPO 1871:230); perhaps for the Americans in Samaná, the "freedom" in this quote should be capitalized as it represents the ideal. Their physical distance from the realities of Reconstruction allowed for a more naïve or romantic view of the United States and the possibilities that would come with Emancipation. This distance also meant that they were able to enjoy full rights of citizenship, albeit within the Dominican Republic. All of this enabled something of a reconciliation between the two selves, or rather more of an integration of their two-ness. Once on the island and legally, physically, emotionally, and intellectually separated from the realities of being black in the United States, the African American settlers and their descendants were able to return to the earliest stage of Du Bois' trajectory of the ideals of American blacks, namely Freedom. In conjunction with the boundary-creating realities of identifying as American, this facilitated the continuation of the community's African American identity during the first five decades of the enclave's development.

Note

1. Du Bois's gendered analysis has been discussed elsewhere (e.g., Zamir 2014).

References Cited

Armstrong, Douglas V., and Kenneth G. Kelly
2000   Settlement Patterns and the Origins of African Jamaican Society: Seville Plantation, St. Ann's Bay Jamaica. *Ethnohistory* 47:369–397.
Berlin, Ira
1998   *Many Thousands Gone: The First Two Centuries of Slavery in North America.* Belknap Press of Harvard University, Cambridge, Massachusetts.

Cazneau, M.W.L.
1878   *Our Winter Eden: Pen Pictures of the Tropics*. The Authors' Publishing Company, New York.

Crassweller, Robert D.
1966   *Trujillo: The Life and Times of a Caribbean Dictator*. Macmillan, New York.

Davis, Martha Ellen
1980   That Old-Time Religion: Tradición y Cambio en el Enclave "Americano" de Samaná. *Boletín, Museo del Hombre Dominicano* 14:165–196.

2007 Asentamiento y vida económica de los inmigrantes afroamericanos de Samaná: testimonio de la profesora Martha Willmore (Leticia). *Boletín del Archivo General de la Nación* 32(119):709–734.

Dixon, Chris
2000   *African America and Haiti: Emigration and Black Nationalism in the Nineteenth Century*. Greenwood Press, Westport, Connecticut.

Du Bois, W.E.B.
2003 [1903] *The Souls of Black Folk*. Reprint. Barnes & Noble Classics, New York.

Fellows, Kristen R.
2013   African Americans from "Back Yonder": The Historical Archaeology of the Formation, Maintenance, and Dissolution of the American Enclave in Samaná, Dominican Republic. Ph.D. dissertation, Department of Anthropology, University of Pennsylvania, Philadelphia.

García, José Gabriel
1894   *Compendio de la Historia de Santo Domingo, Tomo II*. Tercera Edicion. Imprenta de Garcia Hermanos, Santo Domingo, Dominican Republic.

Government Printing Office (GPO)
1871   Report of the Commission of Inquiry to Santo Domingo. United States Government Printing Office, Washington, D.C.

Hazard, Samuel
1873   *Santo Domingo, Past and Present; With a Glance at Hayti*. Harper & Brothers, New York.

Heath, Barbara J., and Amber Bennett
2000   "The little Spots allow'd them": The Archaeological Study of African-American Yards. *Historical Archaeology* 34(2):38–55.

Hidalgo, Dennis R.
2001   From North America to Hispaniola: First Free Black Emigration and Settlements in Hispaniola. Ph.D. dissertation, Department of History, Central Michigan University, Mount Pleasant.

Hoetink, Harry
1962   "Americans" in Samaná. *Caribbean Studies* 2(1):3–22.

Krohn-Hansen, Christian
2009   *Political Authoritarianism in the Dominican Republic*. Palgrave Macmillan, New York.

McQueen, Steve (director)
2013   *12 Years a Slave*. Twentieth Century Fox. Film.

Miller, Floyd J.
1975   *The Search for a Black Nationality: Black Emigration and Colonization, 1787–1863.* University of Illinois Press, Urbana.

Moya Pons, Frank
1998   *The Dominican Republic: A National History.* Reprinted. Markus Wiener Publishers, Princeton, New Jersey. Originally published 1995, Hispaniola Books, New Rochelle, New York.

Nash, Gary B.
1988   *Forging Freedom: The Formation of Philadelphia's Black Community, 1720–1840.* Harvard University Press, Cambridge, Massachusetts.

Newman, Richard S.
2008   *Black Founders: The Free Black Community in the Early Republic. An Exhibition at the Library Company of Philadelphia, March-October 2008.* Phillip S. Lapsanaky, Curator. The Library Company of Philadelphia, Philadelphia.

Northup, Solomon
2012 [1853]   *Twelve Years a Slave.* Derby and Miller, Auburn, New York. 2012 reprint. Penguin Books, New York.

Poplack, Shana, and David Sankoff
1987   The Philadelphia Story in the Spanish Caribbean. *American Speech* 62:291–314.

Ramírez Zabala, Virginia
2005   The Difficult Task of Assimilation: The Case of the Samaná Americans in the Dominican Republic. Master's thesis, College of Liberal and Professional Studies, University of Pennsylvania, Philadelphia.

Richardson, Edgar
1982   The Athens of America: 1800–1825. In *Philadelphia: A 300-Year History*, edited by Russell F. Weigley, pp. 208–257. W. W. Norton, New York.

Schomburgk, R. H.
1853   The Peninsula and Bay of Samaná, in the Dominican Republic. *Journal of the Royal Geographical Society of London* 23:264–283.

Smith, E. Valerie
1986   Mate Selection as an Indicator of Ethnic Identity and Maintenance: A Case Analysis of the "Immigrants" in Samaná, Dominican Republic. Ph.D. dissertation. Department of Sociology. University of Florida, Gainesville.
1987   Early Afro-American Presence on the Island of Hispaniola: A Case Study of the "Immigrants" of Samaná. *Journal of Negro History* 72(1/2):33–41.

Stuart, R.
1878   Haiti, or Hispaniola. *Journal of the Royal Geographical Society of London* 48:234–274.

Torres-Saillant, Silvio
2010   *Introduction to Dominican Blackness.* City University of New York, Dominican Studies Institute, New York.

Weeks, John M., and Virginia Ramírez Zabala
2005   The Samaná Americans. *Expedition* 47(1):38–41.

The Wesleyan Missionary Notices
1858   The Wesleyan Missionary Notices Relating Principally to the Foreign Missions

under the Direction of the Methodist Conference. Third Series, Vol. V. James Nichols, London.

Winch, Julie

1988   American Free Blacks and Emigration to Haiti. Paper presented at the XIth Caribbean Congress, Río Piedras and San Germán, Puerto Rico.

1989   "To Reunite the Great Family": Free Blacks and Haitian Emigration. Paper presented at the Annual Meeting of the Organization of American Historians, St. Louis.

Zamir, Shamoon

2014   The Souls of Black Folk: Thought and Afterthought. In *The Cambridge Companion to W.E.B. Du Bois*, edited by Shamoon Zamir, pp. 7–36. Cambridge University Press, Cambridge.

14

Conclusion

Minding the Gaps in the Diasporic Web

LAURIE A. WILKIE

The essays in this volume seek to understand the Caribbean past by focusing their gazes on "spaces in between." The Caribbean has long been an important "space" in American historical archaeology. The year 1492, when Columbus first struck landfall in a small Bahamian harbor (Hoffman 1987), has historically been cited as the starting date for the discipline in the United States. While we now routinely problematize such hard temporal boundaries on archaeological histories, this date still has a charm-like power for students and the broader public. The Caribbean has historically been an important intellectual space for archaeologists of the recent past as well. When we consider the theoretical and methodological developments of the field, the contributions of Jerome Handler (1994, 1997; Handler and Lange 1978), Kathleen Deagan (1995; Deagan and Cruxent 2002), Merrick Posnansky (1984), and Douglas Armstrong (1985, 1990, 2003, 2010; Armstrong and Hauser 2009) stand out. Caribbean historical archaeology has been at the forefront of developments in discussions of colonialism (Deagan 1995, Deagan and Cruxent 2002), diaspora (Haviser 1999, Kelly and Norman 2006; Wilkie and Farnsworth 2005), landscape (Delle 1998, 2000, 2011; Hicks 2007), and trade (Hauser 2008, 2011), and as we have seen in this volume, it is a space where scholars are now pushing us to consider spaces of postcoloniality, transnationalism, diaspora, and hybridity.

Yet just as the Caribbean has been a space that has allowed for expansive thought and research, it has also too often been a constricted space, a space where some voices are heard more loudly than others in the academy, a space where an emphasis on particular kinds of sites has created distorted narratives, a space where some historical communities or members of communities have been interpretively privileged over others. Before looking more closely at individual studies presented here, I want to briefly discuss how these papers have sought to open up some of these spaces. The research presented in some of these chapters is for some part of long-term commitments to opening up these Caribbean spaces, and in others we can see the how a new generation of scholars are turning their attentions to the Caribbean.

While there are a growing number of Caribbean nationals doing historical archaeological research in the Caribbean (e.g., Gray 1997; Haviser 1999; Haviser and MacDonald 2006; Turner 2006), it is a space that has long been dominated by scholars from outside the region. Many of the authors in this volume have worked extensively with local vocational groups, heritage communities, stakeholders, and descendants as part of their research projects and drawn upon the work of Caribbean-based scholars in their work.

For local and foreign scholars alike, the logistics of organizing research across multiple national boundaries has led to the circumstance that archaeologists who work in the area have often focused on particular individual sets of islands or within single colonial systems. Despite this, the peoples who are the object of the archaeological gaze were not similarly restricted in their movements. During the period of enslavement, people both willingly and unwillingly moved between islands and even colonial systems, as records of probates and slave auctions, slave registers, and other documents demonstrate. Understanding this history of movement across space is essential for understanding the Caribbean as a site of diasporic expression. Several authors in this volume have begun the important work of tracing the movements of specific populations—whether it is the soldiers stationed in West India Regiments or the politically discontented relocating from the United States.

Larger land-management and heritage priorities have often shaped the spaces available for research in the Caribbean. Structures and the areas immediately around them have received the greatest amount of attention, with residences receiving more time and focus than outbuildings. Sugar plantations have similarly received more attention than other economies, inadvertently leading archaeological representations to reify hegemonic narratives of the Caribbean past. Several chapters in this volume successfully challenge those narratives by adding new spaces to the archaeological history of the Caribbean.

While I have introduced some broad spaces that these essays contribute to in Caribbean archaeology, I would like to focus my considerations in this more detailed discussion on the following spaces: spaces and living places; Caribbean peoples; and race, racialization, and diaspora.

Spaces and Living Places

As multiple authors in this volume attest, the colonial spaces of the Caribbean were designed to maximize agricultural production and ensure the control of the labor needed to make that happen. The modifications to the Caribbean landscape undertaken starting in the sixteenth century were massive and enduring. Field walls, wells, cisterns, houses, and plantation works built with enslaved and indentured labor are visible throughout the Caribbean today and in many instances are still used by contemporary populations in a variety of ways.

How landscapes emerged out of colonial processes is of course intimately tied to the economic uses of those lands. In looking at these papers, the authors have done an excellent job of problematizing dominant economic narratives regarding the Caribbean. At any given time, the economy of the Caribbean was more complicated than the mythology of sugar monoculture that dominates the popular imagination and is sometimes enforced through scholarly writing (e.g., Mintz 1985). As someone who worked in an archipelago whose economy was supported by cotton production, salt-raking, wrecking, and slaving (Turner 2006; Wilkie and Farnsworth 2005), I have long been frustrated by that narrative. Even on the island of Jamaica, recognized as a center for sugar production, James A. Delle's (1998, 2014, this volume) long-term study of coffee plantations reveals that a more complex and thriving economic system existed in colonial Jamaica.

Jane Seiter's study (Chapter 6) demonstrates the value of rooting out early pre-sugar economies. Her archaeological work in St. Lucia demonstrates that, predating the sugar industry, the island supported a complex economic mosaic of small estates growing crops as diverse as cassava, indigo, cotton, bananas, coffee, and tobacco. These smaller estates allowed farmers to better use the range of land types available on the island and were owned by a population as diverse as the crops. Free people of color were able to establish themselves as landholders and, often, slaveholders within this economic landscape. It was only once the island was taken over by the British and following the development of steam-powered mill machinery that sugar came to dominate the economic landscape of the island. We see clearly in this example how the shape of the economy shaped opportunity. It is important for historical archaeology to continue to high-light the economic diversity of these colonial enterprises so that non-sugar islands are not rendered invisible in Caribbean history.

Within plantation economies, space was used to control the movement and actions of plantation laborers. Yet multiple chapters in this volume attest to the degree of agency laborers had over the shaping of these land-scapes. Delle's study of Marshall's Pen, Jamaica (Chapter 5), focuses on the existence of housing outside of planned plantation villages. The field houses he tested stood in provisioning grounds—a space in the economic landscape of the plantation that served the economic interests of laborers as much as planters. Archaeological evidence suggested pre-emancipation domestic occupation, clearly illustrating that these were not merely shelter from the sun or places to store tools but habitations. Residents lived here to facilitate work or perhaps to ease the frustrations, tensions, and violences that inevitably arise in oppressive labor regimes. Building habitations in provisioning grounds reflects a kind assertion of ownership over a piece of property—an assertion not to be ignored on a plantation that had several legal disputes over its property boundaries.

Frederick Smith and Hayden Bassett (Chapter 2) render visible another liminal space in the plantation landscapes of Barbados—the caves and "gul-lyscapes" that network across the island. In multiple instances, the inte-riors of Barbadian caves contain evidence of architectural improvement and archaeological evidence of occupation. In the historical narratives of Barbadian planters and administrators, caves were places of anxiety on the landscape: places where runaway slaves hid. From the elite perspective, at the very least, runaways were absenting their labor and the value of their bodies from their owners or, worse, they were using these spaces to plot theft, terrorism, and rebellion. Smith and Bassett found that much of the archaeological evidence suggests these were mainly places of refuge, where people could engage in leisure activities such as drinking, gambling, social-izing, and resting. The removal of oneself from the plantation's day-to-day activities was a mode of resistance that, although not appreciated, was to some degree tolerated by management as long as it didn't last too long. The presence of ceramic artifacts related to food consumption suggests that "pe-tite marronage" could last for days or weeks. Unfair punishments and labor demands could be contested and critiqued in this way, with the added ben-efit of leaving management considering whether worse retaliations were being planned.

The chapters by Krysta Ryzewski and John Cherry (Chapter 7) and Matthew Reilly (Chapter 3) complement one another, each working to render visible the presence of white labor within the plantationscapes of Barbados and Montserrat. Each of these authors notes the ways that people of mixed race and poor whites were, for elites, problematic members of Caribbean society. In the case of Potato Hill, Montserrat, historical documents persistently and stubbornly avoid detailing the people who inhabited this liminal space between estates during successive occupations. Archaeological investigations, however, clearly show that the occupants of these sites were intimately connected to one another socially, economically, and spatially.

Reilly (Chapter 3), in his consideration of the "Redleg" settlement of Clifton Hall, Barbados, shows how poor whites used their fragile position within the racial-economic hierarchies of the island society to take advantage of "spaces in between" on the plantation. By law given the right to reside on plantation lands when serving as militia as well as workers on these plantations, poor whites created spaces on plantations that could be frequented by enslaved Africans without requiring them to leave the borders of the plantations. Goods recovered from the white settlement at Clifton Hall include numerous examples of locally produced coarsewares, as do the goods from Potato Hill (see Chapter 7). While ethnohistoric literature throughout the Caribbean often associates coarsewares with African-descended potters (see Armstrong 1985; Handler 1963; Hauser 2008), sites like Clifton Hall demonstrate the problem of equating the ethnoracial identity of producers with the ethnoracial identity of their users.

While a number of authors refer to the importance of provisioning grounds to the economies of enslaved peoples, poor white tenants, and planters alike, Lynsey Bates' contribution (Chapter 4) provides a unique evaluation of the comparative potential of lands set aside as provisioning grounds on two Jamaican plantations. Using a geographic information system to integrate landscape features, soil maps, and informed by planters' emic understandings of soil types, drainage, and labor productivity, she evaluates the quality, quantity, and location of the provisioning grounds allotted to enslaved Jamaicans. Her analysis reveals that, despite the importance of provisioning grounds to the economic structure of the colonial system, the quality and accessibility of provisioning grounds was varied and often less than ideal. Given these circumstances, she posits, the economic successes that enslaved people derived from these lands (revealed through artifact assemblages) are impressive. To build on the foundation of Bates' work, it is clear that archaeologists should turn some attention to understanding the ways that enslaved, and later free, families worked with soils to increase and maintain the productivity of their provisioning grounds. While botanical preservation is notoriously poor in the Caribbean, it may be that advances in micromorphology, soil chemistry, and phytolith analysis may be productive routes for us to take archaeologically to explore these dimensions of Caribbean life.

A number of the chapters deal with the ways that newly freed people created new relationships with Caribbean economic landscapes. In several of these chapters we see the authors struggling with problematic documentary records. Marco Meniketti's chapter (Chapter 8) on the mysterious 1871 postemancipation-village-that-wasn't provides a number of productive insights for our understanding of freedom and postemancipation bureaucratic administration. The inclusion of a defunct village on an 1871 map is emblematic of increased disinterest on the part of colonial administrators as the economic fortunes of some islands decreased following emancipation. As archaeologists, we know the importance of ground-truthing. It is likely that an administrator who did not want to send a crew out to the bush to make their map simply copied an earlier island map when creating the 1871 document. A space that was seen as economically and politically valuable would have been treated differently. John Chenoweth (Chapter 10), working in the British Virgin Islands, had a different challenge in his work; instead of misleading documents, he found a documentary vacuum for the postemancipation period. His experience is not unusual. Postemancipation records were less attentively maintained by administrators responsible for creating them and less diligently archived by those who followed, if at all. The village studied by Meniketti is fascinating in that the reuse of materials was so extreme as to include the very architecture of the village. It is hard to imagine a more clear assertion of ownership of one's house. Khadene Harris (Chapter 11) confronted the opposite problem from Meniketti at the Bois Collette Estate in Dominica. In her case, the archaeological record demonstrates a larger population continuing to live at and work on the site following emancipation than indicated in administrative records. In each case we see a failure of colonial administrators to care. The problematic documentary record for the postemancipation period illustrates the importance of archaeological work focusing on these periods and suggests the value of oral historical research.

Delle's chapter may provide some interpretive insights into the material patterns seen at Morgan's Village, Nevis, and Bois Collette, Dominica. In the latter, Harris' work shows a clear pattern of movement out of clustered slave villages following freedom to more individually separated landholdings elsewhere on the estate. It is interesting to ponder whether newly freed people, after relocating to new places away from centralized villages, took advantage of proximity of their old housing on a seasonal or opportunistic basis. It may have been convenient to reoccupy the slavery-period dwellings from time to time when access to plantation works was needed. In the case of Morgan's Village, it may be that people were actively using parts of the slavery-period village while simultaneously in the process of moving to a new location. This model would have a different set of implications than one that proposes that individual families occupying single homes were slowly leaving over time. If families were simultaneously using structures in Morgan's Village opportunistically for convenience while simultaneously stripping them down to move, we might expect to see them making decisions about what they took when they left. Objects of greatest value would be removed first to the new location, with lesser-valued objects being left for use at the old houses until they were either abandoned or moved. Such a set of behaviors would result in an assemblage that seemed "poorer." Certainly, such a pattern of material relocation is seen today in Louisiana hunting camps, where the mismatched and "not-so-good" domestic objects are taken from the primary residence to the secondary residence. These chapters demonstrate that more work needs to be done on this vital period to understand the range of strategies employed by freed families.

Caribbean Peoples

When archaeologists examine transformations in the built landscape—material traces of changes in economic systems and artifact assemblages documenting transitions from enslavement to freedom—we are looking at the traces of decisions made by persons or groups of persons. Authors in this volume have engaged with a number of different living people through the course of their archaeological research—government entities, relief organizations, historical trusts, landholders, descendant communities, to name just a few. One of the advantages of these kinds of engaged and collaborative research is that we are forced to learn to talk about archaeological research in different ways. We are forced to think beyond settlement systems, structures of oppression, economic networks, and any range of anthropological jargon and to explain what our work says about the lives of past peoples.

Importantly, these papers add much-needed complexity to historical narratives regarding Caribbean populations by illuminating less-studied aspects of the Caribbean. Seiter renders visible the slave-holding free-black population of St. Lucia, while Ryzewski and Cherry and Reilly, by illuminating marginalized lands within plantation landscapes, have revealed the necessity of considering non-elite white and mixed-race peoples' contribution to Caribbean communities. Helen Blouet (Chapter 9), in her study of enslaved and free-black Moravian populations, introduces us to the diversity in funerary practices employed by members of the same faith community on two different islands. Her work underscores both the impacts that freedom had on something as fundamental as religious practice and the diverse ways that Caribbean peoples have dealt with similar structures of inequality at different places and times. In the chapters by Kristen Fellows (Chapter 13) and Stephan Lenik and Zachary Beier (Chapter 12), which I discuss further shortly, we gain a much-needed consideration of how different Caribbean communities confronted demands of nationalism, race, and diaspora. In adding diversity to our picture of the roots of Caribbean society, the authors of this volume have underscored the complexity of racialized relationships in the area. There is much to be lauded in these works, and I hope I have begun to detail that in the comments above. I did, however, also identify some themes that I think are worth exploring further as Caribbean archaeology moves forward.

New Spaces

Several of the essays in this volume highlight the ingenuity of Caribbean peoples in reusing and repurposing materials. At Potato Hill, Ryzewski and Cherry found knapped glass and worked ceramics. Marshall's Pen included portions of coffee mills being repurposed as graters. Chenoweth found similar reuse and commented on the reuse of architectural materials. Meniketti's chapter provides perhaps the ultimate example of reuse, with freed people picking up and moving an entire village and its architecture. Examples of such reuse throughout the Caribbean are countless and the ingenuity represented limitless and varied. At Clifton Plantation, a nineteenth-century reoccupation of one structure included a brick that had been used as a laundry stone and was worn down from reuse, nails bent to make fishhooks, and conch shell waste from meals used as ingredients in mortar (Wilkie and Farnsworth 2005, 2011).

Chenoweth carefully looks at reuse in his chapter as something that was done selectively, as residents actively manipulated their engagement with the cash economy to best serve their needs. His is an important example of how we need to carefully consider the contexts in which these objects appear and how context may shift meanings. Archaeologists are often quick to attribute these repurposing of objects as evidence of the restricted access to supplies and goods, and I would like to problematize this idea a bit with some examples from my own work. My experiences suggest that reuse is much more complicated and should be contextualized within particular social temporal spaces. I would suggest that we also consider other possibilities, including that perhaps these practices can suggest populations who have not drunk the Kool-Aid of consumer capitalism. Perhaps, just perhaps, sometimes it makes more sense to use something easily available and close at hand than to have a specialized toolkit of things.

Bahamians regularly use the rough skins of triggerfish for scrubbing. Excavating at the beach at Clifton Plantation one season, our enthusiastic crew of excavators had broken the handles of our cheap plastic dustpans by loading too much dirt into them. An ingenious crewmember walked to the beach and found a plastic Draino bottle that had washed up on shore. By cutting away half the bottle with a pocketknife, leaving the spout to serve as a handle, this brilliant inventor created a sturdy dustpan that structurally is stronger than any we could have bought. He saved us time and money, and this tribute to Bahamian ingenuity remains part of my dig kit ten years later. We shouldn't discount the possibility that creative reuse of materials can represent an alternative mindset that embraces self-sufficiency and values creativity, a mindset that contrasts starkly with the blind consumption patterns of elite colonists.

While excavating at Bahamian sites, we found countless examples of glass sherds that seemed to exhibit short-term expedient use as cutting or scraping tools. As we all know, it is easy to dismiss these objects as the result of trampling or other postdepositional processes. Given the large amount of fish consumption at most Bahamian sites, we engaged in some experimental archaeological research. With a team of Berkeley and Louisiana State University students, we decided we would take a break from artifact analysis and use glass sherds to gut and clean fish for our dinner. One student, an avid Louisiana sportsman, had brought fishing gear to the island and declared that he would acquire fish for us.

We went to a local beach we knew to be a popular fishing spot. While our fisherman set up his rig, a group of young Bahamians approached and asked if they could have a hook and some line. I asked if I could watch them fish, and they looked at me quizzically and said sure. They climbed out to a small jetty, and without bait or sinker, gently lowered the small hook into the water, and with careful movements that mimicked the flashing of small shiners, quickly enticed a decent pan-sized fish to take their hook. The children each took turns, and soon each had a fish. They handed the hook and line to me. "Don't you want it for next time?" I asked. They laughed at me and said they didn't want to carry it. They paused long enough to look with concern at our struggling fisherman and skipped off to wherever they were headed next with their fish.

Later that afternoon, after a trip to a fish market where we procured a number of pan-sized grunts and red snappers favored by Bahamians past and present, we broke a Kalik beer bottle to create glass sherds. Each student selected a sherd for their tool to clean their fish. I had experience gutting, cleaning, skinning, and scaling a variety of fish in Louisiana using knives and scaling tools. I randomly picked a sherd and was pleased to realize how the curved body sherd fit comfortably in my fingertips. It was very easy to manipulate and extremely sharp. We learned several things from the experiment. First, a randomly selected unmodified glass sherd can be used to make clean, sharp cuts in fish and makes an excellent scaling tool. Second, it is impossible to make a Berkeley undergraduate willingly gut and clean more than one fish.

Anecdotally, however, the experience solidified for me the idea that just because an artifact is expedient does not mean it is inferior. My finished fish was much prettier than what I usually accomplished with my commercially purchased gear, and I did not have to clean my glass sherd: I could have just tossed it. Reuse represents a certain kind of wisdom—one that is increasingly appreciated in parts of the United States where the green sustainability movements encourage creative reuse of materials otherwise thought of as waste and debris.

The reuse of existing materials can also be seen as representing an active decision not to participate in particular economic networks. Reilly has noted the importance of locally manufactured ceramics in the assemblages that he studied, including recognizing that locally manufactured coarsewares remain important after prices in imported wares drop significantly. There are many ways that materials can be used to indicate membership in a particular community. We should think about what it means when a person decides to purchase a pot made by a neighbor but to not purchase a knife made off-island.

Chenoweth's chapter demonstrates the necessity of contextualizing reuse in a historical setting. In the case of the British Virgin Islands, abandonment of plantations by white planters was so commonplace as to facilitate the development of a robust land-holding freed peoples' community. As plantation estates were abandoned, their buildings became source material for new constructions. The reuse of these materials not only allowed access to better-quality construction materials but also had the added benefit of contributing to the erasure of the white planter presence from the landscape. No small amount of effort was put into acquiring these materials. Chenoweth provides an analysis of shell remains to suggest that residents may have been living within a stressed marine ecosystem. As is done here, we need to not just document creative reuse practices but also must attempt to understand what social and economic work was being done through practices of reuse.

There was one space of Caribbean life that I was surprised to see ignored in this volume. Despite the racial, economic, occupational, national and geographic diversity highlighted in these chapters, I was frustrated that every author chose to bypass the issue of gender as an archaeological analytic. This is particularly perplexing given that enslavement was a system that relied upon sexual terrorism and threats to family integrity as part of its control of enslaved and—later, to a different extent—free labor. We speak of "oppressions" as a vague category of colonial offenses, but it is important to remember that sexual violence has always been part of racialized systems of control, and it is important to render this dimension of colonial systems visible. Barbara Bush (1990) in particular has detailed the abuses experienced by enslaved women in the Caribbean. Sexual violence against women hurt women, their children, and the men who cared about them. It was a means of creating a sense of powerlessness and desperation (Davis 1983; Roberts 1998).

Nonstop sexual violence in a society has material manifestations, particularly in the use of space, as brilliantly illustrated by Barbara Voss (2000). In California, she demonstrated that threat of sexual violence at the hands of the Spanish led to native Californians rearranging village layout so that women's work activities were focused in the protected centers of the villages rather than on the perimeters as they had been in pre-contact-period sites. If nothing more, it would have been useful to see considerations of how spatial arrangements and movement through landscapes was shaped by fear of harassment or abuse. Living in a rape culture means that select members of the community shape their behaviors to avoid violence—we can see this in our own society where education efforts focus more on teaching women what to do to avoid being raped rather than teaching men how not to rape.

The gendered implications of space were driven home to me when talking about house yards and provisioning grounds with Bahamians on Crooked Island back in 1995. I had been fascinated by Mintz's (1974) discussions of house yards and decided to talk to local women about their house yards (Wilkie 1996). As one of the outlying "Family" islands, Crooked has seen massive depopulation as its younger family members move to New Providence in search of economic opportunities. I was told in 1995 that the island was home to about 300 people. The 2000 census listed 350 people as living on the island. Stone houses built during the Loyalist plantation period were often still lived in, or concrete-block houses had been built adjoining these older structures that were used as kitchens or storage buildings. The women I spoke to were no younger than 60 years and had lived their whole lives on Crooked. Not only were women thrilled to talk about the creativity and family histories embedded in the different plantings and layouts of their gardens but they also spoke to these areas as female-shaped and controlled spaces. Men and women alike were firm in declaring that, while house gardens were women's spaces, provisioning grounds were worked and controlled by male members of the household. Likewise, fishing was a male pursuit while families collected land crabs as a group.

As I read the chapters on plantation spaces, I found myself thinking about those gendered landscape task divisions in the Bahamas and how they may have served as responses to the threat of sexual violence. From this perspective, the liminal spaces of Montserrat can be seen as discrete routes for moving along plantation landscapes that allow women and children to minimize contact with white planters and overseers. The white tenant villages located on plantations become places where familiar people can be traded with while minimizing contact with potentially threatening strangers. Further, if we consider women craftsmen, the act of selling goods in urban, publicly visible areas is safer than working agricultural fields. White tenants, like those who occupied Clifton Hall and potentially Potato Hill, further offered a means of reaching broader trade networks as middlemen who resell goods. If we think about the houses in provisioning grounds, we must think about who is living there. Would it be safe for women to ever farm these lands alone, or did concentrating women's labor in house yards serve as a means of maximizing their safety? Are men relocating families to these spaces or are they, like in the Bahamas, working these isolated patches alone so that families are safely housed in the enslaved people's villages where neighbors can track who comes in and out of the settlement? And what of African Caribbean traditions of house yard burials, which Blouet discusses existing also among Moravians? Through their presence, are the ancestors protecting their descendants?

Gender relationships in these communities would not be dictated merely by the threat of violence. Indeed, on islands where white citizens became less common through time, the threat of interracial sexual violence as a means of control would lessen. Freedom, in theory, meant legal recourse against those who would harm one's person. Shifts to new settlement patterns following emancipation—away from caves, provision-ground houses, and other "liminal" spaces where people convened—may also have gendered dimensions. European planters often imposed on enslaved and tenant communities models of housing that failed to account for non-European ideas about gender, cohabitation, and privacy—even within family groups and sexual partners (Wilkie 2000; Wilkie and Farnsworth 2005).

Drinking and gambling in caves may speak to homosocial spaces that provided refuge from home life. Provisioning-ground houses could have been another such space. On Crooked Island, women enjoyed visiting one another's house yards and saw these as spaces where women could work together as well as enjoy homosocial leisure time. We should consider if practices like these shaped the experiences of the everyday in the past. Similarly, children need to be brought back into the landscapes of the Caribbean (Clark and Wilkie 2007). Caribbean demographers speak to the brutal impacts of Caribbean enslavement on African Caribbean families, where high infant mortality rates and low fertility were all too common on sugar estates (Bush 1990). At Clifton, excavations at house yards revealed patterns of cleaning and yard arrangement that would facilitate child care, and we recovered artifacts that in ethnographic settings are associated with protecting the health of newborns and infants (Clark and Wilkie 2007; Wilkie and Farnsworth 2005). There was also evidence of ways that children seemed to be contributing to the household economies of the enslaved people's village.

I am not offering these as answers but as examples of the ways that an engendered gaze can bring additional questions to probe and increase the texture and nuance of our archaeological interpretations. I recognize that many of the studies discussed in these chapters are in very early stages of excavation and research, and I urge these researchers to consider questions of gender and life stage into their developing research projects. If we are going to continue to build upon understanding diverse experiences of colonialism, then certainly we must consider the engendered, embodied experiences of people.

Race, Racialization, and Diaspora

Reilly's chapter illustrates the importance of focusing on the diversity of racialized experiences in the Caribbean and how they intersect with other categories of identification. His study of the Redlegs of Barbados underscores how we might refer to racism as one of the enduring legacies of colonialism. We have done less to study the processes through which race is constructed and constituted in different Caribbean settings. Works by historical archaeologists in North American contexts have demonstrated that much can be learned from interrogating how racialized systems of inequality are constituted and enforced (see Mullins 1999; Orser 2003, 2007; Wilkie 2003). Reilly includes quotes in his essay in which contemporary chroniclers describe the poor whites of the island as "arrogant." If we ponder how race intersected with class, gender, and legal status in the Caribbean, we have to consider whether trade relationships between enslaved people and their white fellow laborers were truly egalitarian or whether they provided a means for poor whites to assert a sense of racial privilege. These are questions that remain to be explored.

Early works in the Caribbean focused on the task of recognizing the unique cultural contributions of African-descended populations to Caribbean culture. Often this work took the form of looking explicitly at material evidence of continuities in African practice (e.g., Armstrong 1985; Handler and Lange 1978; Heath 1999), and the search for African continuities has largely been discarded in the Caribbean as too essentializing; in general, we are quick to lump any study that considers the role of Africanized material culture as part of the search for "African continuities." While I appreciate concerns about essentializing people based on things, it is rather absurd to criticize scholars who study the ways populations use their heritage in social relations when the ethnoracial composition of the people being studied is well documented. Similarly, if we do not engage with the notions of heritage, ancestry, and tradition, it becomes impossible for us to look at constructions of diasporic identification in the Caribbean (see Haviser 1999; Haviser and MacDonald 2006). At a time when African American studies have increasingly turned their attentions toward understanding the creation and politics of diaspora, it seems that anthropologically driven archaeology can contribute to these intellectual debates. Certainly Akinwumi Ogundiran and Toyin Falola's (2007) edited volume demonstrates the powerful analytical lens provided by a focus on diaspora. Following Tiffany Patterson and Robin Kelley (2000), I see diaspora as an emergent process, always in production and situated within global circumstances and debates as well as within other axes of identification and hierarchy.

The social spaces of diaspora and racialization are intimately entwined, feeding one another and creating one another, and each are the products of maneuvering for political, economic, and social power. I was working in the Bahamas when Maria Franklin introduced me to Michael Gomez's (1998) book, *Exchanging Our Country Marks*. In this book, now widely declared a classic of diaspora studies, Gomez documents the emergence of a shift within enslaved African populations from self-identification based on specific African ethnic heritages to a shared, Pan-African, black identity in the early nineteenth century. Paul Farnsworth's and my book-length study (2005) of late-eighteenth- and early-nineteenth-century Clifton Plantation on the island of New Providence, Bahamas, was an attempt to see how material culture was employed by families negotiating those new identities. Clifton was an ideal location for such a study: unlike many plantations in the Bahamas (and elsewhere in the Caribbean), it was so well documented that we could identify families who resided in each house during landowner William Wylly's tenure. The plantation's owner, Wylly, attorney general of the Bahamas, held up the plantation as a showcase for plantation management. His fellow planters, often the object of Wylly's persecuting prosecutions, countered his accusations against them by accusing Wylly of underprovisioning his enslaved population. The resulting trial transcripts include a wealth of information about the plantation's organization and economies, including even details of what crops were grown in each enslaved family's provisioning grounds.

While it was our analytical intent to study diaspora in the past, we were confronted with a powerful lesson in contemporary diaspora politics during the course of the project. Like many of the sites described in this volume, archaeological work at Clifton was shaped by modern-day management concerns. The government of the Bahamas wished to sell the previously undisturbed nearly 300-acre site to an American firm who planned to develop it into a gated community. By 2000, when development seemed certain, a coalition of concerned island preservationists, descendants, and other stakeholders employed our archaeological interpretations to rally support for preservation. Archaeological interpretations that portrayed the people of Clifton as being one of the populations that collectively forged what it was to be African Bahamian resonated with Bahamians. In the process of pressuring the government to halt development, Bahamians drew upon diasporic networks, using Bev Smith's Black Entertainment Television radio show to rally support among African Americans in the United States and Bahamian ex-patriots in Canada and inviting Jesse Jackson's Rainbow Coalition to stage a protest parade (Wilkie 2001).

In a strange tale that deserves a longer telling, the site of Clifton was ultimately "saved" through Bahamian efforts at the ballot box in an election that ousted the ruling party. The opposition party, which had previously been outnumbered in the house of assembly by a ratio of 3:1, won the election based on a party platform centered on saving the site and preserving it as a national park. The party platform was taken directly from the recommendation section of an archaeological report. The site is now indeed a national park whose interpretation is guided under a Bahamian-composed board of supervisors. Although "saving" Clifton did not result in the saving of other threatened sites, it is an interesting example of how the idea of diaspora is employed politically in a Caribbean setting.

Too often, traditionalist Marxist analyses suggest that ethnicity prevents the formation of class identification and frustrates emancipatory change. Instead, we saw racial identity, through the understanding of diaspora, employed to affect political change. Throughout the United States and the Caribbean, African-descended peoples time and again indicate that they are interested in archaeologists conducting research that can contribute to their understanding of their African heritage (see Agbe-Davis 2010; Haviser and MacDonald 2006; McDavid 2002). This is not merely idle curiosity but part of a larger political consciousness that can be employed in activism.

That is not to say that an archaeology of diaspora should present African-descended peoples' as monolithic or hegemonic. As we see in the chapters within this volume, diaspora is a response to the systems of racialization that emerged in distinct colonial and postcolonial spaces. The same Bahamians who employed diaspora to coax support out of African Americans would speak disdainfully of how the Haitian illegal immigrants to the Bahamas would benefit from the low-paying jobs that the gated community would have created. As we see in the papers within this volume, contrasting systems of racialization lead to interesting problems of eth-noracial classification.

Fellows' paper on the community of Philadelphian African Americans who settled in what is now the Dominican Republic is a fascinating study of diasporic processes in motion. Although motivated by a Pan-African senti-ment to relocate to Hispañiola, overcoming entrenched experiences of race made integration into the broader community difficult. Coming from a nation where social mobility arose from a whitening process, the American Samanesa were reluctant to abandon their English language and Protestant religion. We see in this case study the enduring impacts of colonial struc-tures—in this case, language and religion—on diasporic communities. For American immigrants in less isolated parts of the island, the shared experi-ence of racialized educational opportunities led to the quicker adoption of Spanish language and encouraged more rapid integration. The American Samanesa were able create their own religious and educational institutions for 150 years and employed the nationalistic identity of being American to maintain a distance from other diasporic communities on the island, ironi-cally, despite their political embracing of a Pan-African ideology.

If diaspora is one of the lived spaces that emerged out of colonial roots, then we must discuss the tangled branches of nationalism and hybridity as well. This nationalistic identity and a sense of hybridity/double conscious-ness is well illustrated in Lenik and Beier's study of Fort Rocky in Kingston Harbor, Jamaica. The authors situate the occupants of the fort within a con-text of growing nationalistic and diasporic movements within Jamaica (the development of labor unions, Garveyism, and Rastafarianism) and con-trast this context with the subject position of men serving as soldiers in the British military. They argue convincingly that these men occupied a third space, simultaneously representatives of a kind of black nationalism and authority as members of the British West Indies regiments and as Jamaican, yet also occupying the role of representatives of empire. The material cul-ture of the fort demonstrates the uneasiness with which soldiers occupied this colonial third space. Recovery of material culture within the fort dem-onstrates a conformance with hierarchies and material practices of mili-tary life, such as the maintenance of dress uniforms and plain utilitarian ceramics. At the perimeter of the fort, however, the authors found a much wider assortment of decorative forms of ceramics, which they interpreted as introduced to the community by the soldiers. The location of these mate-rials at the outskirts of the fort shows a technical if not complete adherence to protocol. Individuality was asserted through personal artifacts, such as the continued use of pipes among the soldiers at a time when cigars and cigarettes were more popularly used in the broader population. Medicinal and personal hygiene artifacts demonstrate a range of preferences in hair and skin treatments, indicating another means through which individuality was expressed.

Diasporic consciousness is itself a creation of empire. It is easy when thinking of the period of slavery to think of enslaved people as tied to places, yet, as essays in this volume demonstrate, enslaved peoples engaged with multiple scales of landscape in ways both sanctioned and unsanctioned by colonial powers. Meeting spots in caves, gullies, or white tenant neighborhoods provided opportunities to build island-wide networks of support and solidarity. The transfer of enslaved peoples from one part of an empire to another, the stationing of African troops in the Caribbean and Caribbean troops in Africa, the movement of freed people from one island to another, the stationing of black U.S. troops in the Caribbean—these and myriad other examples all served to create a fertile ground for the roots of diaspora. As more archaeologists turn their research attentions to the more recent periods of Caribbean history, we can explore the effects of these movements.

Closing Thoughts: Connecting Spaces, Seeing Webs of Landscape

The contributors to this volume are to be commended for offering a set of consistently strong, engaging, and enlightening essays, and I thank the editors for giving me the opportunity to read and comment on them. It is probably apparent from my comments that they have reignited my desire to work through old excavation materials.

It is often the case in edited volumes that each chapter hangs isolated as a solitary island in a sea of other chapters that surround it. As a discussant, such volumes are hard to think about in a constructive way, and the writer is left to create something unified out of random diversity. Such was not the case in this volume, where, in different places and times, authors were struggling with the same challenges: how to recognize and rethink silent spaces of the Caribbean in a way that meaningfully contributes a new understanding of the past.

Ultimately, these chapters are also part of a growing intellectual landscape. Anthropologists have been increasingly interested in understanding entanglements or complex social webs between human, animal, and material agents across space and landscapes (in particular, see Ingold 2007). For Tim Ingold, it is not any particular animal, person, place, or thing that should be the meaningful focus of our anthropological consideration but the webs of meaning and action that knit those things together. In other words, it is precisely that "in-betweenness" that is anthropologically interesting.

As archaeologists, we are similarly interested in understanding the web of relationships that connect people things and places. It is an interest not only shaped in current theorizing in anthropology but also deeply rooted in our disciplinary intellectual history. Unlike social anthropologists who can enter and observe webs through participant observation, archaeologists, since we work with traces of the past, are in the challenging position of simultaneously entering and reweaving the web we want to understand from the evidence available to us. The very thing we are trying to understand emerges from our archaeological interpretative weavings.

Methodologically, we have to start from a place (an archaeological site or sites or landscape) that itself roots the study in a particular space. We also start our work with a space in time (as often dictated by archaeological materials), a limited set of actors (those who created the sites or landscapes), a set of materials (artifacts), and—importantly—a question. These things collectively form the parameters of any archaeological research project.

To understand any time and place, archaeologists then branch outward from their site, seeking to understand the social historical setting that created the place and ways the site is connected to the broader social worlds. Because we start from one place and attempt to connect it to other places that we or other archaeologists have studied, we inadvertently create analytical distances between sites as both physical places and as spaces of social action. Always seeking to represent our knowledge in space, archaeologists then situate what we know on maps, putting boundaries and edges on features on the landscape. The essays in this volume challenge us to question what we know about Caribbean history and everyday life by turning our gaze from the very things that we have put boundaries on to those things we have not. The result of considering those spaces of "in-betweenness" has been a refreshingly new set of perspectives on Caribbean historical archaeology that should inspire others to do the same.

References Cited

Agbe-Davis, Anna S.
2010   Concepts of Community in the Pursuit of an Inclusive Archaeology. *International Journal of Heritage Studies* 16(6):373–389.

Armstrong, Douglas V.
1985   An Afro-Jamaican Settlement: Archaeological Investigations at Drax Hall. In *The Archaeology of Slavery and Plantation Life*, edited by Theresa A. Singleton, pp. 261–285. Academic Press, New York.
1990   *The Old Village and the Great House: An Archaeological and Historical Examination of Drax Hall Plantation, St. Ann's Bay, Jamaica*. University of Illinois Press, Urbana.
2003   *Creole Transformation from Slavery to Freedom: Historical Archaeology of the East End Community, St. John, Virgin Islands*. University of Florida Press, Gainesville.
2010   Degrees of Freedom in the Caribbean: Archaeological Explorations of Transitions from Slavery. *Antiquity* 84(32):146–160.

Armstrong, Douglas V., and Mark W. Hauser
2009   A Sea of Diversity: Historical Archaeology in the Caribbean. In *International Handbook of Historical Archaeology*, edited by David Gaimster and Teresita Majewski, pp. 583–612. Springer, New York.

Bush, Barbara
1990   *Slave Women in Caribbean Society, 1650–1838*. University of Indiana, Bloomington.

Clark, Bonnie, and Laurie A. Wilkie
2007   Prism of Self: Gender and Personhood. In *Identity and Subsistence: Gender Strategies for Archaeology*, edited by Sarah Nelson. Altamira, Walnut Creek, California.

Davis, Angela
1983   *Women, Race and Class*. Vintage Books, New York.

Deagan, Kathleen
1995   *Puerto Real: The Archaeology of a Sixteenth-Century Spanish Town in Hispaniola*. University Press of Florida, Gainesville.

Deagan, Kathleen, and J. M. Cruxent
2002   *Archaeology at La Isabella: America's First European Town*. Yale University Press, New Haven, Connecticut.

Delle, James A.
1998   *An Archaeology of Social Space: Analyzing Coffee Plantations in Jamaica's Blue Mountains*. Plenum Press, New York.
2000   Gender, Power, and Space: Negotiating Social Relations under Slavery on Coffee Plantations in Jamaica, 1790–1834. In *Lines that Divide: Historical Archaeologies of Race, Class, and Gender*, edited by James A. Delle, Stephen A. Mrozowski, and Robert Paynter, pp. 168–201. University of Tennessee Press, Knoxville.
2011   The Habitus of Jamaican Plantation Landscapes. In *Out of Many, One People: The Historical Archaeology of Colonial Jamaica*, edited by James A. Delle, Mark W.

Hauser, and Douglas V. Armstrong, pp. 122–143. University of Alabama Press, Tuscaloosa.

2014   *The Colonial Caribbean: Landscapes of Power in Jamaica's Plantation System.* Case Studies in Early Societies. Cambridge University Press, Cambridge.

Gomez, Michael A.

1998   *Exchanging Our Country Marks: The Transformation of African Identities in the Colonial and Antebellum South.* University of North Carolina Press, Chapel Hill.

Gray, Dorrick E.

1997   Managing Underwater Archaeological Resources: The Jamaican Experience. Paper presented at the Conference for Historical and Underwater Archaeology, Corpus Christi, Texas, January 8.

Handler, Jerome S.

1963   Pottery Makers in Rural Barbados. *Southwestern Journal of Anthropology* 19(3):314–334.

1994   Determining African Birth from Skeletal Remains: A Note on Tooth Mutilation. *Historical Archaeology* 28:113–119.

1997   An African-Type Healer/Diviner and His Grave Goods: A Burial from a Plantation Slave Cemetery in Barbados, West Indies. *International Journal of Historical Archaeology* 1:91–130.

Handler, Jerome S., and Frederick Lange

1978   *Plantation Slavery in Barbados: an Archaeological and Historical Investigation.* Harvard University Press, Cambridge, Massachusetts.

Hauser, Mark W.

2008   *An Archaeology of Black Markets: Local Ceramics and Economies in Eighteenth-Century Jamaica.* University Press of Florida, Gainesville.

2011   Routes and Roots of Empire: Pots, Power, and Slavery in the 18th-Century British Caribbean. *American Anthropologist* 113(3):431–437.

Haviser, Jay B. (editor)

1999   *African Sites: Archaeology in the Caribbean.* Markus Wiener, Princeton, New Jersey.

Haviser, Jay B. and Kevin C. MacDonald (editors)

2006   *African Re-Genesis: Confronting Social Issues in the Diaspora.* Left Coast Press, Walnut Creek, California.

Heath, Barbara J.

1999   Yabbas, Monkeys, Jugs, and Jars: An Historical Context for African-Caribbean Pottery on St. Eustatius. In *African Sites: Archaeology in the Caribbean,* edited by Jay B. Haviser, pp. 196–220. Markus Wiener, Princeton, New Jersey.

Hicks, Dan

2007   "The Garden of the World": An Historical Archaeology of Sugar Landscapes in the Eastern Caribbean. British Archaeological Report International Series 1632, Studies in Contemporary and Historical Archaeology 3. Archaeopress, Oxford.

Hoffman, Charles

1987   Archaeological Investigations at the Long Bay Site, San Salvador, Bahamas. In *Proceedings of the First Annual San Salvador Conference, Columbus and His*

World, edited by Donald T. Gerace, pp. 237–245. College Center of the Finger Lakes, Bahamian Field Station, Bahamas.

Ingold, Tim
2007   Materials against Materiality. *Archaeological Dialogues* 14(1):1–16.

Kelly, Kenneth G., and Neil L. Norman
2006   Medium Vessels and the Longue Dureé: The Endurance of Ritual Ceramics and the Archaeology of the African Diaspora. In *African Re-Genesis: Confronting Social Issues in the Diaspora*, edited by Jay B. Haviser and Kevin C. MacDonald, pp. 223–233. University College London Press, London.

McDavid, Carol
2002   "Archaeologies That Hurt, Descendants That Matter: A Pragmatic Approach to Collaboration in the Public Interpretation of African-American Archaeology." *World Archaeology* 34(2):303–314.

Mintz, Sidney W.
1974   *Caribbean Transformations*. Aldine, Chicago.
1985   *Sweetness and Power: The Place of Sugar in Modern History*. Penguin, New York.

Mullins, Paul R.
1999   Race and Affluence: An Archaeology of African America a Consumer Culture. Plenum Press, New York.

Orser, Charles E., Jr.
2003   *Race and the Practice of Archaeological Interpretation*. University of Pennsylvania Press, Philadelphia.
2007   *The Archaeology of Race and Racialization in Historical America*. University Press of Florida, Gainesville.

Ogundiran, Akinwumi, and Toyin Falola (editors)
2007   *Archaeology of Atlantic Africa and the African Diaspora*. Indiana University Press, Bloomington.

Patterson, Tiffany Ruby, and Robin D. G. Kelley
2000   Unfinished Migrations: Reflections on the African Diaspora and the Making of the Modern World. *Africa Studies Review* 43(1):11–45.

Posnansky, Merrick
1984   Toward an Archaeology of the Black Diaspora. *Journal of Black Studies* 15(2):195–205.

Roberts, Dorothy
1998   *Killing the Black Body*. Vintage Books, New York.

Turner, Grace
2006   Bahamian Ship Graffiti. *International Journal of Nautical Archaeology* 35(2):253–273.

Voss, Barbara
2000   Colonial Sex: Archaeology, Structured Space, and Sexuality in Alta California's Spanish-Colonial Missions. In *Archaeologies of Sexuality, edited by Robert Schmidt and Barbara Voss*, pp. 35–61. Routledge, New York.

Wilkie, Laurie A.
1996   House Gardens and Female Identity on Crooked Island. *Journal of the Bahamas Historical Society* 18:33–39.

2000   Magical Passions: Sex and African-American Archaeology. In *Archaeologies of Sexuality*, edited by Barbara Voss and Robert Schmidt, pp. 129–142. Routledge, London.

2001   Communicative Bridges Linking Actors through Time: Archaeology and the Construction of Emancipatory Narratives at a Bahamian Plantation. *Journal of Social Archaeology* 1(2):225–243.

2003   *The Archaeology of Mothering: An African-American Midwife's Tale*. Routledge, New York.

Wilkie, Laurie A., and Paul Farnsworth

2005   *Sampling Many Pots: An Archaeology of Memory and Tradition at a Bahamian Plantation*. University Press of Florida, Gainesville.

2011   Living Not So Quietly, Not So on the Edge of Things: A Twentieth Century Bahamian Household. In *The Materiality of Freedom—Archaeologies of Postemancipation Life*, edited by Jodi A. Barnes. University of South Carolina Press, Columbia.

Contributors

Hayden F. Bassett is a Ph.D. candidate in the Department of Anthropology at the College of William and Mary.

Lynsey A. Bates is a senior archaeological analyst for the Digital Archaeological Archive of Comparative Slavery (DAACS).

Zachary J. M. Beier is assistant professor in the Department of History and Archaeology at the University of the West Indies, Mona, Jamaica.

Helen C. Blouet is associate professor of anthropology at Utica College.

John M. Chenoweth is associate professor of anthropology at the University of Michigan-Dearborn and the author of *Simplicity, Equality, and Slavery: An Archaeology of Quakerism in the British Virgin Islands, 1740–1780*.

John F. Cherry is the Joukowsky Family Professor of Archaeology and professor of classics and anthropology at Brown University.

James A. Delle, associate provost at Millersville University, is the editor of *The Limits of Tyranny*.

Kristen R. Fellows is assistant professor at North Dakota State University.

Khadene K. Harris is a Ph.D. candidate in the Department of Anthropology at Northwestern University.

Stephan T. Lenik is visiting assistant professor of anthropology in the Department of Anthropology at St. Mary's College of Maryland.

Marco Meniketti is associate professor of archaeology at San Jose State University and director of the nonprofit Institute for Advanced Interdisciplinary Caribbean Studies.

Matthew C. Reilly is a postdoctoral fellow at the Joukowsky Institute for Archaeology and the Ancient World at Brown University.

Krysta Ryzewski is assistant professor in the Department of Anthropology at Wayne State University.

Jane I. Seiter is co-owner of the Oxford Tree-Ring Laboratory.

Frederick H. Smith is associate professor of anthropology at the College of William and Mary.

Laurie A. Wilkie is professor of anthropology at the University of California, Berkeley.

Index

Tacachale: Essays on the Indians of Florida and Southeastern Georgia during the Historic Period, edited by Jerald T. Milanich and Samuel Proctor (1978)

Aboriginal Subsistence Technology on the Southeastern Coastal Plain during the Late Prehistoric Period, by Lewis H. Larson (1980)

Cemochechobee: Archaeology of a Mississippian Ceremonial Center on the Chattahoochee River, by Frank T. Schnell, Vernon J. Knight Jr., and Gail S. Schnell (1981)

Fort Center: An Archaeological Site in the Lake Okeechobee Basin, by William H. Sears, with contributions by Elsie O'R. Sears and Karl T. Steinen (1982)

Perspectives on Gulf Coast Prehistory, edited by Dave D. Davis (1984)

Archaeology of Aboriginal Culture Change in the Interior Southeast: Depopulation during the Early Historic Period, by Marvin T. Smith (1987)

Apalachee: The Land between the Rivers, by John H. Hann (1988)

Key Marco's Buried Treasure: Archaeology and Adventure in the Nineteenth Century, by Marion Spjut Gilliland (1989)

First Encounters: Spanish Explorations in the Caribbean and the United States, 1492– 1570, edited by Jerald T. Milanich and Susan Milbrath (1989)

Missions to the Calusa, edited and translated by John H. Hann, with an introduction by William H. Marquardt (1991)

Excavations on the Franciscan Frontier: Archaeology at the Fig Springs Mission, by Brent Richards Weisman (1992)

The People Who Discovered Columbus: The Prehistory of the Bahamas, by William F. Keegan (1992)

Hernando de Soto and the Indians of Florida, by Jerald T. Milanich and Charles Hudson (1993)

Foraging and Farming in the Eastern Woodlands, edited by C. Margaret Scarry (1993)

Puerto Real: The Archaeology of a Sixteenth-Century Spanish Town in Hispaniola, edited by Kathleen Deagan (1995)

Political Structure and Change in the Prehistoric Southeastern United States, edited by John F. Scarry (1996)

Bioarchaeology of Native Americans in the Spanish Borderlands, edited by Brenda J. Baker and Lisa Kealhofer (1996)

A History of the Timucua Indians and Missions, by John H. Hann (1996)

Archaeology of the Mid-Holocene Southeast, edited by Kenneth E. Sassaman and David G. Anderson (1996)

The Indigenous People of the Caribbean, edited by Samuel M. Wilson (1997; first paperback edition, 1999)

Hernando de Soto among the Apalachee: The Archaeology of the First Winter Encampment, by Charles R. Ewen and John H. Hann (1998)

The Timucuan Chiefdoms of Spanish Florida, by John E. Worth: vol. 1, *Assimilation*; vol. 2, *Resistance and Destruction* (1998)

Ancient Earthen Enclosures of the Eastern Woodlands, edited by Robert C. Mainfort Jr. and Lynne P. Sullivan (1998)

An Environmental History of Northeast Florida, by James J. Miller (1998)

Precolumbian Architecture in Eastern North America, by William N. Morgan (1999)

Archaeology of Colonial Pensacola, edited by Judith A. Bense (1999)

Grit-Tempered: Early Women Archaeologists in the Southeastern United States, edited by Nancy Marie White, Lynne P. Sullivan, and Rochelle A. Marrinan (1999)

Coosa: The Rise and Fall of a Southeastern Mississippian Chiefdom, by Marvin T. Smith (2000)

Religion, Power, and Politics in Colonial St. Augustine, by Robert L. Kapitzke (2001)

Bioarchaeology of Spanish Florida: The Impact of Colonialism, edited by Clark Spencer Larsen (2001)

Archaeological Studies of Gender in the Southeastern United States, edited by Jane M. Eastman and Christopher B. Rodning (2001)

The Archaeology of Traditions: Agency and History Before and After Columbus, edited by Timothy R. Pauketat (2001)

Foraging, Farming, and Coastal Biocultural Adaptation in Late Prehistoric North Carolina, by Dale L. Hutchinson (2002)

Windover: Multidisciplinary Investigations of an Early Archaic Florida Cemetery, edited by Glen H. Doran (2002)

Archaeology of the Everglades, by John W. Griffin (2002; first paperback edition, 2017)

Pioneer in Space and Time: John Mann Goggin and the Development of Florida Archaeology, by Brent Richards Weisman (2002)

Indians of Central and South Florida, 1513–1763, by John H. Hann (2003)

Presidio Santa Maria de Galve: A Struggle for Survival in Colonial Spanish Pensacola, edited by Judith A. Bense (2003)

Bioarchaeology of the Florida Gulf Coast: Adaptation, Conflict, and Change, by Dale L. Hutchinson (2004)

The Myth of Syphilis: The Natural History of Treponematosis in North America, edited by Mary Lucas Powell and Della Collins Cook (2005)

The Florida Journals of Frank Hamilton Cushing, edited by Phyllis E. Kolianos and Brent R. Weisman (2005)

The Lost Florida Manuscript of Frank Hamilton Cushing, edited by Phyllis E. Kolianos and Brent R. Weisman (2005)

The Native American World Beyond Apalachee: West Florida and the Chattahoochee Valley, by John H. Hann (2006)

Tatham Mound and the Bioarchaeology of European Contact: Disease and Depopulation in Central Gulf Coast Florida, by Dale L. Hutchinson (2006)

Taino Indian Myth and Practice: The Arrival of the Stranger King, by William F.

Keegan (2007)

An Archaeology of Black Markets: Local Ceramics and Economies in Eighteenth-Century Jamaica, by Mark W. Hauser (2008; first paperback edition, 2013)

Mississippian Mortuary Practices: Beyond Hierarchy and the Representationist Perspective, edited by Lynne P. Sullivan and Robert C. Mainfort Jr. (2010; first paperback edition, 2012)

Bioarchaeology of Ethnogenesis in the Colonial Southeast, by Christopher M. Stojanowski (2010; first paperback edition, 2013)

French Colonial Archaeology in the Southeast and Caribbean, edited by Kenneth G. Kelly and Meredith D. Hardy (2011; first paperback edition, 2015)

Late Prehistoric Florida: Archaeology at the Edge of the Mississippian World, edited by Keith Ashley and Nancy Marie White (2012; first paperback edition, 2015)

Early and Middle Woodland Landscapes of the Southeast, edited by Alice P. Wright and Edward R. Henry (2013)

Trends and Traditions in Southeastern Zooarchaeology, edited by Tanya M. Peres (2014)

New Histories of Pre-Columbian Florida, edited by Neill J. Wallis and Asa R. Randall (2014; first paperback edition, 2016)

Discovering Florida: First-Contact Narratives from Spanish Expeditions along the Lower Gulf Coast, edited and translated by John E. Worth (2014; first paperback edition, 2015)

Constructing Histories: Archaic Freshwater Shell Mounds and Social Landscapes of the St. Johns River, Florida, by Asa R. Randall (2015)

Archaeology of Early Colonial Interaction at El Chorro de Maíta, Cuba, by Roberto Valcárcel Rojas (2016)

Fort San Juan and the Limits of Empire: Colonialism and Household Practice at the Berry Site, edited by Robin A. Beck, Christopher B. Rodning, and David G. Moore (2016)

Rethinking Moundville and Its Hinterland, edited by Vincas P. Steponaitis and C. Margaret Scarry (2016)

Handbook of Ceramic Animal Symbols in the Ancient Lesser Antilles, by Lawrence Waldron (2016)

Paleoindian Societies of the Coastal Southeast, by James S. Dunbar (2016)

Gathering at Silver Glen: Community and History in Late Archaic Florida, by Zackary I. Gilmore (2016)

Cuban Archaeology in the Caribbean, edited by Ivan Roksandic (2016)

Archaeologies of Slavery and Freedom in the Caribbean: Exploring the Spaces in Between, edited by Lynsey A. Bates, John M. Chenoweth, and James A. Delle (2016; first paperback edition, 2018)

Setting the Table: Ceramics, Dining, and Cultural Exchange in Andalusia and La Florida, by Kathryn L. Ness (2017)

Simplicity, Equality, and Slavery: An Archaeology of Quakerism in the British Virgin Islands, 1740–1780, by John M. Chenoweth (2017)

CPSIA information can be obtained
at www.ICGtesting.com
Printed in the USA
LVHW110957170119
604272LV00002B/126/P